Library of the

Catholic Foreign Mission Society

of America

18925

天主實義

THE TRUE MEANING
OF
THE LORD OF HEAVEN
(T'ien-chu Shih-i)

Series I. Jesuit Primary Sources, in English Translations

No. 1. St. Ignatius of Loyola. *The Constitutions of the Society of Jesus. Translated, with an Introduction and a Commentary,* by George E. Ganss, S.J.

No. 2. *Documents of the 31st and 32nd General Congregations of the Society of Jesus. An English Translation.* Prepared by the Jesuit Conference and edited by John W. Padberg, S.J.

No. 3. *Jesuit Religious Life Today. The Principal Features of Its Spirit, in Excerpts from Papal Documents, St. Ignatius' Constitutions, the 31st and 32nd General Congregations, and Letters of Father General Pedro Arrupe.* Edited by George E. Ganss, S.J.

No. 4. *Letters from the Mughal Court. The First Jesuit Mission to Akbar (1580-1583).* John Correia-Afonso, S.J., Editor and Translator.

No. 5. *Documents of the 33rd General Congregation of the Society of Jesus.* An English Translation of the Official Latin Texts of the General Congregation and of Related Documents.

No. 6. Matteo Ricci, S.J. *The True Meaning of the Lord of Heaven (T'ien-chu Shih-i).* Translated, with Introduction and Notes, by Douglas Lancashire and Peter Hu Kuo-chen, S.J. A Bilingual Edition. **Edited by Edward J. Malatesta, S.J.**

Matteo Ricci, S.J.

THE TRUE MEANING OF THE LORD OF HEAVEN
(T'ien-chu Shih-i)

Translated, with Introduction and Notes,
by
Douglas Lancashire and Peter Hu Kuo-chen, S.J.

A Chinese-English Edition
edited by
Edward J. Malatesta, S.J.

THE INSTITUTE OF JESUIT SOURCES
St. Louis, 1985

in cooperation with
The Ricci Institute
Taipei, Taiwan

This book is co-published by

The Institute of Jesuit Sources
Fusz Memorial, St. Louis University
3700 West Pine Boulevard
St. Louis, Missouri 63108, U.S.A.

and

The Ricci Institute for Chinese Studies
Hsin Hai Road, Section 1, No. 24, 8F
Taipei 107, Taiwan, Republic of China

with the collaboration of

The Faculty of Theology
Fujen Catholic University
Hsinchuang, Taipeihsien 242
Taiwan, Republic of China

and

The Institute for Chinese-Western Cultural History
The University of San Francisco
San Francisco, California 94117, U.S.A.

This book is volume no. 72 of

Variétés Sinologiques-Nouvelle Série
published by
The Ricci Institute, Taipei

©1985 Institut Ricci
68 Rue de la Tour
75016 Paris, France

Library of Congress Catalog Card Number: 84-80944
ISBN 0-912422-77-7 sewn paperbound
ISBN 0-912422-78-5 clothbound

CONTENTS

Publisher's Foreword ix
Translators' Preface xiii
Abbreviations 2
Translators' Introduction 3
   1. The Life of Matteo Ricci 3
   2. History of the Composition and Publication of *The True Meaning of the Lord of Heaven* 10
   3. The Present English Translation 21
   4. Ricci's Viewpoint and the Contents of the Work 22
   5. A Detailed Outline of *The True Meaning of the Lord of Heaven* 25
   6. The Terminology 32
   7. Reactions to Ricci's Work 38
   8. A Contemporary Evaluation 47

THE TRUE MEANING OF THE LORD OF HEAVEN
The Chinese Text, English Translation, and Notes

Matteo Ricci's Introduction 57
Chapter 1
   A discussion on the creation of heaven, earth, and all things by the Lord of Heaven, and on the way He exercises authority [over them] and sustains them 65

Contents

Chapter 2
An explanation of mistaken views concerning the Lord of Heaven current among men — 99

Chapter 3
The human soul is not extinguished and is greatly different from [the souls] of birds and beasts — 133

Chapter 4
A discussion on spiritual beings and the soul of man, and an explanation as to why the phenomena of the world cannot be described as forming an organic unity — 175

Chapter 5
Refutation of false teachings concerning reincarnation in the Six Directions and the taking of life, and an explanation of the true meaning of fasting — 239

Chapter 6
An explanation as to why man cannot be free of motives, and a discussion of why the good and evil done on earth by man must be rewarded or punished in Heaven and Hell — 285

Chapter 7
A discussion on the [Confucian] teaching that human nature is fundamentally good, and an exposition of the orthodox [Way of] learning of those who adhere to the religion of the Lord of Heaven — 347

Chapter 8
A summary of Western customs, a discussion on the meaning and history of celibacy among the clergy, and an explanation of the reason why the Lord of Heaven was born in the West — 409

Appendix

Ricci's Latin Summary of *The True Meaning of the Lord of Heaven*   **460**

Bibliography   **473**

Index of Chinese Classical Texts   **483**

Illustrations
1. Copper Engraving of Paul Hsü Kuang-ch'i   41
2. Matteo Ricci and the K'ang-hsi Inscription   42
3. Diagram of the Kinds of Being   192
4. A page of the First Chinese Edition   458
5. A page of the Latin Autograph   459

PUBLISHER'S FOREWORD

The nature and importance of Matteo Ricci's work in the sixteenth century meeting of West with East, his genuine esteem of the Chinese people and their culture, and the dedication to his Chinese friends and his ministry by which he endeared himself to them are extensively treated later in this volume and need no further comment here.

But the circumstances and cooperation which have produced this book make a fascinating narrative which will be of interest to many of its readers. The telling of that account, too, will make it possible to point out the respective roles of the persons who cooperated in its publication.

The initiator of the project was Father Douglas Lancashire who was born in China of missionary parents. After nine years of missionary work in Hong Kong, he spent a year as Visiting Lecturer in the History of Chinese Thought and in the Chinese language at the University of Michigan, Ann Arbor. After three and a half years as Senior Lecturer in Chinese at the University of Melbourne, Australia, he proceeded to New Zealand where for fifteen years he held the foundation Chair of Chinese and was head of the Department of Asian Languages and Literatures in the University of Auckland. He is presently Rector of the Anglican Churches of St. Mary the virgin at Langham and St. Peter at Boxted (both first built in the twelfth century), England. He resides at The Rectory, Wick Road, Langham, Colchester C04 5PG, England.

Publisher's Foreword

He prepared the translation of Ricci's *The True Meaning of the Lord of Heaven,* with an introduction, brief notes, and a bibliography. He thought that this work would prove of interest to theologians, sinologists, students of Asian topics or of comparative religion, and also to the non-specialist reading public; further, that it would supplement his other publications (listed in the bibliography below) about Confucian and Buddhist reactions to Christianity in the early seventeenth century. Consequently he submitted it in late 1981 for possible publication by the Institute of Jesuit Sources.

The present writer and Director of this Institute found himself pleased with the ready flow of what seemed to be a sound scholarly work. But knowing no Chinese, he also found himself unable to appraise its accuracy and completeness. Hence in the customary manner of seeking opinions of other scholars, he sent the draft to Father Edward J. Malatesta, a former professor of Scripture and theology in the Gregorian University, Rome, and at that time a professor in Fujen Catholic University, Taipei, Taiwan.

Malatesta offered enthusiastic encouragement, and also pointed out ways in which the book might be improved, particularly by use of a better Chinese text and by taking more account of modern research on problems of terminology and the like. For help he turned to a Chinese Jesuit, Father Peter Hu Kuo-chen, a graduate student already deeply engaged in textual and other studies on Ricci in the Faculty of Theology at Fujen University. Hu readily offered to help. Then Malatesta proposed a cooperative project between Lancashire, Hu, and himself, to which Lancashire graciously agreed.

From that time on Malatesta became the architect, supervisor, and finally the editor of the book. He suggested that it become a bilingual edition, and mediated the collaboration of all who have since become concerned: in England, Father Douglas Lancashire;

Publisher's Foreword

in Taiwan, Jesuit Fathers Peter Hu, Aloysius B. Chang, and Mark Fang of the Faculty of Theology at Fujen Catholic University, and Yves Raguin, Jean Lefeuvre, and Yves Camus of the Ricci Institute, Taipei; Miss Anny Chang, designer of the Hsiang Han Culture Corporation, Taipei—all of whom showed themselves warmly hospitable and helpful as we collaborated in the design, typesetting, and printing of the book.

Mention should be made, too, of the cooperation shown to the Institute of Jesuit Sources by the China Jesuit History Project, founded by the late sinologist Francis A. Rouleau, S.J., in Los Gatos, California, through Malatesta and his research associate, Dr. Theodore N. Foss, the two founders of the Institute for Chinese-Western Cultural History which was established in summer, 1984, at the University of San Francisco.

To all these collaborators who have made possible this book which the Institute of Jesuit Sources is happy to publish, we express our sincere thanks.

> George E. Ganss, S.J.
> Director and General Editor
> The Institute of Jesuit Sources
> September 27, 1984

TRANSLATORS' PREFACE

Recent years have witnessed the appearance of a number of studies of the Jesuit mission in China and, in particular, of Matteo Ricci whose reputation for being the most influential figure during the mission's early years has been shown to be eminently deserved. As the first noteworthy exponent of European religious, philosophical, and scientific thought in China, his Chinese publications on these subjects rightly rank as a landmark in Sino-European relations.

It is generally agreed that his two most important and influential publications were the *T'ien-chu shih-i* (*The True Meaning of the Lord of Heaven*) and his translation of the first six books of Euclid. Although frequent references to the first of these two works have been made in books on Ricci and the Jesuit mission, it has never to our knowledge been translated into English. The present translation, then, is an attempt to make up for this deficiency.

Three points should be made here. First, an interest in Ricci's life and work has not been confined to the specialist and, in consequence, there have appeared excellent books directed as much to the public as to the scholar. It is hoped that this translation will have as wide an appeal. Footnotes and comments, therefore, have been kept to a minimum; where possible, the reader is referred to the most accessible sources of information.

Second, Ricci was a pioneer in attempting to render into Chinese the theological and philosophical ideas of the West. Sometimes he used commonly employed Chinese terms to express Western concepts and at other times he created new combinations of Chinese characters. The English reader should bear in mind how difficult it is to obtain mutual understanding through such a process of communication. In the footnotes we try to explain some of the terms used.

Translators' Preface

Third, Ricci's dialogue takes for granted the philosophical and religious background current in his day in Ming China. Fortunately, in recent years works representative of the two most influential schools of Confucianism in the sixteenth and seventeenth centuries have been translated into English by Professor Wing-tsit Chan under the titles *Reflections on Things at Hand* (New York, 1967) and *Instructions for Practical Living* (New York, 1963). If Ricci's dialogue is studied in conjunction with these two works, the reader will quickly gain a clear picture of the issues at stake and, incidentally, be made aware of the formidable task Ricci and his colleagues had set themselves. It is to be hoped that one will also come to appreciate some of the spiritual riches to be found within the Chinese tradition.

We wish to express our deepest appreciation to Dr. Edel Lancashire who has read the whole manuscript and saved us from some grosser lapses in style. All errors in this text are, however, our own.

We wish also to record our thanks to Mrs. Jane Johnstone for the long hours she devoted to the typing of the manuscript, to Barbara Steffen and Janice Smith for transferring the text onto word processing disk, and to Father Edward J. Malatesta, S.J. who has given of himself unsparingly to the preparation of this work for publication.

Douglas Lancashire
Peter Hu Kuo-chen, S.J.
August 15, 1984

天主實義

THE TRUE MEANING
OF
THE LORD OF HEAVEN
(T'ien-chu Shih-i)

ABBREVIATIONS

ARSI   Archivum Romanum Societatis Iesu
ISCWCI International Symposium on Chinese-Western Cultural Interchange in Commemoration of the 400th Anniversary of the Arrival of Matteo Ricci, S.J. in China. Taipei, Taiwan, Republic of China, September 11-16, 1983. [= Volume containing the papers read at the symposium.]
JS   Japonica et Sinica section of ARSI
n.   note
no.   number
par.   paragraph
vol.   volume

TRANSLATORS' INTRODUCTION

1. The Life of Matteo Ricci

Established in 1534 and given formal recognition by Pope Paul III in 1540, the Society of Jesus declared its aims to be "to strive especially for the defense and propagation of the faith and for the progress of souls in Christian life and doctrine" and also "to go ... to whatsoever provinces they [the popes] may choose to send us—whether they are pleased to send us among the Turks or any other infidels, even those who live in the region called the Indies ..."[1] In a remarkably short space of time members of the Society were to be found in the Americas, India, and East Asia.

Francis Xavier (1506-1552), one of the founding members of the Society, made his way to Japan where, in little over two years, he established a thriving church. Noticing, however, "that whenever the Japanese were hard pressed in an argument, they always had recourse to the authority of the Chinese,"[2] and "that they commonly asserted, that if the Christian religion was really the one true religion, it surely would have been known to the intelligent Chinese and also accepted by them,"[3] Xavier determined to carry the message of Christianity to China and to convert its people.

---

1 See George E. Ganss, S.J., *The Constitutions of the Society of Jesus,* (St. Louis, 1970), pp. 65-68.
2 *China in the Sixteenth Century: The Journals of Matthew Ricci: 1583-1610,* translated from the Latin by Louis J. Gallagher, S.J. (New York, 1953), p.117.
3 Ibid., p.118.

Translators' Introduction

Returning to Goa, Xavier persuaded the viceroy of India and the bishop of Goa to organize an embassy to China to which he himself would be attached. When letters patent and letters of credence had been secured from the viceroy and the bishop, and appropriate presents prepared for the emperor, Xavier set out from Goa on 14 April 1552. Forbidden as a foreigner to enter China, however, Xavier landed on Shangchuan Island which was being used as a trading-post by Chinese and Portuguese merchants. There, at the age of forty-six, he died of a fever on 3 December 1552.[4]

On 16 October of the same year Matteo Ricci was born in Macerata, Italy. Here he began his schooling under a secular priest who was later to enter the Society of Jesus. At the age of seventeen his father sent him to Rome to study law. Believing that he had a religious vocation, however, the young Ricci applied for admittance to the Society and was received into the Order on the Feast of the Assumption, 15 August 1571.

At the time, the acting novice master was Father Alessandro Valignano, who was later to direct the affairs of the Society in India, Japan and China.[5] Ricci studied philosophy and mathematics at the Roman College and was fortunate enough to have as a teacher Christopher Clavius, the distinguished mathematician and friend of Kepler and Galileo. Towards the end of his student days in Rome he may have attended the Course of Controversies which the eminent theologian Robert Bellarmine had recently inaugurated.

At the Roman College Ricci was made very much aware of the Society's emphasis on foreign missions and eventually volunteered for work in the East. Given permission to join the India mission,

---

4 Ibid., pp.118ff.
5 See Josef Franz S.J., *Valignano's Mission Principles for Japan,* translated from the first part of the German original by John J. Coyne, S.J. (St. Louis, 1980).

Ricci, together with several colleagues, made his way in May, 1577, to Portugal, where he spent nine months at the University of Coimbra learning Portuguese and perhaps studying some theology. On 24 March 1578 he paid his respects to King Sebastian of Portugal and then embarked for India together with thirteen other Jesuits, among them Michele Ruggieri with whom he was destined to work for some years. Ricci arrived in Goa on 13 September 1578, and remained in India for four years "completing his course in Theology, acting as professor of Rhetoric, at Goa and at Cochin, and preparing for greater undertakings."[6] He was then assigned to the China mission.

In April, 1582, Ricci sailed from Goa, and when he arrived at the Portuguese enclave of Macao, received a warm welcome from his friend and colleague, Michele Ruggieri, who had preceded him. Also waiting for his arrival was the one who had received him into the novitiate, Valignano, who, as successor to Xavier, was now responsible for the missions in the region. Firm in the opinion that if the Church were to succeed in the Far East it would have to adapt itself, to some degree, to the cultural life of the area, Valignano, following his arrival in Macao in 1578, had set himself the task of learning what he could of the political and religious life of China. He soon came to the conclusion that if his missionaries were to have any chance of success among the Chinese they would have to do what, heretofore, none had done: they would have to master the Chinese language.

Both Ruggieri and, when he also arrived in Macao, Ricci were set the task of acquiring the language. Ricci proved the more adept of the two. It was not until 1583, however, that Ricci and Ruggieri

---

6 *China in the Sixteenth Century,* p.xii.

Translators' Introduction

were able to take up residence in China with official approval.[7] In that year, Wang P'an, prefect of Chaoching, invited Ruggieri to visit him. Unable to take with him Francesco Pasio, a companion on an earlier visit, Ruggieri arranged for Ricci to accompany him. With financial assistance from a Portuguese trader Ruggieri and Ricci set out for Chaoching in September. To make themselves more acceptable to the Chinese they shaved off their hair and beards and dressed themselves in the grey cloaks worn by Buddhist monks. They travelled from Macao by junk to Canton and thence to Chaoching where they were given permission to purchase some land on which to erect a residence.[8]

Ricci spent in all thirteen years in the province of Kwangtung. The results of his work, in terms of converts, were not great during this initial period, but in terms of Ricci's own development this was a time of profound importance. His knowledge of the Chinese language and of the Confucian texts, the teachings of which were normative for Chinese society, advanced to the point where he was able, in 1591, to commence a translation into Latin of the Four Books (the *Confucian Analects,* the *Book of Mencius,* the *Great Learning,* and the *Doctrine of the Mean*).[9] Much earlier than this, however, he had come to realize the importance of the printed word

---

[7] Ruggieri had been in Macao since July, 1579. On his arrival there he was instructed to apply himself to the study of Chinese. In November, 1580, he accompanied a group of Portuguese merchants to Canton and was invited to pay a second visit the following spring. On a third visit in autumn the intendant, sub-prefect, and military commander of the region attended a Mass he celebrated. See George Dunne, S.J., *Generation of Giants* (London, 1962), pp.18-19.

[8] For fuller details of the preparatory period leading up to Ricci's arrival in China the reader is referred to *Generation of Giants,* pp. 15-35; *China in the Sixteenth Century,* pp. 117-153; Vincent Cronin, *The Wise Man from the West* (London, 1955), pp. 16-40.

[9] *The Wise Man from the West,* p.107.

in China. It quickly became obvious to him that if he and his colleagues were to make any lasting impact on the Chinese nation it would have to be through publications. The point was brought home to him most forcefully when, towards the end of their first year in China, he and Ruggieri set out, with the aid of a Chinese convert from Macao who had been given the name Philip, to translate the Ten Commandments. The interest generated by this brief work, once it was in print, was so great that the two missionaries quickly set about producing another pamphlet containing the Lord's Prayer, the Hail Mary, and the Creed.[10]

Maps and clocks, mathematics, astronomy and music, however, were to be the things that would attract the attention of the majority of the educated. Chinese cartography already had a long and respectable history behind it, but whereas considerable accuracy had been achieved in mapping China, the Chinese cartographers' knowledge of other nations and regions was limited and, in consequence, when these other areas were included on Chinese maps they were totally distorted. Wang P'an persuaded Ricci to prepare a map in his own way so that it could be compared with the Chinese view of the world. When Ricci completed it he presented it, along with a clock which he had had built locally, to the prefect who was so pleased with the gift that he had it printed and copies distributed to his friends.[11]

The objective which had always been uppermost in the minds of Valignano and his missionaries in China was the establishment of a mission in Peking and the conversion of the emperor. Ricci decided to move north in 1595 and, after receiving permission from Valignano, took advantage of the occasion to transform his appearance from that of a Buddhist monk to that of a Confucian

10 Ibid., pp. 71-72.
11 Ibid., pp. 73-75.

Translators' Introduction

graduate.

When Ricci reached Nanking he was so impressed with this southern capital that he sought to reside in it and to establish a mission center. Receiving an official rebuff, however, he withdrew to Nanchang, the capital of the province of Kiangsi. Since Nanchang was a center of learning and of strong Buddhist influence, Ricci soon found the atmosphere there to be more relaxed than that in Nanking. Only days after his arrival he was invited to a banquet at which two princes were present.

It was at this banquet that Ricci gave a demonstration of his considerable powers of memory which, once they had become widely known, stimulated such interest in him that he soon found little difficulty in gaining access to some of the most influential men in the city. Despite the congenial atmosphere in Nanchang, however, Ricci's objective of reaching Peking still dominated his thoughts. He therefore proposed to Valignano that a papal embassy be established in Peking. Valignano gave him all the support he could, and Ricci set about making the necessary preparations for his entry into the capital. He travelled first to Nanking and then, by the Imperial Canal, to Peking.

He and a colleague reached Peking on 7 September 1598, only to discover that there was no easy route to the emperor and that political and social circumstances were such that temporary withdrawal from the capital was the wisest policy. Making his way to Soochow on horseback he fell ill and remained in a state of great weakness until the end of January 1599. A visit to Nanking in February convinced Ricci that he should make a further attempt to establish a mission center in that city. Hideyoshi, the Japanese minister who had led a successful campaign against Korea and thereby threatened the security of China, had suddenly died, and, with the withdrawal of Japanese troops from the Korean peninsula, Chinese officials were in a more relaxed and cheerful mood. Sensing the improvement in the situation Ricci rented a house and, having come to the conclusion that he would only win firm friends among the educated through his abilities as a mathematician and scientist, set about finding pupils interested in such skills. Assured, however, through his study of the Confucian classics that Confucianism in its earliest manifestations was a nearly perfect expression of the "natural law" and that it served as a natural foundation for Christian teaching in China, Ricci determined to undermine the hold that Buddhism still had on the minds of so many among both the educated and uneducated. His aim was to counteract the influence of Buddhism while presenting Christianity as the fulfillment of primitive Confucianism.

Although it is commonly asserted that Buddhism began to decline in importance from the middle of the ninth century and that the rise of Neo-Confucianism in the Sung dynasty (960—1278) helped to accelerate this decline, Buddhism in the Ming dynasty (1368—1644) continued to exercise a powerful influence at all levels of society, to dictate developments in Confucian thought, and even to win the allegiance of men of great intellectual ability. The defense of what he felt to be best in Confucianism and the refutation of Buddhism were therefore to demand of Ricci all the mental ingenuity and skill he could muster.

Probably Ricci's most celebrated encounter with Buddhism took place during the time he was resident in Nanking. Invited on one occasion to a banquet he was brought face to face with Huang Hung-en, better known as San Huai, who was one of the leading Buddhist monks in China at that time. As, no doubt, everyone present had hoped, Ricci and Huang soon found themselves engaged in a religious dispute—a dispute in which neither man could have been pronounced the victor, but which was to increase the respect in which Ricci was held, and to have an effect on the arguments Ricci was eventually to put forward against Buddhism in *The True Meaning of the Lord of Heaven.*

Once Ricci had acquired permanent premises for the mission in

Translators' Introduction

Nanking he again turned his attention to the task of establishing himself in Peking. Arriving back in the capital in 1601 Ricci managed, despite considerable difficulties, to have the presents he had prepared, delivered to the emperor. Although the emperor and Ricci were never to meet face to face, the sovereign's interest in certain of the gifts he had received, in particular several clocks, resulted in Ricci's being able to win a foothold in Peking.

The years 1601—1610 marked the peak of Ricci's achievements. It was during these years that he was to witness the conversion of Hsü Kuang-ch'i (1562—1633) and Li Chih-tsao (1565-1630), two of the "three pillars of the early church" in China. With the help of Hsü and Li, scientific works, including the first six books of Euclid's *Elements*, were translated into Chinese, and in 1603, *The True Meaning of the Lord of Heaven* was finally published. Ricci died on 11 May 1610. He was buried in land on the outskirts of Peking which had been designated by the emperor for this purpose and for the erection of a new residence for the mission.[12]

2. History of the Composition and Publication of The True Meaning of the Lord of Heaven

Since the end of the nineteenth century, Chinese and foreign scholars have differed in their opinions regarding the dates of composition and publication of *The True Meaning of the Lord of Heaven*. The most important writers in this field have been Louis Pfister, S.J.,[13] Pasquale M. D'Elia, S.J.,[14] and Hsü Tsung-tse, S.J,

12 For full accounts of Ricci's years in China the reader is again referred to the relevant chapters in *China in the Sixteenth Century, Generation of Giants,* and *The Wise Man from the West*. The definitive edition of Ricci's memoirs was published by Pasquale M. D'Elia, S.J. under the title *Fonti Ricciane,* 3 volumes (Rome, 1942-1949).
13 *Notices biographiques et bibliographiques* (Shanghai, 1932), I, pp. 34-35 (Variétés Sinologiques, no. 59).
14 *Fonti Ricciane,* I, pp. 379-380; II, pp. 292-293.

the twelfth generation descendant of Hsü Kuang-ch'i.[15] Their views have been investigated and analyzed by the historian Lin Tung-yang who concludes that D'Elia has come closest to the truth and that his account of the process by which the work was completed is most in accord with circumstances and reason.[16]

When Francis Xavier felt the urge while in Japan to preach the gospel on Chinese soil, he was already conscious of the important effect that the literary and scholarly dissemination of the faith could have on Chinese culture and on the strata of society which could be reached by these means. Many comments in his extant letters illustrate his thinking in this connection. One such letter was that written to John III, King of Portugal, on 8 April 1552 from Goa. In his letter Xavier begs the king to press the Society of Jesus to send more priests to the East, but not to send those who could only preach. Because the people of China and Japan were well-educated and fond of learning, what was required were priests of high scholastic caliber and of a profound experience of life.[17]

Although Xavier never obtained his wish to enter China, he nevertheless laid the foundation for his successors to preach the gospel through literary and scholarly means. Valignano held to the same policy and it was he, as we have seen, who sent Ruggieri, Ricci, and others to China. This approach provides the ultimate reason for the writing of *The True Meaning of the Lord of Heaven*.

Ruggieri arrived in Macao in 1579 and began at once to study the Chinese language. His aim was to prepare himself to expound Christian thought through books written in Chinese. At first he

---

15 Hsü Tsung-tse, S.J., *An Outline of Jesuit Publications of Late Ming and Early Ch'ing* (Taipei, 1958), pp. 142-143. (In Chinese.)

16 Lin Tung-yang, "Several Problems Concerning Matteo Ricci's *The True Meaning of the Lord of Heaven* and *Ten Chapters by a Non-conformist*," *Ta-lu tsa-chih* 56 (1978), 26-44. (In Chinese.)

17 Felix Zubillaga, S.J., ed., *Cartas y Escritos de San Francisco Javier* (Madrid, 1953), pp. 463-464.

Translators' Introduction

cooperated with Father Piero Gomes in the drawing up of a catechism for the use of Chinese catechumens. The catechism was translated from the Latin into Chinese with the help of a copyist from Fukien, the first draft being completed in 1581 and the final version at the end of 1583. Finally, it was revised over a period of four or five months by Matteo Ricci and a Confucian scholar resident in Chaoching before publication in November 1584. This catechism, written in Chinese and in the form of questions and answers, was called *True Record of the Lord of Heaven - A New Compilation from India*. Its Latin title was *Vera et brevis divinarum rerum expositio*.

In 1596 when Ricci had completed his first draft of *The True Meaning of the Lord of Heaven,* the earlier work of Ruggieri was destroyed. But after 1637, Father João Monteiro and two others revised the text, making additions and subtractions, and published it again, changing its name to *True Record of the Sacred Teachings Concerning the Lord of Heaven*. It is not clear when or where this edition was published, but it must have been sometime during the Ming dynasty. A copy of a later printing of the work was preserved in the Jesuit library of Zikawei in Shanghai.

According to a copy from the first printing of *A True Record of the Lord of Heaven - A New Compilation from India* kept in the Jesuit Archives in Rome, the work consisted of sixteen chapters. The contents can be divided into five sections:

1. There is one Lord of Heaven (preface). His existence (chapter one), His nature, and His mystery (chapters two and three).

2. The Lord of Heaven is the creator of the universe (chapter four), of angels and mankind (chapter five), and of souls which neither die nor are destroyed (chapters five, six, and seven).

3. The Lord of Heaven is a judge who admonished man on three occasions: when He created man and bestowed on him a conscience; when He promulgated the Ten Commandments by the hand of Moses on Mount Sinai; and when He came Himself to earth as man

Composition and Publication

and proclaimed the New Law (chapters eight, nine, ten, and eleven).

4. The Ten Commandments (chapters twelve, thirteen, and fourteen).

5. The Lord of Heaven punishes sinners and rewards the just; moral cultivation and the ascent to Heaven (chapter fifteen). Baptism washes away sin (chapter sixteen).

From the foregoing account of its contents it is clear that *A True Record of the Lord of Heaven* is a catechism. Although incomplete in certain respects—for example, in its failure to make any mention of the Trinity or to treat of any sacraments besides baptism—the work nevertheless gives an excellent account of the heart of the Christian faith: the Incarnation and Redemption.[18]

But because this book was compiled by Ruggieri, Ricci, and others shortly after their arrival in China and before they had had time to understand fully the social concepts and value systems within Chinese culture, they referred to themselves as "bonzes from India" and, in their book, made frequent use of Buddhist terminology paying scant attention to Confucian scholarship and totally ignoring the existence of the religious aspects of Taoism.

The new missionaries eventually made some important discoveries. Buddhist monks were little respected in China and Confucian scholars looked on Buddhism as heterodox. While the polytheism of popular Taoism was not in accord with the basic spirit of original Confucianism, there were many areas of agreement between this spirit and the basic outlook of Christianity. Ricci then began to consider presenting himself as a "Confucian scholar" and introducing the concepts of the Catholic religion in terms of Confucian learning.

This change of attitude and style on the part of Matteo Ricci probably took place about the year 1591. In December of that year he began to translate the Confucian *Four Books* into Latin, and

---

18 *Fonti Ricciane,* I, pp. 197-198. See Joseph Shih, S.J., *Le Père Ruggieri et le problème de l'évangelisation en Chine.* Excerpt from a doctoral dissertation (Rome, 1964).

sometime before 24 October of the following year he decided to stop referring to himself as "bonze" and expressed the wish to change his dress to that of a Confucian scholar.

In 1593 Valignano urged Ricci to begin writing a book of first principles for intellectuals. On 10 December of that same year Ricci wrote to Father General Aquaviva that the friend who had urged him to translate the *Four Books* into Latin was just in the process of helping him to compile a new book on first principles.[19] It can safely be assumed that Ricci was referring to the commencement of work on *The True Meaning of the Lord of Heaven*. Ricci's chief aim in translating the *Four Books* was to search out material directly and genuinely related to China's cultural heritage for the rewriting of the now defunct catechism *True Record of the Lord of Heaven*.

The translation of the *Four Books* was completed in November of 1594, and Ricci immediately went on to study the *Six Classics,* devoting about a year to them. On 4 November 1595 Ricci wrote to Father General Aquavia: "I have noted down many terms and phrases in harmony with our faith, for instance, 'the unity of God,' 'the immortality of the soul,' 'the glory of the blessed,' and the like."[20] Manifestly he was systematically seeking in China's ancient canonical writings for similar doctrines with the highest degree of authority in order to discuss them with China's men of learning.

A comparison of the table of contents of *True Record of the Lord of Heaven* with that of *The True Meaning of the Lord of Heaven* reveals that those sections in the former work which allow for philosophical consideration, explanation, or proof—such as the existence of God, nature and the act of creation, the differences between the human soul and the souls of birds and animals, the im-

---

19 *Fonti Ricciane,* I, p. 379.
20 Ibid., II, p. 295. See Pasquale M. D'Elia, S.J., "Prima Introduzione della Filosofia Scolastica in Cina," *The Bulletin of the Institute of History and Philology, Academia Sinica* 28 (1956), 149-150.

perishability of the human soul—are all preserved in *The True Meaning of the Lord of Heaven*. But the sections which treat of God's revelation and cannot be considered by philosophical methods alone have been totally removed. On the other hand, topics like "intention" and the "goodness of human nature" have been added. These changes clearly show that Ricci was striving to expound Catholic thought with the aid of China's existing cultural heritage. To proceed in such a fashion meant that it was manifestly impossible to give an account of those elements of the faith classed as pure revelation, and also impossible to compile a "catechism." For these reasons *The True Meaning of the Lord of Heaven* can appropriately be called a "pre-evangelical dialogue."

There can be little doubt that as soon as he had completed his search into China's canonical writings and had gathered relevant material from them at the end of 1595, Ricci would have begun immediately to rewrite the usable parts of *True Record of the Lord of Heaven,* removing Buddhist vocabulary and substituting terms and phrases from the Chinese classics. A year later, in October 1596, the first draft of *The True Meaning of the Lord of Heaven* was finished. Ricci then made copies for his Chinese friends to read and sent a Latin rendering to the Bishop of Japan resident in Macao, Don Luis Cerqueira. The visitor, Valignano, and the leader of the Chinese mission, Father Duarte de Sande, examined the text and pointed out places where minor changes were required. When the Chinese draft had been corrected, Valignano handed the text over to de Sande on 16 July 1598, instructing him to return it to Ricci when he went on an inspection tour of the Jesuit residences at Chaochou and Nanchang. Unfortunately, Ricci had already departed for the north on 25 June 1598 and de Sande fell ill and died in the middle of July, 1599. Thus it was not until Ricci arrived in Peking in 1601 that he received the corrected draft.[21]

21 *Fonti Ricciane,* II, p. 292.

Translators' Introduction

Between 1596 and 1601 the handwritten draft was circulated and copied by various people, and quite a number of additional handwritten copies thus went into circulation in a variety of places. It was because Hsü Kuang-ch'i read Father João da Rocha's handwritten copy of the work in Nanking that he decided to be baptized and to enter the Church. Li Chih-tsao, on the other hand, read chapter five of Ricci's manuscript, which was concerned with the subject of fasting, and made his own copy of it.[22] Feng Ying-ching, after reading the first draft, promptly wrote a preface to it expressing his willingness to help defray the cost of printing the book.[23]

While all this was taking place, Ricci was traveling from Nanchang to Nanking, and then to Peking. As his circle of friends steadily increased, he had new opportunities for conversation about ethical and religious questions. Material from a considerable number of significant conversations was incorporated by Ricci into his *Ch'i-jen shih p'ien* (*Ten Chapters by a Non-conformist*) which was eventually published in 1608. The history of this publication allows us reasonably to infer that the ten conversations recorded in it were held with the following persons and at the following times:

1. 1601, Li Tai, "Time past must be thought of as gone forever."
2. 1603, Fêng Chi, "Man is a stranger in this world."
3. 1604, Hsü Kuang-ch'i, "To think of the future life contributes to progress in virtue."
4. 1604-1607, Hsü Kuang-ch'i, "To think of the future life prepares for a favorable judgment after death."
5. 1601-1607, Ts'ao Yü-pien, "The virtuous person speaks little or not at all."
6. 1601, Li Chih-tsao, "The purpose of fasting is not to prevent the slaughter of animals."

---

22 Lin Tung-yang, op. cit. (see above note 16), pp. 29-31; *Fonti Ricciane,* II, pp. 292-293.
23 Lin Tung-yang, ibid., pp. 34-35; *Fonti Ricciane,* II, p. 301.

7. 1599-1600, Wu Tso-hai, "Self-examination and self-reproach prevent mistakes."

8. 1605, Wu Tao-li, "After death, the good are rewarded and the wicked punished."

9. 1589, Mr. Kuo, "Seeking predictions of the future is harmful."

10. 1595-1598, a rich man, "The rich who are greedy and stingy cause the poor to suffer."[24]

A careful investigation of the contents of *Ten Chapters by a Nonconformist* shows that conversations prior to 1603 (namely, nos. 1, 2, 6, 7, 9, and 10) have much of their dialogue reproduced in *The True Meaning of the Lord of Heaven*. The most obvious case is in chapter two of *Ten Chapters* and the beginning of chapter three of *The True Meaning*. Apart from minor changes in vocabulary, the terms and sentences in both are almost identical.[25] Furthermore, in that part of *The True Meaning* the method of reasoning is almost entirely that common in Chinese philosophical circles.[26]

Moreover, chapter seven of *The True Meaning* contains part of a discussion held with the Buddhist monk San-huai in 1599 in Nanking, and chapter four incorporates arguments with the devout Buddhist Huang Hui in 1601 or 1602.[27] Only after all this material had been added and final corrections made did Ricci write his "Introduction" to the whole work, which was completed on 22 August 1603.

When the manuscript was finished, with the financial support of Feng Ying-ching, Ricci arranged for the carving of the printing blocks. At the same time, however, he had several manuscript copies circulated among friends for their perusal and final suggestions for

---

24 *Fonti Ricciane*, II, pp. 302-304.
25 Lin Tung-yang, op. cit., pp. 26-28.
26 Ricci himself writes at the beginning of *The True Meaning of the Lord of Heaven*, par.26: "Now you, Sir, desire to learn the principles of the teachings of the Lord of Heaven. I shall therefore state them plainly for you, and my explanations will be based solely on reason." We have not been able to examine in the present work which European books Ricci might have used in composing *The True Meaning of the Lord of Heaven*.
27 See *Fonti Ricciane*, II, pp. 75-80; 180, n. 6; 182, n. 2.

Translators' Introduction

improvements in content and style. When blocks for the entire text had been carved, Ricci carried out a final review of the text eliminating or changing unsuitable characters.

Evidence that the printing blocks were corrected in the manner described can be seen most clearly in the dialogue recorded near the end of chapter one (see par. 53). Each line on the original printing blocks consisted of twenty character places, one character occupying one place. The layout is exceedingly regular. But in the fourth character place of the first line on the ninth page of a copy of the first edition now held in the Biblioteca Casanatense in Rome, two characters (*shih erh,* "twelve") are to be found. There can only be one explanation for this departure from the norm. A change was made on the block subsequent to its first carving.

According to the reading in the first edition, the minister at first asked his prince to allow him three days for reflection, and then he asked for a further six days and, when this time had elapsed, he asked for twelve days more. Now, when we turn to the same account in the third edition of the book, the text of which was freshly carved in Hangchow in 1607, we discover nothing untoward. One character regularly occupies one character place, but the minister asks his prince only one day for reflection and then two days and, finally, four days. Manifestly, this is the sentence which appeared in the original copy made by hand, and all the handwritten copies would have had twenty character places in a line. Artisans who carved blocks for printing always made faithful copies of the handwritten texts submitted to them. We can therefore deduce that in 1603, when Ricci was preparing his final draft for the carvers, there was assuredly a number of handwritten manuscripts in circulation among his friends, and that the third edition freshly carved in Hangchow in 1607 was not based on the "official" first edition printed and distributed in Peking in 1603. Rather it used another handwritten copy which had not taken account of the final corrections made by Ricci on the printing blocks of his first edition.

It is probable that someone would normally check the carving after the text had been transferred from the manuscript to the wood blocks. Because on the occasion of the first edition Ricci had carried out this task himself, the name of a final inspector is nowhere

Composition and Publication

given. On the other hand, in the case of the third edition, published and distributed by the Yen-i Pavilion, a person attached to that company acted as final inspector of the printing blocks. That is why at the beginning of each of the parts of the work there appears beneath the words "Written by Matteo Ricci, member of the Society of Jesus" the additional statement that "Final examination of the carved blocks was carried out by the Yen-i Pavilion," thus showing who was responsible for this operation.

From what has been said above we can propose the various stages which led to the composition of *The True Meaning of the Lord of Heaven,* its first printing, and distribution:

1579-1584 Composition of Ruggieri's *True Record of the Lord of Heaven.*

1584-1591 Use of Ruggieri's book in evangelization and discovery of its inadequacies for the Chinese mentality.

1591-1594 Ricci translates the *Four Books* into Latin. He realizes that Ruggieri's work must be replaced; Valignano agrees.

1594-1595 Ricci selects quotations from the *Six Classics.*

1595-1596 Ricci writes the first draft of *The True Meaning.*

1596-1600 Ricci's text is examined by ecclesiastical and Jesuit censors, while his friends circulate the manuscript.

1601 Feng Ying-ching writes a preface.

1601-1603 Permission is granted for publication. Ricci adds new material as a result of his conversations.

1603 Preparation of the woodblocks for the first xylographic edition. Ricci himself writes an introduction. Before the actual first printing some changes are made on the wood blocks. The first edition at Peking consists of 200 copies.

1604 Ricci sends a copy of the first edition to Father General Aquaviva in Rome, adding in his own hand a Latin translation of Feng Ying-ching's preface, his own in-

Translators' Introduction

troduction, and a Latin summary of the eight chapters.[28]

Once the first edition was published in Peking, there quickly followed other printings in different places in China during the Ming dynasty. A second xylographic edition was published in Canton in 1605 at the order of Valignano who wished to send it to Japan. The Yen-i Pavilion published a third edition in Hangchow in 1607 which was subsidized by Wang Meng-p'u and for which Li Chih-tsao wrote a preface.[29]

A copy of the third edition exists in the Jesuit Archives in Rome. A second known copy was first deposited in the former Jesuit library of Zikawei, Shanghai and was then transferred to the Order's residence in Taichung, Taiwan. In the heat of the Chinese Rites Controversy, Pope Clement XI in 1704 issued an edict banning the use of the terms *T'ien,* "Heaven," and *Shang-ti,* "Sovereign on High," as designations for God. Thus, in subsequent printings of *The True Meaning of the Lord of Heaven* these terms were always replaced by *T'ien-chu,* "Lord of Heaven."

Besides the editions just mentioned, we know of the following: an undated printing on new woodblocks by Yen-i Pavilion; an undated printing by the Ch'in-i Pavilion in Fukien; a new woodblock printing by Tou-se-we, Shanghai in 1868; another edition at Hsien-hsien, Hopei in 1898. Printings with metal type were made at Tou-se-we, Shanghai in 1904, 1930, and 1935; at Hsien-hsien in 1933; at Yenchow, Shantung in 1938; at Nazareth Retreat House, Hong

---

28 Ricci's Latin summary can be found in the appendix at the end of this volume.

29 An English translation of Li Chih-tsao's preface can be found in *Sources of Chinese Tradition,* compiled by Wm. Theodore de Bary, Wing-tsit Chan, and Burton Watson (New York, 1960), pp. 626-629. D'Elia, in the article cited above in note 20, included his own Italian translation of the prefaces of Feng Ying-ching (1601), Li Chih-tsao (1607), Ku Feng-hsiang (1609), of Ricci's introduction (1603), and of the epilogue by Wang Ju-shun (1607).

Kong, 1939.

Ricci's original text was published together with a rendering into contemporary Chinese by Chu Hsing-yuan and T'ien Ching-hsien, Ch'ung-te Pavilion, Tientsin, 1941; and by Liu Shun-te, Kuang-chi Press, Taichung, Taiwan, 1966.[30]

Over the years translations have been made into Manchu,[31] Korean, Vietnamese, French,[32] and Japanese.[33]

3. The Present English Translation

The present publication represents the first English translation of the entire text of *The True Meaning of the Lord of Heaven* and of Ricci's own introduction to the work. Having compared the third edition with a microfilm copy of the first edition obtained from the Biblioteca Casanatense in Rome the translators found that the third edition printed in Hangchow is not a direct copy or an adjustment of the original text which preceded it. It seems likely that it was based on a current handwritten copy. During more than three hundred years, the various reprints and editions which appeared all over China followed either the text of the first edition or that of the third. There are, therefore, numerous variations in the texts

---

30 The former rendering used a modified edition of the original but succeeded in penetrating Ricci's outlook. The latter rendering used the third edition, but in the view of the present translators did not fully capture Ricci's mind.

31 A copy of the Manchu version exists in ARSI, *JS* I, 48A, 48B.

32 "Entretiens d'un Lettré Chinois et d'un Docteur Européen, sur la vraie idée de Dieu," in *Lettres édifiantes et curieuses, écrites des missions étrangères.* Nouvelle édition. Mémoires des Indes et de la Chine (Toulouse, 1811), pp. 143-385.

33 The most recent Japanese edition, which we were able to consult, is translated and edited by Goto Motomi (Tokyo, Meitaku Shuppansha, 1971). Only the most important sections have been translated and these have been provided with a commentary and footnotes.

Translators' Introduction

of the various editions now extant. The English translation presented here is based on the first edition and it is the Chinese of the first edition which is printed in this volume. The third edition has, however, served as a supplementary text. We also consulted some of the editions and translations listed above for the resolution of minor textual problems.

We have given paragraph numbers to the natural, shorter divisions of the text for the purpose of facilitating citations and cross references.

4. Ricci's Viewpoint and the Contents of the Work

The slogan *Ch'in ju p'ai fo,* "Draw close to Confucianism and repudiate Buddhism," served as a compass bearing for Ricci in his work of disseminating the Christian faith, and in his writing of *The True Meaning of the Lord of Heaven*. What most concerned Confucians was the task of moral self-improvement covering the span of a lifetime, and therefore Ricci's purpose from the beginning to the end of *The True Meaning of the Lord of Heaven* was to expound the nature of self-cultivation. He emphasized that the Confucian gentleman who had set himself the task of self-cultivation had both to believe in and serve God. Similarly, he described how the person who was a believer had to engage in self-cultivation if he was to achieve the greatest good. Ricci drew extensively on the ancient Chinese classics of the Confucian School in order to justify his arguments.

But the Confucian classics are primarily concerned with the relationship between Heaven and man and make little reference to the attributes either of man or of God. Ricci therefore employed theories current in Chinese philosophical circles together with any material he could find concerning God and man in order to clarify these matters. This represented one aspect of his "augmentation of Confucianism." Another is to be found in his attacks on the nihilistic tendencies in Taoism and the pantheistic trends in Buddhism and in the Neo-Confucianism of the Sung and Ming dynasties. He was likewise strongly opposed to the superstitious customs and practices so widespread among the populace.

But *The True Meaning of the Lord of Heaven* is also deeply colored both in its contents and in its structure by the *Spiritual Exercises* of St. Ignatius of Loyola and by the *Constitutions* which he composed for the Society of Jesus. The fact that Ricci's dialogue limits itself to being a "preparation for the gospel" and treats salvation history only towards the end of the work in chapter eight, reflects the basic attitude that one giving the Spiritual Exercises is expected to maintain. "The Spiritual Exercises must be adapted to the nature of those who wish to undergo them, suited, that is, to their age, education or ability...Again, each should be given whatever is proper to what he has in mind, so that he may get help and benefit..."(*Spiritual Exercises*, [18]).

Ricci found himself writing for Confucian scholars who were totally lacking any knowledge of the tenets of Christianity and who therefore could not easily discuss anything like God's revelation of Himself in history. Further, the Chinese had a particular antipathy towards such teachings as the suffering and death of God. Keeping in mind the particular mindset of his readers, Ricci divided his book into two parts with a total of eight chapters.

In *Part One* he begins by setting out the proofs for the existence of God, asserting that God created the universe and all things and giving an account of His attributes (chapter one). Next, Ricci uses the classical Confucianism prior to the Ch'in dynasty (221-206 B.C.) to criticize the Taoist concept *Wu*, "Non-being" and the Buddhist concept *K'ung*, "Voidness." He then employs such terms as *tzu-li-che*, "substance," and *i-lai-che* "accident" concepts current in philosophical circles of the time, to demonstrate the inappropriateness of speaking of God as "Supreme Ultimate" and "Principle," as the Neo-Confucianist philosophers appeared to him

Translators' Introduction

to do. He also gives reasons for equating the traditional Chinese terms for God, *T'ien*, "Heaven," and *Shang-ti*, "Sovereign on High," with *T'ien-chu*, "Lord of Heaven," the term decided upon by the Jesuits to designate God (chapter two).

Ricci turns next to the question of the soul and seeks to demonstrate its existence along with the existence of purely spiritual beings by reference to China's traditional Confucian classics. He also explains that human souls are different from the souls of plants and animals, and that it is impossible to regard Heaven, Earth and all creation as sharing in one body (chapters three and four).

Part Two begins with an attack on the Buddhist doctrine of reincarnation and the Six Ways of sentient existence. He also criticizes the Buddhist prohibition against the killing of non-human living things and explains the true significance of fasting (chapter five). From the doctrine of the imperishability of the soul he deduces the existence and imperishability of thought and intention, and concludes that good and evil actions are respectively the outcome of upright and depraved thought. He then proceeds to prove from the Chinese classics the existence of both Heaven and Hell and that they are the destinations of the good and the evil after death (chapter six).

Ricci next treats the question of human nature and its goodness or depravity. From this he proceeds to the worship of God and states how worshippers should practice self-cultivation (chapter seven). In the same chapter he argues against certain Buddhist practices and opposes a sect called the "Three in One School," which sought to harmonize the teachings of Confucianism, Buddhism, and Taoism.

Finally, Ricci clarifies the manner in which Catholic priests engage in self-cultivation. He discusses celibacy and its relationship to filial piety (chapter eight).

These main themes of Ricci's book show us that he did not set out to discuss in depth God's revelation of Himself in history. The translators of the book, therefore, prefer to describe it as a "pre-evangelical dialogue" rather than as a "catechism." Nevertheless, in a small section at the end of chapter eight the Western scholar gives a brief outline of the Incarnation and of God's saving work as a guide to the Chinese scholar, so that he might accept the faith and be baptized. Obviously, a person who having read this book should wish to be baptized and join the Church, would require further instruction in order to know all the beliefs proper to Christian discipleship.

5. *A Detailed Outline of* The True Meaning of the Lord of Heaven
(In this outline, the number before the comma refers to the chapter, and the number following the comma to the paragraph divisions, for example, I,16-27 indicates chapter one, paragraphs sixteen to twenty-seven.)

Ricci's Introduction: The reason for writing the present work. 1-15

I. *The aims and methods of the writer.* I,16-27
   A. The relationship between the discipline of self-cultivation, the will of God, and life after death. I,16-18
   B. Reason as the principal tool of discussion. I,19-27

II. *A Discussion about God.* I,28—II,116
   A. God as creator and ruler of the universe. I,28-64
      1. The existence of the ruler of the universe. I,28-31
      2. This ruler is the creator of the universe. I,32-40
      3. The self-existence and eternity of God. I,41-42
      4. The manner of God's creative work. I,43-47
      5. The uniqureness of God. I,48-50
      6. The nature of God. I,51-64
   B. Refutation of theories concerning the source of created things in various schools of thought. II,65-101
      1. The basic theories of the three schools of thought (Taoism, Buddhism and Confucianism) governing the discipline of self-cultivation. II,65-66

Translators' Introduction

      2. Rejection of the Taoist concept of "Nothingness" and the Buddhist concept of "Voidness." II,67-76

      3. Rejection of the Neo-Confucian concepts of "Supreme Ultimate" and "Principle." II,77-101

   C. Designation of God in China. II,102-116

      1. Sovereign on High (not the supreme deity of religious Taoism). II, 102-108

      2. Heaven. II,109-116

III. *A Discussion about Man.* III,117—VII,520

   A. The true end of man is not in this world but in the world to come. III,117-130

      1. This world is an animal world. Man is born into it and experiences a lifetime of suffering. III,117-126

      2. Man is born into this world to cultivate the Way and thereby to seek after the joys of everlasting life in Heaven. III,127-130

   B. The condition of man in this life. III,131-300

      1. Man is different from plants and animals. III,131-169

         a. Man possesses a spiritual and animal soul. III,131-132

         b. There are three grades of soul in the world: the vegetative, sensitive, and spiritual. Man's soul is spiritual. III,133

         c. Why vegetative and sensitive souls perish along with the body, whereas the spiritual soul exists forever. III,134-138

         d. Why the animal, sensitive soul is a bodily soul while the soul of man is spirit. III,139-150

         e. Proof that the soul of man is imperishable based chiefly on views concerning rewards and punishments in the hereafter. III,151-169

      2. Man's soul differs from spirits. IV,170-206

         a. Writings of ancient times employed to prove the ex-

A Detailed Outline

       istence of spirits, including the human soul. IV,170-183

    b. Although the soul exists eternally after death it does not remain long in this world unless God causes it to do so. IV,184-187

    c. Spirits and the soul are not *ch'i* (material-energy). Material-energy may accumulate or disperse and possesses physical properties; spirits and the soul do not. IV,188-190

    d. Spirits attached to created things are external to them and are different from the soul which is an internal and integral part of man. IV,191-201

    e. *Ch'i* (material-energy) is different from spirits. IV,202-206

  3. Man as created is distinct from God. IV,207-237

    a. Rejection of the Buddhist and Neo-Confucian teaching that "Heaven, Earth, and all things form one body," and that "God and creation are physically one." IV.,207-209

    b. Man is limited and cannot be equated with God. Man's creative powers are limited by his being aware only of the laws of Heaven and Earth. He can fall into sin and thus his mind and awareness become confused. IV,210-221

    c. Why God cannot be equated with man or be regarded as an inner part of him. IV,222-231

    d. Man's nature is good and his soul is pure insofar as he bears the image of God, but this image is not God Himself. IV,232-237

  4. Man does not share one body with the created world. IV,238-257

    a. Confucians adopted this "one body" teaching to encourage man to follow the path of humanity (*Jen*),

Translators' Introduction

   but some instead turned away from the path of humanity and righteousness. IV,238-248
   b. Why created things cannot all share one body. IV,249-257
5. Human beings do not have a prior existence. V,258-284
   a. Buddhism teaches that individuals have previous existences. This teaching was first promulgated to dissuade people from doing evil. It was not an objective account about the human condition. V,258-262
   b. No one can remember events of a former life; therefore there cannot be a former life. The few accounts of former existences in Buddhist records were designed by the devil to lead people astray. V,263-266
   c. Reasons why the human soul cannot become an animal. V,267-282
   d. The human soul is spiritual; it does not occupy space and it does not require rebirth to transform it. V,283-284
6. Heaven, Earth and all things are created for the use of humans. There is no need to prohibit the killing of animals. V,285-300
   a. The killing of animals and the prohibition against the killing of human persons. V,285-286
   b. Examples of how Heaven, Earth, and all things are meant for our use. V,287-288
   c. Things harmful to our bodies encourage us to practice caution and cause us not to forget Heaven and the afterlife. V,289-293
   d. Vegetation and animals are shown to be creatures possessing life. Eating them and using them are beneficial. V,294-300

C. The Way to eternal life is to become a good and virtuous person. V,301-520

A Detailed Outline

1. The true motives for fasting and cultivating the Way. V,301-320
   a. The three true motives for fasting. V,301-302
   b. The first motive: repentance and atonement for sin. V,303-304
   c. The second motive: to purify the heart and reduce desires. V,305-308
   d. The third motive: to help man cultivate virtue. V,309-315
   e. Methods of fasting, which are not limited to dieting. V,316-320
2. The motivation for doing good and avoiding evil. VI,321-420
   a. Confucianism also advocates purity of intention or sincerity. VI,321-324
   b. Taoists advocate "lack of intention." This is no different from classifying man with metals, stones, vegetation, and animals. VI,325-332
   c. The goodness or evil of actions is determined by one's motives. VI,333-335
   d. Apart from correct motivation, actions themselves must be correct. VI,336-340
   e. Examples from ancient Chinese records adduced to illustrate the connection between motivation and efficacy, gain and loss, reward and punishment. VI,341-352
   f. The need to pursue "the benefits of the world to come." V1,353-364
   g. Three correct motivations. Ordinary people wish to obtain reward in Heaven and avoid punishment in Hell. The Gentleman and the Sage seek to harmonize their wills with the will of God. VI,365-372
   h. The need for rewards for good and evil to be in the

Translators' Introduction

        next life, rather than in this one, and the reasons for the existence of Heaven and Hell. VI,373-385
- i. Rewards and punishments also exist in this life. V1,386-388
- j. Use of ancient Chinese texts to prove the existence of Heaven and Hell. VI,389-395
- k. Standards of judgement related to reward and punishment after death and to Purgatory. VI,396-401
- l. The Gentleman is bound to believe in the existence of Heaven and Hell because God is supremely just and supremely humane. VI,402-410
- m. Descriptions of Heaven and Hell. VI,411-420

3. Persons must apply themselves to the cultivation of virtue. VII,421-520
   - a. Definitions of the terms "nature," "human nature," "good," and "evil" for the purpose of expounding the teaching that "nature is fundamentally good." VII,421-429
   - b. Distinguishing between "natural goodness" and the "goodness of virtue." Good persons, sages, and worthies are people of virtue. VII,430-438
   - c. The difficulty of cultivating virtue. VII,439-444
   - d. The greatest value of learning lies in spiritual self-cultivation in order to be in accord with God's will. VII,445-455
   - e. Perfection of oneself for God and perfection of oneself for self are the same. VII,456-459
   - f. The work of self-cultivation. (This section is related to that above on fasting.) VII,460-487
     1) First, self-examination and repentance. VII,460-465

A Detailed Outline

        2) Second, perception of the principles of Heaven and the principles of action. VII,466-476

        3) Third, worship directed towards God; gratitude for His grace and seeking for His protection. VII,477-487

      g. Mistaken worship of images of the Buddha. VII,488-507

      h. Rejection of eclecticism. VII,508-520

IV. *Additional Considerations.* VIII,521-596

  A. Introduction to social organization in the Western world. VIII,521-526

  B. An explanation of the Jesuit practice of celibacy. VIII,527-573

        1. A single-minded devotion to the cultivation of virtue and the propagation of the faith. VIII,527-550

        2. Filial piety. VIII,551-562

        3. The corruption of the age demands persons with total commitment to saving the world. VIII,563-573

    C. A brief account of the history of God's saving work. VIII,574-591

        1. God creates the world; man's sin and Fall; birth of Jesus, God's Son, to save the world, and His ascension into Heaven. VIII,574-580

        2. Jesus is God. VIII,581-589

        3. The disciples evangelized in all directions. China formerly sent emissaries to the West to obtain the Bible, but they mistakenly acquired Buddhist scriptures. VIII,590-591

    D. The procedure for entering the Church: remorse for past misconduct and baptism. VIII,592-596

Translators' Introduction

6. The Terminology

Like the Nestorian missionaries before them,[34] the Roman Catholic missionaries were faced with the problem of whether to devise a totally new vocabulary to express the ideas unique to Christianity, or whether to appropriate existing religious terminology, infusing fresh meaning into it whenever this was deemed necessary. The problem was felt to be a most serious one among the missionaries in both China and Japan and was to prove a continuing cause for controversy for many years.[35]

Canonical writings

When the first missionaries arrived in China they discovered that they were not alone in possessing a body of canonical writings. Confucians, Buddhists, and Taoists all had collections of literature which they regarded as normative for their philosophical, ethical, and religious positions and to which they constantly referred when out to legitimize or prove a point. The term applied to each of these bodies of literature is *ching,* which originally meant the warp of a piece of cloth, and then rules or norms. Although it was to be many years after the first generation of missionaries before the Christian scriptures were translated in full into the Chinese language,

---

34 For accounts of the Nestorian Church in China, see A.C. Moule, *Christians in China Before the Year 1550* (London, 1930), chapter 2; P.Y. Saeki, *The Nestorian Documents and Relics in China,* second edition (Tokyo, 1951); Paul A. Rule, *K'ung-Tzu or Confucius?,* unpublished thesis (Canberra, 1972), pp. 235-263.
35 See Arnold H. Rowbotham, *Missionary and Mandarin, The Jesuits at the Court of China* (Berkeley, 1942), pp. 119-175; George Dunne, S.J., *Generation of Giants,* pp. 269-301; Paul A. Rule, *K'ung-Tzu or Confucius?,* chapter 4; Francis A. Rouleau, S.J., "Chinese Rites Controversy," *New Catholic Encyclopedia,* III, pp. 611-617.

Ricci found it necessary when seeking to present Christianity to the Chinese to claim the Christian scriptures as a valid repository of truth and to refer to them in order to clinch an argument. He therefore described them as the Christian *ching*. The technique he adopted in his apologetics however, was to discount the *ching* of Buddhism and Taoism and to assert as valid all those passages in the Confucian *ching* which are clearly theistic in outlook.

It is customary, when referring to the Confucian corpus to use the word "classics," and to designate the Buddhist and Christian canonical writings "scriptures." In almost all cases, however, we have translated *ching* by "canonical writings," since, to maintain the distinction between "classics" and "scriptures" would probably result in some distortion because of the way these two terms tend to leave different impressions on the minds of English readers.

God

Understandably, the choice of a suitable term for God was of the utmost importance to the Christian missionary, for, the term chosen was bound to affect the Chinese understanding of what the missionary meant both by God and by Christianity.

In the earliest strata of the Confucian canonical writings the word *Ti* or *Shang-ti* appears as a frequent term for deity. Meaning Lord or Sovereign on High, this deity, who was possibly an ancestor (or ancestors, since the word *ti* may be a collective term) of the Chinese rulers of the time, was believed to watch over human society and to regulate the working of the universe. Beneath this deity were lesser spirits or gods of the sun, moon, stars, wind, and rain and of the mountains and rivers. Working in conjunction with this system were the ancestors of the ruling and artistocratic families who dwelt in Heaven with the Lord on High and who continued to exercise an important influence on human events. The spirit world was, in fact, a reflection of the world below, the counterpart of man's experience

Translators' Introduction

on earth.

However, when the Shang rulers (1766-1123 B.C.) were defeated by the Chou (1122-221 B.C.), a new term, *T'ien,* "Heaven," was introduced, and for some considerable time *T'ien* and *Shang-ti* seem to have been regarded as virtually interchangeable terms. Gradually, however, *T'ien* superceded *Shang-ti* and in the process became less a governing personal deity and increasingly an impersonal natural power.

Committed as they were both to a belief in the natural law and in a special, divine revelation, Ricci and his fellow Jesuits were eager to discover traces of theism in China as well as to assert the uniqueness of their message. In the earliest parts of the Confucian canon and, in particular, in the person of *Shang-ti* or Lord on High, they believed they had found the traces of the early theism they were looking for. The word *T'ien* or Heaven, however, was attractive since it was in wide use as a term equivalent to Heaven as this is sometimes used in the West, that is, as the equivalent of Providence. The dilemma was that to employ the ancient term *Shang-ti* might have led to the mere equation of Christianity with Confucianism, or worse still, with popular Taoism where the term *Shang-ti* had been taken over as a name for a popular deity, whereas to use the term *T'ien* would have opened the way to a degree of imprecision regarding the personal nature of God which the missionaries could not tolerate. In Japan, difficulties experienced in the selection of a suitable term for God finally led to the use of the Latin *Deus,* suitably transliterated. The decision as to what term was to be used in China seems to have been resolved, however, when a young catechumen "saluted the painting of Christ with the title 'Lord of Heaven.' "[36] That this turned out to be a term for a deity found in Buddhist canonical writings[37] did not ultimately deter the

36 *Fonti Ricciane,* I, p. 186; *The Wise Man from the West,* p. 56.
37 *Fonti Ricciane,* I, p. 186; see also Douglas Lancashire, "Anti-Christian polemics in Seventeenth Century China," *Church History* 38 (1969), 235-236.

The Terminology

Catholic missionaries from continuing to use it, and it has remained the official term for God in the Catholic Church in China to the present day. The term, it was felt, preserved continuity with China's religious heritage while, at the same time, emphasizing the personal nature of God. An interesting fact is that whereas Ricci freely employed both the traditional Chinese terminology for God (with a clear preference for *Shang-ti*) as well as the newly coined *T'ien-chu* (Lord of Heaven), in later editions of the dialogue traditional terminology was deliberately reduced by others to a minimum.

Controversy over the term to be used for God broke out afresh when Protestant missionaries arrived in China in the mid-nineteenth century. Rejecting the Roman Catholic solution, some missionaries advocated the use of *Shang-ti* and others, usually the theologically more conservative, insisted on using *shen*, the generic word for "spirit" or "deity." Protestants have never resolved their differences in this matter and, in consequence, versions of the Bible are still printed and circulated to meet their respective requirements.[38]

Heaven, Hell, and the Devil

It is more than a little ironical that the religion which Ricci and his colleagues wished most to displace was the very religion from which they had to borrow much of their religious vocabulary. However inadvertently, the term selected to designate the Christian God had turned out to be a deity known to Buddhists through their own scriptures. It was to be the same story with much of the remaining distinctly religious vocabulary. *T'ien-t'ang*, "Heaven," was a term which the Buddhists had originally employed as the equivalent of the Sanskrit *devaloka*, "mansions of the gods." These "mansions," in Buddhist cosmology, were located between the earth

---

38 Kenneth S. Latourette, *A History of Christian Missions in China* (London, 1929), pp. 432-433.

and the *brahmalokas*, "mansions or heavens of Brahma."

Ti-yü, "Hell," was the Chinese Buddhist equivalent of the Sanskrit *naraka*. In Chinese the term means earth-prison and, in accordance with Buddhist thought, is usually regarded as being composed of three major compartments—the central, the secondary, and the isolated—each of which is then subdivided into hot and cold hells, adjacent hells, and mountain and desert hells. Not surprisingly, the term *mo-kuei*, used by Christians to designate the Devil, has as its first syllable the Chinese equivalent of the Sanskrit *māra*, the tempter of the Buddha. And so the word Christians chose to designate the Devil, was also derived ultimately from Buddhism.

Angels

Although the term *t'ien-shih*, "heavenly messenger," which was later to be adopted by Protestant translators, might seem to us to have been the best equivalent of the Greek *angellos*, Ricci preferred the expression *t'ien shen* (Sanskrit *deva*), a designation for Brahama and the gods in general.

Soul

As one would expect, the European philosophy expressed in Ricci's dialogue is essentially that of St. Thomas Aquinas. When he therefore discussed the soul he spoke of it under three headings: the vegetative, the sensitive, and the intellective. For the word "soul" itself Ricci employed the Chinese *hun* which had always meant the spirit of a person which was capable of existing apart from the physical body. For the vegetative and sensitive souls he merely prefixed the words *chih*, "plant," and *chüeh*, "feeling," "consciousness" to the word "soul." For the intellective soul he accepted the Buddhist term *ling-hun* in which the word *ling*, which can mean "spirit,"

The Terminology

"bright," "clever," or "intelligent," serves as the prefix. We find that Ricci uses a variety of terms, all including the word *ling,* which could equally be translated "soul," but which, because of their association with the intellect, and for variety's sake, we have translated "intellect" and "intelligence."

Holy, Sacred, Saint

In searching for suitable equivalents of the Christian terms "holy," "sacred," and "saint" the Jesuit missionaries in China were naturally attracted to the word *sheng* which, as a noun, meant the perfect or ideal person, and, as an adjective, frequently described the nature of a command or favor handed down by the Throne. It was even employed as an honorific for dynasties.

There is little doubt that the word *sheng* conjured up in Chinese minds a sense of awe which was religious in character, and that there was no other term which, both in its significance and in its usage, so nearly matched the words "holy," "sacred," and "saint." It needs to be borne in mind, however, that the Chinese concepts are not the exact equivalents of Christian ones. The opposite of "saint" in the Christian context is "sinner," and the opposite of "holy" is "profane." These ideas imply the existence of a holy deity and the dependence of human saintliness upon a relationship between a person and that deity. In China, on the other hand, where the emphasis has been on moral self-cultivation with little or no reference to deity, the opposite of *sheng* is essentially "ignorance."[39] This

39 There has, of course, been a development in the Chinese understanding of what constitutes a sage. The Chinese contemporary philosopher, Fung Yu-lan, goes so far as to say that the *sheng* identifies himself with the universe and thereby transcends the intellect and common morality. The earliest Chinese sages were clearly cultural heroes rather than mystics. In Confucian thought, however, they were elevated to such a degree that Arthur Waley translates the term Divine Sage. See Fung Yu-lan, *A Short History of Chinese Philosophy* (New York, 1948), pp. 339-340; *The Confucian Analects,* translated by Arthur Waley (London, 1938), pp. 17-19.

Translators' Introduction

was especially true at the time when Ricci found himself in China. It must also be said that in China those who came to be designated *sheng* by later generations were persons of cultural achievement as well as moral excellence, persons of wisdom and understanding as well as paragons of virtue. Although there are certainly Christian parallels to this, intellectual and cultural achievements have never been essential to holiness and, therefore, to saintliness. It is not surprising, then, that the word "sage" has become the commonly accepted translation of *sheng,* and that this meaning appears more appropriate than "saint," "holy," or "sacred." However, because of the influence of Christianity which, in both its Catholic and Protestant forms, has made free use of *sheng,* modern dictionaries now include among its meanings "saint," "divine," and "holy." Since the average reader of Ricci's dialogue in the early seventeenth century was totally ignorant of Christian terminology, however, we have translated *sheng* as "sage." It is interesting to note that in the first editions of the dialogue, *sheng* is used rather sparingly when it is meant to signify "sacred" or "holy."

Another point of interest is the fact that in the latter half of the book Ricci introduces the term *sheng-shen,* "sage and spiritual" for "saint." This term results from a description of Emperor Yao in the *Book of History* where he is said to be both sage and spiritual.[40] Later writers used the compound term as another expression for the person of supreme virtue. While Catholics came to use it as the equivalent of "Holy Spirit," Protestants preferred *sheng-ling* for the third person of the Trinity.

7. *Reactions to Ricci's Work*

From the compilation of the first draft of *The True Meaning of the Lord of Heaven* and its subsequent circulation in manuscript

---

40 See *Chinese Classics,* III, p. 54.

form, the work had an incomparable effect on the propagation of the Christian faith. The fact that Ricci had already gained a reputation for himself as a mathematician and scientist and that the dialogue quoted liberally from the Chinese classics to support his teachings meant that considerable interest was aroused in the work in scholarly and official circles. While still circulating in manuscript form, a copy came into the hands of the censor, Feng Ying-ching, in 1601. Affected by what he read, he wrote a foreword to the work and urged Ricci to have it printed. A year later he entered the Church.[41]

After the catechism had been printed, a copy was presented to Hsü Kuang-ch'i by João de Rocha in Nanking. So gripped was Hsü by the contents that he spent a whole night reading it and was later reported as saying, "I have always been a doubter; but now my doubts have been dispelled. I have always been fond of argument; but now I find myself silenced. I have made up my mind to receive baptism."[42]

The effects of Ricci's dialogue were not limited only to his own time. It is reported, for example, that the emperor K'ang-hsi (1662-1723) of the following Ch'ing dynasty (1644-1911) studied it for six months and that this was one reason why he issued the edict of toleration in March, 1692.[43] Because of the explanations this book offered, many scholars and officials of the day came to accept the fact that the principles of Catholicism were both compatible with the Confucian outlook and worthy of promotion. Even learned persons outside the Church expressed such views.

The book, as we have seen, stressed self-cultivation, equated God

41 *Fonti Ricciane*, II, pp. 292-293; *T'ien-chu shih-i*, translated by Liu Shun-te (Taipei, 1966), pp. 3-4; Hsü Tsung-tse, S.J., *An Outline of Jesuit Publications of Late Ming and Early Ching* (Taipei, 1958), p. 142. (In Chinese.)
42 See Liu Shun-te, ibid., p. 4.
43 *Fonti Ricciane*, II, p. 295; Liu Shun-te, ibid., p. 4.

Translators' Introduction

with *Shang-ti,* and used the Chinese classics to prove that some of the basic religious concepts of Catholicism were already to be found in the China of ancient times. The work thus provided Christian thought with an entrance into Chinese culture.

Many of the Jesuit missionaries who came to China after Ricci shared his point of view and continued along the same path. Typical examples were Giulio Aleni at the end of the Ming dynasty and Francois Noël and Alexandre de la Charme during the Ch'ing dynasty. Their writings drew even more on the rites and classics of ancient China in an attempt to prove that the scholars of ancient China had faith in God. With ever greater clarity they discussed the principle, still only partly explored in Ricci's dialogue, that Catholicism could augment Confucianism.

In a work entitled *T'ien-hsüeh ch'uan-kai, (A Summary of Teaching about God),* written by Li Tsu-po, a Chinese Christian who lived at the beginning of the Ch'ing dynasty, the author raised the following question:" Why is there agreement between the Confucianism of ancient times and the basic religious ideas of Christianity?" Answering his own question he said: "They both find their origins in mankind as a single family, for both the Chinese and the Jews had the same first ancestors." With this pronouncement a further theoretical view was provided to bolster the opinion that Catholicism was in a position to make up what was lacking in Confucianism.

Although the views put forward in *The True Meaning of the Lord of Heaven* found an echo in the minds of some and so contributed to the growth of the Church in China, it was inevitable they should also encounter opposition. Adverse criticism has come from both within the Roman Catholic Church and from Protestant missionaries and theologians who have either quarrelled with the equation of the Judaeo-Christian God with the Chinese deity, *Shang-ti,* and with the choice of other Chinese terminology for key Christian concepts, or have pointed to the fact that little of what is commonly associated with the word "gospel" can be found in it. That there is truth in the latter view is something Ricci himself would not have denied,

Figure 1. Copper engraving of the famous Chinese convert, Paul Hsü Kuang-ch'i, friend of Ricci and Grand Secretary of the Ming Imperial Government. From Jean-Baptiste Du Halde, S.J. Description ...de la Chine. Paris, 1735, vol. 3. Courtesy of Theodore N. Foss.

41

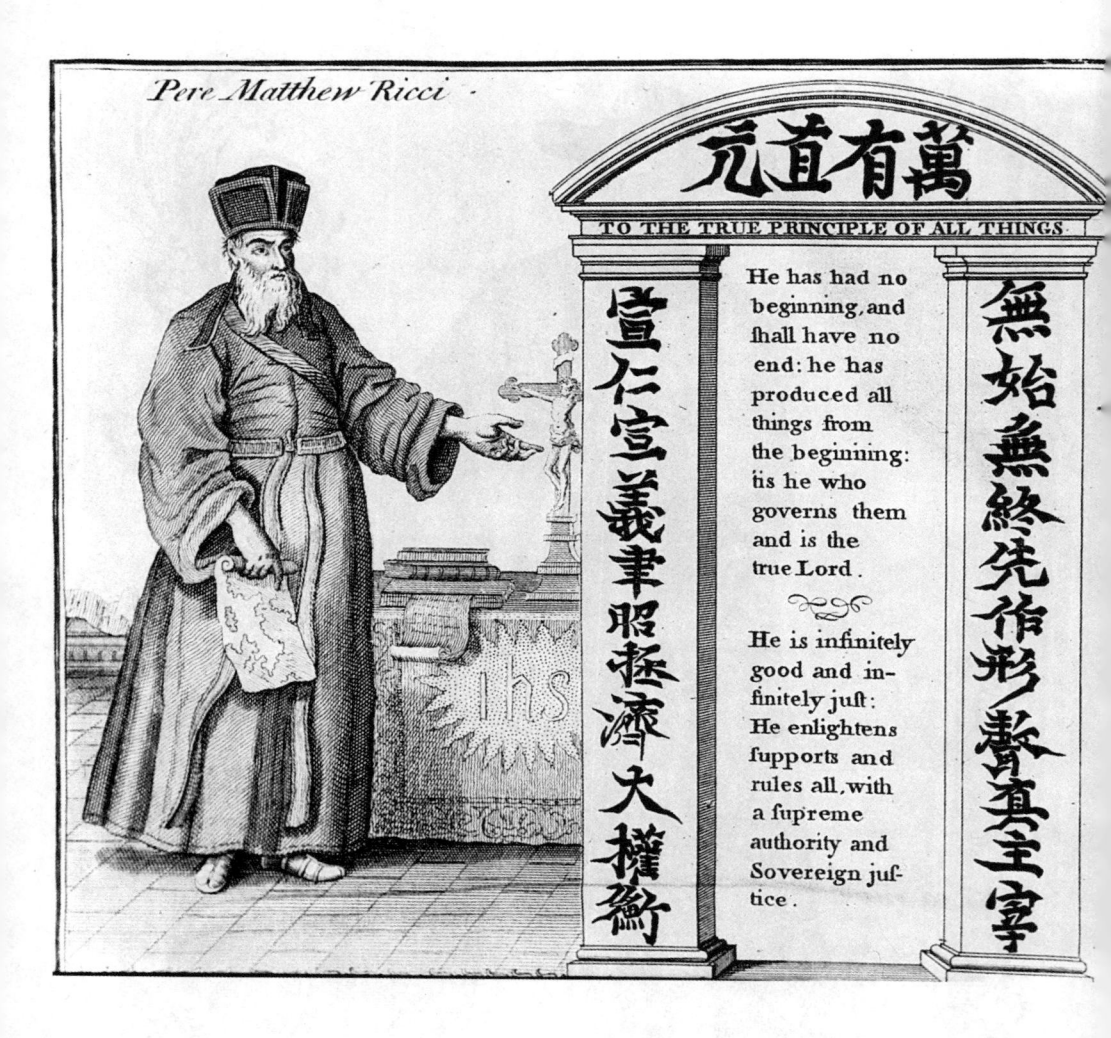

Figure 2. Matteo Ricci at an altar. Superimposed is the inscription composed by the K'ang-hsi Emperor for the dedication of the newly rebuilt Jesuit Nan T'ang, Southern Church, in Peking on 24 April 1711, one hundred and one years after Ricci's death. The Chinese characters in this plate were copied by a Westerner who omitted two strokes from the second character on the top line which should read 真. From Jean-Baptiste Du Halde, S.J. Description ...de la Chine. Paris, 1741, vol. 2. Courtesy of Theodore N. Foss.

for, as he himself stated:

> This catechism does not treat of all the mysteries of our holy faith, which need be explained only to catechumens and Christians, but only of certain principles, especially such as can be proved and understood with the light of reason. Thus it can be of service both to Christians and to non-Christians and can be understood in those remote regions which our Fathers cannot immediately reach, preparing the way for those other mysteries which depend upon faith and revealed wisdom.[44]

Because the book vehemently attacked the teachings of Taoists, Buddhists, and Neo-Confucians, persons committed to these positions were bound to strike back. Between 1616 and 1618, Nanking, and in the years 1637-1638, in Fukien, it even led to legal action being taken against Christians.

The writings which record Buddhist and Neo-Confucian arguments against Christianity have been preserved for posterity by a certain Hsü Ch'ang-chih who, in 1640, gathered them together and published them under the title *Sheng ch'ao p'o-hsieh, (Collection of Writings of the Sacred Dynasty for the Countering of Heterodoxy)*.[45] The *Collection*, which embraces the writings of more than forty authors, includes: (a) memorials to the Throne composed by Shen Ch'üeh, vice-president of the Board of Rites at Nanking in 1616; (b) records of legal actions taken against Christians

---

44 This English translation appears in *Generation of Giants,* p. 96. The original text is found in *Fonti Ricciane,* II, p. 292. For the conflict over terminology, see Arnold H. Rowbotham, *Missionary and Mandarin, The Jesuits at the Court of China* (Berkeley, 1958 reissue), pp. 128-130; *Generation of Giants,* pp. 282-287; *K'ung-Tzu or Confucius?,* pp. 235-263.

45 Douglas Lancashire, "Anti-Christian Polemics in Seventeenth Century China," *Church History* 38 (1969), 218-241 and "Buddhist Reaction to Christianity in Late Ming China," *Journal of the Oriental Society of Australia* 6 (1968-1969), 82-103; E. Zürcher, "The First Anti-Christian Movement in China (Nanking, 1616-1621)," *Acta Orientalia Neerlandica* (Leiden, 1971).

Translators' Introduction

in Nanking between 1616 and 1618; (c) reports on, and action taken against Christianity in Fukien in 1637-1638; (d) anti-Christian polemics largely representative of the Neo-Confucian position; (e) attacks on Christianity by Buddhists.

The attacks on Ricci's writings and, by extension, on the Jesuits and their Chinese converts, were made, broadly, on three fronts: the scientific, the political, and the philosophical-religious. On the scientific front there was clear resentment over the implication, which may be drawn from Ricci's publications, that China was scientifically and technologically backward. It was also asserted, however, by Ricci's opponents that scientific and technological skills contributed nothing to good government, sound education, and the moral welfare of the nation. On the political front, suggestions were made that the Jesuits were the vanguard of European armies which could be expected to invade China in a manner reminiscent of the Spanish conquest of the Philippines. Regarding the philosophical-religious front, we would like to make three points.

First, because men of learning in China did not regard Taoist thought as orthodox, they did not feel the need to make any direct defense of its position, and because the common people to whom religious Taoism chiefly appealed were not intellectuals, they were incapable of making any argued response. Thus there are virtually no representatives of Taoism among the authors of these essays.

Second, by the end of the Ming dynasty exceedingly few Buddhists upheld Buddhist theories in their purest form. Some, though Buddhists, held views very similar to those of Confucians. The fact was that towards the end of the Ming dynasty Neo-Confucianism, and particularly the late Ming expressions of it, had become infused with both Buddhist and Taoist ideas in addition to Confucian concepts to form a philosophico-religious syncretism. For Buddhism to continue to survive and grow in China it had to come to some kind of accommodation with Confucianism, so that when Ricci advocated the principle "Draw close to Confucianism and repudiate

Buddhism," he was advocating an attitude and course of action which could only prove harmful to the status of Buddhism in China. Thus, apart from defending Buddhist theory and teaching, many Buddhists also came to the defense of Neo-Confucianism.

Third, the fiercest opponents of Ricci remained the Confucian traditionalists, and especially those scholars who regarded the transmission of Confucian orthodoxy as of great importance. These had inherited the methodology common to Confucian scholarship since Chu Hsi (1130-1200), but, while giving the impression that they rejected Buddhism, they had in fact substantially accepted certain modes of Buddhist thinking into the body of their own thought. Yen Wen-hui is an example of this. Adopting the stance of the historian he insisted that Confucian thought was complete and that consequently it had no need of any contribution from Catholicism. He deliberately glossed over Buddhism's role in the history of Chinese thought. Such critics adopted a purely Neo-Confucian position when they attacked the affirmation of *The True Meaning of the Lord of Heaven* that "The Supreme Ultimate, being principle, cannot be the source of all creation." Huang Chen, for instance, vigorously countered: "In his teaching on Heaven Ricci...is a traitor and usurper and a rebel against Confucius... By destroying the Supreme Ultimate the demon Ricci destroyed the Mean."

The doctrines which came most under attack were Chinese theism and the doctrine of the soul. However, the Incarnation, human nature, Heaven and Hell, and the problem of evil also attracted attention. Ricci's positions on all these issues were declared indefensible, both in terms of common sense and from the standpoint of the received tradition. It goes without saying that Ricci and his colleagues were shown to be ignorant of the finer nuances of Chinese thought.

Apart from the positive and negative responses it elicited from China's intellectuals, *The True Meaning of the Lord of Heaven* had a profound effect within the Church. Among Ricci's contemporaries as well as among those who succeeded them, there were some missionaries, both Jesuits and others, who were uncertain about or opposed to using *T'ien,* "Heaven," and *Shang-ti,* "Sovereign on High," to designate God. This reticence was to figure as part of the major controversy in which the Confucian outlook adopted by Ricci and his followers and their policy for evangelization were judged to sacrifice Christian truth in favor of traditional Chinese thought. The dispute, which also involved the veneration of ancestors and of Confucius gained momentum in 1637. It became known as the Rites Controversy and was brought to Rome for judgment.

At first, successive popes hesitated to pronounce definitive judgment since both sides were able to present cogent arguments. Finally, in 1704, the Roman Inquisition stated officially that Catholics were forbidden to venerate the ancestors and Confucius, and could not use the terms "Heaven" or "Sovereign on High" as names for God. The K'ang-hsi emperor took the view that the attitude of Ricci was the correct one. The tensions which resulted from the clash between emperor and pope proved a major setback to the growth of Christianity in China for more than two hundred years.

On the other hand, the controversy which resulted in several Roman decrees between 1645 and 1742, could not be limited merely to the missionaries in China. In the major educational institutions of Europe heated discussion took place as to whether ancient Chinese beliefs in any way resembled Christian theology. Such debate stimulated Europe's scholars, whether officials of the Church, philosophers, or students of politics and economics, to concentrate on China, thus creating an excellent opportunity for Chinese thought to be imported into Europe. In philosophical circles, in particular, Chinese thought was to influence the European Enlightenment.

8. A Contemporary Evaluation

The True Meaning of the Lord of Heaven is the first attempt by a Catholic scholar to use a Chinese way of thinking to introduce Christianity to Chinese intellectuals. Although composed at the end of the sixteenth century, this work, in its spirit and purpose, corresponds to the efforts expended by the Catholic Church since the Second Vatican Council (1962-1965) to express the Christian faith in ways appropriate to the many cultures of our planet. Ricci's book exercised a great influence on the evangelization of the Chinese during four hundred years. A study of its contents, its success and its limitations can assist also those who seek to elaborate a contemporary Chinese expression of Christianity.

We attempt here to offer not a detailed consideration of *The True Meaning of the Lord of Heaven,* but rather some general observations.

First, we discover that Ricci did not really grasp the central ideas of the various Chinese schools of thought of his day, or their historical background. The most obvious example is in chapter two where he examines ideas about God in various schools of contemporary thought. Ricci seems not to have understood correctly the Taoist *Wu,* the Buddhist *K'ung,* and the Neo-Confucianist *T'ai-chi, Li,* and *Ch'i.* The *Wu* of Taoism and the *K'ung* of Chinese Mahayana Buddhism describe the absolutely Ultimate Reality itself which has no beginning and no end, which has no visible appearance, and is the Source of the Universe and all within it. These concepts can in fact be understood by Christians as similar to those of the *via negativa,* that is, the negative approach to God in scholastic philosophy and theology, which is the Western counterpart to the apophatic tradition of Eastern Christianity.

The concepts of *T'ai-chi, Li,* and *Ch'i* in the Chu Hsi school of

Neo-Confucianism can be extended to explain the relationship between the Ultimate Reality and the people and things within the universe. Furthermore, these three concepts can serve to express three substantial modes of the Ultimate Reality itself. The notion *T'ai-chi* in a way resembles the Christian notion of God the Father, who is the unoriginated Source, who cannot be understood directly and who enters into relationships with humans and the rest of creation through a mediator. *Li* is somewhat like the Christian concept of God the Son who reveals the Source. Through this Mediator human reason can understand something of the Source, its mystery, and its relationship with all creation. *Ch'i*, provided it is freed from its material associations, is somewhat similar to the Holy Spirit, the creative, transforming power of God at work in creation and leading all things back to their Source. Therefore the Chu Hsi school's theory of *T'ai-chi* is not totally incompatible with the Christian concept of God. The Taoist *Wu* and the Buddhist *K'ung* can also be used to describe the Lord of all things.

Unfortunately Ricci, in examining these concepts, did not take account of their connotations within their original thought systems. He analyzed these terms from the perspective of scholastic philosophy and could see only superficial similarities which he criticized while failing to understand their deeper meaning. For example, Ricci affirms that *Wu* and *K'ung* mean "nothingness" and he explains *Li* as a type of accident. For the ordinary Chinese reader, the sections of *The True Meaning of the Lord of Heaven* which treat these concepts seem somewhat strange and the discussion seems to lack a satisfactory conclusion.

In chapter six, when treating of the motivation that animates moral behavior, Ricci uses the Chinese scholar to express his own ideas. He is of the opinion that Chinese intellectuals maintain that good conduct should not have any motivation. This is a misunderstanding on Ricci's part. In fact, Chinese tradition believes

A Contemporary Evaluation

that human nature is a gift from Heaven and that it is naturally good. Ethical conduct, because it fulfills and gives expression to our nature, is the highest purpose of each person's life. A prerequisite for doing what is right is the wholehearted willingness to allow one's good nature to be fulfilled. This willingness, called *ch'eng-i*, "sincerity," is the motive for good conduct. Without this kind of motivation a person cannot realize his nature and is incapable of doing good. Therefore the Chinese do not maintain that one can accomplish what is good without motivation.

Why, then, was Ricci mistaken on this point, and why did he devote so much space to prove good conduct must have motivation? The reason is that Ricci's understanding of motivation is different from that of Chinese tradition. For the Chinese, since goodness is the manifestation of one's nature, sincerity, the motive for good conduct, does not need an outside purpose of advantage or disadvantage, reward or punishment. But according to Ricci, at least in some passages, such an outside purpose seems to be a necessary part of motivation.

Ricci naturally insists on this way of thinking because of the Christian belief in Heaven and Hell, reward and punishment after death. These realities can and should have an influence on Christian behavior, and therefore Ricci's treatment of these matters has a place in the context of the whole work. But his restricted outlook shows he had not yet completely grasped the root concepts of Chinese ethical thought, otherwise he would have treated the topic of motivation and ethical conduct in another way.

In chapter five, Ricci affirms that the Buddhist concept of reincarnation has its origin in the theory of the Greek philosopher Pythagoras. This affirmation shows that he did not clearly understand the relationship between Chinese Buddhist thought and the Indian philosophical tradition.

However, we should not criticize too harshly Ricci's failure to grasp the central concepts of contemporary schools of Chinese philosophy and their historical background. When he composed *The True Meaning of the Lord of Heaven,* Ricci had not yet completed fifteen years of life in China. It was impossible for him in such a short time to experience and appreciate the richness and beauty of the profoundest insights of Chinese thought. His European education had very naturally shaped his thinking according to the more static concepts of scholasticism and this was a limitation. His attitude towards Taoism and Buddhism was very negative and as a result he rejected outright these systems of thought. He did not fully understand either one. But if he had really understood them, would he have been able to converse with them in a more friendly spirit? We today can hardly answer that question.

In his discussions with Confucian scholars, Ricci's purpose was to show the compatibility between original Confucian thought and Christianity. Unfortunately, he did not appreciate the historical development of the Confucian tradition. He rejected not only contemporary Neo-Confucianism, but also the thought of Mencius, who wrote only one hundred years after Confucius. This radical separation of original Confucian thought from its historical development has resulted in Ricci's being criticized by many Chinese intellectuals from his own time until the present.

Ricci's outright rejection of other religions and his tendency to oppose all Confucian schools except the earliest express an attitude which the Catholic Church of our day cannot approve. The theology of Ricci's time, which owed much to Augustine, affirmed that in the providence of a merciful God, there can be high moral life outside of Christianity. This way of thinking allowed Ricci to recognize the values inherent in pristine Confucianism. But the majority of European theologians in his day also believed that there is only one true religion, namely Christianity, which can teach people communion with God. In other words, outside of Christianity, there is no other truth which brings salvation. Other religions are not only incapable of offering union with God, but they are the result of original sin and therefore have no value for the attainment of salvation. This kind of theology led Ricci to oppose Taoism and Buddhism.

The history of theology demonstrates that the Western systematic theologians of Ricci's day, for the most part, used static rather than dynamic ways of thinking. If we keep this fact in mind, it is not hard to understand why Ricci rejected the results of the historical development of Confucian thought as represented by the Neo-Confucianism he encountered.

The above mentioned defects of *The True Meaning of the Lord of Heaven* should not prevent us from recognizing the merits of this work which far surpass its weak points. First, because the work is in the form of a pre-evangelical dialogue, it does not speak at any length either of revelation or of the faith required to accept revelation. The approach taken is that of natural reason and its ability to think philosophically. Because of this method, Chinese scholars were able for the first time to understand something of the Christian philosophical-theological synthesis and to see how Confucianism had points of contact with Christianity. As a result, Chinese scholars were led by means of this book further to investigate Christian thought. One of the reasons which led Ricci to compose his book as he did was, as mentioned above, the desire to improve upon Ruggieri's catechism which spoke too much of themes drawn from revelation. The correctness of Ricci's approach was demonstrated by its success and was evidenced not only in China itself, but in all the Asian countries subject to the influence of Chinese culture from Ricci's day until the Second World War.

Second, in this book, both the starting-point and the final purpose concern "self-cultivation." This "self-cultivation," every Chinese intellectual believes, is the most important task of life and therefore the truly superior person strives first and foremost for this goal. Ricci, in this book, explained clearly why the superior

Translators' Introduction

person in order to achieve self-cultivation has to worship the Lord of Heaven. Ricci's point of departure for reflecting on self-cultivation is the natural goodness of human nature. Although he used scholastic modes of thought, which are different from those of Chinese tradition, nevertheless many Chinese scholars could accept his teaching on this essential point.

Third, Ricci quoted many sayings from the Chinese classics. If we analyze his use of these quotations in detail, we discover that although he does not attend to their original context, his application of them in his own book is generally correct and serves to show points of contact between Chinese tradition and Christianity. It was a stroke of genius on his part to demonstrate in particular the compatibility of the traditional Chinese concepts of *T'ien,* "Heaven," and *Shang-ti,* "Sovereign on High," with the Christian concept of God. This demonstration is the greatest merit of *The True Meaning of the Lord of Heaven* and Ricci's most important contribution to the Chinese-Christian dialogue. His spirit is that which should animate those who wish to create a Chinese Christian theology.

But in the last analysis, the above evaluation is not intended to be a theological one. If we were to analyze Ricci's work from our own contemporary theological viewpoint, it would be necessary to take issue with many points of his exposition. If we were to do this, our criticisms would be directed not so much against Ricci as against the limitations of the theological trends of his time. In any case, making a necessary distinction between Christian faith and the theological expressions of that faith, we would like to make our own the words of Pope John Paul II: "Just as the Fathers of the Church thought in regard to Christianity and Greek culture, so Matteo Ricci was rightly convinced that faith in Christ would not bring any harm to Chinese culture, but rather would enrich and perfect it."[46]

The True Meaning of the Lord of Heaven, together with Ricci's other publications, and the *Collection of Writings for the Countering of Heterodoxy,* [47] may correctly be regarded as the first lengthy expressions of dialogue between China and the West and, more specifically, between representatives of Chinese and Western value systems. For a variety of reasons which cannot be explored here, the dialogue was either discontinued or failed to make any discernible progress until recent years. There are signs, however, that political events over the past three decades are allowing contemporary thinkers, Chinese and Western, Christian and those of other schools of thought, to engage once again in philosophical and religious dialogue. It is to be hoped that renewed interest in the work of Ricci and the Chinese response to it will throw some light on the manner in which such a dialogue could develop today.

46 Discourse on 25 October 1982, during the concluding session of the International Ricci Studies Congress which was held at the University of Macerata and the Pontifical Gregorian University to commemorate the 400th anniversary of Ricci's arrival in China.
47 See above, note 45.

THE TRUE MEANING OF THE LORD OF HEAVEN

The Chinese Text, English Translation, and Notes

天主實義引

1 平治庸理,惟竟於一,故賢聖勸臣以忠。忠也者,無二之謂也。五倫甲乎君,君臣為三綱之首,夫正義之士此明此行。

2 在古昔,值世之亂,群雄分爭,真主未決,懷義者莫不深察正統所在焉,則奉身殉之,罔或與易也。

3 邦國有主,天地獨無主乎?國統於一,天地有二主乎?故乾坤之原、造化之宗,君子不可不識而仰思焉。

4 人流之抗罔,無罪不犯,巧奪人世,猶未饜足,至於圖僭 天帝之位,而欲越居其

1 These words translate the four characters *ping chih yung li* (平治庸理). *P'ing chih* (平治), the abbreviation of *p'ing-t'ien-hsia* (平天下) and *chih kuo* (治國), represents the highest ideal of the rulers and people of China. Cf. *Ta-hsüeh* (大學), *The Great Learning,* one of the *Four Books.*
2 *Wu-lun* (五倫, "the Five Human Relationships"), between king and minister (or sovereign and subjects), father and son, husband and wife, among brothers, and among friends.
3 *San-kang* (三綱, "the Three Bonds [in human relations]"). They are those between king and minister, father and son, husband and wife.
4 *T'ien-ti* (天地, "heaven and earth"); here it means the whole universe.
5 *Ch'ien-k'un* (乾坤, the first two hexagrams of the *I Ching* (易經, *The Book of Changes*). *Ch'ien* symbolizes heaven or male; *k'un* symbolizes earth or female. Here *Ch'ien-k'un* means heaven and earth, that is the whole universe.
6 *T'ien-ti* (天帝). In the Chinese original of the preface, but not in the body of the text, each time the names for God occur (*T'ien-ti, T'ien-chu, Shang-ti*), a blank space is left before the name as a sign of reverence, according to Chinese custom. To indicate this usage to the English reader, the translations for the names for God are printed in capitals.

Ricci's Introduction to
The True Meaning of the Lord of Heaven

---

1. All doctrines about making the whole world peaceful and governing a country rightly[1] are focussed on the principle of uniqueness. Therefore, worthies and sages have always advised the ministers to be loyal, that is not to have a second [lord in their mind]. Among the Five Human Relationships[2] the most important is that regarding the king, and the first of the Three Bonds in Human Relations[3] is that between the king and the minister. A just man must understand this and act accordingly.

2. In ancient times, whenever a large number of heroes disunited [the country] and fought against each other in times of anarchy, and when it was still uncertain who would be the rightful lord, every just man examined carefully who could be the legitimate lord and then [decided to fight for him and even] to die for him. This decision was irrevocable.

3. Every state or country has [its own] lord; is it possible that only the universe[4] does not have a lord? A country must be united under only one [lord]; is it possible that the universe has two lords? Therefore, a superior man cannot but know the source of the universe[5] and the creator of all creatures, and then raise his mind [to Him].

4. However, there were some people who came to rebel [against the Lord of the universe] and to commit all kinds of sins. They were not satisfied with robbing all [glory] in the human world; they even tried to usurp the seat of the SOVEREIGN OF HEAVEN[6] and

上。惟天之高，不可梯升，人欲難遂，因而謬布邪說，欺誑細民，以泯沒天主之跡，妄以福利許人，使人欽崇而祭祀之；蓋彼此皆獲罪於上帝。

5 所以天之降災世世以重之，而人莫思其故。哀哉！哀哉！豈非認偷為主者乎？聖人不出，醜類胥煽，誠實之理幾於銷滅矣。

6 竇也從幼出鄉，廣游天下，視此屬毒無瘳不及。意中國堯舜之氓、周公仲尼之徒，天理天學，必不能移而染焉。

7 而亦間有不免者。竊欲為之一證，復惟逖方孤旅，言語文字與中華異，口手不能開動，剗材質鹵莽，恐欲昭而彌瞑之。

8 鄙懷久有慨焉，二十餘年，旦夕瞻天泣禱：仰惟天主矜宥生靈，必有開曉匡正之日。忽承二三友人見示

7 *Fu-li* (福利).
8 *Shang-ti* (上帝).
9 Yao (堯, c. 2300 B.C.) and Shun (舜, c. 2200 B.C.), two of the most celebrated sage-kings in ancient China.
10 Chou-kung (周公, around 1100 B.C.), the Duke of Chou, was a brother of Chou Wu-wang (周武王, 1100 B.C.), first ruler of the Chou dynasty (1121-250 B.C.). After Wu-wang died, he became the prime minister of the son of Wu-wang. Confucius and subsequent generations of Chinese thought he was the best and greatest politician.
11 Chung-ni (仲尼), another name of Confucius (551-478 B.C.). In the present translation, Chung-ni and K'ung-tzu (孔子) are both rendered by Confucius, the more common Western usage.
12 *Sheng-ling* (生靈, "living spirits") means human beings.

Ricci's Introduction

place themselves over Him. But the desire of these people was impossible to satisfy because heaven was too high for them to climb to. Therefore, they proclaimed erroneous and evil doctrines, and lied to the common people in order to make disappear every trace of the LORD OF HEAVEN. They also promised to give happiness and benefits[7] in order to make people respect and worship them. They themselves sinned and so they [caused] the people to sin against the SOVEREIGN ON HIGH.[8]

5. Therefore, Heaven sent down great disasters in every age.

However, mankind did not consider the reason [why these disasters occurred]. Alas! Alas! Does this not indicate that [people who believe in them] make thieves their lord? If sages do not appear, these monstrous individuals proclaim even worse [doctrines], with the result that the true doctrine will be almost eliminated [from men's minds].

6. I, Matteo, left my country as a young man and travelled through the whole world. I discovered that doctrines which poison men's minds had reached every corner of the world. I thought that the Chinese, since they are the people of Yao and Shun,[9] and the disciples of the Duke of Chou[10] and of Chung-ni,[11] must not have changed the doctrines and teachings about Heaven and must never have allowed them to be stained.

7. But inevitably, even they sometimes also [fell into error]. I would like to prove this [assertion]. However, because I am only a single traveller from far away and because my spoken and written language is different from Chinese, I cannot begin either to open my mouth or to move my fingers. Furthermore, because of my foolish disposition, I am afraid that the more I try to display [the true doctrines], the less clear they appear.

8. I have deplored this situation for a long time, and so for more than twenty years every morning and evening I prayed to Heaven with tears. I knew that the LORD OF HEAVEN pities living spirits[12] and forgives them. Surely the day would come when [these true doc-

59

，謂雖不識正音，見偷不聲固為不可，或傍有仁惻矯毅，聞聲興起攻之。實乃述答中士下問吾儕之意，以成一帙。

9 嗟嗟，愚者以目所不睹之為無也，猶瞽者不見天，不信天有日也。然日光實在，目自不見，何患無日？

10。天主道在人心，人自不覺，又不欲省也。

11 不知天之主宰雖無其形，然全為目，則無所不見；全為耳，則無所不聞；全為足，則無所不到。在肖子，如父母之恩也；在不肖，如憲判之威也。

12 凡為善者必信有 上尊者理夫世界；若云無是尊，或有而弗預人事，豈不塞行善之門，而大開行惡之路也乎？

13 人見霹靂之響徒擊枯樹，而不即及於不仁之人，則疑上無主焉。不知天之報咎，恢恢不漏，遲則彌重耳。

13 *Shang-tsun* (上尊).

Ricci's Introduction

trines] would be made known [to the Chinese] and [their erroneous doctrines] would be corrected. Finally, one day several friends told me that even if I could not speak perfectly, I could not be silent if I saw a thief, and if I cried out and a good and strong man were nearby, he would chase and attack [the thief]. Therefore, I wrote down these dialogues which I had had with some Chinese scholars, and collected them into a book.

9. A foolish man who thinks that what his eyes cannot see does not exist, is like a blind man who does not believe there is a sun in the sky because he does not see the sky. However, sunlight really exists. Even if your eyes cannot see it, is the sun not there? The truth about the LORD OF HEAVEN is already in the hearts of men. But human beings do not immediately realize this and furthermore they are not prone to reflect about such a matter.

10. Therefore, they do not know that, although Heaven's Providence has no body, it is like a Great Eye that sees everything; it is like a Great Ear that hears everything; and it is also like a pair of Great Feet that reach everywhere. For a good son, it is like his parent's favor; for a bad one, it is like the authoritative power of policemen and ministers of justice.

11. All men who do good believe that there must exist a SUPREMELY HONORED ONE[13] who governs this world. If this Honored One did not exist, or if He exists but does not intervene in human affairs, would this not be to shut the gate of doing good and to open the road of doing evil?

12. When some people see that [during a thunderstorm], lightning only strikes dead trees but not villains, they doubt that there exists a Lord above. However, they do not know that the net of Heaven stretches everywhere, and that no one who has done evil can escape the judgment of Heaven. The later this judgment comes, the more serious it will be.

天主實義引

13 顧吾人欽若上尊，非特焚香祭祀，在常想萬物原父造化大功，而知其必至智以營此，至能以成此，至善以備此，以致各物，以類所需都無缺欠，始為知大倫者云。

14 但其理隱而難明，廣博而難盡知，知而難言，然而不可不學。

15 雖知天主之寡，其寡之益尚勝於知他事之多。願觀實義者，勿以文微而微之也。若夫天主，天地莫載，小篇孰載之？

時萬曆三十一年、歲次癸卯、七月

既望 利瑪竇書

14 *Ta-lun* (大倫, "the Great Relationship"). Ricci in his Latin translation of this preface renders these characters by "maximum rerum Principium et Ordinatorem." Pasquale M. D'Elia, S.J., "Prima Introduzione della Filosofia Scolastica in Cina," *The Bulletin of the Institute of History and Philology, Academia Sinica,* 28 (1956), p. 195. In his Italian translation D'Elia apparently follows Ricci's Latin: "questo Grande Ordinatore," *op. cit.,* p. 163. But *lun* (倫) should be taken as "relationship." See above, par. 1.

15 See Thomas Aquinas who, following Aristotle (*De Part. Anim.*, I,5) affirms: "the slenderest knowledge that may be obtained of the highest things is more desirable than the most certain knowledge obtained of the lowest things" (*Summa Theologica,* I, q. 1, art. 5, ad 1).

16 *Shih-i* (實義), an abbreviation of *T'ien-chu Shih-i,* the title of the present work.

17 *T'ien-ti* (天地).

18 See John 21:25.

19 Wan-li (萬曆). According to traditional usage, each emperor, on ascending the throne, chose one name for his reign and another for himself. "Thus the Ming prince whose family and personal name was Chu I-chün (Chu was the family name of the Ming rulers), assumed the imperial name of Shen-tsung (神宗). To his reign period (1573-1619) was given the title Wan-li (forever). He may properly be referred to as Emperor Shen-tsung or as the Wan-li Emperor." George Dunne, *Generation of Giants* (Notre Dame, 1962), p. 51, n.2.

13. The way that we respect and admire the SUPREMELY HONORED ONE is not only by burning incense and worshiping Him, but also by often meditating upon the great achievement of the first Father who is the creator of all things. By so doing we can understand that because His Omniscience is suffficient to administer this [universe], because His Omnipotence is sufficient to complete this [universe], and because His Infinite Goodness is sufficient to make this [universe] perfect, every creature will have what it needs. By so doing, we begin to understand the Great Relationship[14] [between Heaven and man].

14. However, because this doctrine is so mysterious, it is difficult to understand; because its contents are so immense it is difficult to know exhaustively; and even what is understood is difficult to explain. Nevertheless, we cannot but learn it.

15. Although we know only a little about the LORD OF HEAVEN, the advantage of knowing this little is still more than that of knowing much about other things.[15] It is my hope that those who read this *True Meaning*[16] do not belittle the doctrine about the LORD OF HEAVEN because of the poverty of my writing. The universe[17] cannot contain the LORD OF HEAVEN. How can this slight book contain Him?[18]

Date: the thirty-first year of Wan-li,[19] that is, the year
of *Kuei-mao*,[20] the seventh month, the day after
the full moon.[21]
Written by Matteo Ricci

---

20 *Kuei-mao* (癸卯). This is another way to indicate a date, namely, by calculating not according to the Emperor's reign but according to *T'ien-kan* (天干) and *Ti-chih* (地支), that is, according to the Ten Celestial Stems and the Twelve Terrestrial Branches. Both these are arranged to form a cycle of sixty. *Kuei* is one of the Celestial Stems; *mao* is one of the Terrestial Branches.

21 The twenty-second day of August, 1603.

首篇

論天主始制天地萬物、而主宰安養之

16 中士曰：夫修己之學，世人崇業。凡不欲徒稟生命與禽彙等者，必於是殫力焉。修己功成，始稱君子；他技雖隆，終不免小人類也。成德乃真福祿；無德之幸，謂之幸，實居其患耳。

17 世之人，路有所至而止；所以繕其路，非為其路，乃為其路所至而止也。吾所修己之道，將美所至而歟？本世所及，雖已略明；死後之事，未知何如。

1. For the individual the chief aim of Confucianism is the realization of the *Tao* (道) or Way in oneself. To accomplish this aim one is instructed, among other things, to engage in self-cultivation which, according to the orthodox Neo-Confucian view, involves the "extension of knowledge through the investigation of things." In the idealist wing of Neo-Confucianism, however, it tends to be based on a technique of "quiet-sitting" or meditation akin to the practice of *Ch'an* (禪, Zen) Buddhists. There seems to be little doubt that the Jesuit emphasis on the *Spiritual Exercises* of St. Ignatius of Loyola led Ricci to see in the Confucian doctrine of self-cultivation a point of contact with his own teachings, and a suitable subject with which to begin his pre-evangelical dialogue.
2. *Chün-tzu* (君子). This term, which means "prince" or "sovereign," came, in Confucianism, to mean a princely or superior man who is so, not through an accident of birth, but because of his moral stature and cultural insights and accomplishments. He corresponds, as Arthur Waley pointed out in his introduction to his translation of the Confucian *Analects,* (London, 1938), p. 35, "to the traditional Western conception of a gentleman." In this translation we have sometimes employed the word "gentleman," but, in most cases, "superior man" to translate the term.
3. *Hsiao-jen* (小人). This term, in Confucianism, has the opposite meaning of *chün-tzu*. Sometimes it indicates a person of little worth; sometimes it is used to describe a person whose thinking and acting are very wrong.

Chapter 1

A DISCUSSION ON THE CREATION OF HEAVEN, EARTH, AND ALL THINGS BY THE LORD OF HEAVEN, AND ON THE WAY HE EXERCISES AUTHORITY [OVER THEM] AND SUSTAINS THEM.

16. *The Chinese scholar states:* The study of self-cultivation[1] is a task which all men deem to be of the utmost importance. Anyone who does not wish to show ingratitude for the life with which he has been endowed, and to be classed with animals, must exert himself to the utmost in this [matter of self-cultivation]. Only when he has succeeded in cultivating himself can a man be called a Gentleman.[2] Though a man may have other great abilities, [if he fails to cultivate himself], he will remain a man of little worth.[3] True happiness and wealth is perfected virtue. Good fortune devoid of virtue[4] is falsely named and is assuredly instinct with calamity.

17. When a man travels a road it is bound to be because he wishes to reach his destination. The reason, therefore, for keeping the road in good repair lies not in the road itself but in the terminal point to which the road leads. Now where does the Way[5] of [moral] self-cultivation lead us? Although it is somewhat clear where it takes us in this world, I have no idea what it leads to after death.

4 "Virtue" is the translation of the Chinese *te* (德). Like its Western counterpart, it refers to the inherent power or character of a thing, but has increasingly come to mean moral excellence. Ricci uses it mostly in this latter sense.

5 The *Tao* or Way can, as in the West, have a variety of connotations. In Neo-Confucianism it is frequently the equivalent of "principle" as, for example, the controlling principle of the universe or of individual persons and things.

論天主始制天地萬物、而主宰安養之

18 聞先生周流天下，傳授天主經旨，迪人為善。願領大教。

19 西士曰：賢賜顧，不識欲問天主何情何事？

20 中士曰：聞尊教道淵而旨玄，不能以片言悉。但貴國惟崇奉天主，謂其始制乾坤人物，而主宰安養之者。愚生未習聞，諸先正未嘗講。幸以誨我。

21 西士曰：此天主道，非一人一家一國之道，自西徂東，諸大邦咸習守之，聖賢所傳，自天主開闢天地，降生民物至今，經傳授受無容疑也。但貴邦儒者鮮適他國，故不能明吾域之文語，諳其人物。

6 *T'ien-chu* (天主).
7 *Ch'ien-k'un* (乾坤). See above, Ricci's Introduction, n. 5.
8 *Sheng-hsien* (聖賢).
9 *Ching-chuan* (經傳). In Chinese, *ching* means the basic canonical writings: *chuan* means the authoritative commentaries on the *ching*. Later Chinese Catholics called the Bible *Sheng-ching* (聖經, "holy *ching*"), and the writings of the Church Fathers *Sheng-chuan* (聖傳, "holy *chuan*").

The Lord of Heaven as Creator

18. I have heard it said that you, Sir, have travelled the world; that you teach people concerning the decrees of the Lord of Heaven, and that you encourage people to do good. I would, therefore, like to receive your instruction.

19. *The Western scholar replies:* I am grateful for your patronage, but I do not know what you wish to ask concerning the Lord of Heaven.

20. *The Chinese scholar says:* I have heard it said that the teachings of your revered religion are profound and that its ideas are mysterious and subtle so that it is impossible to expound them in just a few words. Nonetheless, your esteemed country worships only the Lord of Heaven[6] and you say that in the beginning He created heaven and earth,[7] man and all things, and that He exercises authority over them and sustains them. This ignorant scholar has so far heard nothing concerning these matters, and none of our wise men and respected scholars of former times has ever expounded them. I shall regard myself fortunate if you will instruct me.

21. *The Western scholar says:* This doctrine about the Lord of Heaven is not the doctrine of one man, one household, or one state. All the great nations from the West to the East are versed in it and uphold it. That which has been taught by sages and worthies[8] has been handed down, from the creation of heaven and earth, men and all things by the Lord of Heaven, to the present times through canonical writings[9] and in such a manner as to leave no room for doubt. But the scholars of your esteemed country have seldom had contact with other nations, and are therefore unable to understand the languages and culture of our regions and know little of their peoples.

論天主始制天地萬物、而主宰安養之也。

22 吾將譯天主之公教,以徵其為真敎。姑未論其尊信者之眾且賢,與其經傳之所云,且先舉其所據之理。

23 凡人之所以異於禽獸,無大乎靈才也。靈才者,能辯是非,別真偽,而難欺之以理之所無。禽獸之愚,雖有知覺運動,差同于人,而不能明達先後內外之理。緣此,其心但圖飲啄,與夫得時匹配,孳生厥類云耳。

24 人則超拔萬類,內稟神靈,外覩物理,察其末而知其本,視其固然而知其所以然,故能不辭今世之苦勞,以專精修道,圖身後萬世之安樂也。

25 靈才所顯,不能強之以殉夫不真者。凡理所真是,我不能不以為真是;理所偽誕,不能不以為偽誕。捨靈才所是之理,斯于人身,猶太陽於世間,普遍光明。而殉他人之所傳,無異乎尋覓物,方遮日光而持燈燭也。

10 *T'ien-chu chih kung-chiao* (天主之公教) would be translated today "Catholic religion of God." *T'ien-chu chiao* is the Chinese name by which the Roman Catholic Church is now known. The term *chiao*, strictly speaking, means "teaching" or "guiding doctrine." There was no term for religion as such until modern times.

11 *Ling-ts'ai* (靈才). Ricci put these two terms together to translate the Western word "intellect."

12 *Li* (理). This term, which meant the "grain" or "veins" found in stone, came to signify the "principles" or "laws" of nature, "rationality" and "truth." Used extensively in this work there is a certain ambiguity about it in some passages. It is not always possible to determine precisely which meaning was uppermost in Ricci's mind.

13 *Shen-ling* (神靈).

The Lord of Heaven as Creator

22. I shall explain the universal teaching of the Lord of Heaven[10] in order to prove that it is the true teaching. But before I talk about the number of those who believe in it and their goodness or about what its canonical writings have to say, I shall first present the principles upon which it is based.

23. Of all things which mark off all men as being different from animals, none is greater than the intellect.[11] The intellect can distinguish between right and wrong and between that which is true and that which is false, and it is difficult to deceive it with anything which lacks rationality.[12] The stupidity of animals is such that although they possess perception and are capable of motion in much the same way as men, they are incapable of understanding the principles of causality. For this reason their minds are merely concerned with drinking and eating, with mating at appropriate times, and with begetting their own kind.

24. Man, then, transcends all other creatures since he is endowed with a spiritual soul[13] within, and the ability to observe the principles of things without. By examining the outcome of things he is able to know their origins, and by observing their existence he can know that by which they exist. Thus, without leaving this world of toil, he can devote himself to the cultivation of the Way and prepare himself for an eternity of peace and joy following his death.

25. That which is brought to light by the intellect cannot forcibly be made to comply with that which is untrue. Everything which reason shows to be true I must acknowledge as true, and everything which reason shows to be false I must acknowledge as false. Reason stands in relation to a man as the sun to the world, shedding its light everywhere. To abandon principles affirmed by the intellect and to comply with the opinions of others is like shutting out the light of the sun and searching for an object with a lantern.

26 今子欲聞天主教原，則吾直陳此理以對，但仗理剖析。或有異論，當悉折辯，勿以誕我。此論天主正道公事也，不可以私遜廢之。

27 中士曰：茲何傷乎？鳥得羽翼，以翔山林；人稟義理，以窮事物。故論惟尚理焉耳。理之體用廣甚，雖聖賢亦有所不知焉。一人不能知，一國或能知之；一國不能知，而千國之人或能知之。君子以理為主，理在則順，理不在則咈，誰得而異之？

28 西士曰：子欲先詢所謂始制作天地萬物，而時主宰之者。予謂天下莫著明乎是也。人誰不仰目觀天？觀天之際，誰不默自嘆曰：「斯其中必有主之者哉！」夫即天主——吾西國所稱『陡斯』是也。茲為子特揭二三理端以證之。

論天主始制天地萬物、而主宰安養之

70

26. Now you, Sir, desire to learn the principles of the teachings of the Lord of Heaven. I shall therefore state them plainly for you, and my explanations will be based solely on reason. Should you find any proposition unacceptable I hope you will dispute it and not deceive me in any way. Because we are discussing the universal principles of the Lord of Heaven I cannot permit personal modesty to stand in the way of the truth.

27. *The Chinese scholar says:* What harm is there in that? A bird has wings so that it may soar to the mountain forests, and man is endowed with reason so that he can probe things to their depth. Therefore, in any discussion it is essential to put truth above all else. The substance and function of truth are exceedingly extensive, so that even though a man may be a sage or a worthy there will still be aspects of it about which he will be ignorant. What may not be known by one man may nevertheless be known by a nation, and what may not be known by a nation may yet be known by the inhabitants of a thousand nations. The superior man makes truth his standard. Where truth is to be found, he will comply with it, but where there is no truth he will oppose it. No one will think that strange.

28. *The Western scholar says:* You, Sir, wish first to inquire about the One who is said to have created heaven, earth, and all things and to exercise constant authority over them. I assert, then, that there is nothing under heaven which is more evident than the truth of His existence. Is there anyone who has not raised his eyes and gazed at the sky and who has not silently sighed to himself, while gazing at the sky, and said: "There must surely be Someone in the midst of it who exercises control over it." Now this Someone is none other than the Lord of Heaven whom our Western nations term *Deus*. I shall now specially select two or three arguments to prove [His existence].

29 其一曰：吾不待學之能，為良能也。今天下萬國各有自然之誠情，莫相告諭而皆敬一上尊。被難者籲哀望救，如望慈父母焉；為惡者捫心驚懼，如懼一敵國焉。則豈非有此達尊，能主宰世間人心，而使之自能尊乎？

30 其二曰：物之無魂無知覺者，必不能于本處所自有所移動，而中度數。使以度數動，則必藉外靈才以助之。設汝懸石於空，或置水上，石必就下至地方止，不能復動。緣夫石自就下，然皆隨發亂動，動非度之本處所故也。若風發于地，能於本處自動，次至如日月星辰並麗于天，各以天為本處所，然實無魂無知覺者數。今觀上天自東運行，而日月星辰之天自西循逆之，度數各依其則，曾無纖忽差忒焉者。倘無尊主斡旋主宰其間，能免無悖舍各安其位乎哉？譬如舟渡江海，上下風濤而無覆蕩之虞，雖未見人，亦知一舟之中必有掌舵智工撑駕持握，乃可安流平渡也。

14 This is clearly an attempt to describe "the Ptolemaic-Aristotelian theory according to which the geocentric universe was made up of 'solid concentric crystalline spheres.'" See J. Needham, *Chinese Astronomy and the Jesuit Mission: An Encounter of Cultures* (London, 1958), and D. Lancashire, "Anti-Christian Polemics in Seventeenth Century China," *Church History* 38 (1969), 5.

The Lord of Heaven as Creator

29. The first [of these arguments has to do with] our untutored ability which is innate ability. Now [men] of all nations under heaven possess, each of them, a natural capacity by which, without any communication between them, all venerate One who is regarded as worthy of supreme honor. Those in distress call upon Him for pity and look to Him for salvation as to a compassionate father and mother. Those who do evil are gripped by fear, as if afraid of a hostile nation. Does this not indicate that there is One who is highly honored who is able to govern the hearts of men and cause them of themselves to honor Him?

30. My second [argument is as follows]: Objects which lack souls and perception cannot move from their natural habitats by themselves in a regular and orderly manner. If they are to move in a regular and orderly manner, it is necessary that an intelligence external to themselves should come to their aid. Should you suspend a stone in space or place it on water it is bound to fall until it reaches the ground, unable to move a second time. Now the reason why the stone falls of its own accord is because neither water nor space is its natural habitat. A wind which rises from the ground can move within its natural habitat; but its movements will be haphazard and lacking in any orderliness. When we come to the sun, moon, and stars, we find them attached to the heavens, each having the firmament as its natural habitat; but they lack souls and perception. Now, when we observe the supreme heaven we see that it moves from the East while the heavens of the sun, moon, and stars travel from the West.[14] Without the slightest error, each thing follows the laws proper to it, and each is secure in its own place. If there were no Supreme Lord to control and to exercise authority [over these things] would it be possible to avoid confusion? For example, when a boat crosses a river or the sea and is enveloped by wind and waves, if there is no danger of its founder-

31 其三曰：物雖本有知覺，然無靈性，其或能行靈者之事，必有靈者為引動之。試觀鳥獸之類，本冥頑不靈，然饑知求食，渴知求飲，畏矰繳而薄青冥，驚網罟而潛山澤，或吐哺、或跪乳，俱以保身孳子、防害就利，與靈者無異。此必有尊者默教之，纔能如此也。譬如觀萬千箭飛過於此，每中鵠，我雖未見張弓，亦識必有良工發箭，乃可無失中云。

32 中士曰：天地間物至煩至賾，信有主宰。然其原制造化萬物，何以徵也？

33 西士曰：大凡世間許多事情，宰於造物，理似有二。至論物初原主，絕無二也。雖然，再將二三理解之。

ing, and the passage is made in safety, one can be sure there is someone with his hand on the tiller who knows his seamanship, even though one may not have seen anyone.

31. My third [argument] is that should certain things which are endowed with perception, but which lack intelligence, be capable of performing intelligent acts, it is sure to be due to the guidance of something with intelligence. If we observe birds and animals we find them to be basically stupid. Nevertheless, when they are hungry they know how to seek for food, and when thirsty, they know how to search for water. Afraid of arrows they flee into the blue depths of the sky, and alarmed by traps they hide in hills and marshes. Some eject food from their mouths and some kneel to suck, all for the purpose of self-preservation and rearing the young. They ward off evil and turn to that which is beneficial. In this they are no different from intelligent beings. There must be a Supreme Lord who secretly instructs them for them to be able to behave in this fashion. For example, if I see thousands upon thousands of arrows fly by me and each hits a target, even though I may not have seen a bow drawn, yet I recognize the fact that there must be skilled bowmen firing the arrows for them not to miss the target.

32. *The Chinese scholar says:* The things in heaven and earth are most numerous and most complex, and I believe that there must be One who exercises supreme authority over them. But how can one prove that He is in fact the creator of all things?

33. *The Western scholar says:* In the case of many things in the everyday world there would appear to be two principles of overlordship, the one pertaining to creation and the other to control; but when one comes to speak of the original Lord of creation one finds there is absolutely no room for a second principle. Since this is so, I shall employ two or three arguments to clarify [the truth of] it.

34 其一曰：凡物不能自成，必須外為者以成之。樓臺房屋不能自起，恆成於工匠之手。知此，則識天地不能自成，定有所制作者，即吾所謂天主也。譬如銅鑄小毬，日月星宿山海萬物備焉，非巧工鑄之，銅能自成乎？況其天地之體之大，晝夜旋行，日月揚光，辰宿布象，山生草木，海育魚龍，潮水隨月，其間員首方趾之民，聰明出於萬品，誰能自作己，必宜先有一己以為之作；無既已有己，何用自作？如先初未始有己，則作己者必非己也。故物不能自成也。

35 其二曰：物本不靈而有安排，莫不有安排之者？如觀宮室，前有門以通出入，後有園以種花果，庭在中間以接賓客，室在左右以便寢臥，樑柱居下以員棟樑，茅茨置上以蔽風雨，如此乎處置協宜，而後能成也。又觀銅鑄之字，本各為一字，而能接續成句，排成一篇文章，苟非明儒安置之，何得自然偶合乎？

論天主始制天地萬物、而主宰安養之

34. My first argument is that material things cannot come to completion of their own volition, but must have a cause external to them to bring them to fruition. A theater or building cannot rise of its own accord, but is always completed at the hands of artisans. When one comprehends this, one comes to understand that heaven and earth cannot come into being by their own will, but must assuredly have a creator, namely, our so-called Lord of Heaven. Let us take as an example a small globe cast in bronze. Sun, moon, stars, planets, mountains, and seas all appear complete on it. Now if a skilled craftsman had not cast it, would the bronze have been able to take on all these features by itself? How much more must this question apply to bodies the size of heaven and earth. Night follows day; sun and moon shed light; constellations of stars are spread out [across the heavens]; the hills give forth grass and trees; the sea nurtures fish and dragons; the tides follow the moon, and man, the chief resident among all these things, is more intelligent than all ten thousand of them. Yet which of these things is able to come into being of its own volition? If there were any one thing able to create itself, there would first have to be a self to do the creating. But since a self would already exist what need would it have of self-creation? And if there were no self in the beginning, then the creator of self would have to be someone other than this self. Thus, phenomena cannot come into being of themselves.

35. My second argument is that if objects which are devoid of intelligence nevertheless possess order, there must be someone who imposes the order on them. If we look at a mansion we find that it is provided with doors in front to facilitate exit and entry. Behind are gardens in which are planted flowers and fruit trees. A hall is built centrally for the reception of guests, and rooms are placed to the left and to the right to serve as sleeping quarters. Columns are implanted below to support the beams in the roof, and

論天主始制天地萬物、而主宰安養之

36 因知天地萬物咸有安排一定之理，有質有文而不可增減焉者。夫天高明上覆，地廣厚下載，分之爲兩儀，合之爲宇宙；辰宿之天高乎日月之天，日月之天包乎火，火包乎氣，氣浮乎水土，水行於地，地居中處；而四時錯行以生昆蟲草木，水養黿龜蛟龍魚鱉，氣育飛禽走獸，火煖下物。

37 吾人生於其間：秀出等夷，靈超萬物；稟五常以司衆類，得百骨以立本身；目視五色，耳聽五音，鼻聞諸臭，舌啖五味，手能持，足能行，血脈五臟全養其生。

15 *Wu-ch'ang* (五常, "Five Basic Virtues"): *jen* (仁, "humanity"); *i* (義, "righteousness"); *li* (禮, "propriety or sense of decorum"); *chih* (智, "wisdom"); *hsin* (信, "faith or trustworthiness").
16 "A hundred bones," (百骨) 1st ed. Peking, 1603; "a hundred organs," (百官) 3rd ed. Hangchow, 1607.
17 *Wu-se* (五色, "Five Colors"): red, yellow, blue, white and black.
18 *Wu-yin* (五音, "Five Notes of the Chinese musical scale"): *kung* (宮, "do"); *shang* (商, "re"); *chiao* (角, "mi"); *chih* (徵, "sol"); *yü* (羽, "la").
19 *Wu-wei* (五味, "Five Flavors"): sour, sweet, bitter, pungent and salty.
20 *Wu-tsang* (五臟, "Five Viscera"): heart, lungs, liver, kidneys, and stomach.

thatch is placed above to keep out wind and rain. When all these things have been ordered harmoniously the master of the house can dwell securely within it. But if such a building is to be brought to completion, it must be built by a skilled artisan. If we turn next to each of the individual words cast in metal [in preparation for printing] we find that if they are to be joined together to form sentences and to be built up into an essay, they must be arranged by an educated man who understands how to perform this task. They are hardly likely to be able to come together by chance.

36. Thus, it is obvious that heaven and earth and all things have a definite reason for their orderliness; that where there is matter there is form, and that things cannot increase or diminish of their own volition. The brilliant heaven provides a cover above and the earth gives support below. Divided, they are the two polarities; but together, they form the universe. The heaven of the stars is higher than the heaven of the sun and the moon. The heaven of the sun and the moon embraces fire; fire embraces air; air floats above waters and the earth, and the waters flow across the land. The earth resides at the center and the four seasons alternate in such a manner as to produce insects and vegetation. The waters harbor sea-turtles, flood-dragons, fish, and fresh-water turtles; the air supports birds and animals, and fire provides warmth for the creatures of the earth.

37. We human beings, the most excellent and most intelligent creatures in all creation, live in the midst of all this. Man is endowed with the Five Basic Virtues[15] in order that he might control the things of this world. He has been given a hundred bones so that he can stand up;[16] eyes to distinguish the Five Colors;[17] ears to hear the five Notes;[18] the nose to smell every different kind of scent, and the tongue to taste the Five Flavors.[19] His hands can grasp hold of things; his feet are able to walk; the pulse and the five viscera[20] serve to preserve his life.

論天主始制天地萬物、而主宰安養之

38 下至飛走鱗介諸物，為其無靈性，不能自置所用，與人不同，則生而或得毛、或得羽、或得鱗、或得介等當衣服，以遮蔽身體也；或具利爪、或具尖角、或具硬蹄、或具長牙、或具強嘴、或具毒氣等當兵甲，以敵其所害也；且又不待教而識其傷我與否。故雞鴨避鷹，而不忌牛馬；非鷹與豺狼滋巨，而孔雀與牛馬滋小也，知其傷與無傷異也。

39 又下至一草一木，為其無知覺之性，可以護己及以全果種，故植而或生刺、或生皮、或生甲、或生絮，皆生枝葉以圍蔽之。吾試忖度：此世間物安排布置有次有常，非初有至靈之主賦予其質，豈能優游於宇下，各得其所哉？

40 其三曰：吾論衆物所生形性，或受諸胎、或出諸卵、或發乎種，皆非由己制作也。且問胎卵種猶然一物耳，又必有所以為始生者，而後能生他物，果於何而生乎？則必須推及每類初宗，必有元始特異之類化生萬類者──即吾所稱天主是也。

80

The Lord of Heaven as Creator

38. Because birds and beasts, down to the lowest of animals, whether feathered, scaly or shelly, have no spiritual nature, they are unable to arrange for their own needs, and are therefore different from human beings. It is for this reason that they are provided from birth with fur, feathers, scales and shells and the like to serve as clothing and as a cover for their bodies. They are also provided with sharp claws, tapered horns, hard hooves, long teeth, powerful jaws, and poison to serve as weapons and armor with which they can defend themselves against the attacks of enemies; moreover, without any instruction they are able to know whether another creature is likely to harm them. For this reason chickens and ducks naturally hide from eagles, but do not seek to avoid the peacock; sheep are afraid of the wolf, but have no fear of oxen and horses. This is not because the eagle and the wolf have large bodies and the peacock, oxen, and horses have small bodies; it is due to the fact that they know whether these other animals are likely to cause them any harm.

39. Further, even a blade of grass or a tree which has no awareness can protect itself, its fruit, and its seed, and defend itself against harm from bird and beast. Thus, some plants grow thorns and some skin; some grow scales and others catkins; and all have branches and leaves to serve as a protective cover. If we consider the matter carefully we will conclude that the things on this earth are arranged and deployed in an orderly fashion, and that if there had not been a supremely intelligent Lord above at the beginning of creation to bestow various natures on things, they would not be able to exist in the world and each find its appropriate station.

40. My third argument is that when we come to discuss the manner whereby all things propagate themselves, we find that they are born from the womb, from eggs, or grow from seeds, and that none creates itself. Since wombs, eggs, and seeds are themselves things, we must ask what first produced them so that they in turn could

論天主始制天地萬物、而主宰安養之

41　中士曰：萬物既有所生之始，先生謂之天主，敢問此天主由誰生歟？

42　西士曰：天主之稱，謂之原；如謂有所由生，則非天主也。物之有始有終者，鳥獸草木是也；有始無終者，天地鬼神及人之靈魂是也。無始無終，而為萬物始焉，為萬物根柢焉。無天主則無物矣。物由天主生，天主無所由生也。

43　中士曰：萬物初生，自天主出，已無容置喙矣。然今觀人從人生、畜從畜生，凡物莫不皆然；則似物自為物，於天主無關者。

44　西士曰：天主生物，乃始化生物類之諸宗；既有諸宗，諸宗自生物生物，如以人生人，其用人由天，則生人者豈非天主？譬始鋸鑿雖能成器，皆由匠者使之，誰曰成器乃鋸鑿，非匠人乎？吾先釋物之所以然，則其理自明。

The Lord of Heaven as Creator

produce other things. We must trace every kind of thing back to its first ancestor; and since nothing is capable of producing itself, there must be Someone who is both original and unique who is the creator of every kind of thing and object. It is this One whom we term Lord of Heaven.

41. *The Chinese scholar says:* Since you, Sir, say that the Lord of Heaven is the beginning of all things, may I ask by whom the Lord of Heaven was produced?

42. *The Western scholar says:* The Lord of Heaven is referred to as the source of all things. If there were another who produces Him, the Lord of Heaven would cease to be the Lord of Heaven. The birds and beasts, grass and trees are things with a beginning and an end. The ghosts and spirits in heaven and earth and the souls of men have a beginning but no end. The Lord of Heaven has no beginning and no end and is therefore the beginning of all things and the root of all things. If there were no Lord of Heaven there would be nothing else. All things were produced by the Lord of Heaven, but the Lord of Heaven was not produced by anything else.

43. *The Chinese scholar says:* That all things were first produced by the Lord of Heaven leaves no further room for argument. However, we can see that men are born from men, and animals from animals, and that all things are produced in this way. Thus, the birth of things from things would seem to have nothing to do with the Lord of Heaven.

44. *The Western scholar says:* When the Lord of Heaven created all things he created the first ancestors of all categories, and once the first ancestors had come into existence, each first ancestor itself transmitted life; so now things produce things in much the same manner as humans beget humans. Since Heaven makes use of man, how could anyone but the Lord of Heaven have created man? For example, the saw and the hammer are employed to make furniture, but only the craftsman can cause these instruments to

83

45 試論物之所以然有四焉。四者維何？有作者，有模者，有質者，有為者。夫作者，造其物而施之為物也；模者，狀其物置之於本倫，別之於他類也；質者，物之本來體質所以受模者也；為者，定物之所向所用也。此於工事俱可觀焉，所以乘於人為者，輿人為作者；於生物亦可觀焉，樹木料為質者，所以乘於人為作者；熱乾氣為模者，薪柴為質者，然：有生火之原火為作者，熱乾氣為模者，薪柴為質者，所以燒爇物為者。

46 天下無有一物不具此四者；四之中，其模者、質者此二者在物之內，為物之本分，或謂陰陽是也；作者、為者此二者在物之外，超於物之先者也，不能為物之本分者。吾按天主為物之所以然，但云作者、為者、不云模者、質者。蓋天主渾全無二，胡能為物之分乎？

論天主始制天地萬物、而主宰安養之

21 The "four causes" are concepts proper to scholastic philosophy based largely upon Aristotle. Ricci was the first to express the term "four causes" in Chinese and he used the characters 四所以然:作者, 模者, 質者, 爲者; contemporary Chinese philosophers use 四因:動因, 型因, 質因, 目的因

22 Though most likely of non-Confucian origin, the concepts of *yin* (陰) and *yang* (陽) came to play an important part in Confucian thought. They signify the first two opposite, yet complementary, forces which emerge from the one undifferentiated whole. As the two prime complementary forces they are seen to permeate all things making them hard and soft, hot and cold, male and female, etc. It should be pointed out that *contemporary* Neo-Confucian scholars would not identify *yin* and *yang* with Western formal and material causes which they call *li* (理) and *ch'i* (氣).

complete the furniture. Is there anyone who would say that it is the saw or the hammer which completes the furniture and not the craftsman? When we explain why things are as they are, their governing principles become self-evident.

45. When we attempt to discuss why things are as they are, we find that there are four causes. And what are the four causes? They are the "active cause," the "formal cause," the "material cause," and the "final cause."[21] The active cause is that which makes a thing to be. The formal cause gives form to a thing and places it in its own class, thereby distinguishing it from other classes of things. The material cause is the original material of a thing which is given form. The final cause determines the end and purpose of a thing. These causes can be seen operating in every event and in every piece of work. For example, the maker of a carriage is the active cause; the sum total of characteristics specific to a carriage is its formal cause; timber is its material cause, and the final cause for which the carriage is made is to carry passengers. One can see these causes at work in everything that is produced. Let me take fire as an example. The original fire which gives rise to fire is the active cause. Heat, dryness, and air are the formal cause. Fuel is the material cause; and the using of fire to burn and cook things is the final cause.

46. There is nothing in the world which does not combine within itself these four causes. Of these four, the formal cause and the material cause, as found in phenomena, are internal principles of phenomena or, if one wishes to state it in that way, are the *Yin* (negative) and *Yang* (positive) principles.[22] The active and final causes lie outside phenomena and exist prior to phenomena, and therefore cannot be said to be internal principles of phenomena. The Lord of Heaven we speak of is the reason for things being as they are, and we refer to Him only as the active and final cause.

47　至論作與為之所以然，又有近遠公私之別；公遠者大也，近私者其小也。天主為物之所以然，至公至大；而餘之所以然，近私且小也。私且小者必統于大者、公者。夫雙親為子之所以然，稱為父母，近也，私也；使無天地覆載之，安得產其子乎？使無天主掌握天地，天地安能生育萬物乎？則天主固無上至大之所以然也。故吾古儒以為所以然之初所以然。

48　中士曰：宇內之物眾而且異，竊疑所出必為不一，猶之江河所發，各別有源。今言天主惟一，敢問其理？

49　西士曰：物之私根原，固不一也；物之公本主，則無二焉。何者？物之公本主，乃眾物之所從出，備有眾物德性，德性圓滿超然，無以尚之。使疑天地之間，物之本主有二尊。不知所云二者，是相等乎？否乎？如非相

He is not their formal or material cause. Because the Lord of Heaven is perfectly whole, unique, and with none other beside Him, He cannot be a part of matter.

47. As to the active and final causes, we find distinctions within them between what is distant and what is proximate and between what is universal and what is special. What is distant and universal is a great cause, and what is proximate and special is a lesser cause. The Lord of Heaven is the most universal and the most supreme cause, other things are proximate and special and therefore lesser causes. Special and lesser causes are of necessity subordinate to great and universal causes. Parents are the cause of children; they are termed fathers and mothers, and are the proximate and special cause; but if there were no heaven to cover them and no earth to sustain them, how would they be able to beget and nurture their children? If there were no Lord of Heaven to superintend heaven and earth, how would heaven and earth be able to produce and nurture all things? Therefore, the Lord of Heaven is the supreme and greatest cause. Thus, our learned men of ancient times regarded Him as the first of all causes.

48. *The Chinese scholar says:* The things in this world are many and dissimilar, and, in my humble view, they cannot emerge from a single source any more than can the rivers and streams, the sources of which are located in a variety of different places. Now, however, you assert that there is only one Lord of Heaven. Will you kindly give me your reason for this?

49. *The Western scholar says:* The special sources of things are assuredly dissimilar, but the Lord who is the universal source of things has none beside Him. Why? Because the universal and fundamental Lord of things is He from whom all phenomena proceed; who furnishes all things with their natures and to whose surpassing perfection nothing can be added. If one were to suppose that there were two fundamental lords of phenomena in heaven and

等，必有一微，其微者自不可謂公尊，其公尊者大德成全，莢以加焉；如曰相等，一之已足，何用多乎？又不知所云二尊，能相奪滅否？如不能相滅，則其能猶有窮限，不可謂圓滿至德之尊；如能奪滅，則彼可以被奪滅者，非天主也。

50 且天下之物，極多極盛，苟無一尊維持調護，不免散壞：如作樂大成，苟無太師集衆小成，完音亦幾絕響。是故一家止有一長，一國止有一君，有二，則國家亂矣；一人止有一身，一身止有一首，有二，則怪異甚矣。吾因是知乾坤之內雖有鬼神多品，獨有一天主始制作天地人物，而時主宰存安之。子何疑乎？

51 中士曰：耳聽至敎，蓋信天主之尊，眞無二上。雖然，願竟其說。

---

23 Kuei-shen（鬼神，"ghost and spirit"）. Here it means all spiritual beings.
24 Ch'ien-k'un（乾坤）. See above, Ricci's Introduction, n. 5.

The Lord of Heaven as Creator

earth, it would be difficult to know whether these so-called lords were equal or not. If not, one would have to be smaller than the other, and the smaller of the two could not then be called "universal" and "supreme." One who is universal and supreme is by nature perfect to the point where nothing can be added to him. If we were to say they were equal, then one would be sufficient. Why the need for two? It would also be hard to know whether the two lords you refer to would be capable of destroying each other. If they were unable to destroy each other, this would demonstrate that the power of each was limited, and that neither could be said to be whole, or to be endowed with the highest virtue attributable to a supreme lord. If they were able to destroy each other it would prove that the one who could be destroyed was not the Lord of Heaven.

50. Further, the things in this world are exceedingly numerous, and if there were no supreme lord to keep and maintain order among them, they would inevitably disperse and be destroyed. It is like a musical performance: even though the musicians might wish to make music, without a maestro, there would be no music. Therefore, each family has but one head, and each nation has but one sovereign. Should there be two, a nation will find itself in a state of anarchy. A man has only one body; a body has only one head. If it had two heads the man would be a freak. We know, therefore, that although there are many kinds of spiritual beings[23] in the universe,[24] there is only one Lord of Heaven who is the first creator of heaven and earth, mankind and all phenomena and who constantly controls and sustains them. What room is there for doubt, Sir?

51. *The Chinese scholar says:* Now that I have personally heard your teaching, I believe that the Lord of Heaven is supreme, and that there is genuinely none beside Him. Although [I already believe], I should like to hear the whole doctrine about Him.

論天主始制天地萬物、而主宰安養之

52 西士曰：天下至微蟲如蟻，人不能畢達其性，矧天主至大至尊者，豈易達乎？如人可以易達，亦非天主矣。

53 古有一君，欲知天主之說，問於賢臣。賢臣答曰：「容退三日思之。」至期，又問。答曰：「更六日方可對。」君怒曰：「汝何戲？」答曰：「臣何敢戲。但天主道理無窮，臣思日深，而理日微，亦猶瞠目仰瞻太陽，益觀益昏，是以求十二日以對。君怒曰：『如是已六日，又難對也。』」

54 昔者又有西士賢人，名謂嶴梧斯悌諾，一概通天主之說，而書之於冊。一日，浪遊海濱，心正尋思，忽見一童子掘地作小窩，手執蠔殼汲海水灌之。聖人曰：「子將何為？」童子曰：「吾欲以此殼盡汲海水傾入窩中也。」聖人笑曰：「若何甚愚？欲以小器竭大海入小窩。」童子曰：「爾既知大海之水，小器不可汲，小窩不盡容，

25 "Three days...six days...twelve days," 1st ed. Peking, 1603; "one day...two days...four days," 3rd ed. Hangchow, 1607.
26 Ricci, the first to put Augustine's name into Chinese, used five characters, "Ao-wu-ssu-ti-no" (嶴梧斯悌諾). Today Chinese Catholics use three, "Ao-ssu-ting" (奧斯定), while others use four, "Ao-ku-ssu-ting" (奧古斯丁).

52. *The Western scholar says:* People are unable to understand completely the nature of even the smallest insect in the world, like the ant. How much less easy, then, must it be to understand completely the Lord of Heaven who is supremely great and supremely to be honored. If it were easy for man to understand Him He would not be the Lord of Heaven.

53. In ancient times there was a certain king who wanted to know the truth concerning the Lord of Heaven, and therefore enquired of his good minister. The good minister said: "Allow me three days to consider your question." When three days had passed the king again put his question, and the minister replied: "You must allow me a further six days before I can give you an answer." When another six days had passed, the minister demanded another twelve days[25] before giving his answer. The king grew angry and said: "Are you not making fun of me?" The minister replied: "How would your minister dare make fun of you; it is simply that the truth about the Lord of Heaven is inexhaustible, and that for every day I devote myself to deep consideration of Him, the truth about Him appears ever more subtle. It is like staring at the sun; the more one looks at it the more blurred becomes one's vision. It is for this reason that I find it difficult to give you an answer."

54. Formerly there was also a sage of the West called Augustine[26] who wanted to understand completely the truth about the Lord of Heaven so that he could write a book about it. One day he went for a walk beside the sea, and was just searching in his mind for this truth when he suddenly saw a child digging the ground to make a small pool and using a shell to scoop up sea water to fill his pool, the sage said: "What are you doing?" The child replied: "I am using this shell to scoop all the water in the sea into this pool." The sage laughed and said: "Why are you so foolish that you use so small a vessel to scoop all the water in the sea into a small pool?" The child replied: "Since you know that the waters of the great ocean

論天主始制天地萬物、而主宰安養之

55 蓋物之列於類者，吾因其類，考其異同，則知其性也；有形聲者，吾視其容色，聆其音響，則知其情也；有限制者，吾度量自此界至彼界，則可知其體也。若天主者，非類之屬，超越眾類，比之於誰類乎？既無形聲，豈有迹可入而達乎？其體無窮，六合不能為邊際，何以測其高大之倪乎？庶幾乎舉其情性，則莫若以『非』者，『無』者舉之；苟以『是』、以『有』，則愈遠矣。

56 中士曰：夫『極是』、『極有』者，亦安得以『非』、以『無』」闡之？

57 西士曰：人器之陋，不足以盛天主之巨理也。惟知事有缺陷，天主所非是，然而不能窮其所為尊貴也；惟知物有卑賤，所無有，然而不能稽其所為全長也。

又何為勞心焦思，欲以人力竟天主之大義，而入之微冊耶？」語畢不見。聖人亦驚悟，知為天主命神以警戒之也。

27. *Liu-ho* (六合, "the Six Directions") — north, south, east, west, up and down — here means the whole breadth and depth of the universe, i.e., the whole material universe.
28. *Fei* (非, "not"); *wu* (無, "lack"). On the "via negativa," see Thomas Aquinas, *Summa Theologica*, I, q. 12, especially art. 9, ad 3.
29. *Shih* (是, "is"); *yu* (有, "has").
30. *Chi-shih* (極是, "Ultimate Being").
31. *Chi-yu* (極有, "Ultimate Possessor").

92

cannot all be drawn with a shell and that a small pool cannot contain them, why are you engaging in such mental labor, trying to use man's powers to understand completely the truth concerning the Lord of Heaven and then to write it down in a small book?" When the child had finished speaking he disappeared. At this moment the sage suddenly apprehended the truth, and knew that the Lord of Heaven had commanded a spirit to come and caution him.

55. Because things fall into different categories, I can determine their dissimilarities and similarities on the basis of these categories, and thereby know the natures of things. I can see the forms and hear the sounds of those things which possess form or sound, and thereby know their natures. Things which are limited can be measured from one boundary to another, and one can thereby come to know their physical size. The Lord of Heaven, however, transcends all categories, and does not belong to any common category. To what category, then, can He be compared? Since the Lord of Heaven has no form or sound, by what traces can He be apprehended? His substance is inexhaustible and the material universe[27] cannot contain Him within its boundaries. How then can one discover a clue as to how great He is? If one wishes to give some indication as to His nature, one can find no better way to do so than by employing words like "not" and "lack,"[28] because, if one uses words like "is" and "has"[29] one will err by too great a margin.

56. *The Chinese scholar says:* How can the "Ultimate Being"[30] and the "Ultimate Possessor"[31] be described with words like "not" and "lack"?

57. *The Western scholar says:* Man is a lowly vessel and is incapable of containing the great doctrine concerning the Lord of Heaven. We only know that things are base and that the Lord of Heaven cannot be base, but we have no way of fully expressing His nobility. We only know that things are deficient and that the Lord of Heaven cannot be deficient, but we cannot investigate the perfection of the Lord of Heaven.

58 今吾欲擬指天主何物，曰：非天也，非地也，而其高明博厚較天地猶甚也；非鬼神也，而其神靈鬼神不啻也；非人也，而遐邁聖睿也；非所謂道德也，而為道德之源也。

59 彼實無往無來，而吾欲言其以往者，但曰無始也；欲言其以來者，但曰無終也。

60 又推而意其體也，無處可以容載之，而無所不盈充也。不動，而為諸動之宗。無手無口而化生萬彙、教諭萬生也。

61 其能也，無毀無衰，而可以無之為有者；其知也，無昧無謬，而已往之萬世以前，未來之萬世以後，無事可逃其知，如對目也；其善純備無滓，而為眾善之歸宿，不善者雖微而不能為之累也；其恩惠廣大，無壅然塞，無私無類，無所不及，小蟲細介亦被其澤也。

論天主始制天地萬物、而主宰安養之

The Lord of Heaven as Creator

58. If we now wish to say what the Lord of Heaven is we can only say He is not heaven and not earth; His loftiness and intelligence are much more extensive and much more ample than that of heaven and earth. He is not a ghost or a spirit; His spiritual essence transcends all ghosts and spirits. He is not man; He totally surpasses all sages and men of wisdom. He is not morality; He is the source of morality.

59. He has no past or future. Should I wish to speak of His past, I can only do so by saying that He lacks any beginning, and should I wish to speak of His future, I can only do so by saying that He lacks any end.

60. If I wish to infer the nature of His essence, I find that no place can contain Him and yet there is no place where He is not present; that He is unmoving and yet that He is the active cause of all movement; that He has no hands or mouth, and yet that He creates all things and instructs all people.

61. His power has never been able to be destroyed or to decline and can create all things out of nothing. His knowledge is neither partial nor mistaken. Things which took place more than ten thousand generations ago and matters ten thousand generations hence are to Him as events before our eyes; there is nothing He does not know. He is perfectly good and without a blemish and is the final resting place of all goodness. He cannot harbor any evil whatsoever. His graciousness is broad and without limit, open to all and impartial and reaches everywhere. Even the smallest insect is a recipient of His benefits.

62. When we come to speak of all the good things and good deeds in the universe, there is not one of them which does not come from the Lord of Heaven. Yet, when we compare them with [the Lord of Heaven who is] the source [of goodness], they are not even equivalent to a drop of water falling into the ocean. The Lord of Heaven's happiness and prosperity, virtue and ability, abundance

論天主始制天地萬物、而主宰安養之

62 夫乾坤之內，善性善行無不從天主稟之；雖然，比之于本原，一水滴於滄海不如也。天主之福德，隆盛滿圓，洋洋優優，豈有可以增，豈有可以減者哉？故江海可盡汲，濱沙可計數，宇宙可充實，而天主不可全明，況竟發之哉？

63 中士曰：嘻！豐哉論矣。釋所不能釋，窮所不能窮矣。某聞之而始見大道，以歸大元矣。願進而及終。今日不敢復瀆，詰朝再以請也。

64 西士曰：子自聰睿，聞寡知多，余何力焉？然知此論，則難處已平，要基已安，餘工可易立矣。

32 Ricci usually uses *yüan* (原) to express "source" or God as Creator. Here he uses *yüan* (元).

The Lord of Heaven as Creator

and completeness are so vast that they can neither be added to nor subtracted from. Thus, even if the waters of rivers and oceans could be totally drawn off, the sands on the sea shores counted or the universe filled, it would still be impossible to understand the Lord of Heaven completely. How, then, could one ever completely explain Him?

63. *The Chinese scholar says:* What a rich doctrine! It explains what man is unable to explain and tells exhaustively what man is unable to tell exhaustively. As I listened to you I saw the great Way for the first time and returned to the Supreme Source[32] of all phenomena. But I should like to continue my studies to the very end and dare not trouble you further today. I shall come again another day to receive your instruction.

64. *The Western scholar says:* You are very perceptive. Without any effort on my part you are able to infer much from the little you have heard. Since you understand these principles all areas of difficulty have disappeared. Once the important foundations have been firmly laid the rest is easy.

第二篇 解釋世人錯認天主

65 中士曰：玄論飫耳醉心，終夜思之忘寢，今再承教，以竟心惑。

66 吾中國有三教，各立門戶：老氏謂物生於無，以無為道；佛氏謂色由空出，以空為務；儒謂易有太極，故惟以有為宗，以誠為學。不知尊旨誰是？

67 西士曰：二氏之謂，曰無曰空，於天主理大相剌謬，其不可崇，尚明矣。夫儒之謂，曰有曰誠，雖未盡聞其釋，固庶幾乎？

68 中士曰：吾國君子亦痛斥二氏，深為恨之。

1. An abridged version of the words "For though all creatures under heaven are the products of Being, Being itself is the product of Non-Being," from the *Tao-te ching* (道德經, *Classic of the Way and Its Power* [*Virtue*]). See *The Way and its Power*, trans. by Arthur Waley, (London, 1934), p. 192. Here Ricci thought *Wu* (無, "Non-Being") meant "Nothing" but many Chinese scholars both past and present would speak of "Non-Being" as the Absolute without form or body.

2. This assertion brought an angry response from Fei-Yin, author of one of the ripostes in the *Collected Documents for the Countering of Heterodoxy*, since it appears to involve the Absolute in causation, a notion which is anathema to Buddhists. See Lancashire, "Buddhist Reaction to Christianity in Late Ming China," *Journal of the Oriental Society of Australia* 6 (1968-1969), 97.

3. Fung Yu-lan (馮友蘭), in his *A Short History of Chinese Philosophy* (New York, 1948), p. 170, translates the whole passage which appears in "Appendix III" of the *Book of Changes* as follows: "In the *Yi* (易) there is the Supreme Ultimate which produces the Two Forms. The Two Forms produce the Four Emblems, and these Four Emblems produce the eight trigrams."

4. See above, Translators' Introduction, pp. 47-48.

5. See above, ibid., p. 49.

Chapter 2

AN EXPLANATION OF MISTAKEN VIEWS CONCERNING THE LORD OF HEAVEN CURRENT AMONG MEN.

65. *The Chinese scholar says:* Your profound doctrine satisfies the ear and intoxicates the mind. I thought about it the whole night long and quite forgot to go to sleep. Now I would like to ask you for further instruction in the hope that the doubts lingering in my mind can be thoroughly dispelled.

66. In our China there are three religions, each with its own teaching. Lao Tzu said: "Things are produced from nothing,"[1] and made "nothing" the Way [of Life]. The Buddha taught that "the visible world emerges from voidness,"[2] and made "voidness" the end [of all effort]. The Confucians say: "In the processes of *Yi* there exists the Supreme Ultimate"[3] and therefore make "existence" the basic principle [of all things] and "sincerity" the subject of the study of self-cultivation. I wonder who, in your revered view, is correct?

67. *The Western scholar says:* The "nothing" spoken of by Lao Tzu and the "voidness" taught by the Buddha are totally at variance with the doctrine concerning the Lord of Heaven;[4] and it is therefore abundantly clear that they do not merit esteem. When it comes to the "existence" and "sincerity" of the Confucians, however, although I have not heard a complete explanation of the meaning of these words, they would seem to be close to the truth.[5]

68. *The Chinese scholar says:* The superior men of my country too are vehement in their dismissal of Buddhism and Taoism and have a deep hatred of them.

69 西士曰：恨之不如辯之以言，辯之不如析之以理。二氏之徒，並天主大父所生，則吾弟吾兄矣。譬吾弟病狂，顛倒怪誕，吾為兄之道，恤乎？恨乎？在以理喻之而已。

70 余嘗博覽儒書，往往憾嫉二氏，夷狄排之，謂斥異端，而不見揭一鉅理以非之。我以彼為非，彼亦以我為非，紛紛為訟，兩不相信，三家歸一耳。西鄉有諺曰：「堅繩可繫牛角，理語能服人心。」儆國之鄰方，上古不止三教，纍纍數千百枝，後為我儒以正理辨喻，以善行默化，今惟天主一教是從。

6 Here Ricci probably refers to the writings of Neo-Confucians who severely criticized the doctrines of Buddhism and Taoism, although some of their own teachings derived from these two systems of thought.

100

Mistaken Views About the Lord of Heaven

69. *The Western scholar says:* It is better to refute [the teachings of Buddhists and Taoists] than to hate [the men who hold these opinions]; and it is better still to use clear reasoning than to refute them merely with many words; for Taoists and Buddhists are all produced by our great Father, the Lord of Heaven, and we are therefore all brothers. For example, if my younger brother goes mad and falls to the ground, should I, as his elder brother, pity him or hate him? What is most important is that we should employ reason to explain the truth and make things clear to them.

70. I have read a great number of Confucian books[6] and have noticed that they never cease to express animosity towards Buddhism and Taoism. They are condemned as being barbarian, and the rejection of them is described as attacks on heresy; nevertheless, I have never seen anyone expose their errors with any overriding principle. The result has been that if one says the other is wrong, the other says his opponent is wrong, and so they have attacked one another, neither party being willing to yield, for one thousand five hundred years; and they are still unable to reconcile their different points of view. If they were able to argue with each other in a rational manner they would naturally be able to distinguish between truth and falsehood; and the three schools would be able to return to the one and only correct Way. There is a Western proverb which runs: "Strong rope can tether the horns of an ox and rational speech can subdue men's minds." In ancient times, in the states neighboring on my own humble nation, there were not merely three religions but hundreds of thousands of heterodox schools of thought; because our scholars later clarified the truth with the aid of correct reasoning and influenced people by means of good works, these states now all follow the religion of the Lord of Heaven.

解釋世人錯認天主

71 中士曰：正道從一耳，烏用眾？然佛老之說持之有故，凡物先空後實，先無後有，故以空無為物之原，似也。

72 西士曰：上達以下學為基，天下以實有為貴，以虛無為賤，若謂萬物之原貴莫尚焉，奚可以虛無之賤當之乎？況己之所無，不得施之於物以為有，此理明也。今，日空曰無者絕無所有於己者也，則胡能施有性形以為物體哉？物必誠有，方謂之有物焉；無誠，則為無物。設其本原無實無有，則是并其所出物者，無之也。世人雖聖神，不得以無物為有；則彼無者安能以其空無為萬物有、為萬物實哉？試以物之所以然觀之，亦安能以無為物之作者、模者、質者、為者乎？既謂之空無，則不能為物之所以然，此於物尚有何者歟？

73 中士曰：聞教固當，但謂物者先無而後有，是或一道也。

---

7 *Sheng-shen* (聖神). *Sheng* means "holy" or "holiness." *Shen* can mean, among other things "god" (divinity), "divine power," and "spirit." Ricci combined these two terms to make an adjective modifying "man" or "sage." However, later on the Chinese Catholic Church used *Sheng-shen* (聖神) as a proper noun to indicate the Holy Spirit, the third person of the Trinity. So, in all editions of the present work after the 18th century, the original phrase was changed to *Shen-sheng* (神聖) or *Sheng-jen* (聖人), *jen* meaning "person" or "man."

8 Ricci manifests here his misunderstanding of the Buddhist and Taoist doctrine.

Mistaken Views About the Lord of Heaven

71. *The Chinese scholar says:* There is only one orthodox doctrine; how can there be many? Nevertheless, the teachings of Buddhism and Taoism are not without some foundation. All things, they say, are first void and then later actualized; at first they do not exist, and it is only later that they come into existence. Thus, they seem to regard "voidness" and "nothingness" as the sources of things.

72. *The Western scholar says:* If one wishes to gain a thorough understanding [of the profound principles of things] one must begin by laying a foundation of elementary knowledge. [Those who live] below heaven value the real and the existing and despise the non-existent. When we come to speak of the source of all phenomena we are clearly speaking of that, the value of which is beyond all comparison. How, then, can one employ despicable [words like] "voidness" and "nothingness" to represent it? Moreover, one cannot give to another what one does not have oneself. This is an obvious principle. What is now called "voidness" or "nothingness" possesses abolutely nothing of its own. How then can it give nature and form to something else and thereby cause it to come into being? A thing must genuinely exist before it can be said to exist. What does not genuinely exist does not exist. If the source of all things were not real or did not exist then the things produced by it would naturally also not exist. Even the divinest[7] among all people on earth would not be able to make nothing a being. How can things which are essentially nothing or void employ their voidness and nothingness to cause all things to come into being and to continue in existence? If we look at things in terms of their causes, we must conclude that since these causes are called "voidness" and "nothingness," they cannot be the active, formal, material and final causes of things; and since this is so, of what use are they to things?[8]

73. *The Chinese scholar says:* Having listened to your instruction I find it unquestionably correct and proper; but perhaps there is truth in the claim that things are first nothing and only later exist?

103

74 西士曰：有始之物，曰先無而後有，可也；無始之物，非所論矣。無始者，無時不有，何時先無焉？特分而言之，謂每物先無後有，可耳；若總而言之，則否也。譬始某人未生之先，果無某人，旣生而後，有也；然未生某人之先，却有某人之親以生之。天下之物，莫不皆然。至其渾無一物之初，是必有天主開其原也。

75 中士曰：人人有是非之心，不通此理，如失本心，寧聽其餘誕哉？借如空無者，非人、非神、無心性、無知覺、無靈才、無仁義、無一善足嘉，卽草芥至卑之物猶不可比，而謂之萬物之根本，其意誠悖。但吾聞空無者，非真空無之謂，乃神之無形無聲者耳，則于天主何異焉？

76 西士曰：此屈於理之言，請勿以斯稱天主也。夫神之有性、有才、有德，較吾有形之彙益精益高，其理益實，何得特因無此

---

9 *Pen-hsin* (本心). This expression is used by Mencius and refers to that moral mind with which he believed every person to be endowed, and which, when lost, he held to be recoverable. See James Legge, tr., *The Chinese Classics* (Hong Kong, 1960), vol. II, p. 414.

10 The Chinese scholar here takes an approach similar to that of the "via negativa" mentioned earlier by Ricci himself, but Ricci does not seem to see the parallel. See above, notes 1 and 2 of this chapter.

Mistaken Views About the Lord of Heaven

74. *The Western scholar says:* One may say of things which have a beginning that they are at first nothing, and that only later do they come into existence. Things without a beginning we shall not discuss here. Things which are beginningless have always existed. How could there be a time when they were non-existent? Of some individual things we can say that initially they were nothing and only subsequently they came into existence. But one must not make too sweeping a generalization. For example, before a person is born, he, of course, does not exist, and after he is born he does exist. But before a person is born the parents of this person are in existence; and so it is with everything else in the world. At the beginning, when not a single thing was in existence, there had of necessity to be a Lord of Heaven to serve as the source of all things.

75. *The Chinese scholar says:* People all possess a mind capable of distinguishing between right and wrong, truth and falsehood. Anyone who is unable to understand this truth which you have just expounded is like a person who has lost his root-mind.[9] No one would want to listen to any other of his absurdities. If voidness and nothingness are neither man nor spirit and are without mind, awareness, and intellect, and if they are devoid of humanity and righteousness, and lack anything worthy of being called good, then voidness and nothingness cannot be compared even with the humblest and smallest of plants. To call these the root of all phenomena is truly to be perverse. But the voidness and nothingness of which I have heard tell are not a real voidness and nothingness; they are rather the formlessness and soundlessness of spirit.[10] What difference, then, is there between these and the Lord of Heaven?

76. *The Western scholar says:* This is a most unseemly way of speaking; kindly do not equate these terms with the Lord of Heaven. This spirit has a nature, talent, and virtue. He profoundly excels all things possessed of form, and His reason is more suffi-

解釋世人錯認天主

形，隨謂之無且虛乎？五常之德，無形無聲，孰謂之無哉？無形者之於無也，隔霄壤矣。以此為教，非惟不能昭世，愈滋惑矣。

77 中士曰：吾儒言太極者是乎？

78 西士曰：余雖末年入中華，然竊視古經書不怠，但聞古先君子敬恭于天地之上帝，未聞有尊奉太極者。如太極為上帝—萬物之祖，古聖何隱其說乎？

79 中士曰：古者未有其名，而實有其理，但圖釋未傳耳。

80 西士曰：凡言與理相合，君子無以逆之。太極之解，恐難謂合理也。吾視夫無極而太極之圖，不過取奇偶之象言，而其象何在？太極非生天地之實可知已。天主之理，從古實

11 *Wu-ch'ang* (五常). See chapter 1, n. 15.
12 *T'ai-chi* (太極). The Supreme or Great Ultimate is a term derived from the Han dynasty appendices to the *Book of Changes*. It is the first principle from which all things emerge and are differentiated. Although the *Changes* is essentially a divination manual, the appendices provided the raw material for Neo-Confucian cosmological and metaphysical speculation.
13 *T'u-shih* (圖釋). In Chinese tradition "diagrams" were used to illustrate the relationships between the universe and the Supreme Ultimate. Some Chinese scholars thought that although there were many diagrams of the Supreme Ultimate (太極圖 , *T'ai chi t'u*), only a few of them had been handed down.
14 This refers to the diagram of the Supreme Ultimate employed by Chou Tun-yi (周敦頤 , 1017-1073) to illustrate his theory of emanation. Chou sought to identify his Supreme Ultimate with the Taoist concept of Non-Being and the Buddhist notion of voidness by referring to it also as the Ultimateless. He also combined his theory with that of *Wu-hsing* (五行), according to which the cosmos is composed of Five Elements: metal, wood, water, fire, and earth. Neo-Confucian cosmology and metaphysics were elaborated according to this diagram.
15 Some contemporary Chinese scholars, both Christians and non-Christians, consider that the Supreme Ultimate, when recognized as personal, could be a correct representation of God. Ricci did not see this.

Mistaken Views About the Lord of Heaven

cient. How can one call Him nothingness and emptiness because He is without form? The morality implicit in the Five Basic Virtues[11] is also without form or sound, but who would say of it that it is nothing? The difference between something that is formless and nothingness is as great as that between heaven and earth. If the theory of nothingness is taught it will not only fail to illuminate mankind, but will increasingly mislead it.

77. *The Chinese scholar says:* Are the Confucian scholars of my country right in what they say about the Supreme Ultimate?[12]

78. *The Western scholar says:* Although I arrived in China late in life, I have assiduously studied the ancient records of China and discovered that the superior men of ancient times worshipped and revered the Sovereign on High, [the Supreme Lord] of Heaven and earth, but I have never heard of them paying respect to the Supreme Ultimate. If the Supreme Ultimate is the Sovereign on High and ancestor of all things, why did not the sages of ancient times say so?

79. *The Chinese scholar says:* Although the term did not exist in ancient times, there is no doubt that teaching concerning it did exist. It is simply that the diagram[13] of this teaching has not been handed down to the present day.

80. *The Western scholar says:* Superior men have no reason to oppose any theory which accords with the truth, but I am afraid it is difficult to harmonize explanations of the Supreme Ultimate with the truth. The theory, from what I have seen of the diagram illustrating the Ultimateless and the Supreme Ultimate,[14] is based on symbols representing *Yang* and *Yin;* and what is [the reality of which] these symbols [are an expression]? It is obvious, then, that the Supreme Ultimate cannot be the reality which produced heaven and earth.[15] The truth concerning the Lord of Heaven has been handed down from ancient times. It is complete, and is deficient in nothing. When we write it down in books so that it may be

解釋世人錯認天主

傳至今，全備無遺；而吾欲誌之于冊，傳之于他邦，猶不敢不揭其理之所憑，況虛象無實理之可依耶？

81 中士曰：太極非他物，乃理而已。如以全理為無理，尚有何理之可謂？

82 西士曰：嗚呼！他物之體態不歸于理，可得將理以歸正議；若理之本體定以其理，又將何以理之哉？吾今先判物之宗品，以置理於本品；然後明其太極之說不能為萬物本原也。

83 夫物之宗品有二：有自立者，有依賴者。物之不恃別體以為物，而自能成立，如天地、鬼神、人、鳥獸、草木、金石、四行等是也，斯屬自立之品者；物之不能立，而託

16 Ch'eng I (程頤, 1033-1107) and his brother Ch'eng Hao (程顥, 1032-1085) were early contributors to the Confucian revival of the Sung dynasty. Ch'eng I's rationalistic thought was taken up and developed by Chu Hsi (朱熹, 1130-1200). Ch'eng Hao and Ch'eng I used the term *li* (理), "principle," as the Absolute in cosmology and metaphysics and as the "form" of beings. This concept derives from a Chinese Mahayana Buddhist school, *Hua-yen Tsung* (華嚴宗).

17 *Tsung-p'in* (宗品). Ricci introduced scholastic philosophy into China and used this term to translate the concept "category" of Aristotelean and scholastic philosophy. Contemporary Chinese scholars use *fan-ch'ou* (範疇).

18 Ricci used *tzu-li-che* (自立者) and *i-lai-che* (依賴者). Contemporary Chinese scholars use *tzu-li-t'i* (自立體) and *i-fu-t'i* (依附體).

19 Here Ricci used the concept of the ancient Greek philosopher Heraclitus (c. 544-484 B.C.), who taught there were four elements in the cosmos: fire, air, water and earth. Chinese tradition recognized five. See above, n. 14.

20 *Wu-ch'ang* (五常). See chapter 1, n. 15.
21 *Wu-sê* (五色). See chapter 1, n. 16.
22 *Wu-yin* (五音). See chapter 1, n. 17.
23 *Wu-wei* (五味). See chapter 1, n. 18.
24 *Ch'i-ch'ing* (七情, "the Seven Emotions"): happiness, anger, sorrow, joy, love, hate, desire.
25 The question of the existence or otherwise of a white horse is debated in the *Kung-sun Lung Tzu* (公孫龍子), a work dating from the first half of the third century B.C.

transmitted to other nations, we dare not but produce the principles upon which it depends. These empty symbols, however, are not based on any real principle.

81. *The Chinese scholar says:* But the Supreme Ultimate is nothing other than principle.[16] If you say that principle, in all its perfection, lacks principle, can there be any principle to talk about?

82. *The Western scholar says:* Dear me! If the form of a thing does not conform to its principle, it is possible to correct it by means of that principle. But if the principle itself is wrong, by what means can it be corrected? I shall now distinguish between the various categories[17] of things and relate their principles to them. When I have done this you will understand that the way the Supreme Ultimate is described precludes it from being the source of all things.

83. There are two categories of things: substance and accident.[18]

Things which do not depend on other things for their existence, such as heaven and earth, ghosts and spirits, men, birds and beasts, vegetation, metals, stones, the four elements,[19] and the like, are all classed as substance. Things which cannot stand on their own and which can only be established subject to other things, as, for example, the Five Basic Virtues,[20] the Five Colors,[21] the Five Notes,[22] the Five Flavors,[23] the Seven Emotions,[24] and the like, are all classed as dependent. Let us take a white horse as an illustration.[25] Here there are two things: whiteness and horse. Horse is substance. Whiteness is an accident, since even without its whiteness the horse could continue to exist. If there were no horse, however, the whiteness of the horse would be totally incapable of continued existence. We therefore say that it is an accident. When we compare these two categories we find that substance has prior existence and is of value, whereas accident is comparatively secondary and of little consequence. There can only be one substance in any one thing, whereas there can be many accidents. For example, a man has only one body, which is substance; but this body contains numerous accidents such as the emotions, sound, appearance, color, moral obligations, and the like.

他體以為其物，如五常、五色、五音、五味、七情等是也，斯屬依賴之品者。且以白馬觀之：曰白，曰馬，馬乃自立者，白乃依賴者。雖無其白，猶有其馬；如無其馬，必無其白，故以為依賴也。比斯兩品：凡自立者，先也、貴也；依賴者，後也、賤也。一物之體，惟有自立一類；若其依賴之類，不可勝窮。如人一身固為自立，其間情聲、貌色、彝倫等類俱為依賴，其類甚多。

84 若太極者，止解之以所謂理，則不能為天地萬物之原矣；蓋理亦依賴之類，自不能立，曷立他物哉？中國文人學士講論理者，只謂有二端：或在人心，或在事物。事物之情合乎人心之理，則事物方謂真實焉；人心能窮彼在物之理，而盡其知，則謂之格物焉。據此兩端，則理固依賴，奚得為物原乎？

85 二者皆在物後，而後豈先者之原？夫理在何處？依屬何物乎？依賴之情不能自立，故無自立者以為之託，則依賴者了無矣。如曰賴空虛耳，恐空虛非足賴者，理將不免于僵墮也。試問盤古之前既有理在，何故閒空不動而生物乎？其後誰從激之使動？況理本無動靜，況自動乎？如曰昔不生物乎？後乃願生物，則理豈有意乎？何以有欲生物，有欲不生物乎？

解釋世人錯認天主

26 This passage seems to indicate the root of Ricci's misunderstanding of Neo-Confucianism.
27 The teaching that the extension of knowledge lies in the investigation of things is found in the *Great Learning*. See Wing-tsit Chan, *A Source Book in Chinese Philosophy*, (Princeton, 1963), pp. 84-94.
28 In popular Taoism P'an Ku (盤古) is regarded as the one "who chiselled the universe out of Chaos." He is said to have been produced by the two forces of *yin* and *yang* and to have devoted eighteen thousand years to the forming of the sun, moon, stars, heavens, and earth. See E.T.C. Werner, *Myths and Legends of China* (London, 1922), pp. 76-83.

Mistaken Views About the Lord of Heaven

84. When we come to the Supreme Ultimate we find that it is only explained in terms of principle. It cannot therefore be the source of heaven, earth, and all things because principle also falls into the category of accidents. Since it is not substance how can it establish other things?[26] When men of letters and learned men in China discuss principle they only speak of it in two ways: they either say that principle resides in the minds of men, or else they say it is to be found in things. They only say that things are real when their mode of being harmonizes with the principles in men's minds. When the human mind is able to study, penetrate and completely understand the principles inherent in things this is called "the investigation of things."[27] It is clear, on the basis of these two ways of speaking about principle, that principle is dependent and cannot be the source of things. Principles, whether in the human mind or in things, are all subsequent to those things; and how can that which is subsequent be the source of that which exists prior to it?

85. Further, in the beginning, before anything existed, who said that there had to be principles? Where were those principles located and on what did they depend? Accidents cannot stand by themselves; if there are no substances for them to rely on, then the accidents are void and non-existent. If you say that they rely on voidness and emptiness, I am afraid I can only say that voidness and emptiness are not adequate to serve as their supports. Thus, one can come to no other conclusion than that principle must fall. Let me ask you: If principle existed prior to *P'an Ku*,[28] why did it remain at leisure and not move to produce things? Who later stimulated it into activity? If, as has been said, principle originally was neither active nor inactive, how could it possibly move of its own accord? If you say that principle at first did not produce anything but that later it wished to produce things, is this not tantamount to saying that principle possesses will? Why is it that at times it desires to produce things, and at other times it does not desire to produce things?

111

解釋世人錯認天主

86 中士曰：無其理則無其物，是故我周子信理為物之原也。

87 西士曰：無子則無父，而誰言子為父之原乎？相須者之物情恒如此：本相為有無者之物之理；無此物之實，即無此理之實。有物，則有物之理；無此物之實，即無此理之實。若以虛理為理之原，是無異乎佛老之說，以攻佛老之實，是以燕伐燕，以亂易亂矣。今時實理不得生物，昔者虛理安得以生之乎？譬如今日有輿人於此，何不即動發一乘車？而必待有樹木之質，斧鋸之械，匠人之工，然後成車。何初之神奇能化天地之大，而今之衰微不能發一車之小耶？

88 中士曰：吾聞理者，先生陰陽五行，然後化生天地萬物，故生物有次第焉。使於須臾生耳，非其譬矣。

29 Chou-tzu (周子). Here the Chinese scholar erroneously states that Chou-tzu, that is, Chou Tun-yi (see n. 14), believed that principle was the source of things. The origins of the doctrine are to be found in the teaching of Chou's students, Ch'eng Hao and Ch'eng I.
30 Yen (燕), one of the principal contenders for power during the period of the Warring States (戰國時代, 403-221 B.C.).
31 *Wu-hsing* (五行, "Five Elements"); see n. 14.
32 This doctrine was originated by Chu Hsi, the great synthesizer of Neo-Confucian thought, who has dominated Confucian thinking until modern times. He combined the doctrine of the diagram of the Supreme Ultimate, which comes from Chou Tun-yi, and the theory that principle was the Absolute in cosmology, which came from the brothers Ch'eng. He thus made principle the equivalent of the Supreme Ultimate.

86. *The Chinese scholar says:* Without principle there can be nothing; it was for this reason that Chou-tzu[29] of our country believed that principle was the source of things.

87. *The Western scholar says:* If there is no son there can be no father; yet who would say that a son is the source of his father? Things necessary to each other are always like this—they depend on each other for their existence and non-existence. Only when there is a sovereign can there be a minister; if there is no sovereign there can be no minister. Only when there are things can there be principles of things; without the real existence of things their principles cannot exist. If you make empty principle the source of things, there will be no difference between your teachings and those of the Buddhists and Taoists. If you employ this kind of exposition to attack Buddhism and Taoism it will be like the state of Yen[30] attacking itself or like substituting one disorderly government for another. If real principles now in existence cannot produce things, how could the empty principles of the past produce anything? For example, we have here a carriage maker with the principles governing the making of carriages in his mind. Now why can these principles not produce a carriage? Why must there be timber, hammers, saws, and the like, as well as the work of the craftsman before the carriage can be manufactured and completed? Why is it that in the beginning principle was so ingenious that it was able to produce the enormous heaven and earth, whereas now it has declined to the point where it cannot even produce something as small as a carriage?

88. *The Chinese scholar says:* I have heard it said that principle first produced the *Yin* and *Yang* and the Five Elements,[31] and that only later did these evolve into heaven, earth and all things.[32] There was therefore a definite order of sequence in the production of things. If you are implying that principle should produce a carriage in an instant, your illustration is not apposite.

解釋世人錯認天主

89 西士曰：試問於子：陰陽五行之理，一動一靜之際轍能生陰陽五行；則今有車理，豈不動而生一乘車乎？又理無所不在，彼既是無意之物，性必直遂任其所發，自不能已；何今不生陰陽五行於此？孰禦之哉？

90 且『物』字為萬實總名，凡物皆可稱之為『物』。太極圖註云：「理者，非物矣。」物之類多，而均謂之物：或為自立者，或為依賴者；或有形者，或無形者。理既非有形之物類，豈不得為無形之物品乎？

91 又問理者靈覺否？明義者否？如靈覺明義，則屬鬼神之類，曷謂之太極，謂之理也？如否，則上帝鬼神夫人之靈覺由誰得之乎？彼理者以己之所無，不得施之于物以為之有也；理無靈無覺，則不能生靈生覺。請子察乾坤之內，惟自靈覺而出不靈覺者，則有之矣；未聞有自不靈覺而生有靈覺者也。子固不踰母也。

33 This commentary was written by Chu Hsi.
34 *Ch'ien-k'un* (乾坤). See above, Ricci's Introduction, n. 5.

114

Mistaken Views About the Lord of Heaven

89. *The Western scholar says:* May I ask you, Sir, if the principles of *Yin* and *Yang* and the Five Elements produced *Yin* and *Yang* and the Five Elements at the moment between action and quiescence, how is it that the principles of a carriage now in existence are unable to produce a carriage at the moment they become active? Further, principle is everywhere, and since it is devoid of will, its self-manifestation must be spontaneous. It must be incapable of self-restraint. Why, then, does it not produce the *Yin* and *Yang* and the Five Elements at this moment and in this place? Who is restraining it?

90. Further, the word "thing" is the general term for all things which actually exist; all things can, therefore, be called "things." The *Commentary to the Diagram of the Supreme Ultimate*,[33] however, says: "Principle is not a thing." There are numerous categories of things, but they are all termed "things." There are substances and there are accidents, and there is a distinction between things with form and things without form. Since principle is not a thing with form, must it not be a thing without form?

91. May I further ask you whether principle has intelligence and consciousness? Can it comprehend the principle of righteousness? If it has intelligence and consciousness and can comprehend the principle of righteousness then it must fall within the category of ghosts and spirits, in which case why call it Supreme Ultimate or principle? But if this is not the case, then where did the intelligence and consciousness of the Sovereign on High, of spiritual beings and of mankind come from? Principle cannot give what it does not possess. Because principle does not have intelligence and consciousness, it cannot produce intelligence and consciousness. I would ask you, Sir, to look carefully at everything in the universe.[34] Only things with intelligence produce intelligence, and only things with consciousness produce consciousness. It does happen that things with intelligence and consciousness produce

解釋世人錯認天主

92 中士曰：靈覺為有靈覺者所生，非理之謂，既聞命矣。但理動而生陽，陳乃自然之靈覺，或其然乎？

93 西士曰：反覆論辯，難脫此理。吾又問：彼陽者何由得靈覺乎？此于自然之理，亦大相悖。

94 中士曰：先生謂天主無形無聲，而能施萬象有形有聲；則太極無靈覺，而能施物之靈覺，何傷乎？

95 西士曰：何不云「無形聲者精也、上也；有形聲者粗也、下也」？以精上能施粗下，分不為過。以無靈覺之粗下，為施靈覺之精上，則出其分外遠矣。

96 又云，上物能含下物，有三般焉：或窮然包下之體，如一丈載十尺，一尺載十寸之體是也；或渾然包下之性，如人魂混有禽獸魂，禽獸魂混有草木魂是也；或粹然包下之德，如天主含萬物之性是也。

---

35 *Chang* (丈), *ch'ih* (尺), *ts'un* (寸) are units in the Chinese system of linear measurement. One *chang* equals ten *ch'ih*; one *ch'ih* equals ten *ts'un*. One *ch'ih* is slightly longer than one foot.

stupid and unintelligent things, but I have never heard it said that things lacking intelligence and consciousness are able to produce things with intelligence and consciousness, for a result cannot be greater than its cause.

92. *The Chinese scholar says:* I accept your point that it is not principle but something possessing intelligence and consciousness which produces things possessing intelligence and consciousness. But when principle moves it produces *Yang*; and does not *Yang* naturally possess intelligence and consciousness?

93. *The Western scholar says:* We may argue back and forth but you will not be able to escape the truth. Let me ask you instead: Where did the *Yang* you refer to gain intelligence and consciousness? Such a thing is totally opposed to natural reason.

94. *The Chinese scholar says:* You said before, Sir, that the Lord of Heaven, though without form or sound, was able to create all things having form and sound. Why should not the Supreme Ultimate, which is devoid of intelligence and consciousness, be able to produce things with intelligence and consciousness?

95. *The Western scholar says:* Why don't you say that something which lacks form and sound is refined and superior, whereas something which has form and sound is gross and inferior? There is absolutely nothing wrong in the refined and superior bestowing something on that which is gross and inferior; but for a gross and inferior thing which is lacking in intelligence and consciousness to bestow something on a thing which is refined and superior and which possesses intelligence and consciousness is to transcend its own powers by too wide a margin.

96. Furthermore, it is said that there are three ways in which superior things can incorporate inferior things. They may totally and physically embrace the forms of inferior things as, for example, one *chang* encompasses ten *ch'ih* and one *ch'ih* encompasses ten *ts'un*;[35] or they may wholly embrace the natures of inferior

解釋世人錯認天主

97 夫天主之性最為全盛,而且穆穆焉非人心可測,非萬物可比倫也。雖然,吾姑譬之。如一黃金錢有十銀錢及千銅錢價,所以然者,惟黃金之性甚精,大異於銀銅之性,故價之幾倍如此。天主性雖未嘗截然有萬物之情,而以其精德包萬般之現,含眾物之性,其能無所不備也;雖則無形無聲,何難化萬象哉?

98 理也者,則大異焉。是乃依賴之類,自不能立,何能包含靈覺為自立之類乎?理卑於人,理為物,而非物為理也,故仲尼曰:「人能弘道,非道弘人也。」如爾曰「理含萬物之靈,化生萬物」,此乃天主也,何獨謂之『理』,謂之『太極』哉?

99 中士曰:如此,則吾孔子言太極何意?

---

36 *Analects*, XV, 28.
37 Actually, Confucius never said anything about the Supreme Ultimate in his *Analects* or in his other writings. The term comes from *I chuan* (易傳, *The Commentary on the Book of Changes*), which was written about 300 years after Confucius.

118

Mistaken Views About the Lord of Heaven

things as, for example, man's soul wholly embraces the souls of birds and beasts; and the souls of birds and beasts wholly embrace the souls of vegetation; or they may selectively embrace the virtues of the inferior, as, for example, the Lord of Heaven embraces the natures of all things.

97. The nature of the Lord of Heaven is most perfect, most complete and supremely serene. It cannot be fathomed by the minds of men, nor can it be compared with anything. I shall attempt, nevertheless, to give you a temporary illustration. A gold coin is worth ten silver coins and one thousand copper coins. Because gold is by nature the purest of metals and is greatly superior to silver and copper, its value is many times greater than that of the other metals. Similarly, the nature of the Lord of Heaven has never shared in all aspects of phenomena; yet, His perfect virtue embraces the principles of all things and harbours the natures of all things. He is without form or sound, yet, because there is nothing with which He is not provided He has no difficulty in creating all things.

98. When we come to principle, however, we find a totally different situation. Since principle falls into the category of accident and cannot stand and exist on its own, how can it embrace intelligence and consciousness and become substance? Principle is more lowly than man. Its final purpose is to become actualized in phenomena; phenomena do not have principle as their final purpose. Thus Confucius says: "A man can enlarge his Way; but there is no Way that can enlarge a man."[36] If you say that principle embraces the intelligence of all things and produces all things, then you are talking about the Lord of Heaven and not about principle or the Supreme Ultimate.

99. *The Chinese scholar says:* In that case, what did Confucius mean when he talked of the Supreme Ultimate?[37]

解釋世人錯認天主

100 西士曰：造物之功盛也，其中固有樞紐矣；然此為天主所立者。物之無原之原者，不可以理，以太極當之。夫太極之理，本有精論，吾雖曾閱之，不敢雜陳其辯，或容以他書傳其要也。

101 中士曰：吾國吾臣，自古迄今，惟知以天地為尊，敬之如父母，故郊社之禮以祭之。如太極為天地所出，是世之宗考妣也，古先聖帝王臣祀典宜首及焉；而今不然，此知必太極之解非也。先生辯之最詳，于古聖賢無二意矣。

102 西士曰：雖然，天地為尊之說，未易解也。夫至尊無兩，惟一焉耳；曰天、曰地，是二之也。

103 吾天主，即華言上帝；與道家所塑玄帝玉皇之像不同，彼不過一人，修居於武當山，俱亦人類耳，惡得為天帝皇耶？

38 Unfortunately it seems Ricci never wrote such a book. If he had had occasion to re-examine these themes, perhaps he would have had a more positive understanding of them.
39 Ricci's Chinese scholar gives up too easily. In reality, both in Ricci's time and since, up to the present day, other Chinese scholars have defended their positions more vigorously.
40 For information on popular Taoist deities and other aspects of Chinese religious life the reader should consult such works as the following: J.J.M. De Groot, *The Religion of the Chinese* (New York, 1910); Henri Doré, *Researches into Chinese Superstitions* (Shanghai, 1914-1938); Lewis Hodous, *Folkways in China* (London, 1929); C.K. Yang, *Religion in Chinese Society* (Berkeley, 1961); Michael Saso, *Taoism and the Rite of Cosmic Renewal* (Pullman, 1972) and *The Teachings of Taoist Master Chuang* (New Haven, 1978).

Mistaken Views About the Lord of Heaven

100. *The Western scholar says:* The work of creation is an enormous undertaking and it must have its own pivot; but this is established by the Lord of Heaven. If there were no first cause to serve as the source of phenomena, neither principle nor the Supreme Ultimate would be able to fill this role. I am sure that there initially must have been very profound reasons for the teachings concerning the Supreme Ultimate. I have read them, and I would not dare to cast aside these arguments in any casual manner. Perhaps I shall later be able to write another book in which I can discuss their important ideas.[38]

101. *The Chinese scholar says:* From ancient times to the present the sovereigns and ministers of my country have known only that they should pay reverence to Heaven and Earth as if they were reverencing their fathers and mothers. They have therefore employed the ceremonial of state worship to sacrifice to them. If the Supreme Ultimate were the source of heaven and earth it would be the first ancestor of the world; and the first sages, emperors, and ministers of ancient times ought to have given priority to the worship of it. But, in fact, this was not the case. It is obvious, then, that the explanation given of the Supreme Ultimate is incorrect. You have argued the matter exhaustively, Sir, and your views are the same as those of the sages and worthies of ancient times.[39]

102. *The Western scholar says:* Despite what you say, the teaching that Heaven and Earth are the two things most honored is by no means easy to explain, since that which is most deserving of honor is unique and unparalleled. If we speak of "heaven" and "earth" we are talking about two things.

103. He who is called the Lord of Heaven in my humble country is He who is called *Shang-ti* (Sovereign on High) in Chinese. He is not, however, the same as the carved image of the Taoist Jade Emperor who is described as the Supreme Lord of the Black Pavilions of Heaven, for he was no more than a recluse on Wu-tang mountain.[40] Since he was a man, how could he have been the Sovereign of heaven and earth?

104 吾天主，乃古經書所稱上帝也。中庸引孔子曰：「郊社之禮以事上帝也。」朱註曰：「不言后土者，省文也。」竊意仲尼明一之，以不可為二，何獨省文乎？

105 周頌曰：「執兢武王，無兢維烈。」又曰：「於皇來年，將受厥明，明昭上帝。」商頌云：「聖敬日躋，昭假遲遲，上帝是祇。」雅云：「維此文王，小心翼翼，昭事上帝。」

106 易曰：「帝出乎震。」夫帝也者，非天之謂，蒼天者抱八方，何能出於一乎？

41 Chan, *A Source Book in Chinese Philosophy*, p. 104.
42 See above, n. 16.
43 *Hou-t'u* (后土).
44 Chung-ni (仲尼), another name of Confucius.
45 The majority of Chinese scholars, past and present, agree with Chu Hsi's comment.
46 *The Chinese Classics*, vol. IV, p. 578, slightly altered.
47 Ibid., IV, pp. 582-583, slightly altered.
48 Ibid., IV, p. 640, slightly altered.
49 Ibid., IV, p. 433, slightly altered.
50 See *I Ching: Book of Changes*, trans. by James Legge and edited by Ch'u Chai with W. Chai (New York, 1969), p. 425.

Mistaken Views About the Lord of Heaven

104. Our Lord of Heaven is the Sovereign on High mentioned in the ancient [Chinese] canonical writings [as the following texts show]: Quoting Confucius, the *Doctrine of the Mean* says: "The ceremonies of sacrifices to Heaven and Earth are meant for the service of the Sovereign on High."[41] Chu Hsi[42] comments that the failure to mention Sovereign Earth[43] [after Sovereign on High] was for the sake of brevity. In my humble opinion what Chung-ni[44] intended to say was that what is single cannot be described dualistically.[45] How could he have been seeking merely for brevity of expression?

105. One of the hymns to the Chou sovereigns in the [*Book of Odes*] runs as follows:

> The arm of King Wu was full of strength;
> Irresistible was his ardor.
> Greatly illustrious were Ch'eng and K'ang,
> Kinged by the Sovereign on High.[46]

In another hymn we read:

> How beautiful are the wheat and the barley,
> Whose bright produce we shall receive!
> The bright and glorious Sovereign on High
> [Will in them give us a good year.][47]

In the "Hymns to the Shang Sovereigns" there is the following:

> And [T'ang's] wisdom and virtue daily advanced.
> Brilliant was the influence of his character [on Heaven] for long,
> And the Sovereign on High appointed him
> To be a model to the nine regions.[48]

In the "Major Odes" we read:

> This King Wen, watchfully and reverently, with entire intelligence served the Sovereign on High.[49]

106. The *Book of Changes* has the following:

> The Sovereign [Lord] emerges from Chen in the East.[50]

This word "Sovereign" or "Emperor" does not connote the material heavens. Since the blue sky embraces the eight directions how can it emerge from one direction only?

123

107 禮云：「五者備當，上帝其饗。」又云：「天子親耕，粢盛秬鬯，以事上帝。」

108 湯誓曰：「夏氏有罪，予畏上帝，不敢不正。」又曰：「惟皇上帝，降衷于下民，若有恒性，克綏厥猷，惟后。」金縢周公曰：「乃命于帝庭，敷佑四方。」上帝有庭，則不以蒼天為上帝可知。歷觀古書，而知上帝與天主特異以名也。

109 中士曰：世人好古，惟愛古器、古文，豈如先生之據古理也？善教引人復古道焉。然猶有未諳者，古書多以天為尊，是以朱註解帝為天，解天為理也；程子更加詳曰：「以形體謂天，以主宰謂帝，以性情謂乾。」故云奉敬天地，不誠如何？

---

51 *Li Chi: Book of Rites*, trans. by James Legge and edited by Ch'u Chai with W. Chai, (New York, 1967), vol. I, p. 288, slightly altered.
52 Ibid., II, p. 338, slightly altered.
53 *Chinese Classics*, III, p. 174, slightly altered.
54 Ibid., III, p. 185, slightly altered.
55 Ibid., III, p. 345, slightly altered.

Mistaken Views About the Lord of Heaven

107. In the *Book of Rites* it is stated:
> When all these points are as they ought to be, the Sovereign on High will accept the sacrifices.⁵¹

It continues:
> The son of Heaven himself ploughs the ground for the rice with which to fill the vessels, and the black millet from which to distil the spirit to be mixed with fragant herbs, and for services of the Sovereign on High.⁵²

108. In the "Oath of T'ang" [in the *Book of History*] it is stated:
> The sovereign of Hsia is an offender, and, as I fear the Sovereign on High, I dare not but punish him.⁵³

It also says [in the "Announcement of T'ang"]:
> The great Sovereign on High has conferred even on the inferior people a moral sense, compliance with which would show their nature invariably right. But to cause them tranquilly to pursue the course which it would indicate, is the work of the sovereign.⁵⁴

In the "Metal-bound Coffer" of the *Book of History* the Duke of Chou says:
> And moreover he was appointed in the hall of the Sovereign to extend his aid to the four quarters of the empire...⁵⁵

The fact that the Sovereign on High has his hall makes it obvious that the speaker is not referring to the physical blue sky.

[Therefore], having leafed through a great number of ancient books, it is quite clear to me that the Sovereign on High and the Lord of Heaven are different only in name.

109. *The Chinese scholar says:* Man's love of the past amounts to no more than an affection for the objects and writings of ancient times. No one has investigated the principles of ancient times as you have in order to provide methodical teaching designed to lead men back to the Way of the past. But there is still something I do not understand. In the ancient writings Heaven is frequently regarded as worthy of honor; Chu Hsi therefore commented that

解釋世人錯認天主

110 西士曰：更思之，如以天解上帝，得之矣：天者一大耳。理之不可為物主宰也，昨已悉矣。上帝之稱甚明，不容解，況妄解之哉？蒼蒼有形之天，有九重之析分，烏得為一尊也？上帝索之無形，又何以形之謂乎？天之形圓也，而以九層斷焉，彼或東或西，無頭無腹，無手無足，使與其神同為一活體，豈非甚可笑訝者哉？況鬼神未嘗有形，何獨其最尊之神為有形哉？此非特未知論人道，亦不識天文及各類之性理矣。

111 上天既未可為尊，況于下地乃眾足所踏踐，汙穢所歸寓，安有可尊之勢？要，惟此一天主化生天地萬物，以存養人民。宇宙之間，無一物非所以育吾人者，吾宜感其天地萬物之恩主，加誠奉敬之可耳，可捨此大本大原之主，而反奉其役事吾者哉？

56 See above, n. 16.
57 *Ch'ien* (乾, "Heaven"); see Ricci's introduction, n. 5.
58 *I-ta* (一大). The Chinese character for "Heaven" 天, *T'ien*) was traditionally held to be composed of the words "one" (一) and "great" (大). This analysis of the character has been shown in more recent times to be erroneous.

the word "Sovereign" was to be understood as signifying "Heaven," and that the word "Heaven" was to be understood to mean "principle." Providing an even more detailed explanation Ch'eng I[56] said: "when we think in terms of form we speak of sky; when we think in terms of the exercising of control over things we speak of 'Sovereign' or 'lord,' and when we think in terms of nature we speak of *ch'ien*."[57] Is it possible, therefore, to talk of serving Heaven and Earth with reverence?

110. *The Western scholar says:* If one thinks more deeply on the matter and explains the Sovereign on High in terms of Heaven, then you may do as you suggest, because Heaven basically means "one great."[58] Principle cannot exercise control over all things for the reasons I gave yesterday. The term Sovereign on High is very clear and has no need of exposition, much less a misleading explanation. The blue sky which has form is in nine layers ranging from the highest to the lowest. How, then, can it be the same as He who is unique and supremely honored? When we investigate the Sovereign on High we find that He is without form; how, then, can He be called by a name which applies to something with form? The sky is circular and is limited to nine layers. Whether one looks East or West one finds that the sky has no head and no stomach; neither has it hands or feet. Is it not laughable to say that it shares a living body with deity? If all spiritual beings are without form, how can the Lord of Heaven, who is most to be honored and who is without peer, possess form? To assert this is not only to fail to understand the nature of human existence, but also to be ignorant of astronomy and the natures of all phenomena.

111. If heaven above or the sky cannot be reverenced, how much less can the earth beneath, which is trodden on by man and where filth accumulates? Therefore, only the one true Lord of Heaven who creates all things and who produces and preserves mankind may be reverenced. There is not a created thing in the

112 中士曰：誠若是，則吾儕其猶有蓬之心也夫，大抵擡頭見天，遂惟知拜天而已。

113 西士曰：世有智愚差等各別，中國雖大邦，諒有智，亦不免有愚焉，以目可視為有，以目不能視為無，故但知事有色之天地，不復知有天地之主也。遠方之氓，忽至長安道中，驚見皇宮殿宇巍峩藏業，則施禮而拜曰：吾拜吾君。智者乃能推見至隱，視此天地高廣之形，而遂知有天主主宰其間，故肅心持志以尊無形之先天，孰指茲蒼蒼之天而為欽崇乎？

114 君子如或稱天地，是語法耳。譬若知府縣者，以所屬府縣之名為己稱：南昌太守，稱謂南昌府；南昌縣大尹，稱謂南昌縣。比此，天地之主，或稱謂天地焉，非其以天地為體也，有原主在也。吾恐人誤認此物之原主而實謂之天主。不敢不辨。

59 Ch'ang-an (長安), the comtemporary Hsi-an or Xian (西安), a famous city in central China, which was the capital during several dynasties.

Mistaken Views About the Lord of Heaven

universe which is not there for the nourishment of mankind; we ought therefore to thank the gracious Lord of Heaven and earth and all creation, and serve Him reverently with the utmost sincerity. How can we abandon this Lord, who is the Supreme Source of all creation, and serve instead created things which have really been provided for our use?

112. *The Chinese scholar says:* If what you say is really so, then we are still in a state of mental confusion. When the great majority of people lift their heads and see the sky, they think only of worshipping it.

113. *The Western scholar says:* People are different from each other, some being wise and some foolish. Although China is a great country, yet, she not only has men of wisdom but, inevitably, men of stupidity as well, who regard what they can see with their eyes as existent, and what they cannot see with their eyes as nonexistent. For this reason they only think they should serve the physical heaven and earth, and are unaware that there is a Lord of Heaven and earth. When travellers from afar suddenly reach the streets of Ch'ang-an[59] and see the imposing and splendid royal palace, they bow their heads to the ground and say: "I bow my head to the ground to reverence my emperor." But those who now reverence heaven and earth reverence the palace in place of the emperor! The intelligent are able to know things which are hidden through inference; thus, when they see the loftiness of the heavens and the breadth of the earth, they know there is a Lord of Heaven within them, exercising control over them; and respectfulness arises in their minds, and they come and reverence the Lord of Heaven who is without form. How can anyone suggest that the blue sky is worthy of worship?

114. When superior men speak of heaven and earth, they are merely employing a figure of speech. For example, officials in charge of prefectures and districts call themselves by the names of the prefectures and districts under their control. The prefect of Nanchang is called Nanchang Prefecture, and the Magistrate of the district of Nanchang is called Nanchang District. On the basis of

115 中士曰：明師論物之原始，既得其實，又不失其名；可知貴邦之論物理，非苟且疏略之談，乃割開愚衷，不留疑處。天主之事又加深篤。愧吾世儒彿彷要地，而詳尋他事，不知歸元之學。夫父母授我以身體髮膚，我固當孝；君長賜我以田里樹畜，使仰事俯育，我又當尊；矧此天主之為大父母也，大君也，為眾祖之所出，眾君之所命，生養萬物，奚可錯認而忘之？訓諭難悉，願以異日竟焉。

116 西士曰：子所求，非利也，惟真道是問耳。大父之慈，將必佑講者以傳之；祐聽者以受之。吾子有問，吾敢不惟命？

this analogy, the Lord of Heaven and earth is sometimes called "Heaven and Earth." This is not a reference to the heaven and earth which have form, but to the Lord of creation. Afraid lest people be under a misapprehension regarding the true Lord of Heaven, I speak of Him directly as the Lord of Heaven, and therefore find it necessary to clarify this point.

115. *The Chinese scholar says:* Perspicacious Teacher, in your discussion of the origin of things you have not only reached reality, but you have also clarified terminology. One can conclude from this that in your esteemed country, discussion of the principles of things is not careless and superficial talk, but, rather, opens up the hearts of the foolish, freeing them from doubt. You have applied profound study and faith to the matters and principles concerning the Lord of Heaven. I am ashamed that we Confucian scholars have not been able to see clearly the important matters in life. We have investigated other things in detail, and have been unaware of that learning which is concerned with the end of human existence. Our parents give us the various parts of our bodies, and we ought, therefore, to be filial towards them. Our sovereign and his ministers give us land, places to live, trees and animals so that we can practice filial piety towards our elders, and instruct and nurture our children. We ought therefore to honor them as well. But how much more should we honor the Lord of Heaven who is the great Father and Mother, the great Sovereign, the first Cause of all first ancestors, the One from whom all sovereigns derive their mandate and the Producer and Sustainer of all things? How can one be mistaken about Him or forget Him? Your teaching cannot be completed all at one time, and I would therefore like to hear the rest of it another day.

116. *The Western scholar says:* What you seek, Sir, is not profit, but only the true Way. The compassion of our great Father is sure to protect this exponent of the Way, so that he can transmit its teachings, and the enquirer so that he can receive them. If you have any questions, Sir, I dare not do otherwise than answer them.

第三篇

論人魂不滅大異禽獸

117 中士曰：吾觀天地萬物之間，惟人最貴，非鳥獸比；故謂人參天地，又謂之小天地。

118 然吾復察鳥獸，其情較人反為自適，何者？其方生也，忻忻自能行動；就其所養，避其所傷；身具毛羽爪甲；不俟衣履，不待稼穡；無倉廩之積藏，無供饟之工器；隨食可以育生，隨便可以休息；嬉遊大造，而嘗有餘閑；其間豈有彼我貧富尊卑之殊？豈有可否、先後、功名之慮，操其心哉？熙熙逐逐，日從其所欲爾矣。

119 人之生也，母嘗痛苦；出胎赤身，開口先哭，似已自知世之難；初生而弱，步不能移，三春之後，方免懷抱。壯則各有所役，無不苦勞：農夫四時

---

1 See Chan, *A Source Book in Chinese Philosophy*, pp. 281, 458.

132

Chapter 3

THE HUMAN SOUL IS NOT EXTINGUISHED AND IS GREATLY DIFFERENT FROM [THE SOULS OF] BIRDS AND BEASTS.

117. *The Chinese scholar says:* When I examine heaven and earth and all things I find that only man merits the highest esteem, and that neither birds nor beasts can compare with him; that is why it is said: "Man forms a trinity with heaven and earth," and, "Man is a microcosm of heaven and earth."[1]

118. But when I look at the birds and beasts and note their circumstances I find that they enjoy greater freedom and comfort than man. Why is this? The moment they are born they are able to move happily about, forage for food and hide from harm. Their bodies are supplied with fur and feathers, talons and scales so that they have no need of clothes and shoes and are not dependent on ploughing, sowing, and harvesting. They have no need of granaries to store supplies of grain or of tools to cook their meals. They can find food anywhere to keep themselves alive and can rest wherever they please. They roam the wilds and still have time for leisure. Do they have any distinctions of poverty, wealth, and rank as we have? Do they have any need to consider or take pains over right and wrong, precedence or honor? In all their comings and goings they spend each day doing what they enjoy.

119. When men are born their mothers experience intense pain and suffering; and when a child emerges naked from its mother's womb it cries the moment it opens its mouth, as if it already knows the hardships of life on earth. A newly-born baby is very weak; it has feet but cannot walk; and only after two or three years

反土于畎畝;客旅經季徧度于山海;百工勤動手足;士人晝夜劇神殫思焉:所謂「君子勞心,小人勞力」者也。五旬之壽,五旬之苦。至如一身疾病,何啻百端,嘗觀醫家之書,一目之病,三百餘名,況罄此全體,又可勝計乎?其治病之藥,大都苦口。

120

即宇宙之間,不拘大小蟲畜,肆其毒具,能為人害,如相盟詛;不過一寸之蟲,足殘九尺之軀。人類之中,又有相害;作為凶器,斷人手足,截人肢體;非命之死,多是人戕。今人猶嫌古之武器不利,則更謀新者益凶;故甚至盈野盈城殺伐不已。縱遇太平之世,何家成全無缺?有財貨而無子孫;有子孫而無才能;有才能而身無安逸;有安逸而無權勢:則每自謂虧醜,極大喜樂而為小不幸所泯。蓋屢有之。

is it able to leave the arms of its mother. When it attains the strength of youth it becomes involved in the complexities of work, and each has his task to perform. The peasant spends the four seasons in the fields and ditches turning the soil. The man of commerce experiences a life in which he spends months and years traversing mountains and crossing seas. Men in the various trades work painstakingly with hands and feet; and scholars apply mind and spirit [to their studies] day and night. The so-called Gentleman or superior man engages in mental labor, whereas the inferior engages in physical labor. A man who reaches fifty years of age will have undergone fifty years of suffering. If we speak of the illnesses which afflict men's bodies, we find that they come in their hundreds. I have read medical books and know that there are more than three hundred diseases of the eyes. The diseases of the whole body are quite incalculable. The majority of the medicines used to effect a cure are bitter to the taste.

120. Within the universe, whether insects or beasts be large or small, the poisons they release are all capable of causing man harm. It is as if they were all man's deadly enemies. An insect less than an inch in length can harm a man nine feet tall. Men also harm each other. They make weapons with which they can sever men's hands and feet and truncate their bodies and limbs. People who die unnatural deaths are, in most cases, killed by others. And yet people today despise the weapons of ancient times for not being sharp enough, and have devised ways of manufacturing new weapons of even greater cruelty which can destroy the people of a whole city and of the whole countryside. Even in years of peace what home is complete and lacking in nothing? Those with wealth will have no sons; those with sons will find them untalented; those with talent find themselves without leisure, and those with leisure have no authority; all claim that their happiness is incomplete. Over and over again great joy is marred by small misfortunes.

121 終身多愁,終為大愁所承結以至于死,身入土中莫之能逃。故古賢有戒其子者曰:「爾勿欺己,爾勿昧心。人所競往,惟于墳墓。」吾曹非生,是乃常死。入世始死,曰死則了畢已,曰過一日吾少一日,近墓一步。

122 夫此只訴其外苦耳,其內苦誰能當之?凡世界之苦辛,為真苦辛;其快樂,為偽快樂;其勞煩為常事,其娛樂為有數。一日之患,十載訴不盡;則一生之憂事,豈一生所能盡述乎?人心在此為愛惡忿懼四情所伐,譬樹在高山,為四方之風所鼓,胡時得靜?或溺酒色,或惑功名、或迷財貨,各為欲擾,誰有安本分而不求外者?雖與之四海之廣,兆民之眾,不止足也。愚矣!

123 然則,人之道人猶未曉,況乎他道?而或從釋氏,或由老氏,或師孔氏,而折斷天下之心于三道也乎。又有好事者另立門戶,載以新說,不久而三教之

The Human Soul is not Extinguished

121. During his lifetime man mostly experiences grief; and at the very end of his life there comes the greatest grief of all—his own death. In the end his corpse is buried in the ground—something which no man can escape. For this reason the worthies of ancient times warned their sons saying: "Do not deceive yourselves; do not act contrary to your conscience; the end to which man struggles is nothing more nor less than the grave!" We do not live, but are in a constant state of death. The moment man is born into the world he begins to die. What we commonly call death is therefore the end of the process of dying. Every day that passes means a loss of a day for me and a step in the direction of the grave.

122. All this is merely a description of external suffering; who can sufficiently tell the nature of suffering within? The suffering of this world is real suffering, but its joy is false joy. Toil and vexation are common, whereas moments of joy are few and far between. It would take more than ten years to describe the suffering of one day, so how can a lifetime of heartache be narrated in the space of one lifetime? The mind of man is constantly assailed by the four emotions of love, hate, anger, and fear, just like a tree on a lofty mountain which is blown hither and thither by winds from all sides and is never permitted a moment of peace. Some people are addicted to wine and women; some are led astray by honor and ambition, and some are deluded by wealth. Each person is troubled by his desires. Who is contented with his lot, and who does not seek for things external to him? Man's stupidity is such that although he may gain the whole world and be given [control over] millions of people he will still be dissatisfied.

123. Man still fails to understand the truth concerning himself; how much less, then, can he understand other truths? But believers in Sakyamuni, followers of Lao Tzu and imitators of Confucius have divided men's minds into three schools of thought, and other meddlesome people have established further sects, inventing

岐必至于三千教而不止矣。雖自曰：「正道！正道！」而天下之道日益乖亂，上者陵下，下者侮上，父暴子逆，君臣相忌，兄弟相賊，夫婦相離，朋友相欺，滿世皆詐諂誑誕，而無復真心。

124 嗚呼！誠視世民，如大洋間著風浪，舟舶壞溺，而其人蕩漾波心，沉浮海角，緊操不捨，而相繼以死，良可惜也。不知天主何故生人于此患難之處？則其愛人反似不如禽獸焉？

125 西士曰：世上有如此患難，而吾癡心猶戀愛之不能割。使有寧泰，當何如耶？世態苦醜至如此極，而世人昏愚，欲于是為大業，闢田地，圖名聲，禱長壽，謀子孫，篡弒攻併，無所不為，豈不殆哉？

The Human Soul is not Extinguished

new teachings, so that before long the three schools will be divided into three thousand schools at least. Although each calls itself the correct Way, the more ways there are the more strange and confused they become. The superior insult the inferior, and the inferior profane the superior. The father behaves violently and the son wilfully. Sovereign and ministers are suspicious of each other, and brothers murder each other. Husbands and wives divorce, and friends cheat each other. Mankind is filled with deceit, flattery, arrogance, and lies and is devoid of sincerity.

124. Alas! Men appear like persons in a vast ocean who see their ship buffeted by wind and wave and about to break up and sink. Their minds are troubled as they drift to the very corners of the ocean. Each person is concerned over the desperate straits he himself is in, and no one is willing to come to the aid of another. Some cling to broken planks and others clamber onto dilapidated sails and awnings; some grasp at bamboo cases and boxes and hold on tightly to whatever comes into their hands, dying one after the other—a most pitiable sight! I cannot think why the Lord of Heaven should want to create man in such a world of adversity. It is as if the Lord of Heaven has a greater love for birds and beasts than for man!

125. *The Western scholar says:* Despite the fact that there is so much adversity in the world we still dote on it and cannot cast it aside. What would we be like, then, if the world were constantly at peace and we were always in perfect health? Even when the ugliness and suffering in the world is at its worst people still refuse to wake from their dull stupidity, wishing to lay up great treasure on earth, to open up land for cultivation, to scheme for fame, to pray for long life, and to plan for their sons and grandsons. They will do anything including usurpation of the throne, assassination, aggression, and annexation—all most perilous activities.

126 古西國有二聞賢：一名黑蠟，一名德牧。黑蠟恒笑，德牧恒哭，皆因視世人之逐虛物也；笑因譏之，哭因憐之耳。又聞近古一國之禮（不知今尚存否）：凡有產子者，親友共至其門哭而吊之，為其人之生于苦勞世也；凡有喪者，至其門作樂賀之，為其人之去勞苦世也。則又以生為凶，以死為吉焉。夫夫也，太甚矣！然而可謂達現世之情者也。

127 現世者，非人世也，禽獸之本處所也，所以于是不寧、不足也。賢友儒也，請以儒喻。人之在世，試，是曰士子似勞，徒隸似逸；有司豈厚徒隸而薄士子乎？蓋不越一日之事，而以定厥才品耳。試畢，則尊自尊，卑自卑也。

128 吾觀天主亦置人于本世，以試其心而定德行之等也，故現世者，吾所僑寓，非長久居也。吾本家室，不在今世，在後世；不在人，在天，當于彼創本業

2 *He-la* (黑蠟).
3 *Te-mu* (德牧).

The Human Soul is not Extinguished

126. In ancient times, in a nation of the West, there were two famous men, one called Heraclitus,[2] and the other Democritus.[3] Heraclitus was always laughing, whereas Democritus was constantly weeping. One ridiculed and laughed at man and the other pitied and wept over him, because they both saw the way he pursued the vain things of this world. I have also heard it said that in more recent times one country had a custom (though I do not know whether it still exists or not) according to which, whenever a son was born into a family, parents and friends would gather at the gate to mourn the fact that a boy had been born into this cruel world, whereas whenever anyone died they would all gather at his gate to rejoice and to congratulate him because he had departed this world of suffering. This is to regard life as evil and death as a piece of good fortune. Now although this attitude would seem to be unduly extreme, one can at least say that it represents an understanding of the things of this world.

127. This world is not man's world but is the dwelling place of birds and beasts! Therefore, birds and beasts lead a contented life in it. Man lodges only temporarily in this world, and is therefore ill-at-ease and dissatisfied in it. You, my good friend, are a Confucian scholar, and I shall therefore draw on the scholarly world to provide you with an illustration. The present can be compared with the day of an examination. The scholars attending the examination appear wearied and burdened whereas their attendants seem unhurried and at ease. It would be absurd to suggest that this is because the officials in charge of the event treat the attendants with kindness and the scholars with harshness. The grades of the examinees are posted in less than a day! When the examination is over it becomes clear who is to be honored and who is inferior.

128. As I see it, the Lord of Heaven has placed man in this world to test him and to determine the level of his conduct. Thus, the present world is our place of sojourn and not a place of con-

馬。今世也，禽獸之世也，故鳥獸各類之像俯向於地；人為天民，昂首向順于天。以今世為本處所者，禽獸之徒也，以天主為薄於人，固無怪耳。

129 中士曰：如言後世天堂地獄，便是佛教，吾儒不信。

130 西士曰：是何言乎？佛民戒殺人，儒者亦禁人亂法殺人，則儒佛同歟？鳳凰飛，蝙蝠亦飛，則鳳凰蝙蝠同歟？事物有一二情相似，而其實大獲不同者。天主教，古教也；釋氏西民，必竊聞其說矣。凡欲傳私道者，不以三四正語雜入，其誰信之？釋氏借天主、天堂、地獄之義，以傳己私邪意；吾傳正道，豈反置弗講乎？釋氏未生，天主教人已有其說：修道者後世必登天堂受無窮之樂，免墮地獄受不之殃。故知人之精靈常生不滅。

---

4 See Tung Chung-shu's (董仲舒, 179-104 B.C.) comments on man in Chan, *A Source Book in Chinese Philosophy,* p. 281. See also St. Basil, *Ascetical Works* (Washington, D.C., 1962), p. 44 (= The Fathers of the Church, vol. 9).
5 Ricci would seem to imply here that the religion of the Lord of Heaven includes Judaism as well as Christianity.
6 Other writers besides Ricci also held that Sakyamuni borrowed from Judaism.

tinued residence. Our home is not in this world, but in the life to come; not among men, but in Heaven. We ought to establish our inheritance in that place. This world is the world of birds and beasts and therefore the bodies of each incline earthwards. Man is born to be a citizen of Heaven and therefore his head is lifted heavenwards.[4] It is the birds and beasts which treat this world as their own dwelling place; it should not surprise us, then, that the Lord of Heaven should treat people with greater severity [than he treats the birds and beasts].

129. *The Chinese scholar says:* If you say that there is a Heaven and a Hell in the world to come, then that is Buddhism. We Confucians do not believe this teaching.

130. *The Western scholar says:* What words are these? Buddhism forbids the killing of man and Confucianism also forbids the illegal killing of man. Does this imply that Buddhism and Confucianism are the same? The phoenix flies, and so does the bat. Does this mean that the phoenix and the bat are the same? Things may be similar in one or two respects yet quite different in reality. The Religion of the Lord of Heaven is a very ancient religion,[5] and Sakyamuni lived in the West. He must secretly have heard of this teaching. Anyone wishing to promote his own school of thought must insert two or three elements of orthodoxy into it otherwise no one will believe him. Sakyamuni borrowed the doctrines concerning the Lord of Heaven, Heaven and Hell [from us] in order to promote his private views and heterodox teachings;[6] we transmit the correct Way. Does this mean that we have to put this [dogma] aside and say nothing about it? Before Sakyamuni was born members of the religion of the Lord of Heaven were putting forward the following teaching: those who devote themselves to the [correct] Way and train themselves in it will ascend to Heaven, experience inexhaustible happiness, and will avoid Hell and unending misery. Thus we know that man's soul lives forever and is never extinguished.

論人魂不滅大異禽獸

131 中士曰：夫常生而受無窮之樂，人所欲無大於是者。但未深明其理。

132 西士曰：人有魂魄，兩者全而生焉；死則其魄化散歸土，而魂常在不滅。吾入中國嘗聞有以魂為可滅，而等之禽獸者；其餘天下名教名邦，皆省人魂不滅，而大殊於禽獸者也。吾言此理，子試虛心聽之。

133 彼世界之魂有三品：下品名曰生魂，即草木之魂是也，此魂扶草木以生長，草木枯萎，魂亦消滅；中品名曰覺魂，則禽獸之魂也，此能附禽獸長育，而又使之以耳目視聽，以口鼻啖嗅，以肢體覺物情，但不能推論道理，至死而魂亦滅焉；上品名曰靈魂，即人魂也，此兼生魂，覺魂，能扶人長養及使人知覺物情，而又使之能推論事物，明辨理義。

---

7 *Hun-p'o* (魂魄). According to Chinese tradition, each person has two souls while alive: *hun* and *p'o*. After death, *hun*, which belongs to Heaven, ascends to Heaven and is called *shen* (神, "spirit"). *P'o*, which belongs to Earth, descends into the Earth and is called *kuei* (鬼, "ghost"). See *the Chinese Classics*, vol. V, pp. 611-619. In the present passage Ricci understands *hun*, "soul," as the soul of Christian thought, but sees *p'o*, "baser spirit," as a part of man's body which would disintegrate with the body.

8 Ricci here follows scholastic philosophy: there are three kinds of souls in the world. He translated "Vegetative soul" as *Sheng-hun* (生魂); "sentient soul" as *Chüeh-hun* (覺魂); "intellectual soul" as *Ling-hun* (靈魂). These Chinese terms have been used until now.

131. *The Chinese scholar says:* Eternal life and the enjoyment of inexhaustible happiness are man's greatest desires; but he does not have a very clear understanding of the principles which underly them.

132. *The Western scholar says:* Man has both a soul and a baser spirit,[7] and when these are united he has life. When a man dies his baser spirit is transformed and dispersed and returns to the earth, whereas his soul continues to exist and is not extinguished. When I came to China I once heard someone say that the soul ceases to exist exactly like the [souls of] birds and beasts. All well-known religions and countries in the world are aware that the soul is not extinguished and that it is quite different from the [souls of] birds and beasts. I would ask you, Sir, to listen with humility whilst I explain this doctrine.

133. In this world there are three kinds of souls.[8] The lowest is called the life principle—the vegetative soul. This kind of soul supports vegetation in its growth, and when the vegetation withers the soul is also destroyed. The second class of soul is called the sentient soul. This soul is possessed by birds and beasts. It allows the birds and beasts to be born, to develop and to grow up, and causes their ears and eyes to be able to hear and see, their mouths and noses to be able to taste and smell, and their limbs and bodies to be aware of things, though not to be able to infer truth. When these creatures die their souls are destroyed along with them. The most superior of the souls is called the intellectual soul. This is the soul of man which includes [the powers of] the vegetative soul and the sentient soul. It enables people to grow to maturity; it causes people to be aware of things outside themselves, and it allows people to make inferences as to the nature of things and to distinguish between one principle and another.

論人魂不滅大異禽獸

134 人身雖死，而魂非死，蓋永存不滅者焉。凡知覺之事，倚賴于身形，身形死散，則覺魂無所用之，故草木禽獸之魂依身以為本情，身雖歿，形雖渙，其靈魂仍復能用之也。若推論明辨之事，則不必依據于身形而其靈自在；身雖歿，形雖渙，其靈魂仍復能用之也。故人與草木禽獸不同也。

135 中士曰：何謂賴身與否？

136 西士曰：長育身體之事，無身體則無所長育矣。視之以目司焉，聽之以耳司焉，嗅之以鼻司焉，啖之以口司焉，知覺物情之以四肢知覺焉。然而，色不置目前，則不見色矣；聲不近于耳，則聲不聞矣；臭近于鼻則能辨，遠則不辨也；味之鹹酸甘苦入口則知，不入則不知也；冷熱硬軟合於身，我方覺之，遠之則不覺也。況聲，同一耳也，聾者不聞；色，同一目也，瞽者不見。故曰覺魂賴乎身，身死而隨熄也。

The Human Soul is not Extinguished

134. Although the body of man dies his soul does not because it is eternal and inextinguishable. All awareness is dependent on bodies. When bodies die and are dispersed the sentient soul is of no further use. The vegetative soul and [the sentient soul] of birds and animals are attached to their bodies as their final abodes. When these bodies die, they die with them. But a thing which can infer and distinguish is not dependent on a fleshly body, and such a soul can, therefore, exist on its own. Though the body may perish, a man's soul still has its functions. Thus, man is different from vegetation, birds and beasts.

135. *The Chinese scholar says:* What is meant by the expression "dependent on a body?"

136. *The Western scholar says:* [That which is dependent] is something which is born, develops and matures through attachment to a body. If there were no body it would not be able to be born and to grow. For example, the eyes can see, ears can hear, noses have a sense of smell, mouths drink and eat, and the four limbs have the sense of touch. Nevertheless, if there were no color before the eyes they would not see anything; if a sound were not close to the ears, it would not be heard. Only when a scent is near can the nose distinguish it. The saltiness, pungency, sweetness, and bitterness of a flavor can only be known when it enters the mouth. If it does not enter [the mouth] one would not know about it. A body is required if I am to be aware of cold and heat, softness and hardness; but if these are at some distance from me I cease to be aware of them. Moreover, a deaf person cannot hear [what I can hear], though both of us have ears, and a blind person cannot see [what I can see], though both of us have eyes. Therefore I say that the awareness of the sentient soul is dependent on the body, and that when the body dies it is destroyed as well.

論人魂不滅大異禽獸

137 若夫靈魂之本用，則不恃乎身焉，蓋恃身則為身所役，不能擇其是非。如禽獸見可食之物即欲食，不能自己，豈復明其是非？人當饑餓之時，若義不可食，立志不食，雖有美味列前，不屑食矣。又如人身雖出遊在外，而此心一點猶念家中，常有歸思。此明理之魂賴身為用者哉？

138 子欲知人魂不滅之緣，須悟世界之物，凡見殘滅，必有殘滅之者。殘滅之因，從相悖起；物無相悖，決無相滅。凡天下之物，莫不以火氣水土四行相結以成，而卒無殘滅者，因無相悖故也。然火性熱乾，則背于水，水性冷濕也；氣性濕熱，則背於土，土性乾冷也。兩者相對相敵，自必相賊，即同在相結一物之內，其物豈得長久和平？其

137. The activities of the intellectual soul, however, are not dependent on the body. What is dependent on the body is controlled by the body and cannot choose between right and wrong. When birds and beasts, for example, see things that are edible, they go ahead and eat them, being incapable of self-control. How could such creatures begin to distinguish between the rightness or wrongness [of such an action]? If a man, on the other hand, is told that it would be wrong for him to eat something, he will choose not to eat [even though he may be hungry]. The food set before him may be delicious, but he will still refuse to eat. A person who travels abroad but who pines for home and constantly thinks of returning home would be another example. Now, how can an intelligent soul [which causes men to behave in such ways] be said to function in dependence on the body?

138. But if you, Sir, wish to know why man's soul is not destroyed, you must first understand the things of this world. For everything injured and destroyed there must be a reason. The cause of injury and destruction is rebelliousness; if things did not rebel against each other they would definitely not destroy each other. The sun, moon and stars are attached to the heavens without any distinctions of rank; yet they are not destroyed. This is because there is no conflict between them. Everything in the world comes into existence through the combination of the four elements: fire, air, water, and earth. It is the nature of fire to be dry and hot, so that it is in conflict with water which is by nature cold and wet. Air is by nature moist and hot and is therefore the exact opposite of earth which is naturally dry and cold. Any two of these mutually antagonistic elements are bound to harm each other; and if they are combined in one thing, it is impossible for them to remain in harmony over a long period of time. There will inevitably be a constant struggle between them, and when one is victorious, the product of their union will come to an end. Thus, anything composed

139 中士曰：神誠無悖也。然吾烏知人魂為神，而禽獸則否耶？

140 西士曰：徵其實何有乎？理有數端，自悟則可釋疑也。

141 其一曰：有形之魂不能為身之主，而恆為身之所役，以就墮落。是以禽獸常行本欲之役，徇其情之所導，而不能自檢。獨人之魂能為身主，而隨吾志之所縱止，故志有專向，力即從焉。雖有私欲，豈能達公理所令乎？則靈魂信專一身之權，屬于神者也，與有形者異也。

142 其二曰：一物之生惟得一性，一乃神性也。若人則兼有二性：一乃形性，一乃神性也。故舉凡情之相背，亦由所發之性相背焉。如吾或惑酒色，既似人之遇一事也，且同一時也，而有兩念並興，屢覺兩逆，迷戀欲從，又復慮其非理。從彼，謂之獸心，與禽獸無別；從此，謂之人心，

---

9 In the following texts of par. 142, the term "mind" apparently means the human soul.

150

of the four elements is bound to be destroyed. The intelligent soul, however, is spirit and has no connection with the four elements. There is no reason, therefore, for it to be destroyed.

139. *The Chinese scholar says:* There is no doubt that spirit is incapable of harboring conflicting elements within itself which would destroy it; nevertheless, how can we know that man's soul is spirit and that the souls of birds and beasts are not?

140. *The Western scholar says:* There is ample evidence. Numerous reasons can be advanced to demonstrate the truth of it; reasons which, when understood, will dispel all doubts.

141. First, bodily souls cannot be masters of their bodies but must always be their servants, finally perishing with them. Thus, birds and beasts always accord with the desires [of their fleshly bodies] and follow wherever their feeling leads them, unable to exercise any self-control. Only the soul of man is capable of being the master of his body causing it to act or arresting it, in accordance with its intentions. Thus, when the [soul] resolves on a certain course of action, [the body] immediately responds with vigor. Men may have selfish desires, but it is impossible for them to defy the commands of universal reason. Thus the human soul really does hold authority over the whole body, pertains to spirit, and is quite distinct from animal souls.

142. Second, a living creature has only one mind, but man has two at the same time: an animal mind and a human mind. Thus, he also has two natures; a nature appropriate to a body, and a spiritual nature. Opposing emotions must derive from two opposing natures. When a man is confronted by something, he can react toward it in two apparently opposing ways at one and the same time. A man misled by wine and women will simultaneously be besotted by them and wish to pursue them, and be mindful of the unprincipled nature of his action. To follow [after wine and women] is to be "animal-minded," and, in this, man is no different from

論人魂不滅大異禽獸

與天神相同也。人于一心、一時視一物，而並不觀之也；如耳也，也不能一時聽一聲，而並不聽之也。是以兩相悖之情，必由兩相背之心；兩相悖之心，必由兩相悖之性也。試嘗二江之水，一鹹一淡，則雖未見源泉，亦證所發不一矣。

143 其三曰：物類之所好惡，恆與其性相稱焉，故著形之性，以無形之事為愛惡。吾察萬生之情，凡禽獸所貪娛，惟味、色、四肢安逸耳已，所驚駭，惟饑、勞、四肢傷殘耳已，是以斷曰：人之性，兼得有形無形兩端者也。此靈魂之類之性不神，乃著形之性也。若人之所喜惡，雖亦有形之事，然德善、罪惡之事甚，皆無形者也；是以斷曰：人之性，兼得有形無形兩端者也。此靈魂之為神也。

144 其四曰：凡受事物者，必以受者之態受焉，譬如瓦器受水，器圓則所受之水圓，器方則所受之水方。世間所受，無不如是。則人魂之神，何以疑乎

10 In this sentence we follow the third edition.

152

birds and beasts. To follow [after the rational] is to be "human minded," and, in this, man is the same as the angels.[9] Whenever man is devoted with singleness of mind to one thing, two incompatible dispositions cannot exist together. It is like the eyes which cannot both see and not see at the same time, or the ears which cannot both hear and fail to hear a certain sound at the same time. Thus, two opposing feelings must be derived from conflicting minds, and two conflicting minds must stem from two opposing natures. If we taste the waters of two rivers and find that one is salty and the other tasteless, we have sufficient proof that they do not spring from the same source, even though we may never have seen the place whence they sprang.

143. Thirdly, there is a natural affinity between a thing and the object of its love or hate. Things with bodily form always love or hate things with bodily form. Things which transcend bodily form love or hate things which are free of bodily form. When we examine the circumstances of living creatures we find that what birds and beasts covet is merely food, sex, and physical freedom. What they fear is nothing more than hunger, toil and harm to their limbs. Thus, one can assert with certainty that the natures of all the varieties of living creatures are not spiritual, but physical natures. When we come to the objects of man's loves or hates we find that although these include things with bodily form, [he has special feelings for] what is virtuous and good, criminal and hateful, and these are all things which lack physical form.[10] One can, therefore, assume that human nature is a combination of that which has physical form and that which is free of physical form. This is sufficient proof that the soul is spirit.

144. Fourthly, anything which accepts things must do so in a manner appropriate to itself. For example, water poured into a round vessel becomes round, and water poured into a square vessel becomes square. Everything in the world that accepts things is like

145 又如人觀百雉之城，可置之于方寸之心，非人心至神，何以方寸之地能容百雉之城乎？能神所受者，自非神也，未之有也。

146 其五曰：天主生人，使之有所司官者，固與其所屬之物相稱者也。目司視，則所屬者色相；耳司聽，則所屬者音聲；鼻口司臭、司嗜，則所屬者臭、味；耳、目、口、鼻有形，則併色、音、臭、味之類均有形焉。

147 吾人一心，乃有司欲，司悟二官，欲之所屬善者耳，悟之所屬真者耳，善與真無形，則司欲、司悟之為其官者，亦無形矣，所為神也。神之性能達形之性，而有形者固未能通無形之性也。夫人能明達鬼神及諸無形之性、非神而何？

11 *Kuei-shen* (鬼神). See chapter 1, n. 22.

The Human Soul is not Extinguished

this. Why, then, should the fact that the human soul is spirit be so surprising? If I wish to understand something, it is like using my mind to accept it; and if that something possesses bodily form, I must first rid it of that and spiritualize it; only then will I be able to receive it into my mind. For example, if there were a yellow ox in this place and I wanted to think of the nature of the ox on seeing its yellowness, I would say: "This is not the ox; it is merely its color." On hearing its sound, I would say: "This is not an ox; it is merely the lowing of an ox." On tasting its flesh, I would say: "This is not an ox, this is the flavor of the flesh of an ox." Thus it is obvious that an ox can be abstracted from such physical details as its sound, color, and flavor, and spiritualized.

145. It is also like a person who, having seen a city wall with a hundred parapets, can retain it in his mind. If the mind of man were not spiritual how could a "square inch of mind" contain a city wall of such major proportions? If man himself were not spirit he would never be able to spiritualize the things he accepts.

146. Fifthly, when the Lord of Heaven created man he bestowed certain organs on him which pair off nicely with things of their own category. The eyes are responsible for the sense of sight, the ears for the sense of hearing, the nose for the sense of smell and the mouth for the sense of taste. Everything with a color, a sound, a smell, or a taste is an object which falls within their range. Ears, eyes, mouths and noses are all physical things, and therefore all colors, sounds, smells, and tastes are physical.

147. In the minds of men there are two kinds of controlling powers: the will and the rational faculty. The object of the will is goodness; the object of the rational faculty is truth. Goodness and truth are both without form; will and the rational faculty are also without form and are spirit. The nature of spirit can permeate the nature of physical things, but that which is physical definitely cannot penetrate the nature of the non-physical. Since people can

148 中士曰：設使吾言世無鬼神，則亦言無形之性，而人豈能遽明之乎？則此五理似無的據。

149 西士曰：雖人有言無鬼神、無無形之性，然此人必先明鬼神無形之情性，方可定之曰有無焉。苟弗明曉其性之態，安知其有無哉？如曰雪白非黑者，必其明黑白之情，然後可以辨雪之為白而非黑矣。

150 其六曰：肉心之知猶如小器，有限不廣，如以線繫雀于木，不能展翅高飛，線之阻也。是以禽獸雖得知覺有形之外，情不能通，又弗能反諸己而知其本性之態。若無形之心，最恢最宏，非小器所限，直通乎無礙之境。如雀斷其所束之線，則高飛戾天，誰得而禦之？故人之靈非惟知其物外形情，且暢曉其隱體，而又能反觀諸己，明己之本性之態焉，此其非屬有形，益可審矣。

The Human Soul is not Extinguished

understand spiritual beings[11] and the natures of many things which are non-physical, what are they if not spiritual?

148. *The Chinese scholar says:* If we say there are no spiritual beings in the world, we are also asserting that there are no non-physical natures. How then can people understand them? The five reasons you have given would seem to be totally unsupportable.

149. *The Western scholar says:* There are those who say there are no spiritual beings and no non-physical things, but such people need first to understand the nature of spiritual beings and non-physical things before determining whether they exist or not. If one knows nothing of the condition of the nature of spiritual beings, how can one know whether they exist or not? If a person says that snow is white and not black, he must know what white and black are before he can assert without doubt that the snow is white and not black. Thus, it becomes even more obvious that the mind of man is able to understand the nature of the formless and non-physical.

150. Sixthly, the mind of the flesh is like a small utensil: what it can know is small and limited. It is like a sparrow tied to a tree by a thread. Because of the limitations imposed on it by the thread it cannot spread its wings and fly high in the sky. Thus, although birds and beasts have awareness they cannot understand things beyond the world of form and are incapable of reflecting on themselves in order to know the condition of their own natures. The [spiritual and] formless mind, however, is most great and comprehensive. There is nowhere it does not penetrate, and it cannot be limited by a small vessel. It is like the sparrow which, having severed the thread which bound it, is able to fly high in the sky, unable to be hindered by anyone. So it is that the human soul not only knows the external appearance of things, but also is able to understand thoroughly the hidden secrets of things. It can also reflect on itself, coming to know the condition of its own nature. Thus,

151 所以言人魂為神，不容泯滅者也。因有此理，實為修道基焉。又試揭三、四端理，以明徵之。

152 其一曰：人心皆欲傳播善名，而忌遺惡聲，殆與還生不侔。是故行事期協公評，以邀人稱賞：或立功業，或輯書冊，或謀術藝，或致身命，凡以求令聞廣譽，顯名于世，雖捐生不惜，此心人大概皆有之。而愚者則無，愈愚則愈無焉。

153 試問死後，吾聞知吾所遺聲名否？如以形論，則骨歸土，未免朽化，何為能聞？然靈魂常在不滅，所遺聲名善惡實與我生無異。若謂靈魂隨死銷滅，尚勞心以求保譽，譬或置妙畫，以己旣盲時看焉，或備美樂，以己旣聾時聽焉。此聲名何與于我？而人人求之，至死不休。

we know with even greater clarity that [the human soul] does not belong to the realm of things having form.[11]

151. For the above reasons we say that man's soul is spiritual and that it cannot be destroyed. This doctrine is truly the foundation necessary for the cultivation of the Way! I shall now proceed to provide three or four more reasons as proof of this:

152. First, all men have minds that like to spread a good reputation and to prohibit the handing down of a bad reputation to later generations. This is different from the foolish birds and beasts. Thus, whenever they do anything, men always hope that their actions will accord with public opinion in order to invite men's praise. Anyone who hopes to win a good reputation in this world either tries to accomplish something outstanding, or [to establish his teaching] by writing a book, or to become an expert in the arts, or to risk his life to the point of death, and even though he should sacrifice his life he will not regret it. Probably most people have this kind of mind; but foolish people do not, and the more foolish they are the less they have it.

153. Let me ask you, shall I be able to hear or know of the reputation I have left behind me after I have died? From the point of view of my physical body, how can I hear of it once my bones and flesh have rotted away and turned to dust? But the soul continues to exist and is not extinguished; and the goodness or baseness of the reputation I leave behind remains entirely the same as when I was living. If you say the soul is destroyed after a person dies, then to trouble one's mind about a good reputation is like preparing a beautiful painting for viewing after we are blind, or a beautiful piece of music so that we can listen to it after we have turned deaf. What has such a reputation to do with us? Yet people seek after it and are unwilling to give it up even at death.

154 彼孝子慈孫，中國之古禮四季修其祖廟，設其裳衣，薦其時食，以說考妣。使其形神盡亡，不能聽吾告哀，視吾稽顙，知吾「事死如事生，事亡如事存」之心，則固非自國君至於庶人大禮，乃童子空戲耳。

155 其二曰：上帝降生萬品，有物有則，無徒物，無空則。是以魚鱉樂潛川淵，而不冀遊于山嶺；兔鹿性喜走山嶺，而不欲潛于水中。故鳥獸之欲非在常生，不在後世之躋天堂受無窮之樂，其下情所願不踰本世之事。

156 獨吾人雖習聞異論，有神身均滅之說，亦無不冀愛長生，願居樂地享無疆之福者。設使無人可得以盡實情，豈天主徒賦之于眾人心哉？何不觀普天之下多有拋別家產，離棄骨肉，而往深山窮谷誠心修行？此輩俱不以今世為重，祈望來世真福，若吾魂隨身而歿，詎不枉費其意乎？

12 See *The Chinese Classics*, vol. I, p. 403.
13 Ibid., vol. II, p. 403, and vol. IV, p. 541.

The Human Soul is not Extinguished

154. According to the ancient rites of China, filial sons and worthy grandsons must keep the ancestral temples in good repair throughout the year, make clothes, enter the temples and present food appropriate to the time of the year in order to win the approval of parents already departed from this world. If the flesh and spirits of these parents have all been destroyed, they cannot listen to our importunings and cannot see our heads striking the ground in worship. It will be obvious that "serving the dead as if they were living and serving those who have perished as if they still existed"[12]—important rites practiced by all, from the sovereign of the nation down to the common man—will amount to no more than games played by children.

155. Second, in producing all things the Sovereign on High provided them with laws.[13] There is nothing void of law, and no law which exists in a void. I shall now provide you with a few examples from things around us. They all behave in accordance with their own natures and do not seek to attain to untenable positions. Thus, fish and turtles live submerged in rivers and deep waters, and have no wish to roam the hills. Hares and deer love to race over mountain ranges and have no desire to secrete themselves in water. So it is that the desires of birds and beasts are not for unending life, a paradise in a world to come, or the experience of inexhaustible joy. What their natures enjoy does not go beyond the things of this present world.

156. It is only we human beings who, though used to listening to extraordinary arguments to the effect that both soul and body perish, persist, each one of us, to delight in the thought of unending life, wanting to dwell in a place of joy, and to enjoy unlimited happiness. If no one can achieve this aim, has not the Lord of Heaven bestowed this tendency on man in vain? Have you not observed how many people in this world give up home and posses-

157 其三曰：天下萬物惟人心廣大，窮本性之事物弗克充滿，則其所以充滿之者在後世，可曉矣。蓋天主至智至仁，凡厥所為人不能更有非議。彼各依其世態以生其物之態。故欲使禽獸止于今世，則所付之願不越此一世墜落事，求飽而飽則已耳；欲使人類生乎千萬世，則所賦之願不徒在一世須臾之欲，於是不圖止求一飽，而求之必莫得者焉。

158 試觀商賈殖貨之人，雖金玉盈箱，富甲州縣，心無慊足。又如仕者，躡身世之浮名，趨明時之捷徑，惟圖軒冕華袞為榮，即至于垂紳朝陛，晉職台階，心猶未滿，甚且極之奄有四海，臨長百姓，福貽子孫，其心亦無底極。

The Human Soul is not Extinguished

sions, leave family and relations and enter deep into mountains and valleys in order to devote themselves in all seriousness to the cultivation of morality? They all despise this world and hope for the genuine blessings of the world to come. If our souls die and perish with our bodies, have these people not wasted the sincerity of a lifetime?

157. Thirdly, of all the things in this world, the mind of man is the greatest, so that even if one should gain everything in this world, it would not be sufficient to satisfy one's mind. Well, then, it is clear that only in the world to come can the mind of man be satisfied. Because the Lord of Heaven is most wise and most compassionate his actions are beyond human description. He created each thing according to its nature. He willed that the life of birds and beasts be limited to this world, so the desires He bestowed on them do not go beyond things of this world. When these desires are fulfilled, these creatures are satisfied. He wants people to obtain eternal life, and therefore the desires and hopes He has bestowed on them are not centered merely on the temporary things of this world. For this reason man does not merely seek to eat his fill; what he does seek for is something he cannot have [in this world].

158. Look at the men of commerce; although gold, silver, and precious stones fill their boxes, and there are those whose wealth transcends that of anyone else in district and country, their minds are still incapable of being satisfied. Then there are officials who wish to procure the empty fame offered by this world and take advantage of every opportunity which presents itself to crown themselves with the glories of ever higher rank. But even when they become high officials at court and are appointed to the emperor's entourage, their minds are still not fully satisfied. And even if one gains control over all within the four seas and is able to rule the people as their sovereign, and the fruits of one's beneficence are

159 此不足怪，皆緣天主所稟情欲原乃無疆之壽、無限之樂，姑為饜足者？一蚊之小，不可飽龍象；一粒之微，弗克實太倉。西土古聖曾悟此理，瞻天嘆曰：「上帝公父，爾實生吾人輩于爾，惟爾能滿吾心也，人不歸爾，其心不能安足也。」

160 其四曰：人性皆懼死者，雖親戚友朋，既死則莫肯安意近其屍，然而猛獸之死弗懼者，則人性之靈自有良覺：自覺人死之後尚有魂在，可懼；而獸魂全散無所留以驚我也。

161 其五曰：天主報應無私，善者必賞，惡者必罰。如今世之人，亦有為惡者富貴安樂，為善者貧賤苦難，天主固待其既死，然後取其善魂而賞，取之惡魂而罰之。若魂因身終而滅，天主安得而賞罰之哉？

14 See Augustine, *Confessions*, Book I, ch. 1.

The Human Soul is not Extinguished

transmitted to one's sons and grandsons, one's mind will still not be fully satisfied.

159. Nor is this to be wondered at, because the desires bestowed on man by the Lord of Heaven are, in fact, for immeasurable life and unlimited joy. How then can the small joys of this life ever satisfy the minds of men? A mosquito can never be an adequate meal for a dragon or an elephant; a minute grain of food cannot fill a granary. The Western sage of ancient times, [Augustine], understood this truth and, therefore, looking up to Heaven he sighed and said: "Supreme Ruler and Father of all men, you have produced us men for yourself, and only you can satisfy our minds. When man does not turn to you, his mind cannot be at peace and be satisfied!"[14]

160. Fourthly, all men are by nature afraid of the dead, and although a dead person may be a relative or friend no one will dare approach his corpse with equanimity. [It is quite the opposite when birds and beasts die]; no one is afraid of a dead wild beast. Because of the intelligence of human nature and of the fact that it can know things intuitively; and because the soul continues to exist after death, people naturally fear it. Souls of birds and beasts, however, are totally dispersed, so that there is nothing to fear.

161. Fifthly, the rewards and punishments meted out by the Lord of Heaven are fair and impartial; goodness is rewarded and evil is punished. But in the present world there are those who do evil and yet enjoy wealth and honor, security and happiness, and those who do good who suffer poverty, live in humble circumstances, experience suffering and undergo hardship. This is because the Lord of Heaven waits until men have died before rewarding good souls and punishing the souls of evil men. If the soul and the body were both reduced to nothing, how would the Lord of Heaven be able to reward or punish a man?

論人魂不滅大異禽獸

162 中士曰：君子平生異于小人，則身後亦宜異于小人；死生同也，則所以異者必在于魂也。故儒有一種言善者能以道存聚本心，是以身死而心不散滅，惡者以罪敗壞本心，是以身死而心之散滅隨焉。此亦可誘人於善焉。

163 西士曰：人之靈魂，不拘善惡皆不隨身後而滅，載之，余以數端實理證之矣。此分善惡之殊，則不載于經，不據于理，未敢以世之重事輕為新說，而簧鼓滋惑也。勸善沮惡有賞罰之正道，奚捐此而求他詭遇？

164 人魂匪沙匪水可以聚散：魂乃神也，一身之主，四肢之動宗焉。以神散身，猶之何可哉？使惡行能散本心，則是小人必不壽矣。然而自少至老為惡不止，何以散其心猶能生耶？心之于身重乎血，血既散

162. *The Chinese scholar says:* On earth a Gentleman or man of superior worth is distinguished from the small man. This distinction ought to be continued after death. Things are the same whether alive or dead, so that where distinctions exist, they must exist in the souls of men. Thus, Confucian scholars say that a good man is able to preserve the "Way" in his mind, and that therefore, after he dies, his mind is not dissolved and extinguished. Evil people destroy their own minds with wrong-doing, and, therefore, when their bodies die, their souls are dissolved and extinguished with them. This, too, can encourage people to do good.

163. *The Western scholar says:* Whether men's souls are good or evil they are not extinguished with the death of the body. Men of all nations believe this teaching, and it is recorded in the canonical writings of the Religion of the Lord of Heaven. I have also provided you with several substantial reasons to prove that this is so. Your theory concerning the distinction to be made between good and evil is not found in the [Confucian] canonical writings, and is not grounded on any principle. I would not be so bold as to create a new theory about such an important matter in this world and be so careless as to deceive the people. There is a correct way to persuade people to avoid evil and to do good, and that way is the way of reward and punishment. How can one cast aside [this correct way] in favor of some other theory?

164. The souls of men are not sand or water which can be accumulated or dispersed at will. A soul is a spirit; the master of the body and the cause of movement in the four limbs. One can talk of the soul departing and of the consequent dissolution of the body, but how can one talk of the dissolution of the soul along with the body? If wrong-doing can dissolve the human mind, then the small man will certainly not be able to live very long. But some people engage in wrong-doing from youth to old age. How is it that

，身且不能立，則心旣散，身又焉能行？況心堅乎身，積惡于己不能散身，何獨能散其心乎？若生時心已散，何時死後乎？

165 造物者因其善否不易其性：如鳥獸之性非常生之性，則雖其間有善，未緣俾鳥獸常生；魔鬼之性乃常生之性，縱其爲惡，未緣俾豈能因其惡而散滅焉？使惡人之魂槪受滅亡之刑，則其刑亦未公，固非天主所出。蓋重罪有等，豈宜一切罰以滅亡哉？況被滅者，旣歸于無，則亦必無患難、無苦辛、無所受刑，而其罪反脫，則是引導世人以無懼爲惡，引導爲惡者以無懼增其惡也。

166 聖賢所謂心散、心亡乃是譬詞。如吾汎濫逐于外事，而不專一，是謂心散；如吾所務不在本性內事，而在外逸，卽謂心亡；非必眞散、眞亡也。善者藏

The Human Soul is not Extinguished

having dissolved their minds they are still able to go on living? The mind in the body of a man is more necessary to the body than is blood. If the blood is dissolved it is no longer possible to sustain the body; but if the mind is dissolved can the body still function? And how much more pertinent is this question when [it is realized that] the mind which is in the body is stronger than the body? If the whole body accumulates evil and yet is not dissolved by it, how can evil dissolve the human mind? If the mind is already dissolved when a man is alive, why should destruction have to be delayed until after his death?

165. The Lord of creation does not change the natures of created things because of the good or evil they might have done. For example, the natures of birds and beasts are not destined from birth for eternal life, so that although there are times when they chance to do good, the Creator does not on this account cause birds and beasts to be changed into creatures with natures destined for eternal life. Devils by nature have eternal life, but although they do evil He does not for this reason cause devils to be destroyed. Well then, how can the minds of evil men be dissolved because of the evil they have done? A punishment which destroys the souls of evil men cannot be reckoned a just punishment; and the Lord of Heaven would certainly not act in this manner. Do you mean to say that wrong-doings which fall into differing categories of seriousness are all punished with the one kind of destruction? Further, since what is destroyed ceases to exist, it can experience neither grief nor suffering, and cannot be punished. Will the wrong-doer, then, not in fact have escaped [what is justly due to him]? Such a view will only encourage men not to fear wrong-doing and will cause evil-doers not to fear adding to their evil deeds.

166. Any reference to the dispersal or destruction of the mind made by sages and worthies is merely figurative; as, for ex-

169

論人魂不滅大異禽獸

心以德，似美飾之；惡者藏心以罪，似醜污之。此本性之體，兼身與神，非我結聚，乃天主賦之，以使我為人。其散亡之機亦非由我，常由天主。天主命其身期年而散，則期年以散，而吾不能永久。命其靈魂常生不滅，而吾焉能滅之耶？

167 顧我所用何如：善用之，則安泰；誤用之，則險危云耳。吾稟本性如得兼金，吾或以之造祭神之爵，或以之造藏穢之盤，皆我自為之。然其藏穢盤獨非兼金乎？增光于心，則辛騰天上之大光；增瞑于心，則辛降地之大瞑。誰能排此理之大端哉？

168 中士曰：吁！今吾方知人所異於禽獸者，非幾希也。靈魂不滅之理，甚正也，甚明也。

---

15 Compare Mencius' saying: "That whereby man differs from the birds and beasts is but small." See See *The Chinese Classics*, vol. II, p. 325.

170

ample, when we fail to concentrate our minds on our external duties and call this being "scatter-brained." It is also like our use of the expression "the mind is dead to it" when we are engaged in some activity which falls outside the sphere of our natural disposition; neither of these ways of speaking suggest that the mind is really scattered or dead. Virtue hidden in the minds of good men is like an adornment of beauty on the mind. Sin hidden in the minds of evil men is like the defilement of the mind with loathsome filth. The basic nature of man is a combination of matter and spirit. It is not assembled by ourselves, but is bestowed by the Lord of Heaven so that we may become men. Thus, the destruction of mind and spirit does not rest with us, but always with the Lord of Heaven. If the Lord of Heaven commands that the body of a man be destroyed in a certain year, it will be destroyed in that year, and we cannot make it exist for ever. [If the Lord of Heaven] wills that the soul of a man should continue in existence and not die, how can we destroy it?

167. Everything depends on how we make use of [our body and soul]. If we use them well they will enjoy good health and peace; if we misuse them, then they will be in danger. Our being furnished with a basic nature is like being in possession of gold. I can use it to manufacture a chalice for sacrificing to God (*Shen*) or I can use it to make a plate on which filth can be placed. It all depends on me. But does the plate on which filth has been put cease to be gold? If a man adds light to his mind he will in the end ascend to the great light which is in Heaven. If, on the other hand, a man adds darkness to his mind, he will, finally, descend into the great darkness of Hell. Who can oppose this great truth?

168. *The Chinese scholar says:* Well! Now I know for the first time that there are not a few ways in which man differs from the birds and beasts.[15] The teaching concerning the indestructibili-

169　西士曰：期己行于禽獸，不聞二性之殊者，頑也。高士志浮人品之上，詎願等己乎鄙類者哉？賢友得契尊旨，言必躍如，然性逈異矣，行宜勿過焉。

ty of the soul is very just and very clear.

169. *The Western scholar says:* It is sheer obstinacy to wish one's actions to be like those of birds and beasts and to refuse to hear about the distinctions between their natures and that of man. How can refined, educated men with superior ambitions want to be regarded as being in the same class as lowly birds and beasts? Since, my good friend, you already agree in substance with the superior view, your speech will certainly be different in future. Since the natures of men and beasts are so greatly different, their actions and deportment ought also to be clearly distinguishable.

第四篇

辯釋鬼神及人魂異論,而解天下萬物不可謂之一體

170 中士曰:昨吾退習大誨,果審其皆有真理,不知吾國迂儒何以攻折鬼神之實為正道也?

171 西士曰:吾遍察大邦之古經書,無不以祭祀鬼神為天子諸侯重事,故敬之如在其上、如在其左右,豈無其事而故為此矯誣哉?

172 盤庚曰:「失于政,陳于茲,高后丕乃崇降罪疾,曰:『何虐朕民?』」又曰:「茲予有亂政同位,具乃貝玉。乃祖乃父丕乃告我高后。曰:『作丕刑於朕孫。』迪高后丕乃崇降弗祥。」西伯戡黎,祖伊諫紂曰:「天子,天既訖我殷命;格人元龜,罔敢知吉。非先王不相我後人,惟王淫戲用自絕。」

1 *Kuei-shen* (鬼神). See chapter 1, n. 23.
2 See *The Chinese Classics*, vol. I, p. 398.
3 Ibid., vol. III, p. 238.
4 Ibid., vol. III, p. 240.

174

Chapter 4

A DISCUSSION ON SPIRITUAL BEINGS AND THE SOUL OF MAN, AND AN EXPLANATION AS TO WHY THE PHENOMENA OF THE WORLD CANNOT BE DESCRIBED AS FORMING AN ORGANIC UNITY.

170. *The Chinese scholar says:* After taking my leave of you yesterday I went over what you had taught me and, sure enough, discovered truth in it. I cannot understand why the doctrinaire scholars of my country should attack the existence of spiritual beings[1] and regard their view as being orthodox.

171. *The Western scholar says:* I have examined the ancient Chinese canonical writings in great detail and all regard the offering of sacrifices to ghosts and spirits as one of the most important functions of the Son of Heaven and the feudal lords. They reverenced these spiritual beings as if they were above them and all around them.[2] It would be absurd to say that they deliberately acted deceitfully, knowing that there were no such beings!

172. P'an Keng said: "Were I to err in my judgment, and remain long here, my High Sovereign, the founder of our House, would send down great punishment for my crime, and say, "Why do you oppress my people?"[3] And he went on to say: "Here are those ministers of my government, who share with me the offices of the State; —and yet only think of hoarding up cowries and gems! Your ancestors and fathers urgently represent to my High Sovereign, saying, 'Execute great punishments on our descendants.' So they intimate to my High Sovereign that he should send down great calamities."[4] In the section headed "The Chief of the West's Conquest of Li" [the minister of King Chou of the Shang dynas-

173 盤庚者，成湯九世孫，相違四百祀而猶祭之，而猶懼之，而猶以其能降罪、降不祥，勵己勸民，則必以湯為仍在而未散矣。祖伊在盤庚之後，而謂殷先王既崩而能相其後孫，則以死者之靈魂為永在不滅矣。

174 金縢周公曰：「予仁若考，能多才多藝，能事鬼神。」又曰：「我之弗辟，我無以告我先王。」召誥曰：「天既遐終大邦殷之命，茲殷多哲王在天，越厥後王後民，于天……文王陟降，在帝左右。」詩云：「文王在上，於昭

5 Ibid., vol. III, pp. 268, 271.
6 T'ang (湯), the first king of the Shang dynasty (1766-1122 B.C.).
7 See *The Chinese Classics*, vol. III, p. 354.
8 Ibid., vol. III, p. 358.
9 Ibid., vol. III, p. 426.
10 Wen Wang (文王), father of Wu Wang (武王), the first king of the Chou dynasty.
11 See *The Chinese Classics*, vol. IV, pp. 427-428.

ty], Tsu I, went to remonstrate with King Chou and said to him: "Son of Heaven, Heaven is bringing to an end the destiny of our dynasty of Yin; the wisest of men and the great tortoise equally do not venture to know anything fortunate for it. It is not that the former kings do not aid us, the men of this after time; but by your dissoluteness and sport, O King, you are bringing on the end yourself."[5]

173. P'an Keng was the descendent in the ninth generation of King T'ang,[6] the Successful, and nearly four hundred years separated them; yet he still sacrificed to him, still feared him, and still believed that he could send down calamities and misfortune as a warning to him and as an encouragement to the people. It is obvious that he believed that the soul of T'ang had not been destroyed and continued to exist. Tsu I followed P'an Keng, and he said that after the former kings of the Shang dynasty had departed this life, they were still able to help their sons and grandsons in later generations, thereby affirming that the souls of the dead eternally exist and are not destroyed.

174. In "The Metal-bound Coffer" of the *Book of History* the Duke of Chou says: "I have been lovingly obedient to my father; I am possessed of many abilities and arts which fit me to serve spiritual beings."[7] He goes on: "If I do not take the law to these men, I shall not be able to make my report to our former kings."[8] In the "Announcement of the Duke of Shao" it says: "When Heaven rejected and made an end of the decree in favor of the great State of Yin, there were many of the former intelligent kings of Yin in heaven. They finally cast King Chou and his ministers and people aside."[9] In the *Book of Odes* it says: "King Wen[10] is on high; Oh! bright is he in heaven ... King Wen ascends and descends, on the left and the right of the Sovereign [on High]."[11]

175 周公、召公何人乎？其謂成湯文王既崩之後，猶在天陟降而能保佑國家，則以人魂死後為不散泯矣。貴邦以二公為聖，而以其言為誑，可乎？

176 論鬼神之性，其庶幾矣。異端熾行，譸張為幻，難以攻詰，後之正儒其奈何？必將理斥其邪說，明

177 中士曰：今之論鬼神者，各自有見。或謂天地間無鬼神之殊；或謂信之則有，不信之則無；或謂如說有則非，如說無則亦非，如說有無，則得之矣。

178 西士曰：三言，一切以攻鬼神，而莫思其非，將排詆佛老之徒，而不覺忤古聖之旨。且夫鬼神，有山川、宗廟、天地之異名異職，則其不等著矣。所謂二氣良能、造化之迹、氣之屈伸，非諸經所指之鬼神也。

辯釋鬼神及人魂異論，而解天下萬物不可謂之一體

12 That is, the two *ch'i* (氣) which are *yin and yang*.
13 See *The Chinese Classics*, vol. II, p. 456 for Mencius' description of innate or intuitive ability and knowledge.
14 Ways of speaking of phenomena in the creative process.

Spiritual Beings and the Human Soul

175. What kind of men were the Dukes of Chou and Shao? They both said that following the deaths of T'ang, the Successful, and King Wen these two sovereigns continued in Heaven, ascending and descending, and that they were able to protect the nation; that is to say, after their death their souls were not destroyed. Your noble country regards the Duke of Chou and the Duke of Shao as two sages; can one treat their sayings as being deliberately deceptive?

176. False doctrines flourish everywhere defrauding and deceiving the people; and it is difficult to attack and destroy them in such a way as to eradicate them entirely. What must scholars of the orthodox school of Confucianism today do? They must employ reason to condemn these heresies and to explain as nearly as possible the nature of spiritual beings.

177. *The Chinese scholar says:* These days, when people discuss spiritual beings, each person has his own point of view. Some say there are no such things as spiritual beings in the world; others say they exist if you believe in them, and do not exist if you do not believe in them; others again say it is incorrect to say they exist, and also incorrect to say they do not exist, and that the only thing that can be said is that they both exist and do not exist!

178. *The Western scholar says:* All three ways of speaking represent attacks on spiritual beings without any thought being given as to where these attacks might be wrong. Eager to condemn the adherents of Buddhism and Taoism the exponents of these three points of view have failed to realize that they have defied the main ideas of the ancients and sages. Moreover, spiritual beings were classified as spirits of hills and streams, spirits of the ancestral temples, spirits of heaven and earth, and so forth. They thus bore different names and played different roles, and were therefore not on an equal footing. The so-called "two primary material forces,"[12] "innate ability,"[13] "fluctuations of material-energy" and "traces of the production of things"[14] are not the spiritual beings referred to in the canonical writings.

辯釋鬼神及人魂異論，而解天下萬物不可謂之一體

179 吾心信否，能有無物者否？講夢則或可，若論天地之大尊，奚用此恍惚之辭耶？譬如西域獅子，知者信其有，愚人或不信，然而獅子本有，彼不信者，能滅獅子之類哉？又況鬼神者哉？

180 凡事物，有即有，無即無。蓋小人疑鬼神有無，因就學士而問以釋疑，如答之以有無，豈非愈增其疑乎？諸言之旨無他，乃郊野之誕耳。無色形之物，而欲以肉眼見之，比方欲以耳啖魚肉之味，可乎？誰能以俗眼見五常乎？誰見生者之魂乎？誰見風乎？

181 以目觀物不如以理度之。夫目，或有所差，惟理無謬也。觀日輪者，愚人測之以目，謂大如甕底耳；儒者以理而計其高遠之極，則知其大乃過于普天之下也。置直木于澄水中而漫其半，以目視之如曲焉；以理度之，則仍自為直木非曲也。任目觀影，則以影為物，謂能動靜；然以理細察，則知影實無光者耳

15 *Wu-ch'ang* (五常). See chapter 1, n. 15.

Spiritual Beings and the Human Soul

179. Can a belief or unbelief in these things on my part determine whether they exist or not? In my dreams perhaps! How can one employ such vague talk when discussing the Supreme Honor of Heaven and Earth? For example, lions exist in the West and intelligent people believe in their existence whilst the stupid refuse to believe in them. Since lions really do exist, can those who refuse to believe in them thereby eliminate them? And how much more must this be so with spiritual beings!

180. Things either exist or do not exist. When ignorant people are in doubt as to the existence or otherwise of spiritual beings they turn to learned men to have their doubts dispelled; if some of these then answer that "they both exist and do not exist," are they not simply adding to the doubts of the ignorant? The whole purport of their argument is that if spiritual beings exist it must be possible to see them, and if the human eye cannot see them, they must therefore not exist. But such talk cannot serve as the arguments of learned men. It represents the erroneous thinking of the untutored. To expect the physical eye to be able to see things devoid of color or form is like expecting the ear to taste the flavors of fish and meat. This way of thinking is incorrect, is it not? Who can see the Five Basic Virtues[15] with his physical eye? Who has ever seen the soul of a living person? Who has seen the wind?

181. It is better to consider things by means of reason rather than to look at them with the eyes, because the eyes can be mistaken, whereas reason cannot. When people examine the sun the foolish infer with their eyes that it is no larger than the bottom of a jar, whereas the learned calculate with their reason that the sun is at a great distance from the earth and that it is bigger than the whole world. If a straight stick is half inserted in clear water it appears bent to the eye, but if looked at carefully, the stick is obviously as straight as ever, because the wood has no curve. If one looks at the shadows of things with one's eyes one is likely to treat shadows

辯釋鬼神及人魂異論，而解天下萬物不可謂之一體

已，決非有物，況能動靜乎？

182 故西校公語曰：「耳目、口鼻、四肢所知覺物，必撥之于心理。心理無非焉，方可謂之真；若理有不順，則捨之就理可也。」人欲明事物之奧理，無他道焉，因外顯以推內隱，以其然驗其所以然，如觀屋頂烟騰，而屋內之必有火者可知。

183 昔者，因天地萬物而證其固有天地萬物之主也，因人事而證其有不能散滅之靈魂也；則以證鬼神之必有，亦無異道矣。如云死者形朽滅而神飄散泯然無迹，此一二四夫之云，無理可依，奈何以議聖賢之所既按乎哉？

184 中士曰：春秋傳載：鄭伯有為厲。必以形見之也。人魂無形，而移變有形之物，此不可以理推矣。夫生而無異于人，豈死而有越人之能乎？若死者皆有知，則慈母有深愛子，一旦化去，獨不日在本家顧視向者愛子乎？

16 *Cheng* (鄭), a country in the Spring and Autumn Period (722-484 B.C.).
17 Part of the passages referred to here gives an excellent account of the traditional Chinese view concerning the nature of the soul. See *The Chinese Classics*, vol. V, p. 618.

182

as things and to assert that they can both move and be still; but if one investigates them carefully with reason one soon realizes that shadows are due entirely to a lack of light rays and that they have no real existence whatsoever; how then can they move?

182. Thus, the learned academics of the West have a maxim which runs as follows: Things experienced by the ears, eyes, mouth, nose, and four limbs must be weighed by reason, and only if they accord with reason can they be termed true. If they do not accord with reason they ought to be cast aside in favor of the rational. If people want to understand the profound principles of things, there is only one way to do so, and that is by inferring what is hidden within from that which is external and easy to see; to employ things as they are to figure out the reasons for their being as they are. If one sees smoke ascending from the roof of a house one can know that there is a fire in the house.

183. A few days ago we proved [that there is a lord and controller of heaven and earth and all phenomena] because there are heaven and earth and all phenomena. We also proved that man has an indestructible soul because of his activities. The same principle applies when one sets out to prove the existence of spiritual beings. It is said that following a man's death his body is destroyed and his spirit is scattered to the winds, leaving no trace behind. It should be noted that this is merely the indiscriminate chatter of one or two commonplace men, and that it has no foundation in reason; how then can it be used to dispute the judgment of sages and worthies?

184. *The Chinese scholar says:* In *The Commentary to the Spring and Autumn Annals* it is recorded that following the death of the Earl of Cheng[16] he appeared as a spirit.[17] This must mean that there is such a thing as a manifested spirit. If a person's soul which has no form can be transformed into a thing with form, then we have something which defies reason. If he were the same as everyone else when he was alive, how could he possess powers

185 西士曰：春秋傳既言伯有死後為厲，則古春秋世亦已信人魂之不散滅矣。而俗儒以非薄鬼神為務，豈非春秋罪人乎？夫謂人死者，非魂死之謂，惟謂人魄耳、人形耳。靈魂者，生時如拘縲紲中；既死，則如出暗獄而脫手足之拳，益達事物之理焉，其知能當益滋精，踰于俗人，不宜為怪。君子知其然，故不以死為凶懼而忻然安之，謂之歸于本鄉。

186 天主制作萬物，分定各有所在，不然則亂。如死者之魂仍可在家，豈謂之死乎？且觀星宿居於天上，不得降於地下而雜乎草木，草木生於地下，亦不得升於天上而雜乎星宿。萬物各安其所不得移動，譬水底魚饑將死，雖有香餌在岸，亦不得往而食之。人之魂雖念妻子，豈得回在家中？凡有回世界者，必天主使之，或以勸善，或以懲惡，以驗人死之後其魂猶存，與其禽獸之散而不回者異也。

18 *Hun* (魂). See chapter 3, n. 7.
19 *P'o* (魄). See chapter 3, n. 7.

辯釋鬼神及人魂異論，而解天下萬物不可謂之一體

184

Spiritual Beings and the Human Soul

superior to those of ordinary men after his death? If all those who die possess awareness, would not a mother, who deeply loves her son and who one day passes away, continue daily in the home to watch over the son she had formerly loved?

185. *The Western scholar says:* Since *The Commentary to the Spring and Autumn Annals* states that the Earl of Cheng appeared as a spirit following his death, it is clear that in ancient times, during the Spring and Autumn period, people believed that the human soul was not destroyed. Does not the common scholar who regards contempt for the spiritual a right and proper attitude stand condemned by *The Spring and Autumn Annals?* On the question of human death, it is not the soul[18] that dies, but only man's baser animal spirits[19] and his bodily form. While a man is alive his soul is like a fettered prisoner; after he dies it is like someone who leaves the darkness of prison and is freed from his manacles. He will understand the principles of things even more clearly. His consciousness will be even more acute. One should not think it strange that it should be superior to that of any ordinary person in the world. The superior man understands this truth and therefore does not look on death as an evil or as something to be feared; rather, he leaves this world, joyfully saying that he is returning to his hometown.

186. The Lord of Heaven creates all things and allots each its own place. If this were not so there would be confusion. If the soul of a dead person remained in the home, how could he be said to be dead? If we examine the stars in the heavens, we find that they are not permitted to descend to earth to mingle with the vegetation. We also find that the grass and trees growing on earth are unable to ascend to the heavens to mingle with the stars. Thus, all things have their own determined dwelling places and cannot move from these at will. Fish in water, for example, may be dying of hunger, but although there may be tasty bait on shore, they cannot climb the banks to eat it. Although a man's soul may long for his wife and children, how can he return home? If there are souls which

辯釋鬼神及人魂異論，而解天下萬物不可謂之一體

187 魂本無形，或有著顯於人，必托一虛像而發見焉，此亦不難之事。天主欲人盡知死後魂存，而分明曉示若此，而猶有罔誕無忌、亂教惑民，以己所不知，妄云人死魂散，無復形跡，非但悖妄易辯，且其人身後之魂必受妄言之殃矣。可不慎乎？

188 中士曰：謂人之神魂死後散泯者，以神為氣耳。氣散有速漸之殊，如人不得其死，其氣尚聚久而漸泯，鄭伯有是也。

189 又曰陰陽二氣為物之體，而無所不在；天地之間無一物非陰陽，則無一物非鬼神也。如尊教謂鬼神及人魂如此，則與吾常所聞無大異焉。

20 Ch'i (氣).
21 Kuei-shen (鬼神). See chapter 1, n. 22. These two characters recur frequently in par. 174-178, 190-193.

Spiritual Beings and the Human Soul

return to this world it will only be because the Lord of Heaven has so ordered them, using them to persuade people to do good or to restrain them from doing evil. They serve as proof of the continued existence of the soul after death and are totally different from the sentient souls of birds and beasts which, after being dispersed, do not return.

187. The soul is essentially without form, and if it appears to man, it must be by assuming the image of a phantom—something which is not in any way difficult. The Lord of Heaven wants people to know that the soul continues to exist after death and tells them this clearly in this fashion. But there are some people who have no scruples about lying, who are careless in the teaching of others, and who deceive the common people. Being ignorant themselves they talk nonsense, saying that after a person quits this world his soul is destroyed without a trace. Not only is such talk unprincipled, wanton, and unworthy of refutation, but when this kind of careless talker eventually quits the world, his soul is sure to receive punishment commensurate with the foolishness of his speech. One should therefore be cautious in all one says.

188. *The Chinese scholar says:* Those who assert that the soul is extinguished and scattered after death simply regard the soul as material energy.[20] The dispersal of material energy can be either fast or slow. If a person dies before his time his material energy continues to hold together and does not disperse immediately. Only after a long period of time has passed is it gradually dissolved. Men like the Earl of Cheng are good examples of this.

189. Further, the two kinds of material energy of *Yin* and *Yang* are the substance of all matter and they are everywhere present. There is not a thing in the world which is not *Yin* and *Yang*, and there is therefore not a thing which is not spiritual.[21] If what your revered Church calls spiritual beings and the human soul are like this, then there is no great distinction between them and what we habitually hear about.

辯釋鬼神及人魂異論，而解天下萬物不可謂之一體

190 西士曰：以氣為鬼神靈魂者，索物類之實名也。立教者，萬教之理當各類以本名。古經書云氣、云鬼神，文字不同，則其理亦異。有祭鬼神者矣，未聞有祭氣者，何今之人紊用其名乎？云氣漸散，可見其理已窮，而言之盡妄。吾試問之：夫氣何時散盡？何病疾使之散？鳥獸常不得其死，其氣速散乎？漸散乎？則死後之事皆未必知之審者，奚用妄論之哉？何其不回世乎？

191 中庸謂：「體物而不可遺。」以辭迎其意可也。蓋仲尼之意謂：鬼神體物，其德之盛耳；非謂鬼神即是其物也。且鬼神在物與魂神在人大異焉。

192 魂神在人為其內本分，與人形為一體，故人以是能論理而列於靈才之類；彼鬼神在物，如長在船非船之本分者，與船分為二物而各列於各類，故物雖有鬼神而弗登靈才之品也。但有物自或無靈、或無知覺，則天主命鬼神引導之以

22 Chan, *A Source Book in Chinese Philosophy*, p. 102.

188

190. *The Western scholar says:* People who hold that material energy is to be equated with spiritual beings and the human soul are confusing the names by which categories of things are known. Those who seek to establish their teachings as a guide to others must provide appropriate names for each kind of thing. In the canonical writings of ancient times different words are used for *"Ch'i"* (material energy) and *"kuei-shen"* (spiritual beings). Their meaning, therefore, are also regarded as being different. I have heard of sacrifices being offered to ghosts and spirits, (*kuei-shen*), but never to material energy (*ch'i*). Why do people today confuse these terms with one another? If one says that material energy can gradually dissolve, it is obvious that it no longer has any principle to speak of, and any reference to it is absurd. Let me ask you: when is material energy totally dissolved? What severe sickness causes it to be dissolved? Birds and beasts constantly come to an untimely end; does their material energy disperse immediately, or gradually? Why do they not come back to life? It is obvious that one may not entirely understand what takes place after death; what purpose is served, then, by such foolish talk?

191. Discussing spiritual beings the *Doctrine of the Mean* states: "They form the substance of all things and nothing can be without them."[22] We must penetrate these words, and fathom their true meaning. By asserting that spiritual beings form the substance of all things, Confucius meant to say that the virtue of spiritual beings greatly [affects things]. He was not saying that spiritual beings are things. However, there is a great difference between the way in which spiritual beings reside among things and the way in which the soul resides in a man.

192. The soul as an internal ingredient of a man is organically one with the human form. Because of this man can reason and takes his place among things having an intellectual nature. The residence of spiritual beings among things, however, is like the long residence of people in boats. These people are not necessary con-

辯釋鬼神及人魂異論，而解天下萬物不可謂之一體

適其所，茲所謂體物耳矣，與聖君以神治體國家同焉。不然，是天下無一物非靈也。

193 蓋彼曰天下每物有鬼神，而每以鬼神為靈，如草木金石豈可謂之靈哉？彼文王之民感君之思，謂其臺曰「靈臺」，謂其沼曰「靈沼」，不足為奇；今桀紂之臺、沼亦謂之靈矣，豈不亦混亂物之品等而莫之顧耶？

194 分物之類，貴邦士者曰：或得其形，如金石是也；或另得生氣而長大，如草木是也；或更得知覺，如禽獸是也；或益精而得靈才，如人類是也。

195 吾西庠之士猶如詳焉，觀後圖可見。但其依賴之類最多，難以圖盡，故略之，而特書其類之九元宗云。

23 See *The Chinese Classics*, vol. II, pp. 127-128.
24 Ibid., p. 128-129. King Wen was a good emperor, but Chieh（桀, the last emperor of Hsia, 2205-1766 B.C.), and Chou（紂, the last emperor of Shang, 1766-1122 B.C.), were reputedly the worst emperors in Chinese history.
25 See the chart on page 192.

stitutents of the boats but are quite distinct from them, people and boats falling into separate categories. Thus, even though there may be spiritual beings in some things, they cannot be placed in the category of things having intellectual natures. But there are some things which are essentially lacking in any intellectual nature or which have no perception. The Lord of Heaven therefore commands spiritual beings to guide them so that each finds its own place. This is what is meant by the statement: "[The Lord of Heaven] helps and rules all things." It is like the emperor who rules nature with his spirit. If this were not so, everything in the world would have an intellectual nature.

193. Now, they say that everything in the world possesses spiritual beings, and that every spiritual being is intelligent. But can one say that things like grass, trees, metal, and stone all have intelligence? There is really nothing strange in the fact that the people who lived under King Wen, and who were grateful for the favors he bestowed on them, should call his tower The Intelligent Spirit Tower and his ponds The Intelligent Spirit Ponds.[23] But if one were now to call the towers and ponds of Chieh of the Hsia dynasty and Chou of the Shang dynasty[24] Intelligent Spirit Towers and Ponds, would this not indeed be to confuse the classes of things?

194. When the learned men of your noble country divide things up into various categories they commonly say that there are things with form such as metal and stone and the like; that there are things with the power of growth such as grass and trees and the like; that there are things with awareness such as birds and beasts and the like; and that there are things which are even more refined and which have an intelligent and spiritual nature such as man.

195. Our learned men of the West have made even more detailed distinctions. If you look at the accompanying "Chart of the Categories of Things"[25] you will see that the classes of accidents are the most numerous, so much so that it is difficult to list them exhaustively. I have therefore only provided a general survey and made reference to nine major classes.

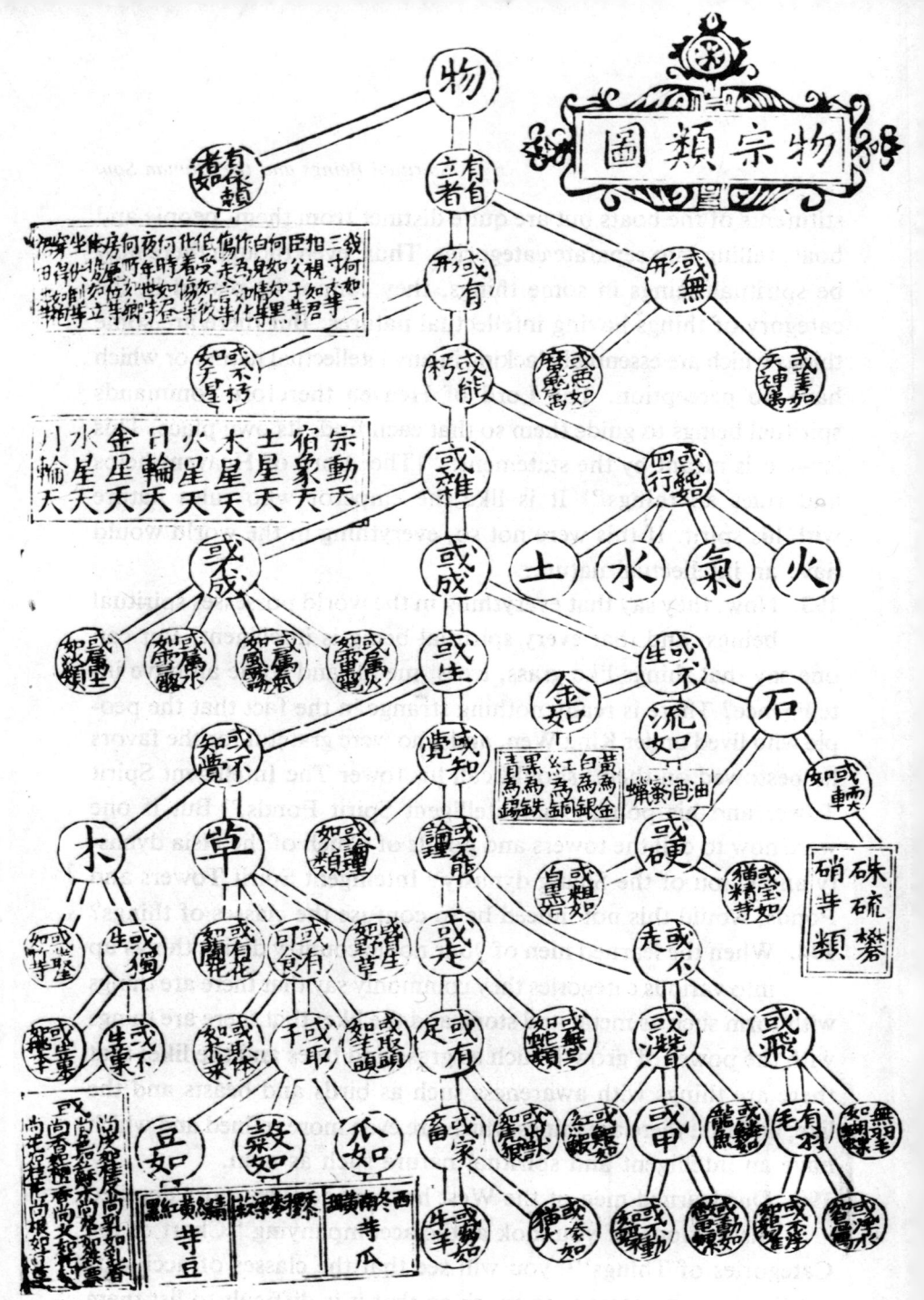

Figure 3. Diagram of the Kinds of Being, as it appears in The True Meaning of the **Lord of Heaven,** *first Peking edition, 1603. With permission of Biblioteca Casanatense, Rome.*

A Diagram of the Kinds of Being

Being is divided into accident and substance. Accident includes quantity (two, three, inch, foot), relationship (king/minister, father/son), quality (black, white, cold, hot), activity (to create, wound, walk, speak), passivity (to be created, wounded), time (day, night, year, century), place (country, house, hall, seat), posture (standing, sitting, lying), dress (robe, cloth, field, pool). Substance includes those things which have a body and those things which are pure forms. Pure forms are divided into those which are good, such as good spirits, angels, and the rest, and those which are evil, such as evil spirits, devils, and the rest.

Bodies are either eternal or perishable. Eternal bodies include celestial bodies and their heavens, such as the heavens, the constellations, Saturn, Jupiter, Mars, the sun, Venus, Mercury, the moon, and their heavens. Perishable bodies are either in a pure state, like the four elements fire, air, water, and earth, or they are not in a pure state. The latter are divided into solids or non-solids. Non-solids are thunder and lightning (related to fire), clouds and fog (related to air), snow and dew (related to water), sand (related to earth).

Solids either have life or are lifeless. Lifeless solids can be divided into stones, fluids, and metals. Stones are either hard or soft. Hard stones are precious like jewels and gems, or common like black and white stones. Some stones are soft like vermillion, sulphur, nitre, and alum. Fluids include wine, oil, honey, and wax, while metals include yellow gold, white silver, red copper, black iron, and blue tin.

Living things either have consciousness or do not. Those which have consciousness are intelligent, such as man, or they lack intelligence. Unintelligent beings either move on the ground, in the air, or in the water. Those which move on the earth are either footless like the snake or they are footed. Footed creatures are wild like the tiger and the wolf, or they are domesticated. Domesticated animals are of two kinds: the cat and the dog, which do not chew the cud, and the cow and the sheep, which chew the cud.

Creatures which fly are without feathers, like the butterfly, or they have feathers. Some of the latter, like the duck and the goose can also move on water, or they cannot like the crow and the sparrow. Of the things which swim, some have scales like dragons and fish; some have shells and move, like the turtle and the conch, or are stable, like the oyster; some are like the shrimp.

Beings which lack consciousness can be divided into types of trees and kinds of grass. Grass includes ordinary grass, flowers, and edible plants. Edible plants are roots, like the potato; leaves, like mustard; seeds, such as melons (watermelon, vegetable marrow, pumpkin, cucumber, honeydew), grains (corn, rice, wheat, sorghum), or beans (blue, green, yellow, red, black).

Trees are either shrublike, such as bamboo, or free-standing. The latter either bear fruit, such as the peach and the plum, or they do not. Some non-fruitbearing trees are useful for their bark or color. Others are fragrant, like sandalwood; have good blossoms, like cassia; produce sap; are especially hard, like teakwood; have good roots, like liquorice; or are beautiful to look at, like pear blossoms.

196 凡此物之萬品，各有一定之類，有屬靈者，有屬愚者。如吾於外國士傳：中國有儒謂鳥獸草木金石皆靈，與人類齊。豈不令之大驚哉？

197 中士曰：雖吾國有謂鳥獸之性同乎人，但鳥獸性偏而人得其正，雖謂鳥獸有靈，然其靈微渺，人則得靈之廣大也，是以其類異也。

198 西士曰：夫正偏大小不足以別類，僅別同類之等耳，正山、偏山、大山、小山並為山類也。智者獲靈之大，愚者獲靈之小，賢者得靈之正，不肖得靈之偏，豈謂異類者哉？如大小偏正能分類，則人之一類，靈之巨微正僻其類甚多。

辯釋鬼神及人魂異論，而解天下萬物不可謂之一體

196. Although there are tens of thousands of different kinds of things, each has its own fixed category. There are some things which belong to the category of the intellectual, and there are those things which belong to the category of the insensate. If I were to inform foreign scholars that a number of Confucian scholars in China assert that birds, beasts, grass, trees, metal, and stone are all endowed with an intellectual nature and are to be put in the same category as human beings, would this not cause them considerable surprise?

197. *The Chinese scholar says:* There are people in China who advocate the view that the nature of birds and beasts is the same as human nature, but that the nature of birds and beasts is one-sided or oblique whereas that of humans is upright. Although they say that birds and beasts have intelligence, the intelligence of birds and beasts is very small; man, on the other hand, is endowed with an intelligence of great magnitude, and for this reason he falls into a different category.

198. *The Western scholar says:* The qualities of uprightness and obliquity, of greatness and of smallness cannot serve as norms for the sorting out of categories; they can only distinguish between classes in a given category. Whether mountains are upright or oblique, large or small, they are all mountains. The intelligence of the wise man is developed to a comparatively greater degree, whereas the intelligence of one who is stupid is developed to a comparatively lesser degree. A good man has an upright intelligence, whereas a depraved man possesses an intelligence which is oblique; but does this mean that they can be said to belong to different categories? If smallness, greatness, obliquity and uprightness are to be regarded as separate categories, then the single category of human intelligence would have to be divided into numerous categories because of the greatness, smallness, uprightness and obliquity of men's individual intelligences.

辯釋鬼神及人魂異論，而解天下萬物不可謂之一體

199 苟觀物類之圖，則審世上固惟「有」「無」二者可以別物異類焉耳。試言之：有形者為一類，則無形者異類也；生者為一類，則不生者異類也；能論理者惟人類本份，故天下萬類然與能論也。

200 人之中，論有正偏小大，均列於會論之類，而惟差精粗。如謂鳥獸之性本靈，則夫其偏、其小，固同類于人者也，但不宜以似為真，以由外來者為內本，譬如因見銅壺之漏能定時候，即謂銅水本靈可乎？將軍者有智謀以全軍而敗敵，其士卒順其令而或進、或退、或伏、或突，以成其功，誰曰士卒之本智不從外導者乎？

201 明于類者，視各類之行動，熟察其本情，而審其志之所及，則知鳥獸者有鬼神為之暗誘，而引之以行上帝之命，出于不得不然，而莫知其然，非有自主

196

Spiritual Beings and the Human Soul

199. If you examine the "Chart of the Categories of Things" you will see that there are only two qualities to be looked for when distinguishing between the different categories of things: the qualities of "existence" and "non-existence." If things which have form constitute one category, then those things which are formless constitute another; and if things which have life fall into one category, then things which are lifeless fall into another. Only man is capable of discussing principles; therefore nothing else in the world can be compared with man.

200. Although rationality in men may be upright or oblique, great or small, all expressions of it take their place within the category of rational thought, the differences between them being nothing more than degrees of refinement and coarseness. If one says that birds and beasts are by nature essentially intelligent, then, although their intelligence be oblique and small, it will fall into the same category as human intelligence. One ought not, however, to regard things which seem to be the same as being genuinely so; or to treat that which is external as internal. For example, when one sees a clepsydra which is manufactured out of copper and is capable of reckoning the hours, is it right to say that the water in the clepsydra is possessed of intelligence? Because of the clever strategy of high-ranking military leaders, troops are able, by following their commands, to advance and retreat, lay ambush and attack and defeat the enemy.

201. Who would say that the strategems of the troops did not derive from the external commands of their military leaders? When one understands categories and then takes cognizance of the activities of each category, and when one thoroughly examines the nature of each category and understands the direction taken by it, one realizes that birds and beasts enjoy the secret guidance of spiritual beings, and that they are led to accept the commands of the Sovereign on High as being necessary, without knowing the

197

之意。吾人類則能自立主張，而事爲之際皆用其所本有之靈志也。

202 中士曰：雖云天地萬物共一氣，然物之貌像不同，是以各分其類。如見身水，其外水與肚裏之水同，鰻魚肚裏之水與鯉魚肚裏之水同，獨其貌像常不一，則魚之類亦不一焉。故觀天下之萬像，而可以驗萬類矣。

203 西士曰：設徒以像分物，此非分物之類者也，是別像之類者耳。像固非其物也，以像分物，不以性分物，則犬之性猶牛之性，犬牛之性猶人之性歟，是告子之後又一告子也。以泥塑虎塑人二者，惟以貌像謂之異，宜也；活虎與活人，謂止以其貌異焉，決不宜矣。以貌像別物者、大概相同，不可謂異類

辯釋鬼神及人魂異論，而解天下萬物不可謂之一體

26 The philosopher Kao-tzu (告子) was one of those with whom Mencius discussed the problem of human nature. See *The Chinese Classics,* vol. II, p. 394.

Spiritual Beings and the Human Soul

reasons for them, and without any thought of independence. We humans can make independent decisions and can employ the intelligent wills with which we are endowed in order to carry out those decisions.

202. *The Chinese scholar says:* Although it is said that heaven, earth, and all pheonomena share one material energy, the forms and images of things are, nevertheless, different, and for this reason they are divided into a variety of categories. The human body may simply appear as a physical body, but both within it and outside it there is the material energy of *Yin* and *Yang* which fills heaven and earth. Through creation material energy becomes all things, and because of the existence of categories, things become different from one another. It is like fish in water; the water outside the fish is the same as the water in the fish's stomach; the water in the stomach of a mandarin fish is the same as the water in the stomach of a carp. It is only the appearances of the fish which persist in being different, so that the fish fall into separate categories. One has only to look at the differing forms and appearances of all the things in the world to be able to know each of the different categories.

203. *The Western scholar says:* To distinguish between things on the basis of appearance is not to distinguish between the various categories of things, but only between their external appearances. External appearances are not the things themselves. If one distinguishes between things on the basis of their appearances rather than on the basis of their natures, then must not the nature of dogs be regarded as being the same as the nature of oxen, and the natures of dogs and oxen be regarded as being the same as human nature? If this is so, we have the emergence of a new Philosopher Kao.[26] If one moulds a tiger and a man out of clay it is appropriate to assert that only their external appearances are dissimilar;

辯釋鬼神及人魂異論,而解天下萬物不可謂之一體。

;如以泥虎例泥人,其貌雖殊,其為泥類則一耳。

204 靈魂,亦不足怪;若知氣為一行,則不難說其體用矣。內外猶然充滿,何適而能離氣?何患其無氣而死?故氣非生活之本也。傳云:「差毫釐,謬千里。」未知氣為四行之一,而同之于鬼神及

205 若以氣為神,以為生活之本,則生者何由得死乎?物死之後,氣在

且夫氣者,和水火土三行,而為萬物之形者也;而靈魂者,為人之內分,一身之主,以呼吸出入其氣者也。蓋人與飛走諸類皆生氣內,以便調涼其心中之火,是故恒用呼吸,以每息更氣,而出熱致涼以生焉。魚潛水間,水性甚冷,能自外透涼于內火,所以其類多無呼吸之資也。

27 *Li Chi,* II, p. 260. *Li* (里), a unit of linear measure, about one third of a mile.
28 Since the term *ch'i* (氣, "material energy" or "material force") also means "air," Ricci naturally equates it with one of the four elements.
29 That is, *ch'i*.

Spiritual Beings and the Human Soul

but it is definitely not appropriate to say of a living tiger and a living man that only their looks are different. If one distinguishes between things on the basis of their appearances, and these are largely alike, it will not be possible to place them in separate categories. If one takes the example of the clay tiger and the clay man, however, although their external appearances are very different from each other, they must both be classified as clay.

204. If material energy is regarded as spirit and the basis of life, how can living things ever die? If, after living things have died, they continue to be imbued with and surrounded by material energy, where can they go to escape from material energy? How can one die from any disaster which is not material in character? Therefore, material energy is not the basis of life. In one ancient work we read: "A mistake of a hair's breadth, will lead to an error of a thousand *li*."[27] Men are not aware that material energy is one of the four elements,[28] and that it does not merit being equated with spiritual beings or with the soul. If they knew that material energy was an element they would cease to find it difficult to explain its essence and its function.

205. Material energy together with the three elements: water, fire, and earth, provide the bodily forms of all things, and the soul is an internal constituent of man. It is the lord and master of the body, and ventilates the body with air[29] by causing it to breathe in and out. Because men, birds, and beasts all live in air, they all make use of breathing to regulate their internal temperatures. They use the unceasing process of breathing to change their air, and thereby to expel heat and to draw in coolness. Fish lie hidden in water, and the nature of water is to be cold. Since it is possible for this coldness to enter into fish from outside and to regulate their internal heat, the majority of them do not have to breathe to aid this process.

206 夫鬼神非物之分,乃無形別物之類。其本職惟以天主之命司造化之事,無柄世之專權,故仲尼曰:「敬鬼神而遠之。」彼福祿、免罪非鬼神所能,由天主耳。而時人諂瀆,欲自此得之,則非其得之之道也。夫「遠之」意與「獲罪乎天,無所禱」同,豈可以「遠之」解無之而陷仲尼于無鬼神之惑哉?

207 中士曰:吾古之儒者,明察天地萬物本性皆善,俱有宏理,不可更易。以為物有巨微,其性一體,則曰天主上帝即在各物之內而與物為一,故勸人勿為惡以玷己之本善焉,勿違義以犯己之本理焉,勿害物以侮其內心之上帝焉。又曰人物壞喪,不滅本性而化歸于天主,此亦人魂不滅之謂,但恐於先生所論天主者不合。

30 *Analects*, V, 20.
31 Ibid., III, 13.

Spiritual Beings and the Human Soul

206. Spiritual beings are not constituents of matter, and fall into the category of things which lack bodily forms. The fundamental duty of spiritual beings is to carry out the will of the Lord of Heaven: to supervise created things. They do not possess absolute power over the world. Thus Confucius said: "By respect for the spirits [he] keeps them at a distance."[30] When we come to happiness, prosperity and the forgiveness of sin, we find that the granting of these things does not lie within the power of spiritual beings, and that they come solely from the Lord of Heaven. These days people like to curry favor with spiritual beings, hoping to receive happiness, prosperity and forgiveness from them; but this is not the way to obtain what they seek. What is implied by the words "keeps at a distance" in the above quotation is the same as what is implied in the statement: "He who has put himself in the wrong with Heaven has no means of expiation left."[31] Can one really explain the words "keeps at a distance" by saying that they are equivalent to the term "non-existent," and then assert uncompromisingly that Confucius advocated the view that there are no spiritual beings, thereby deceiving people?

207. *The Chinese scholar says:* Our scholars in ancient China were clearly aware that the natures of heaven, earth, and all things are good and they all held to the great and unchangeable principle that whether things are large or small, their basic natures are organically one. It is possible, therefore, to say that the Lord of Heaven who is the Sovereign on High is within all things, and that he forms a unity with all things. Our scholars therefore exhort people not to do evil and thereby to soil the goodness which is essentially their own; not to violate righteousness and thereby to offend the rational faculty which is an essential part of themselves, and not to harm other things, thereby insulting the Sovereign on High who dwells in their hearts. They also say that although men and creatures die and are destroyed, their basic natures are not extinguished, but submit to the Lord of Ḥeaven. This is another way of saying that

辯釋鬼神及人魂異論，而解天下萬物不可謂之一體

208 西士曰：茲語之謬，比前所聞者愈甚，曷敢合之乎？吾不敢以此簡吾上帝之尊也。天主經有傳：昔者天主化生天地，卽化生諸神之彙，其間有一鉅神，名謂輅齊拂兒，其視己如是靈明，便傲然曰吾可謂與天主同等矣。天主怒而幷其從者數萬神變為魔鬼，降置之於地獄。自是天地間始有魔鬼，有地獄矣。夫語物與造物者同，乃輅齊拂兒鬼傲語，孰敢述之歟？

209 世人不禁佛氏誑經，不覺染其毒語。周公仲尼之論、貴邦古經書，孰有狎后帝而與之一者？設恒民中有一匹夫，自稱與天子同等，其能免乎？人之稱人謂曰：「爾為爾，我為我。」而今凡溝壑昆蟲與上帝曰：「爾為爾，我為我。」豈不謂極抗大悖乎哉？

32 *Lu-ch'i-fu-erh* (輅齊拂兒).
33 *T'ien-tzu* (天子 , "Son of Heaven"), means the emperor.

a man's soul is not extinguished; but perhaps there is some difference between this and your teaching concerning the Lord of Heaven, Sir.

208. *The Western scholar says:* The error in what you have just said is greater than any I have previously heard you utter. How dare I hold a similar view? How dare I slight the dignity of our Sovereign on High in this fashion? In the canonical writings of the Lord of Heaven we are told that before the Lord of Heaven produced heaven and earth he created all the spirits, and that one great spirit among them, called Lucifer,[32] on observing his own intelligence, arrogantly said: "I can say that I am the equal of the Lord of Heaven!" Filled with anger the Lord of Heaven caused him and tens of thousands of spirits who followed his lead to be changed into devils and cast into Hell. From that time onwards creation has included devils and Hell. To say that what is created is on an equal footing with the creator is to use the arrogant words of the Devil, Lucifer. Who dares to speak in this manner?

209. Because people do not ban the lying canonical writings of the Buddha they have become involuntarily infected with his poisonous words. Where in the teachings of the Duke of Chou and Confucius or in the ancient canonical writings of your noble country is there a person who cares to show disrespect to the sovereign or emperor and to insist that he is on an equal footing with him? If an ordinary citizen asserts that he is as noble as the emperor,[33] can he avoid being guilty of a crime? If people in this world are not permitted recklessly to compare themselves with the kings of this world, how can they regard themselves as being the same as the Heavenly Sovereign on High? Among themselves people say: "You are you and I am myself"; but now an insect in a ditch says to the Sovereign on High: "You are I and I am you." Is this not to carry opposition to the truth to the utmost limit?

210 中士曰：佛氏無遜于上帝也。其貴人身，尊人德，有可取也。上帝之德固厚，而吾人亦具有至德；上帝固具無量能，而吾人心亦能應萬事。試觀先聖調元開物，立教明倫，養民以耕鑿機杼，利民以舟車財貨，其肇基經世，垂萬世不易之鴻猷，而天下永賴以安，未聞蔑先聖而上帝自作自樹，以臻至治。由是論之，人之德能，雖上帝罔或踰焉。詎云叔造天地獨天主能乎？

211 世不達己心之妙，而曰心局身界之內；佛氏見其大，不肯自屈，則謂：「是身也，與天地萬物咸蘊乎心。」是心無遠不逮，無高不升，無廣不括，無細不入，無堅不度，故具識根者宜知：方寸間儼居天主；非天主，寧如是耶？

Spiritual Beings and the Human Soul

210. *The Chinese scholar says:* The Buddha is not inferior to the Sovereign on High: he places great value on man and esteems the virtue of man. There is much that one can learn from him. The virtue of the Sovereign on High is undoubtedly profound, but we men are possessed of supreme virtue too. The Sovereign on High is assuredly imbued with immeasurable capabilities, but men's minds are also able to deal with all things in the world. Just look at the sages of ancient times: they regulated the vital energies, opened up all things, established teachings, expounded ethics, invented the tilling of the land and the weaving of cloth for the nurture of the people, and they built boats and vehicles, amassed wealth, and transported goods for the benefit of the people. They laid a good foundation, winning eternal ease with one supreme effort, and handing down a great unchanging plan to ten thousand successive generations so that the world might long enjoy peace and tranquillity. I have never heard it said that the Sovereign on High neglected these sages of the past and that he established everything by Himself to the point where He exercised supreme control. Since this is the case, even the Sovereign on High has no way of transcending man's virtue and ability. Who said that the creation of heaven and earth is the work of the Lord of Heaven alone?

211. Because people in this world do not understand the extraordinary power of their own minds they say that the mind is confined within the boundaries of the body. Seeing the greatness of the mind the Buddha was unwilling to submit to any external force and asserted that the body together with heaven and earth and all phenomena are stored within the mind. Only the mind is free to go wherever it wishes; to ascend to any height; to embrace everything no matter what its size; to penetrate anything, no matter how small, and to cross anything, no matter how substantial. Thus, anyone with a foundation of knowledge ought to know that

212 西士曰：佛氏未知己，奚知天主？彼以眇眇躬受明于天主，偶畜一材、飭一行，矜誇傲睨，肆然比附于天主之尊，是豈貴吾人身、尊吾人德？乃適以賤人喪德耳。傲者諸德之敵也，一養傲於心，百行皆敗焉。

213 西士聖人有曰：「心無謙而積德，如對風堆沙。」聖人崇謙讓；天主之弗讓，如遜人何哉？其視聖人，翼翼乾乾，畏天明威，身後天下，不有其知，殆天淵而水火矣。聖人不敢居聖，而令恒人擬天主乎？

214 夫德基于修身，成于事上帝。周之德必以事上帝為務；今以所當凜然敬事者而曰吾與同焉，悖何甚乎？

辯釋鬼神及人魂異論，而解天下萬物不可謂之一體

34 St. Gregory the Great, *In Evangelia*, I, 7, 4.

Spiritual Beings and the Human Soul

the mind, no greater than a square inch in size, is indwelt by the Lord of Heaven. If it were not the Lord of Heaven, how could it be as it is?

212. *The Western scholar says:* The Buddha failed to understand himself, so how could he understand the Lord of Heaven? He, in his small body, was illumined by the light of the Lord of Heaven; but, happening to be possessed of some talent, and having been given a task to perform, he became boastful and arrogant, and recklessly, and with no inhibitions whatsoever, considered himself to be as worthy of honor as the Lord of Heaven. Can such behavior be regarded as raising our value or as honoring our virtue? Rather is it to cheapen man and to cause him to lose his virtue! Arrogance is the enemy of all virtue. The moment an arrogant thought is conjured up in our minds, all our conduct is corrupted.

213. A sage in the West once said that if the mind is devoid of humility any attempt to accumulate virtue is as impossible as trying to heap up sand before a wind.[34] The sage emphasizes humility; if a person refuses to yield to the Lord of Heaven, is he likely to show any humility towards men? The difference between such a person and a sage who is careful and discreet; who stands in awe of the spirits; who places himself after everyone else in the world, and who does not boast of his own knowledge is as great as the distance between the sky and the ocean depths and the difference between water and fire. A sage does not dare regard himself as a sage; would he then compare a common man with the Lord of Heaven?

214. Virtue is founded on self-cultivation, and its fulfilment on the service of the Sovereign on High. Thus, the virtue of the Chou dynasty undoubtedly considered the service of the Sovereign on High as its prime duty. To say that the Sovereign on High, who was originally deserving of respectful service, is now on an equal footing with ourselves is just too absurd and irrational for words!

215 至於裁成庶物,蓋因天主已形之物而順材以成之,非先自無物而能創之也;如製器然,陶者以金,斲者以木,然金木之體先備也,無體而使之有體,人孰能之?人之成人,循其性而教之,非人本無性而能使之有性也。

216 若夫天主造物,則以無而為有,一令而萬象即出焉。故曰無量能也,於人大殊矣。且天主之造物也,如硃印之印楮帛,楮帛之印非可執之為印,斯乃印之蹟耳。人物之理皆天主蹟也,使欲當之原印而復以印諸物,不亦謬乎?

217 智者之心含天地、具萬物,非真天地萬物之體也。惟仰觀俯察,鑑其形而達其理,求其本而遂其用耳,故目所未睹,則心不得有其像。若止水、若明鏡影諸萬物,乃謂明鏡、止水均有天地即能造作之,豈可乎?

辯釋鬼神及人魂異論,而解天下萬物不可謂之一體

210

215. As to your comment that man can create things, the fact is that anything manufactured by man is achieved through things already created by the Lord of Heaven. They are made out of ready-made material and are not created out of what was originally non-existent. It is like the manufacturing of implements: The metal-worker uses metals and the carpenter uses timber, but the metals and the timber are all ready-made materials. Who among men can cause materials to exist where they do not already exist? The reason why a man can bring other men to maturity is that they have human natures which can be instructed; it is not because one can make human natures for men devoid of such natures.

216. When we come to the creation of all things by the Lord of Heaven, however, we find that He caused what was non-existent to exist. With one word of command all things were created. He is therefore said to be all-powerful and is very different from man. Moreover, the creation of all things by the Lord of Heaven is like the making of an imprint with a crimson seal. The seal on the paper cannot be used to seal anything else because it is no more than the imprint of the seal. Rationality in man is an imprint of the Lord of Heaven. Is it not therefore a great mistake to try to treat it as an original seal and to seek to make an imprint on other things?

217. The fact that the minds of wise men can embrace heaven, earth, and all phenomena does not imply that the real heaven, earth, and all phenomena are held in their minds. All that is meant is that having raised one's head in personal investigation and then bowed oneself in contemplation, one mirrors their forms and comprehends their principles, and that having investigated their principles one can put them to practical use. Thus, if there is nothing for the eyes to see, no impression is made on the mind. For example, a pool of pure, still water or a brightly polished mirror can reflect all the things in the world; but can one say that the bright mirror or the still water can create heaven and earth because they reflect them?

辯釋鬼神及人魂異論，而解天下萬物不可謂之一體

218 必言顧行乃可信焉。天主萬物之原，能生萬物。若人即與之同，當亦能生之，然誰人能生一山一川于此乎？

219 中士曰：所云生天地之天主者，與存養萬物天上之天主者，佛氏所云「我」也。古與今，上與下，無間焉，蓋全一體也。第緣四大沈淪昧晦，而情隨事移，「真元」曰鑿，「德機」曰弛，而「吾」、天主并溺也；則吾之不能造養物，非本也，其流使然耳。夜光之珠，以蒙垢而損厥值，追究其初體，昉可為知也。

220 西士曰：吁，咈哉！有是毒唾，而世人競茹之，悲歟。非淪昧之極，孰敢謂萬物之原、天地之靈為物淪昧乎哉？夫人德堅白，尚不以磨涅變其真體；物用凝固，不以運動失其常度；至大無偶、至尊無上，乃以人生幻軀能累及而污惑之？是人斯勝天，欲斯勝理，神為形之役，情為性之根，于識

35 *Ti-yüan-szu-ta* (第緣四大): love, hate, anger, and fear. See above, page 108, n. 24.

Spiritual Beings and the Human Soul

218. Words and facts must accord with each other before they can be believed. The Lord of Heaven is the source of all things and He can produce all things. If He and man are the same, then men also ought to be able to produce all things. But who can produce a mountain or a river in this place?

219. *The Chinese scholar says:* The so-called Lord of Heaven who produces heaven and earth and the Lord of Heaven who is in Heaven and who preserves and nurtures all things is what the Buddha called the "self." From ancient to modern times this "self" has existed continuously because it is entirely one in essence. But because of the four basic emotions,[35] man is sunk in darkness and his circumstances have changed accordingly. Day by day his vital spirit is whittled away, and day by day his springs of virtue are weakened, and the "self" and the Lord of Heaven decay together. Thus, the fact that we cannot create and nurture all things is not a true indication of our original capabilities. Our present state is due to the process of decay. It is because the luminescent pearl is obscured by filth that it cannot shine forth and its value is diminished. One has to search out its original state before one can know its true brilliance.

220. *The Western scholar says:* Alas! It is sad indeed that men should vie with each other to swallow such poison. Unless he were totally sunk in darkness, who would dare say that the Source of all things—the most spiritual and intelligent thing in heaven and earth—has been obscured by things? If a man's virtue can be so resolute and unsullied that his character cannot be changed by persecution, and if a material thing is so solid that its condition cannot be altered despite its being moved about, yet He who is supremely great and deserving of supreme honor can be inconvenienced and sullied by man's physical body, then man will have triumphed over Heaven, and desire will have conquered reason; spirit will have become the slave of matter, and the emotions will have become the root of human nature. Anyone capable of understand-

辯釋鬼神及人魂異論，而解天下萬物不可謂之一體

本末者，宜不喻而自解矣。且兩間之比，孰有踰於造物者，能圍之，陷之于四大之中，以昧溺之乎？

221 夫天上之天主，於我既共一體，則二之澄徹混淆無異焉。譬如首上靈神於心內靈神同為一體也，故適痛楚之遭、變故之值，心之神鈞混淆馬，必不得一亂一治之矣。今吾心之亂，固不能混天上天主之永攸澄徹，又不免我心之混淆，則吾於天主非為一體，豈不驗乎？

222 夫曰天主與物同：或謂天主即是其物，而外無他物；或謂物為天主所使用，此三言皆傷理者，吾逐逐辯之也。

223 其云天主即是各物，則宇宙之間雖有萬物，當無二性，既無二性，是無萬物，豈不混淆物理？況物有常情，皆欲自全，無欲自害，如水滅火，火焚木，大魚食小魚，強禽吞弱禽，既天主即是各物，豈天主自為戕害而不及一存護乎？然天主無可戕害之理，

Spiritual Beings and the Human Soul

ing the truth about things will recognize the illogicality of such assertions even before they are explained to him. Moreover, who in this world can transcend the Lord of creation? Do you mean to say that He can be kept within the confines of the four basic emotions, and thus suffer obscuration?

221. If the Lord of Heaven (in Heaven), and I are organically one, then it will be impossible to distinguish the clear from the confused. For example, the spirit in a man's head and the spirit in his heart both share the one body so that when the man experiences pain or change both the spirit in his head and the spirit in his heart feel disturbed and confused. It is impossible for the one to be confused and not the other. But the confusion in my mind at the present time cannot trouble the eternal clarity of the Lord of Heaven in Heaven, and his eternal clarity does not rid me of the confusion in my mind. Is it not therefore true to claim that I and the Lord of Heaven do not share one and the same body?

222. To assert that the Lord of Heaven and all things are the same; or that the Lord of Heaven is all things, and that apart from the Lord of Heaven there is nothing; or that the Lord of Heaven is within all things, and is one internal constituent of all things; or that all things are there for the Lord of Heaven to use as instruments and tools are there for craftsmen to use, is to distort the truth, and I shall now proceed to explain why.

223. If you say that the Lord of Heaven is each and every thing, then, although there are many kinds of things in the universe, there ought only to be one nature; but if there were only one nature, there could be no variety of things. Have you not created confusion among the principles of things? Further, all things have one thing in common: they all seek for self-preservation and have no desire to harm themselves. Yet when I look upon the things of this world I find that they do indeed harm each other and destroy each other; water, for example, extinguishes fire; fire burns wood; big fish eat little fish, and strong beasts devour weak beasts. If the Lord

224 從是說也,吾身即上帝,吾祭上帝即自為祭耳,豈無是禮也。果爾,則天主可謂木石等物,而人能耳順之乎?

225 其曰天主為物之內本分,則是天主微乎物矣。外者包乎內。凡全者,皆其大于各分者也。斗大于升,升乃斗十分之一耳。若天主在物之內為其本分,則物大于天主,而天主反小也;萬物之原乃小乎其生之物,其然乎?豈其然乎?

226 且問天主在人內分,為尊主歟?為賤役歟?為賤役而聽他分之命固不可也;如為尊主而專握一身之柄,則天下宜無一人為惡者,何為惡者滋眾耶?天主為善之本根,德純無渣,既為一身之主,猶致敵於私欲,欲為邪行,德何衰耶?

辯釋鬼神及人魂異論,而解天下萬物不可謂之一體

216

of Heaven is every kind of thing, does this mean that the Lord of Heaven sets out to harm Himself and refrains from protecting Himself? But there is no principle whereby the Lord of Heaven harms Himself.

224. Further, according to this way of putting things, my body is the Sovereign on High, and when I sacrifice to the Sovereign on High I am sacrificing to myself. There can surely be no such rite as this! If what you say really is true, then the Lord of Heaven can be said to be on an equal footing with wood and stone and the like. Does this sound pleasing to the ear?

225. If you insist that the Lord of Heaven is an internal constituent of things, then the Lord of Heaven must be regarded as smaller than things since the whole is greater than its parts. A pint is only one tenth of a bushel and the bushel is therefore larger than the pint. What is external embraces what is within. If the Lord of Heaven is within things and is a portion of these things, these things are larger than the Lord of Heaven and the Lord of Heaven is reduced to size. Is it possible for the source of all things to be smaller than the things He has created? How can it be possible?

226. Let me further ask you: If the Lord of Heaven is merely an element within man, is He lord or servant? It is certainly not fitting that He should be a servant obedient to the commands of other elements. On the other hand, if He is the honored lord in man and exercises authority over his whole body, then there ought not to be a single evil-doer in the world. How is it, then, that there are still so many evil men? Because the Lord of Heaven is the root of all goodness, His virtue is perfectly whole and is lacking in nothing. If He is the lord of the whole body and yet suffers the obscuration of selfish desires and gives free rein to evil conduct, does this mean that His virtue has suffered a decline?

227 當其制作乾坤，無為不中節，美今司一身之行，乃有不守戒者，不能乎？不識乎？不思乎？不肯乎？皆不可謂也。

228 其曰物如軀殼，天主使用之若匠者使用其器械，則天主尤非其物矣。石匠非其鑿，漁者非其網，非其舟。天主非其物，何謂之同一體乎？循此辯焉，其說謂萬物行動不係於物，皆天主事，如機器之事皆使機器者之功：夫不曰耜來耕田，乃曰農夫耕之；不曰斧劈柴，乃曰樵夫劈之；不曰鋸斷板，乃曰梓人斷之。

229 則是火莫焚，水莫流，鳥莫鳴，獸莫走，人莫騎馬乘車，乃皆惟天主者也。小人穴壁踰牆，禦旅于野，非其罪，亦天主使之罪乎？何以當惡怨其人，懲戮其人乎？為善之人亦悉非其功，何為當賞之乎？亂天下者，莫大於信是語矣。

辯釋鬼神及人魂異論，而解天下萬物不可謂之一體

227. When He first created heaven and earth there was nothing that was not regulated. Is there something which He does not regulate, now that He exercises control over the conduct of the body? Further, the Lord of Heaven is the source of all rules of moral conduct. If conduct not in keeping with these rules should develop, is this because there is nothing He can do about it, that He knows nothing about it, that He does not think about it, or that He is unwilling to stop it? Not at all.

228. If, however, you assert that things are like bodies and that the Lord of Heaven makes use of them as a craftsman makes use of tools and mechanical applicances, then the Lord of Heaven is even less to be equated with all things. A stone mason is not the chisel he uses, and a fisherman is not his net or his boat. If the Lord of Heaven is not the things He has created, how can one then go on to say that He is organically one with them? According to this kind of explanation, there is no need for things to take responsibility for their own actions since their actions are all performed by the Lord of Heaven, just as the performance of implements and tools is referred back to the one who uses them. One does not say that a hoe ploughs the land but that a farmer ploughs his fields; one does not say that an axe splits wood, but that a wood-cutter chops firewood; one does not say that a saw severs a wooden plank, but that a carpenter cuts a wooden plank in two.

229. Therefore it is not fire which burns, it is not water which flows, it is not birds that sing, it is not beasts that walk, it is not men who ride horses and travel in carriages; in all these instances it is the one and only Lord of Heaven doing all these things. The inferior man digs tunnels and clambers over walls and forcibly robs travellers in the wilds, but none of these actions are his crimes, since it is again the Lord of Heaven who causes him to commit crime. But why then should one loathe and resent such people, punishing and putting them to death? If good works too may not be attributed to the men who perform them, why should they be rewarded for

辯釋鬼神及人魂異論，而解天下萬物不可謂之一體

230 且凡物不以天主為本分，故散而不返歸于天主，惟歸其所結物類爾矣。如物壞死而皆歸本分，則將返歸天主，不謂壞死，乃益生全，人亦誰不悅速死以化歸上帝乎？孝子為親厚置棺槨，何不令考妣速化為上尊乎？

231 嘗證天主者，始萬物而制作之者也。其性渾全成就，物不及測，則謂之同？

232 吾審各物之性善而理精者，謂天主之迹可也，謂之天主則謬矣。試如見大跡印於路，因驗大人之足曾過于此，不至以其跡為大人。觀畫之精妙，慕其畫者曰高手之工，而莫以是為即畫工。

220

Spiritual Beings and the Human Soul

them? Nothing is more calculated to bring confusion into the world than belief in such teaching.

230. If the Lord of Heaven is not regarded as a constituent of all things, then, when they are eventually destroyed, they will not return to the Lord of Heaven but only to those categories of matter to which they belong. If on the other hand, the Lord of Heaven is regarded as a constituent of all things, then, when they die and are destroyed, they will return to the Lord of Heaven. They ought not, therefore, to be spoken of as dead but as things which have obtained perfect life. If this is the case, who would not wish to die as soon as possible so that he might be transformed into, and return to the Sovereign on High? Filial sons make strong, thick coffins for their parents when they die. Why do this and thus prevent their parents obtaining an early transformation into Him who is Supremely Honored?

231. [In the first section of this work] I proved that the Lord of Heaven is the creator and controller of all things; that His nature is perfect and lacking in nothing, and that He cannot be measured by the things in this world. One can hardly say, then, that all things share a common body with Him!

232. We know that the natures of every kind of thing are good and that their principles are fine. One may speak of them, therefore, as traces of the Lord of Heaven; but to say that they are the Lord of Heaven is wrong. For example, when one sees the imprint of the foot of a great man on the road, one can regard this as proof that the foot of the great man has passed this way, but one would not equate the foot-print with the body itself of the great man. When one looks at a fine painting, one admires the painter and praises his skill and craftsmanship, but one does not for this reason confuse the painting with the painter.

233 天主生萬森之物，以我推徵其原，至精極盛，仰念愛慕，無時可釋。使或泥于偏說，忘其本原，豈不大誤？

234 夫誤之原非他，由其不能辨乎物之所以然也。所以然者，有在物之內分者，則在物之外分矣。

235 第其在物，且非一端：或在物如在其所，若人在家、在庭焉；或依賴之在自立者，如白在馬為白馬，寒在冰為寒冰馬；或在物如所以然之在其已然，若日光之在其所照水晶焉，火在其所燒紅鐵焉。

236 以末揆端，可云天主在物者耶。如光雖在水晶，火雖在鐵，然而各物各體本性弗雜，謂天主之在物如此，固然所妨也。

辯釋鬼神及人魂異論，而解天下萬物不可謂之一體

222

233. The Lord of Heaven produced all things, and when we carefully trace things to their source we find it to be supremely fine and great, and we can only look up to it in unceasing admiration. Is it not a great mistake to adopt a bigoted and narrow opinion of the Lord of Heaven and thus to forget the true and original source of creation?

234. The reason why men have a mistaken understanding of the source of creation is that they cannot comprehend why things are as they are. The reasons for things being as they are include those inherent in things, such as the principles of *Yin* and *Yang,* and those external to things, such as the active cause, and the rest. The Lord of Heaven who created all things is the universal active cause of all things, so He must be external to all things.

235. There is more than one way to describe the Lord of Heaven's relationship to all things: (1) He can be said to be in things in the sense that He resides in them in the way that a man resides in his home. (2) He can be said to be a part of things, just as a hand or foot is part of the body or the *Yin* and *Yang* principles are part of a person. (3) He can be said to stand in relation to a thing as an accident stands in relation to a substance. This is like the whiteness in a horse, which makes that horse a white horse, or coldness in ice, which makes it cold ice. (4) He can be said to be in things, as a cause resides in its effects, or as the light of the sun is found within the crystal on which it shines, or as fire resides in iron red with burning.

236. Because one can infer a cause from its effects, one can say that the Lord of Heaven is in things. Although light is in the crystal and fire within the iron, nevertheless, each has its own substance, and each its own nature which cannot be confused with any other. There is certainly no reason why one should not speak of the Lord of Heaven residing in things in this fashion.

辯釋鬼神及人魂異論，而解天下萬物不可謂之一體

237 但光可離水晶，天主不可離物。天主無形而無所不在，不可截然分而別之。故謂全在於所，可也；謂全在各分，亦可也。

238 中士曰：聞明論，先疑釋矣。有謂人於天下之萬物皆一，如何？

239 西士曰：以人為同乎天主，過尊也；以人與物一，謂人同乎土石，過卑也。由前之過，懼有人欲為禽獸；由今之過，懼人不欲為土石。夫率人類為土石，子從之乎？其不可信，不難辯矣。

240 寰宇間，凡為同之類者，多矣：或有異物同名之同，如柳宿與柳樹是也[36]；或有同群之同，如一寮之羊皆為同群，一軍之卒皆為同軍是也；或有同理之同，如根、泉、心三者相同，蓋若根為百枝之本，泉為百派之源，心為百脈之由是也。此三者姑謂之同，而實則異。

36 In Chinese the tones of "willow star" and "willow tree" are similar, "*liu-hsiu*" (柳宿) and "*liu-shu*" (柳樹), but their characters are different.

224

Spiritual Beings and the Human Soul

237. But light can divorce itself from crystal, whereas things cannot separate themselves from the Lord of Heaven. The Lord of Heaven is without bodily form and is omnipresent. Nothing can be separated from Him or leave Him. Therefore one can say that the whole resides in the whole body of things, and that the whole resides in each part.

238. *The Chinese scholar says:* Now that I have heard your brilliant exposition, any doubts that I had in the past have all been dispelled. But there are some people who say that man is an organic unity with all things in the world. What do you say to that?

239. *The Western scholar says:* To regard man as being the same as the Lord of Heaven is to esteem him too highly; but to regard man as being one with all things is to say that he is the same as clay and stone, in which case he is being abased. Because the former view rates man too highly, I fear there are some who wish to treat him as an animal. Because [these people] overstate man's lowliness, I should imagine there are some who are anxious not to regard him as clay or stone. Would you, Sir, agree to mankind being regarded as falling within the category of clay and stone? It is not difficult to show that this kind of argument is untenable.

240. In the universe many things are alike: there are things which do not fall within the same category, the names of which, however, are similar, as, for example, the "willow star" and "willow tree."[36] Then there is the word *"chün"* (flock). If you gather a large number of people together they will form a flock, just like a pen of sheep; and an army of soldiers all form a *"chün"* (army). Then there are things the meanings of which are similar such as the root of a tree, a spring and the heart. The root of a tree is the basis of a large number of branches; a spring is the source of many rivers, and the heart is the center of a whole complex of veins. These three kinds of things may all be said to be similar; but, in reality, each is different.

辯釋鬼神及人魂異論，而解天下萬物不可謂之一體

241 或有同宗之同，如鳥獸通為知覺，列于各類是也；或有同類之同，如此馬與彼馬共屬馬類，此人與彼人共屬人類是也。此二者略可謂之同矣。

242 或有同體之同，如四肢與一身同屬一體焉；或其名不同而實則同，如放勳、帝堯二名總為一人焉。茲二者乃為真同。

243 夫謂天下萬物皆同，于此三等何居？

244 中士曰：謂同體之同也。曰：君子，以天下萬物為一體者也；間形體而分爾我，則小人矣。君子一體萬物非由作意，緣吾心仁體如是。豈惟君子，雖小人之心亦莫不然。

37 The opening words of the "Canon of Yao" assert that Ti Yao (帝堯), or the emperor Yao, was called Fang Hsün (放勳). See *The Chinese Classics*, vol. III, p. 15.
38 This is a Buddhist point of view.
39 This was a common tenet of Chinese scholars in the time of Ricci.

241. Next there are things which are similar in the sense that they belong to the same family, as, for example, birds and beasts, both of which possess awareness, and both of which fall into the category of things having awareness. Then there are things which are similar in the sense that they are of the same category as, for instance, this horse and that horse which, though different, both belong to the category "horse," and this person and that person, both of which belong to the "human" category. These two kinds of things can be said to be similar.

242. Then there are things which are similar in the sense that they share the same body as, for example, the four limbs in their relationship to one body—all similarly belonging to one body. Or one may have a situation in which names are dissimilar, yet that to which they refer is in fact the same, as, for instance, the two names Fang Hsün and Ti Yao,[37] both of which refer to one man. These two kinds of things can be said to be examples of genuine similarity.

243. To which of the three kinds of similarities mentioned above does the statement "All things in the world are the same" belong?

244. *The Chinese scholar says:* The "similarity" to which that statement belongs is the "similarity of belonging to one body." The superior man sees all things in the world as being organically one. It is the inferior man who distinguishes between bodily forms and divides you from me. When a superior man asserts that all things are organically one, he is not thinking in terms of creation;[38] what he means is that he is showing consideration to all things with his sense of humanity.[39] This is the case not only with superior men but also with inferior persons.

245 西士曰：前世之儒借萬物一體之說，以翼愚民悅從于仁，所謂一體，僅一原耳已。如信之為真一體，將反滅仁義之道矣。何為其然耶？仁義相施必待有二；若以眾物實為一體，則是以眾物實為一物，而但以虛像為之異耳，彼虛像焉能相愛相敬哉？故曰為仁者推己及人也。

246 仁者以己及人也，義者人老老、長長也，俱要人己之殊；除人己之殊，則畢除仁義之理矣。設謂物都是己，則但以愛己、奉己為仁義；將小人惟知自己，不知有人，獨得仁義乎？書言人己，非徒言形，乃兼言形性耳。

247 且夫仁德之厚在遠不在近。近愛本體，雖無知覺者亦能之。故水恒潤下，就濕處，合同類，以養存本體也；火恒升上，就乾處，合同類，以養全本性也。近愛所親，鳥獸亦能之，故有跪乳、反哺者；近愛己家，小人亦能之，故常有

辯釋鬼神及人魂異論，而解天下萬物不可謂之一體

245. *The Western scholar says:* The Confucians of former times made use of the assertion that all things are organically one to encourage the common people to put their sense of humanity into operation. What they meant when they used the expression "organically one" was simply that things emerge from one source. But, if you believe that all things really are organically one, then this will result in the destruction of the great Way of humanity and righteousness. And why should this be so? Because for humanity and righteousness to operate there must be at least two persons. If all things are really regarded as organically one, then that is to treat all things as if they were really one thing, and to say that the differences between them are mere empty images. If they are only empty images, how can there be mutual love and respect? Therefore it is said that he who treads the path of humanity extends it from himself to others.

246. Humanity is the extension of one's own feelings towards others; righteousness is the treatment of the old with respect and honor; but in both cases there must be a distinction between oneself and others. If there is no distinction between oneself and others there can be no principles of humanity and righteousness. If you say that all things are you, then humanity and righteousness will be equivalent to self-love and self-service; you will become an inferior man who is only aware of himself and knows nothing of anyone else, and who is aware of humanity and righteousness only as names. When books speak of the distinction between others and the self they are not only speaking of bodily forms, but of both bodily forms and their rational natures.

247. When we speak of the greatness of humanity it is in terms of what is distant and not of what is at hand. When we think of what is at hand, such as the love of one's own body, we find that even things devoid of awareness can accomplish this; thus, water always flows downwards, heading in the direction of places that are wet and congregating with its own kind in order to nurture and

辯釋鬼神及人魂異論，而解天下萬物不可謂之一體

苦勞行險阻、為竊盜以養其家屬者；近愛本國，庸人亦能之，故常有群卒致命以禦強寇奸宄者。

248 獨至仁之君子能施遠愛，包覆天下萬國而無所不及焉。君子豈不知我一體、彼一體，此吾家吾國、彼異家異國；然以為皆天主上帝生養之民物，即分當兼切愛恤之，豈若小人但愛己之骨肉者哉？

249 中士曰：謂以物為一體乃仁義之賊，何為中庸切「體群臣」於九經之內乎？

250 西士曰：體物以譬喻言之，無所傷焉；如以為實言，傷理不淺。中庸令君體群臣，君臣同類者也，豈草木瓦石皆可體耶？吾聞君子於物也，愛

40 See Chan, *A Source Book in Chinese Philosophy*, p. 105, and *The Chinese Classics*, vol. I, p. 408.

preserve itself. Fire always flies upwards, reaching for dry places and congregating with its own kind in order to nourish its basic nature. Birds and beasts are capable of loving their next of kin; there are therefore those which kneel to feed on their mother's milk, and those which feed and support their old, weak parents. Inferior people are capable of loving their own families and will frequently suffer the hardships of a difficult terrain in order to commit robbery, and thereby to care for members of their families. Ordinary people can love their fatherland, and many soldiers constantly sacrifice their lives to resist rapacious enemies.

248. But only superior men of the utmost humanity can extend their love to distant places so that it embraces all nations in the world and reaches everywhere. How can a superior man fail to know that he has one body and that another man has another body; that this is my family, my nation, and that that is someone else's family and someone else's nation whilst, at the same time, recognizing that all are men and things produced and nourished by the Lord of Heaven who is the Sovereign on High, and that he therefore has a duty to love and have compassion on all men. How can he be like the inferior man who merely loves his own kindred?

249. *The Chinese scholar says:* So the belief that all things are organically one is harmful to humanity and righteousness. Why is it that the *Doctrine of the Mean* lists "identifying oneself with [the welfare of] the whole body of officers"[40] among the nine standards by which the empire should be governed?

250. *The Western scholar says:* I have nothing against the expression "to identify with the body of things" if it is used in its figurative sense; but if you use it in its literal sense, you will be doing great violence to the meaning of the passage. The *Doctrine of the Mean* wants the ruler to sympathize with his ministers, implying that ruler and ministers belong to the same category. Can grass and trees, tiles and stones all be said to feel sympathy? I have heard it said that the superior man must show care but not humanity in

辯釋鬼神及人魂異論，而解天下萬物不可謂之一體

251 之弟仁，今使之於人為一體，必宜均仁之矣。

251 墨翟兼愛人，而先儒辯之為非；今勸仁土泥，而時儒順之為是，異哉！天主之為天地及其萬物，萬有繁然：或同宗異類，或同類異體，或同體異用；今欲強之為一體，逆造物者之旨矣。

252 物以多端為美，故聚貝者欲貝之多，聚古器者欲器之多，嗜味者欲味之多。令天下物均紅色，誰不厭之？或紅、或綠、或白、或青，日觀之不厭矣。如樂音皆宮，誰能聆之？乍宮、乍商、乍角、乍徵、乍羽，聞之三月食不知味矣。外物如此，內何不然乎？

253 吾前明釋各類以各性為殊，不可徒以貌異，故石獅與活獅貌同類異，石人與石獅貌異類同，何也？俱石類也。嘗聞吾先生解類體之情

41 The teachings of Mo Ti (墨翟) or Mo Tzu (墨子) represented the greatest challenge to Confucianism from the fifth to the third century B.C. See Chan, *A Source Book in Chinese Philosophy*, pp. 211-231.

42 See chapter 1, n. 18.

Spiritual Beings and the Human Soul

his dealings with non-intelligent things. To cause unintelligent things to become one body with men is to insist that everything be treated with humanity.

251. Mo Ti[41] loved all men impartially, and the early Confucians argued that he was wrong. If you now persuade people to treat earth and clay with humanity, present-day Confucians will be agreeing with Mo Ti—a very odd thing indeed. When the Lord of Heaven created heaven and earth and all things each had its own form and appearance, some things being of one kind, and some being of a different kind; some being of one kind but with different bodies, and some having similar bodies but with different functions. If you now insist that all things are organically one, you will be opposing the initial intentions of the creator.

252. The beauty of things rests in the fact that they are numerous and varied, and therefore a man who collects treasure desires many precious objects. The man who collects ancient vessels wants as many as he can get; a person who is fond of good food will want as many flavors as possible. If everything in the world were red everybody would loathe red things; but if things are red and green, white and blue, no one will weary of them even though they look at them every day. Who would want to listen to music if it were all on one note? But if the note *kung* is suddenly followed by *shang* and then by *chiao,* by *chih,* and by *yü*,[42] a man who hears this melody will cease to be aware of the flavors of his food for three months. If this is true of things outside the body, it is also true of things in the mind.

253. I have already clearly explained that every category of things ought to be distinguished on the basis of its nature, and that distinctions can not be made solely on the strength of external appearances. Thus, although a stone lion and a living lion have both the same external form, they really belong to different categories. Although a stone man and a stone lion have different external forms they are, in fact, in the same category. Why is this? Because they are both stone! I once heard my teacher explain the significance

曰：自立之類，同體者固同類，同類者不必同體。

254 又曰：同類者之行為皆歸全體，而并指各肢。設如右手能救助患難，則一身兩手皆稱慈悲；左手習偷，非惟左手謂賊，右手全體皆稱為賊矣。推此說也，謂天下萬物一體，則世人所為盡可相謂；跖一人為盜，而伯夷并可謂盜，武王一人為仁，而紂亦謂仁，因其體同而同之，豈不混各物之本行乎？

255 學士論物之分，或有同類，或有各體，連則同體也，相絕則異體也。若一江之水，何用駢衆物為同體？蓋物相既注之一勻中之水於江內之水惟可謂同類，豈仍謂同體焉？況天地萬物一體之論，簡上帝，混賞罰，除類別，滅仁義，雖高士信之，我不敢不詆焉。

43 Chih (跖) is the name of a well-known robber of ancient times; Po I (伯夷), on the other hand, was known for his virtue. King Wu (武王) was a founder of the Chou dynasty and is known for his humanity, whereas Chou (紂) was the last ruler of the Shang dynasty and is remembered for his evil ways.

辯釋鬼神及人魂異論，而解天下萬物不可謂之一體

234

Spiritual Beings and the Human Soul

of categories and bodies by saying that in the category of substances, those with similar bodies undoubtedly belonged to the same category, but that those which belonged to the same category did not necessarily belong to the same body.

254. [My teacher] also said that the actions of a single body do not only belong to the whole body, but also to each limb. If it is said that the right hand saved someone from disaster, then the whole body and both hands are said to be compassionate. If the left hand has become habituated to stealing, then not only is the left hand called a thief, but also the right hand and the whole body. But if you conclude from this that all things under heaven are organically one, then every man's actions in the world must be said to be the actions of everyone. Chih was a robber, so Po-I may also be called a robber; King Wu of the Chou dynasty practiced humanity, so Chou of the Shang dynasty may also be called humane.[43] To say that actions are the same merely because things have similar bodies is surely to confuse the essential actions of each individual thing.

255. When scholars discuss the differences between things they say that some have similar bodies and others do not. What need is there to unite all things in one body? Things which are connected with each other belong to the same body, but things which are unconnected have different bodies. It is like water in a river; so long as it is in the river it shares in the body of the river, but once it is poured into a ladle, the water in the ladle and the water in the river can only be said to fall into the same category. How can they still be said to form one body? If you obstinately persist in your assertion that heaven, earth, and all things are one body, then you are treating the Sovereign on High with disdain, and bringing confusion into the system of rewards and punishments. If you refuse to distinguish between categories you destroy humanity and righteousness. Even though scholars with high moral standards should believe in such a notion, I cannot but stand on my feet and denounce it.

256 中士曰：明論昭昭，發疑排異，正教也。人魂之不滅、不化他物，既聞命矣。佛氏輪廻六道、戒殺之說，傳聞聖教不與，必有所誨，望來日教之。

257 西士曰：丘陵既平，蟻垤何有？余久願折此，子所嗜聞，亦吾喜講也。

辯釋鬼神及人魂異論，而解天下萬物不可謂之一體

256. *The Chinese scholar says:* Your great exposition is very clear and is able to dispel doubt and explain the nature of strange theories. It is correct teaching. I have already received your instruction concerning the fact that the soul of man neither dies nor is destroyed and that it does not change into anything else. I understand that your honored religion does not agree with the teaching of Buddhism concerning reincarnation in the Six Directions, nor with its prohibitions against the taking of life. I am sure you have important views on this which I hope you will make known to me on another day.

257. *The Western scholar says:* I have already dealt with the most difficult subject of all, and these minor questions certainly pose no problem. I have long wished to deal with them, however, and if you are willing to listen, I shall certainly be happy to expound them for you.

第五篇

辯排輪廻六道、戒殺生之謬說，而揭齋素正志

258 中士曰：論人類有三般。一曰人之在世，謂生而非由前跡，則死而無遺後跡矣。一曰夫有前後與今三世也，則吾所獲福禍於今世，皆由前世所為善惡，吾所將逢於後世吉凶，皆係今世所行正邪也。

259 今尊教曰，人有今世之暫寄，以定後世之永居，則謂吾暫處此世，特當修德行善，令後世常享之。而以此為行道路，以彼為至本家；以此如立功，以彼如受賞焉。夫後世之論是矣；前世之論，將亦有從來乎？

1. The Six Directions of reincarnation are those of the hells, hungry ghosts, animals, malevolent nature spirits, human existence, and gods.

238

Chapter 5

REFUTATION OF FALSE TEACHINGS CONCERNING REINCARNATION IN THE SIX DIRECTIONS[1] AND THE TAKING OF LIFE, AND AN EXPLANATION OF THE TRUE MEANING OF FASTING.

258. *The Chinese scholar says:* There are three views concerning man. The first asserts that prior to a man's being born on earth he does not exist, and that therefore he is unable to leave anything of himself behind after he dies. The second view is that man has three existences: one prior to his birth, one following his death, and his present existence. Thus, the happiness or misfortune experienced by me in this life both stem from the good or evil deeds performed in my previous existence; and the fortune or misfortune I shall experience in the next life will be determined by the correctness or depravity of my actions in this life.

259. Now your revered religion teaches that a man has only a temporary existence in this life, and that this life determines his final dwelling place in the life to come. It therefore goes on to teach that while we are temporarily resident in this world, we ought to make a special point of cultivating our virtue and doing good so that we may enjoy happiness in the life to come. Man is born into this world to be a pilgrim, and his next life is a return to his native heath. This present world is the place in which he establishes his merit, and the next world is the place in which he is rewarded. You are certainly right about the life to come, but what is the source of the theory that there is a former existence?

辯排輪廻六道、戒殺生之謬說，而揭齋素正志

260 西士曰：古者吾西域有士，名曰閉他臥剌，其豪傑過人，而質樸有所未盡，常痛細民為惡無忌，則乘己聞名，為奇論以禁之，為言曰行不善者必來世復生有報，或產艱難貧賤之家，或變禽獸之類：暴虐者，變為虎豹；驕傲者，變為獅子；淫色者，變為犬豕；貪得者，變成牛驢；偷盜者，變作狐狸、豺狼、鷹鷂等物；每有罪惡，變必相應。君子斷之曰，其意美，其為言不免玷缺也，沮惡有正道，奚用棄正而從枉乎？

261 既沒之後，門人少嗣其詞者。彼時此語忽漏國外，以及身毒釋氏圖立新門，承此輪廻，加之六道，百端誑言，輯書謂經。數年之後，漢人至其國而傳之中國。此其來歷，殊無真傳可信、實理可倚，身毒微地也，未班上國，無文禮之教，無德行之風，諸國之史未之為有無，豈足以示普天之下哉？

2 "Pi-t'a-wo-la" (閉他臥剌 , Pythagoras), now more commonly rendered "Pi-ta-ke-la-ssu" (畢達哥拉斯).

3 Here Ricci errs because of his ignorance of the history of Buddhist theory. The theory of reincarnation did not come from Pythagoras but from the philosophy of ancient India.

4 It is possible that Ricci speaks this way about India because some Chinese of his time, just as some in preceding ages, thought little of Buddhism and of India.

260. *The Western scholar says:* In ancient times, in our Western region, there was a scholar called Pythagoras[2] who was a man of uncommon, heroic abilities, but who was not always as artless as he might have been. He loathed the unrestrained evil-doings of the inferior men of his own day, and taking advantage, therefore, of his personal fame, he created a strange argument to restrain them, insisting that those who did evil were bound to experience retribution when reborn in a subsequent existence: they might be born into a family engulfed in hardship and poverty or be transformed into an animal; tyrannical men would be changed into tigers and leopards; arrogant men into lions; the licentious into pigs and dogs; the avaricious into oxen and mules, and thieves and robbers into foxes, wolves, eagles, and other birds and beasts. The transformation was bound to correspond to the evil done. Other superior men criticized this teaching saying that, although the intention behind it was excellent, there were faults in the teaching itself. There was a true way which could curb evil, so what purpose was served by abandoning the true and following the distorted?

261. After the death of Pythagoras few of his disciples continued to hold his teaching. But just then the teaching suddenly leaked out and found its way to other countries. This was at the time when Sakyamuni happened to be planning to establish a new religion in India. He accepted this theory of reincarnation and added to it the teaching concerning the Six Directions, together with a hundred other lies, editing it all to form books which he called canonical writings.[3] Many years later some Chinese went to India and transmitted the Buddhist religion to China. There is no genuine record of the history of this religion in which one can put one's faith, or any real principle upon which one can rely. India is a small place, and is not considered to be a nation of the highest standing. It lacks the arts of civilization and has no standards of moral conduct to bequeath to posterity. The histories of many countries are totally ignorant of its existence. Could such a country adequately serve as a model for the whole world?[4]

262 中士曰：觀所傳坤輿萬國全圖，上應天度，毫髮無差，況又遠自歐邏巴書，信其淨土，甚有願蚤死以復生彼國者，良可笑矣。其國之陋如彼也，世人誤讀佛域，故其事恆未詳審；雖然，壤雖褊，人雖陋，苟所言之合理，從之無傷。

263 西士曰：夫輪迴之說，其逆理者不勝數也，茲惟舉四、五大端。

264 一曰：假如人魂遷往他身復生世界，或為別人，或為禽獸，必不失其本性之靈，當說記念前身所為；然吾絕無能記焉，幷無聞人有能記之者焉，則無前世明甚。

265 中士曰：佛老之書所載能記者甚多，則固有記之者。

辯排輪迴六道、戒殺生之謬說，而揭齋素正志

5 The Paradise of the West in which the Buddha Amitābha is lord.

242

Reincarnation, Killing, and Fasting

262. *The Chinese scholar says:* I have seen your "Map of the World and All Nations" and its contents accord precisely with the celestial degrees; there is not the slightest error in it. Moreover, you have personally come a great distance, from Europe to China, so that what you say about what you have seen and heard of the Buddha's country must certainly be reliable. Since India is such a mean and lowly nation, it really is laughable that people should mistakenly study Buddhist books, believe in Buddhism's Pure Land,[5] and even wish to enjoy an early death in order that they might be born again in that Land. We Chinese are not in the habit of travelling great distances to foreign lands, so that we are usually rather ignorant of events outside our nation. Nevertheless, although a place may be small and its people mean and lowly, there is no reason why one should not believe what they say, provided it is reasonable.

263. *The Western scholar says:* There is so much that is unreasonable in the theory of reincarnation that I would not be able to give you an exhaustive account of it. I shall simply refer to four or five major points, and you will see what I mean.

264. First, if a person dies and his soul is transferred to another body, becoming another person, a bird, or an animal when he is reborn into the world, he is bound to retain his original intelligence and ought to be able to remember his activities from his previous existence. But we absolutely cannot remember these things, and I have never heard of anyone who was able to remember them. It cannot be more obvious, then, that there is no so-called "former existence" prior to a man being born.

265. *The Chinese scholar says:* In the writings of Buddhism and Taoism there are many records of people who were able to remember events from their former existences, so there must be people who are able to remember such things.

266 西士曰：魔鬼欲誑人而從其類，故附人及獸身，詒云為某家子，述其家事，以徵其謬，則有之；記之者必佛老之徒或佛教入中國之後耳。萬方萬類生死眾多，古今所同，何為自佛氏而外，異邦異門雖齊聖廣淵，可記千卷萬句，而不克記前世之一事乎？人善忘，羹至忘其父母？幷忘己之姓名？獨其佛老之子弟以及畜類得以記而述之乎？夫詭談以欺市井，或有順之者；在英俊之士、辟雍庠序之間，當論萬理之有無，不笑且譏之，鮮矣。

267 中士曰：釋言人魂在禽獸之體，本依前靈，但其體不相稱，故泥不能達。

268 西士曰：在他人之身，則本體相稱矣，亦何不能記前世之事乎？吾昔已明釋人魂之為神也。夫神者行其本情，不賴于身，則雖在禽獸亦可以用本性之靈

辯排輪廻六道、戒殺生之謬說，而揭齋素正志

244

Reincarnation, Killing, and Fasting

266. *The Western scholar says:* The Devil wishes to deceive people so that they will follow him. He therefore attaches himself to the bodies of humans and animals, causing them to say that they are the sons of certain families and to give accounts of events in those families in order to prove his lies. Those mentioned in the records you refer to are bound to be disciples of the Buddha and Lao Tzu, or the records are bound to be of events subsequent to the transmission of Buddhism to China. In all places hosts of living creatures of every kind have come into existence and then died; why is it, then, that from ancient times until the present, although there have been numerous sages in countries with religions other than the Buddhist whose learning has been both broad and deep and who have been able to commit thousands of books and tens of thousands of words to memory, they have not been able to remember a single event from a former existence? Although people easily forget things, how could they forget their parents and their own names? Is it only the adherents of Buddhism and Taoism, and the animals, who are capable of remembering such things and of telling others about them? Perhaps there are some who will accept unfounded statements made to deceive the ignorant, but among the learned, and in the academies and schools where the existence or otherwise of all principles is debated, very few will find it possible not to ridicule such claims.

267. *The Chinese scholar says:* The Buddhists say that the human soul which attaches itself to an animal's body is, in fact, dependent on its former intelligence, but that because an animal's body does not exactly fit a human soul, the soul is circumscribed and therefore unable to express itself.

268. *The Western scholar says:* But when it was attached to the previous person's body it was in perfect harmony with it; why, then, was it still unable to remember events of a former existence? I have already explained that a man's soul is spirit, and a spirit, by its very nature, is not dependent on a body. This being the case,

辯排輪廻六道、戒殺生之謬說，而揭齋素正志

，何不能達之有？若果天主設此輪廻美醜之變，必以勸善而懲惡也，設吾弗明記前世所為善惡，何以驗今世所值吉凶，果由前世因？而勸乎？懲乎？則輪廻竟何益焉？

269 二曰：當上帝最初生人以及禽獸，未必定以有罪之人變之禽獸，亦各賦之本類魂耳。使今之禽獸有人魂，則今之禽獸魂與古之禽獸魂異，當必今之靈而古之蠢也。然吾未聞有異也，則今之魂與古者等也。

270 三曰：明道之士皆論魂有三品：下品曰生魂，此只扶所賦者生活長大，是為草木之魂；中品曰覺魂，此能扶所賦者生活長大，而又使之以耳目視聽，以口鼻啖嗅，以肢體覺物情，是為禽獸之魂；上品曰靈魂，此兼生魂、覺魂，能扶植長大及覺物情，而又俾所賦者能推論事物，明辨理義，是為人類之魂。

6 "Vegetative soul," "sentient soul," and "intelligence-soul" represent literal translations of the Chinese terms used by Ricci. See translations of the same terms in par. 133.

246

it should be able to use its natural intelligence even though it may be resident in a bird or an animal. How could it possibly be incapable of expressing itself? If the Lord of Heaven really did devise the transformations of reincarnation it must have been for the purpose of persuading people to do good, or to serve as a warning to evil-doers. If I do not clearly remember the good and evil I did in a former existence, how can I determine whether the good or evil fortune met with in this life really does stem from a former existence? Can this be called persuading people to do good or warning them against evil? What benefit, then, accrues from reincarnation?

269. Secondly, when the Sovereign on High first produced men and beasts, there was no need for men to be changed into animals because of sinning, and he therefore gave to each creature a soul which would accord with its own category. If there are now a number of animals to which human souls have become attached, then the souls of animals today are no longer the same as the souls of animals in ancient times, and animals today ought to be intelligent, whereas those of ancient times would be doltish. Yet, I have never heard that there is any difference; therefore, the souls of animals have remained the same from ancient times until the present.

270. Thirdly, all men of learning assert that there are three classes of souls: the lowest class is called the vegetative soul, and this kind of soul can only support the life and growth of that to which it has been given. This is the soul of grain and trees. The second class of soul is called the sentient soul. This kind of soul can support the life and growth of that to which it is given, but can also enable creatures to hear with their ears, to see with their eyes, to taste with their mouths, to smell with their noses, and to be aware of things with their limbs [through the sense of touch.] This is the soul of birds and animals. The highest soul is called the intelligence-soul.[6] This soul, together with the vegetative soul and sentient soul can aid the body in its growth, cause it to be aware

271　若令禽獸之魂與人魂一,則是魂特有二品,不亦紊天下之通論乎?凡物非徒以貌像定本性,乃惟以魂定之。始有本魂,然後為本性;有此本性,然後定於此類;既定此類,然後生此貌。故性異同,由魂異同焉;類異同,由性異同焉;貌異同,由類異同焉。

272　鳥獸之貌既異乎人,則類、性、魂豈不皆異乎?人之格物窮理無他路焉,以其表而徵其內,觀其現而達其隱。

273　故吾欲知草木之何魂,視其徒長大而無知覺,則驗其內特有生魂矣;欲知鳥獸之何魂,視其徒知覺而不克論理,則驗其特有覺魂矣;欲知人類之何魂,視其獨能論萬物之理,明其獨有靈魂矣。

辯排輪廻六道、戒殺生之謬說,而揭齋素正志

of things, and enable men to reason things out and to clarify the truth. This is man's soul.

271. If you now cause the animal and human souls to be the same, then there will only be two kinds of soul, and will this not introduce confusion into a universally accepted theory? The natures of most things are not only determined by their appearances, but by their souls, Only when it has its essential soul does a thing have its essential nature, and only when it has its essential nature can its category be determined. Only when the category of a thing has been determined does it develop its appearance and physical form. Therefore, differences or similarities in natures rest on differences or similarities of soul; differences or similarities of category rest on differences or similarities of nature, and differences or similarities of appearance depend on differences or similarities of category.

272. Since the appearances of birds and beasts are differrent from those of men, it follows that their categories, natures and souls are also different. There is no other way in which man can investigate things and probe exhaustively into their principles except to employ the external appearances of things as proof of their inner nature; to observe what is evident in things in order to understand their innermost secrets.

273. Thus, if we wish to know what kind of souls are possessed by grass and trees, we observe the fact that grass and trees are only capable of growth and are devoid of consciousness, and this provides proof that all they have within them is the vegetative soul. If we wish to know the nature of the souls of birds and beasts we observe the fact that they are only possessed of consciousness and are incapable of rational thought, and from this we know that they only possess the sentient soul. If we wish to know the nature of man's soul we notice the fact that man alone is able to understand the principles of all things, and from this we know that only he possesses an intelligence-soul.

274 理如是明也，而佛氏云禽獸魂與人魂同靈，傷理甚矣。吾常聞殉佛有謬，未嘗聞從理有誤也。

275 四曰：人之體態奇俊，與禽獸不同，則其魂亦異；譬匠人欲成椅桌必須用木，欲成利器必須用鐵，器物各異，則所用之資亦異。既知人之體態不同禽獸，則人之魂又安能與禽獸相同哉？

276 故知釋氏所云人之靈魂，或託於別人之身，或入於禽獸之體，而回生於世間，誠誑詞矣。夫人自己之魂只合乎自己之身，烏能以自己之魂，而合乎他人之身哉？又況乎異類之身哉？亦猶刀只合乎刀之鞘，劍只合乎劍之鞘，安能以刀合劍鞘耶？

277 五曰：夫云人魂變獸，初無他據，惟疑其前世淫行曾效某獸，天主當從而罰之，俾後世為此獸耳。然此非刑也；順其欲，孰謂之刑乎？

辯排輪廻六道、戒殺生之謬說，而揭齋素正志

274. These truths are so obvious, yet Buddhists perversely assert that the souls of birds and beasts are intelligent just as men's are—an assertion which is too irrational for words. I often hear it said that it is a mistake to follow the Buddha; I have never heard it said that it is a mistake to follow after truth.

275. Fourthly, man's bodily form is particularly handsome and different from those of birds and beasts; it follows, then, that his soul is also different. It is like the artisan who must use wood to manufacture a chair, and iron to manufacture a sharp implement. The objects are different, and consequently the material he uses is also different. Since we know that man's bodily form is different from those of the birds and beasts, how can man's soul be the same as the souls of birds and beasts?

276. From all this we know that the Buddhist teaching that men's souls are entrusted to the care of other persons' bodies, or that they are attached to the bodies of birds and beasts to be born again into the world, is a totally erroneous doctrine. Since a man's soul only harmonizes with his own body how can it be made to harmonize with someone else's body, or, even more, with the body of something in a different category? The sheath of a knife is only suitable for holding knives and a scabbard is only suitable for holding swords. How can one relate a knife to a scabbard?

277. Fifthly, there is, in fact, no evidence for the assertion that human souls are transformed into animals. The belief is simply due to perplexity as to whether a person in a former existence lived the wanton life of some animal or other and whether, in consequence, the Lord of Heaven is punishing him by causing him to be transformed into a certain kind of beast in his later existence. But this can hardly be termed punishment. Who would say that to be able to satisfy one's desires is punishment.

278 奸人之情，生平滅己秉彝，以肆行其所積內惡，而尚只痛其具人面貌，若有防礙，使聞後世將改其形容，而憑己流恣，詎不大快？如暴虐者常習殘殺，豈不欲身着利爪鋸牙，為虎為狼，晝夜以血污口乎？倨傲者習于欺人，不識遜讓，豈不樂長大其形，生為獅子，為眾獸之王乎？賊盜者以偷人財貨度活，何憂化為狐狸，稟百巧媚以盡其情乎？此等輩非但不以變獸為刑，乃反以為恩矣。天主至公至明，其為刑必不如是也。

279 如曰自人之貴類入獸之賤類卽謂之刑，吾意為惡之人却不自以生居人類為貴，大抵不理人道而肆其獸情，所羞者具此人面耳已，今得脫其人面而雜於獸醜，無恥無忌甚得志也。故輪廻之謊言蕩詞，於沮惡勸善無益，而反有損也。

Reincarnation, Killing, and Fasting

278. If an evil man spends his life destroying his own virtuous nature and gives free rein to the evil stored up in his mind, only regretting that his human appearance seems to offer some hindrance to the full implemenation of his desires, and if such a person should hear that in a later life he could change his form and thus indulge the wishes of his mind and give full rein to his passions, would this not cause him great contentment? Will not a cruel man who is habituated to slaughter be even happier if he can grow the sharp claws and saw-like teeth of tigers and wolves and if his mouth can run with blood night and day? An arrogant man is used to browbeating other men and knows nothing of humility or of yielding to others. Would such a person not be overjoyed if he were able to grow a large body, be born as a lion and be king of all the beasts? Robbers and thieves live by stealing and robbing others of their wealth and goods. Are they likely to grieve over being transformed into foxes and being able to rely on their cunning in order to follow their own natures? Such men would not only fail to regard transformation into an animal as a punishment, but they would even consider it a favor. The altogether just and wise Lord of Heaven could not employ punishments in this manner.

279. If you say that to descend from the honored category of man to the lowly category of beasts is a punishment, I can only say that anyone who practices evil is, to my mind, not likely to regard birth as a human being to be a thing of honor. The majority of such persons pay no heed to the way a man ought to behave to be a true man, and give free rein to their animal natures. The only difference between them and animals is that they have the appearance of man. If they could now rid themselves of their human looks and mingle with animals, engaging in ugly conduct, they would feel very satisfied indeed, since they would have no need of a sense of shame, and nothing would be taboo for them. I say, therefore, that the lies and dissolute talk concerning reincarnation are of no help whatsoever in restraining evil and encouraging goodness; on the contrary, they are positively harmful.

280 六曰：彼言戒殺生者，恐我所屠牛馬即是父母後身，不忍殺之耳。果疑于此，則何忍驅牛耕畎畝或駕之車乎？何忍羈馬而乘之路乎？吾意栽其親，與勞苦之於耕田，罪無大異也。栽其親，與恒加之以鞍而鞭辱之於市朝，又等也。然農事不可廢，畜用不可免，則何疑于戒殺之說？而云人能變禽獸，不可信矣。

281 中士曰：夫人魂能為禽獸者，誠誑語也，以欺無知小民耳，君子何以信吾騎馬為吾父母、兄弟、親戚、或君、或師、朋友乎？信之而忍為之，亂人倫；信之而不為之，是又廢畜養，而必使不用於世，人無所容手足矣。故其說不可信也。然，若但言輪廻之後復為他人，乃皆同類，亦似無傷。

282 西士曰：謂人魂能化禽獸，信其說則畜用廢；謂人魂能化他人身，信其說將使夫婚姻之禮與夫使令之役皆有窒礙難行者焉。何者？爾所娶女子，誰知其

辯排輪廻六道、戒殺生之謬說，而揭齋素正志

254

Reincarnation, Killing, and Fasting

280. Sixthly, the rules forbidding the taking of life are due to the fact that people are fearful lest the oxen and horses they slaughter are later incarnations of their parents, and they cannot bear to kill them. But if this is the case, how can they bear to yoke oxen to the plough to till their fields, or to harness them to carts? How can they bear to place a halter on a horse and ride on it? In my view there is not too great a difference between the crime of killing one's relations and the crime of making them labor in the fields. Killing one's relations and causing them to be constantly in harness and cruelly humiliating them by beating them with whips in the business quarters of cities are equally heinous. But farming cannot be abandoned, neither can the use of draught-animals be avoided. What further doubt can one have that the theory which forbids the killing of animals is absurd? It is obvious that the assertion that men can be tranformed into animals cannot be believed.

281. *The Chinese scholar says:* To say that the soul of man can be transformed into a bird or a beast is certainly to talk nonsense and to deceive the ignorant common people. How could a superior man believe that the horse he is riding is his own father, mother, brother, relative, king, teacher, or friend? If a person believed this and yet persisted in what he was doing, he would be introducing confusion into the rules governing human relationships; and if he desisted from what he was doing as a consequence of his belief, he would also have to stop rearing animals and cease making use of them; in fact there would be nothing to which such a man could apply either hands or feet. Thus, such a theory is untrustworthy. Nevertheless, if it were stated that in reincarnation a man was transformed only into another man, then he would remain in the same category, and no harm would ensue.

282. *The Western scholar says:* Belief in the view that the human soul can be transformed into a bird or beast results in the need to desist from making use of animals. To believe that the human soul can be transformed into another person means that there must

辯排輪廻六道、戒殺生之謬說，而揭齋素正志

283 中士曰：前言人魂不滅，是往者俱在也。有疑使無輪廻以銷變之，宇內豈能容此多鬼哉？

284 西士曰：疑此者，弗識天地之廣濶者也，則意若易充也；又弗通神之性態者也，以為其有充所也。形者在所，故能充于所；神無形，則何以滿其所乎？一粒之大，而萬神宅焉，豈惟往者，將來靈魂並容不礙也，豈用因是而為輪廻妄論哉？

285 中士曰：輪廻之說，自二氏出，吾儒亦少信之。然彼戒殺生者，若近於仁，天主為慈之宗，何為弗與？

非爾先化之母，或後身作異姓之女者乎？誰知爾所役僕、所署責小人，非或兄弟、親戚、君師、朋友後身乎？此又非大亂人倫者乎？總之，人旣不能變為禽獸，則亦不能變化他人，理甚著明也。

256

be hindrances to marriage and to the use of servants. And why? Who can tell whether the woman you take to be your wife is not a reincarnation of your mother who has become a daughter in a household of a different name? Who can tell whether the servant you use and the underling you abuse is not the reincarnation of your brother, relative, sovereign, teacher, or friend? Is this not again to introduce great confusion into the rules governing human relations? To sum up, since men cannot be tranformed into birds and beasts, it is obvious that they likwise cannot be transformed into other persons.

283. *The Chinese scholar says:* Previously you said that the soul of man is not destroyed and that the souls of the dead continue to exist. If there is no reincarnation to bring about their transformation, one may wonder how the universe can contain so many ghosts?

284. *The Western scholar says:* To be perplexed about this is to fail to realize the breadth of heaven and earth and to think that heaven and earth can easily be filled up. It is also to fail to understand the nature of spirit and to assume that it fills the place it is in. Things which have bodily form occupy space and can therefore fill the places they occupy. Spirit lacks bodily form, so how can it fill the place it occupies? A space the size of a seed can serve as the residence of ten thousand spirits, so that whether they be the souls of the departed or of those of the future, there is nothing to hinder their being all together in one place. Why should one have to manufacture a false doctrine of reincarnation to solve this problem?

285. *The Chinese scholar says:* The theory of reincarnation was created by two men, Pythagoras and the Buddha, and few of us Confucians believe in it. But the Buddhist prohibition against the taking of life seems to come very close to Confucian teaching concerning humanity. The Lord of Heaven is the source of compassion; is he likely, then, to be hostile to this?

286 西士曰：設人果變為禽獸，君子固戒殺小物如殺人比，彼雖殼貌有異，均是人也。但因信此誕說，朔望齋素以戒殺生，亦自不通。譬有人日日殺人而食其肉，且復歸依仁慈而曰：「朔望我不殺人，不食其肉。」但以餘日殺而食之，可謂戒哉？其心忍恣殺于二十八日，彼二日之戒何能增、何能減其惡之極乎？夫吾既明證無變禽獸之理，則并著無殺生之戒也。

287 試觀天主生是天地及是萬物，無一非生之以為人用者。夫日月星辰麗天以我照也，照萬色以我看也，生萬物以遂我用也。五色悅我目，五音娛我耳，諸味諸香之彙以甘我口鼻，百端輭煖之物以安逸我四肢，百端之藥材以醫療我疾病，外養我耳，內調我心。故我當常感天主尊恩，而時謹用之。

7 *Wu-se* (五色). See chapter 1, n. 17.
8 *Wu-yin* (五音). See chapter 1, n. 18.

辯排輪廻六道，戒殺生之謬說，而揭齋素正志

286. *The Western scholar says:* If people really were transformed into birds and beasts then the superior man ought, of course, to forbid the killing of small living creatures in the same way as the killing of humans is forbidden, because, although their external appearances are different, they would all be people. But when we turn to those who believe this false teaching, we find that they only refrain from killing living creatures when they fast and abstain on the first and fifteenth of the month. It is therefore patently an illogical doctrine. It is like a person who kills people daily and devours their flesh, but who then, wishing to join the camp of the compassionate, says: "I shall refrain from killing and eating people on the first and fifteenth of the month." On other days he continues to kill and eat people. Can this be called refraining from taking life? He can bear to take life on twenty-eight days of each month, so how can two days of prohibition add to or detract from his guilt as a taker of life? But since I have already proved that there is no truth [in the doctrine that man is] transformed into birds and beasts, it is clear that there is no need to forbid the taking of life.

287. Look at heaven and earth and all things created by the Lord of Heaven; there is not one of these things which is not produced for the use of man.

The sun, the moon, and the stars are suspended in the heavens to shed light on us, to illuminate all things so that we might observe them, and to nourish all things so that we may have them for our use. The Five Colors[7] give pleasure to our eyes; the Five Notes[8] bring enjoyment to our ears. Flavors and scents delight our mouths and noses, and every kind of thing which is soft and warm provides comfort for our four limbs. The varieties of medicinal herbs have been provided to cure our illnesses, healing our external bodies and repairing our inner minds. We ought therefore constantly to thank the Lord of Heaven for his graciousness, and constantly to be careful to make good use of his gifts.

辯排輪廻六道、戒殺生之謬說，而揭齋素正志

288 鳥獸或有毛羽皮革，可為裘履；或有寶牙角殼，可制奇器；或有妙藥，好治病疾；或有美味，能育吾老幼。吾豈不取而使之哉？借使天主不許人宰翕莩而付之美味，豈非徒付之乎？豈非誘人犯令，而陷溺之於罪乎？且自古及今，萬國聖賢咸殺生食葷，而不以此為悔，亦不以此為違戒，亦豈宜罪聖賢以地獄，而嘉與二三持齋無德之輩，擠之天堂乎？此無乃非達者之言歟！

289 中士曰：世界之物多有無益乎人，且害之者如毒蟲、蛇、虎、狼等。所言天主生萬物一一以為人用，似非然。

290 西士曰：物體幽眇，其用廣繁，故凡人或有所未能盡達，而反以見害，此自人才之蔽耳。

288. Birds and animals have feathers, fur, and hides which can be used to make winter clothing and shoes; they have ivory tusks from which can be made wonderful utensils or which can be used as marvellous medicines to cure sickness. Then, there are some animals with excellent flavors which can serve to nurture both old and young. Why should we not select what we want from among them and make use of them? If the Lord of Heaven does not permit men to kill animals for food, has he not endowed them with excellent flavors to no avail? Further, could it not be said that he has deliberately tempted man to break his commandments and caused them to commit a deadly crime? Moreover, from ancient times to the present, the sages or worthies of all nations have killed animals and eaten a diet of meat without displaying any need to repent and without regarding what they have done as contrary to any prohibition. Can one honestly say that sages and worthies have committed a crime, and that they ought to be consigned to Hell, whilst two or three people who lack virtue, but who have observed rules of abstinence, are to be commended and sent to Heaven? This is not the kind of argument one expects from wise men.

289. *The Chinese scholar says:* There are many things in the world which are not only of no benefit to man, but which are positively harmful to him, as, for example, poisonous insects and snakes, tigers, wolves, and the like. Your assertion that the Lord of Heaven created all things for man's use would seem to be untrue in certain instances.

290. *The Western scholar says:* Material bodies are mysterious and subtle, and their uses extensive and complicated; therefore, ordinary people may not be able completely to understand everything about them; they may in fact only see the harm they do. This is because man's talents have been clouded over.

辯排輪廻六道、戒殺生之謬説，而揭齋素正志

291 人固有二：曰外人，所謂身體也；曰內人，所謂魂神也。比此二者，則內人為尊。毒蟲、虎、狼險外人而寧內人，卒可謂益於人焉。夫傷身體之物，俗稱惡物，而其警我畏天主之怒，使知以天、以水、以火、以蟲皆能責人之犯命者。吾于是不得不戒懼，以時祈乞其助，時念望之，豈非內正人者之大資乎？

292 且天主悲惜小人之心全在於地，惟泥於今世而不知悝望天堂及後世高上事情，是以兼置彼醜毒于本界，欲極拔之焉。

293 況天主初立世界，俾天下萬物或養生，或利用，皆以供事我輩，原不為害，自我輩忤逆上帝，物始亦忤逆我，則此害非天主初旨，乃我自招之耳。

294 中士曰：天主生生者，必愛其生，而不欲其死，則戒殺生順合其尊旨矣。

262

Reincarnation, Killing, and Fasting

291. Man has two aspects: his body, which is external, and his soul, which is internal. When a comparison is made between these two aspects, the inner man is, of course, accorded greater honor. Poisonous insects, tigers, wolves, and the like, may harm the external man, and yet bring peace to the inner man, and may therefore be said to be of benefit to man. Things that harm the body are commonly said to be evil, but they can also serve to warn us of the need to fear the anger of the Lord of Heaven, causing man to realize that the weather, floods, fire, and poisonous insects can all be employed to punish those who offend against the commandments of the Lord of Heaven. Thus, men must ever be on the alert, and constantly beseech [the Lord of Heaven] for His support, remembering Him and yearning for Him. Are these not the greatest resources for the correction of the inner man?

292. Moreover, the Lord of Heaven regrets the fact that the minds of inferior men are entirely centered on this earth and are only concerned to accord with the things of this world, never yearning for Heaven or the superior things of the world to come. The Lord of Heaven has therefore permitted the existence of ugly, evil, poisonous, and harmful things in this world, His intention being to rescue and raise men by means of them.

293. Further, when the Lord of Heaven first established the world, He caused all things under heaven to contribute to the nurture of man's life or to be of benefit to him in some other way. His original intention was not that they should harm men. From the time we rebelled against the Lord of Heaven, things have reacted by rebelling against us. These harmful things, therefore, held no place in the Lord of Heaven's original intention; we have brought them on ourselves.

294. *The Chinese scholar says:* The Lord of Heaven is bound to want the things He has produced to live and not to die. A prohibition against the taking of life must surely accord with His honored will.

辯排輪廻六道、戒殺生之謬說，而揭齋素正志

295 西士曰：草木亦稟生魂，均為生類，爾曰取菜以茹，折薪以焚，而殘忍其命，必將曰：「天主生此菜薪以憑人用耳，則用而無妨。」我亦曰天主生彼鳥獸以隨我使耳，則殺之而使之以養人命，何傷乎？仁之範惟言：「無欲人加諸我，我勿加諸人耳。」不言勿欲加諸禽獸者。

296 且天下之法律但禁殺人，無制殺鳥獸者。夫鳥獸、草木與財貨並行，惟用之有節足矣。故孟軻示世主以「數罟不可入洿池」而「斧斤以時入山林」，非不用也。

297 中士曰：草木雖為生類，然而無血無知覺，是與禽獸異者也。故釋氏戕之而無容悲。

298 西士曰：謂草木為無血乎？是僅知紅色者之為血，而不知白者、綠者之未始非血也。夫天下形生者，必以養；而所以得養者，津液存焉。則凡津液

9 Analects, V, 11.
10 Chinese Classics, II, p. 130.

264

295. *The Western scholar says:* Grass and trees also possess a vegetative soul and belong to the category of living things; but each day you prepare vegetables for your meals and cut firewood for burning you are harming their lives. Yet you are bound to say: "The Lord of Heaven created these vegetables and firewood for man to use; therefore there can be no harm in using them." I must add that the Lord of Heaven created birds and beasts for us to use at will. What, then, can be wrong with slaughtering animals and using them to nourish man's life? Humanity is limited to the area covered by the saying: "What I do not want others to do to me, I have no desire to do to others."[9] It does not say that we should not do these things to animals.

296. Moreover, the laws of every country in the world only prohibit the killing of human beings; there is none which prohibits the killing of birds and beasts. Because birds, beasts, grass, and trees are to be grouped together with wealth and goods, all that is required is that they should be used economically. Thus, Mencius instructed the king of his own day not to cast close-meshed nets into the pools to catch fish, and to use axes to cut down trees on the hills only at fixed times.[10] He never prohibited the use of these things.

297. *The Chinese scholar says:* Although grass and trees fall into the category of living things, they have no blood and no awareness, and so are different from birds and beasts. Thus, Buddhists cut down vegetation without any feeling of pity.

298. *The Western scholar says:* You say that grass and trees have no blood because you are only aware of red blood. You do not know whether what is white or green might not after all be blood. All living things in the world must be nourished, and that by which they receive their nourishment is the liquid within them. Thus, every kind of liquid which flows through them is blood. Why must it always be red? If you try to observe prawns, crabs, and the like in water, you will find that many of them do not have red blood,

辯排輪廻六道、戒殺生之謬說，而揭齋素正志

299 之流貫皆血矣。何必紅者？試觀水族中，如蝦、如蟹，多無紅血，而釋氏弗茹，蔬菜中亦有紅液，而釋氏茹之不禁，則何其重愛禽獸之血，而輕棄草木之血乎？

且不殺知覺之物，以其能痛也已，我誠不欲其痛，寧獨不殺。卽勞之、役之，將有所不可。凡牛之耕野，馬之駿乘，未免終身之患，豈伊不長有痛乎？較殺之之痛止在一時者，又遠矣。

300 況禁殺牲；反有害於牲，蓋禽獸為人用，故人飼畜之而後，禽獸益蕃多也。如不得之以為用，人豈畜之乎？朝捐不急之官，飼畜之僕，黜無能之僕，而況畜類乎？西虜懼食豕，天下而皆西虜，則豕之種類滅矣。故愛之而反以害之，殺之而反以生之。是禁殺牲者，大有損于牧牲之道矣。

301 中士曰：如此則齋素無所用耶？

302 西士曰：因戒殺生而用齋素，此殆小不忍也。然齋有三志，識此三志，滋崇矣。

266

yet Buddhists refrain from eating them. Some vegetables, on the other hand, do have red liquid within them, yet Buddhists do not prohibit the eating of them. Why should [the Buddhists] assign such importance to the blood of animals and pay so little heed to the blood of grass and trees?

299. Moreover, it is said that one should not kill conscious creatures because they can experience pain. If we sincerely do not wish them to experience any pain, we should not only cease to slaughter them, but should also prohibit their being employed in any way. Every ox which tills the fields and every horse which draws a cart suffers in this fashion during the whole of its lifetime. Is this not to subject them to prolonged suffering? Is not the suffering they undergo greater than the momentary suffering they experience when slaughtered?

300. Further, to forbid the slaughter of animals is in fact harmful to animals. Because birds and animals are of use to men, men feed and rear them and they multiply speedily. If men are not permitted to use them, why bother to pasture them? The court gets rid of useless officials, and households cease to employ incompetent servants; how much more should this apply to animals? In the West there is a place where people are afraid to eat pork, and the result is that there is not a pig in the country. If the whole world were like that pigs would cease to exist. Thus, love for them results in harm, and the slaughter of them results in their proliferation. This is the truth concerning the prohibition of the slaughter of animals and the consequent great harm it does to the rearing of cattle.

301. *The Chinese scholar says:* In that case, fasting is useless, is it not?

302. *The Western scholar says:* If fasts are introduced on account of a prohibition against the slaughter of animals, then they represent no more than the smallest expression of pity. But, there

303

夫世固少有今日賢而先日不為不肖者也，少有今日順道而昔日未嘗違厥道者也。厥道者也，天主銘之於心，而命聖賢布之板冊，犯之者，必得罪于上帝。所從得罪者益尊，則罪益重。君子雖已遷善，豈恬然于往所得罪乎？曩者所為不善，人或赦，弗追究，而己時記之，愧之，悔之。設無深悔，吾所旣失於前，烏可望免之于後也？

304

況夫今之為善，君子不自滿足，將必以闚己之短為離婁，以視己之長為盲瞽焉。所責備諸己者精且厚，人雖稱以俊傑，而己愧怍如不置也；所省疲於心者密且詳，人雖謂其備美，而己勤敬如猶虧也。詎徒謙于言乎？詎徒悔于心乎？深自羞恥，奚堪歡樂？則貶食減餐，除其穀味，而惟

11　Here Ricci is alluding to the natural law and to the ten commandments given through Moses. See Deuteronomy 5:1-22 and Exodus 20:1-17.
12　Li-lou (離婁), name of an ancient man, who had an extraordinary power of vision. Cf. *Chinese Classics*, II, p. 288.

are three reasons for fasting which are very much more to the point and very much more admirable.

303. There are a few people in the world who, though good now, always behaved morally in the past, and who, though following the truth now, never flouted it in the past. The truth I am speaking of is the truth which the Lord of Heaven has engraved on men's minds, and which He ordered sages and worthies to carve on tablets of stone and to record in books.[11] Those who violate this truth are bound to offend the Sovereign on High. The more highly esteemed the person offended, the more severe the crime. Although superior men may have changed for the good, can they remain unperturbed over their past wrong-doings? Men may have forgiven them for the bad things they did in the past and may have ceased to pursue matters any further, but they themselves will frequently remember them and will be driven to shame and repentance. If I have no deep remorse for my former transgressions how can I hope not to repeat them in the future?

304. Further, even if he is doing good at the present time, a superior man will not be satisfied on this account. He will have need to examine his own shortcomings carefuly like Li-lou[12] and ignore his own good points like a blind man. He always tries to **reprove himself in detail and with severity; and although others** might call him a hero, he himself will feel only shame at receiving such praise and believe it to be unjustified. Any examination of causes for shame in the mind will be carried out with thoroughness and in detail, and although others may say he is perfect, he himself will be diligent and serious in all that he does as if he were still deficient in some way. Nor can such humility merely be a matter of words or remorse which remain only in the mind. Because of profound, personal shame there can be no room for happiness. On this account he will reduce his intake of food and drink and refrain from meat, eating only vegetables. He will select only the meanest of foods essential for the body. He will inflict suffering on himself and reprove himself severely in order to atone for his former transgres-

取其淡素，凡一身之用，自擇粗陋，自苦自責以贖己之舊惡及其新罪，晨夜惶惶稽顙于天主臺下，哀憫涕淚冀洗己污。敢妄自居聖而誇無過，妄自饒己而須他人審判其非也乎？所以躬自懲詰，不少姑恕，或者天主惻恤而免宥之，不再鞫也。此齋素正志之說一也。

305 夫德之為業，人類本業也。聞其說無不悅而願急事焉。但彼私欲所發者，先已簒入心而擅主之，反相壓難，憤激攻伐，大抵平生所行悉供其役耳。是以凡有所事，弗因義之所令，惟因欲之所樂。

306 睹其面容則人，觀其行，於禽何擇乎？蓋私欲之樂，乃義之敵，塞智慮而蒙理竅，與德無交，世界之瘟病，莫凶乎此矣。他病之害止于軀殼，欲之毒藥通吾心髓而大殘元性也。若以義之仇對，攝一心之專權，理不幾亡？而厥德尚有地可居乎？嗚呼！私欲之樂，微賤也，處過也，而屢貽長悔于心，以卑短之樂售永久之憂，非智之謂也。

辯排輪廻六道、戒殺生之謬說，而揭齋素正志

270

sions and for any new offences committed. He will be troubled day and night, striking his head on the ground before the Lord of Heaven and weeping and wailing in the hope that he might be able to cleanse himself of his impurity. Would he ever rashly dare to assume that he occupied the status of a sage and boast that he was without fault? Must not someone else first judge the nature of his error should he rashly wish to pardon himself? Therefore, not the slightest degree of pardon can result from the punishment and cross-examination of oneself. But one might perhaps win the pity of the Lord of Heaven and His forgiveness for one's offences, with no further cross-examination. This is the first true reason for fasting.

305. The practice of virtue is man's fundamental task. When people hear it explained, there is not one who is not made glad by it and who is not eager to apply himself to it. But on the contrary, selfish desires and passions that have usurped men's minds and have exercised unlawful control over them, always oppress them and make them bitterly attack one another in a fury. Therefore almost everything a man does during his lifetime he does as a slave to selfish desires. Thus, no matter what a person might do, if it is not in accordance with the dictates of righteousness, then it is in obedience to the wishes of selfish desires.

306. The face of such a person may be human, but when one observes his behavior, one finds it to be no different from that of birds and beasts. The things in which selfish desires delight are the enemy of righteousness; they obstruct wisdom and obscure truth and can have nothing to do with virtue. There is no plague in the world more virulent than this. The harm caused by other errors is merely to the body, but the poison of selfish desires penetrates to the very marrow of our minds, causing great harm to our original natures. Should the enemy of righteousness exercise full authority over the mind, will not the rational faculty be almost totally destroyed? Will there be any room left for virtue? Alas! The pleasure of selfish desire is mean and short-lived, leaving behind long-lasting remorse in the mind. To purchase eternal suffering with paltry and brief pleasure is hardly wise.

辯排輪廻六道、戒殺生之謬說，而揭齋素正志

307 然私慾惟自本身藉力逞其勇猛，故過其私欲當先約其本身之氣。學道者願寡欲而豐養身，比方願減火而益加新，可得哉？君子欲飲食，特所以存命；小人欲存命，特所以飲食。夫誠有志於道，怒視是身若寇讐，然不獲已而姑畜之。且何云不獲已歟？吾雖元未嘗為身而生，但無身又不得而生，則服食為腹饑之藥，服飲為口渴之藥耳。誰有取藥而不惟以其病之所要為度馬者？性之所嗜，寡而易營；多品乏味，佳而難遂。蓋人欲者之所圖，而以其所養人，頻反而賊人，則謂飲食殄人多乎刀兵可也。

308 今未論所害于身，只指所傷乎心。僕役過健，恐忤抗其主也；血氣過強，定傾危乎志也。志危卽五欲肆其惡，而色慾尤甚。豐味不恣腹，色慾何從發？淡飲薄食，色氣潛餒，一身旣理約，諸欲自服理矣。此素齋正志之說二也。

---

13 *Wu-yü* (五慾). The Five Desires, understood in a pejorative sense, arise from the objects of the five senses.

272

307. Selfish desires act recklessly in dependence on man's bodily strength alone. If one wishes, therefore, to suppress selfish desires one must first restrain man's energy. A person who cultivates morality will want to have few desires. If such a person pampers his body he will be like someone who wishes to dampen a fire and yet adds fuel to it. Will such a person be able to fulfil his ambition? A superior man will only drink and eat to preserve his life; an inferior man will want to preserve his life merely to drink and eat. A man who is genuinely determined to cultivate morality will look with anger on his body as if it were his enemy, and will temporarily nurture it because he has no alternative. And why do I say because he has no alternative? Because, although he was not in fact born into this world for the sake of his body, he will not be able to live without it. I therefore regard eating as a medicine for the relief of hunger and drinking as a medicine for the relief of thirst. Who does not take only as much medicine as the circumstances of his illness demand? What the body needs is, in fact, very little, and is easy to obtain. There are many fine flavors, but the best are hard to come by. The things selfish desires strive for frequently harm the persons they care for; thus, some say that there are more people killed by eating and drinking than with weapons of war.

308. But I shall now say no more concerning the harm done to the body and speak only of the damage done to the mind. When servants are too healthy there is the possibility that they will rebel against their master, and when a man's animal spirits are unduly strong there is no doubt that they can endanger his firm resolve. When his resolve wavers, the Five Desires[13] give themselves up to evil, lust being the most virulent of the five. If the stomach is not filled with an abundance of flavors, lust will not manifest itself; and if food and drink is simple, lust will steadily diminish. If the whole body is restrained by the rational faculty, then the desires will naturally submit to reason. This is the second true reason for fasting.

309 且本世者，苦世也，非以奉悦此肌膚也，然吾無能竟辭諸樂也。無清樂，必求淫者；無正樂，必尋邪者；得彼則失此。

310 故君子常自習其心，快以道德之事，不令含憂困而有望乎外，又時簡略體膚之樂，恐其透于心，而侵奪其本樂焉。夫德行之樂乃靈魂之本樂也，吾以茲與天神侔矣；飲食之娛乃身之竊愉也，吾以茲與禽獸同矣。吾益增德行之娛於心，益近至天神矣；益減飲食之樂于身，益遐離禽獸矣。吁！可不慎哉？

311 仁義令人心明，五味令人口爽。積善之樂甚，即有大利乎心，而于身無害也；豐膳之樂繁，而身心俱見深傷矣。腹充飽以穀饌，必垂下而墜己志於污賤，如此則安能抽其心於塵垢，而起高曠之慮乎哉？

14 *Wu-wei* (五味). See chapter 1, n. 19.

辯排輪廻六道、戒殺生之謬説，而揭齋素正志

309. Further, the present world is a world of suffering; it is not a place of amusement. The time the Lord of Heaven allots us in this world is extraordinarily short, and we have insufficient time [to win merit through] the cultivation of virtue. [He has not sent us into the world] so that we might enjoy physical happiness. But we do not have the power completely to deny ourselves happiness. If we do not strive for the purest joy, then we are bound to seek after the pleasures of lust. If we do not possess seemly joy, then we are bound to search out unseemly pleasures—in other words, you may gain the one, but you will lose the other.

310. The superior man therefore constantly cultivates his mind; finds happiness in moral actions; does not permit himself to suffer anxiety, and is outward-looking. He constantly curtails his physical happiness, fearful lest one day it should penetrate to his mind and rob him of his essential happiness. For the happiness of moral conduct alone is the happiness of the soul. By means of it one achieves equality with the angels. The pleasures of eating and drinking are the stolen pleasures of the body, and by means of them we become the same as birds and beasts. The more we increase the joys of moral conduct in our minds, the closer we are to the angels; and the more we reduce the pleasures of physical drinking and eating, the more distant we shall be from the birds and beasts. Dare we be injudicious?

311. Humanity and righteousness clarify the human mind; the Five Flavors[14] harm the mouths of men. The more one amasses the happiness of goodness, the greater will be its benefit to the mind, and it will do no harm to the body. The more one indulges in the pleasures of drinking and eating, the more both body and mind will suffer harm. If one fills one's stomach with meat one will easily sink into moral decay and cause one's will to fall into the realm of impurity and baseness. When that happens, how can a person raise his mind out of the mire and have noble thoughts?

275

312　惡者觀人盤樂而己無之,斯嫌妬之矣;善者視之,則反憐恤之,而讓己曰:「彼殉汙賤事,而猶好之如此,懇求之如此;吾既志於上乘,而未能聊味之,未能略備之,且寧如此懈惰而不勉乎哉。」

313　世人之災無他也,心病而不知德之佳味耳。覺其味,則膏梁可輕矣,謂自得其樂也。此二味者,更迭出入於人心,而不可同住者也,欲內此,必先出彼也。

314　古昔有貢我西國二獵犬者,皆良種也。王以一寄國中顯臣家,以其一寄郊外農舍,並使畜之。已壯,而王出田獵試馬,二犬齊縱入圍。農舍之所畜犬,身懼體輕,走鷇禽跡疾趨,獲禽無算;顯家所養犬,雖潔肥容美足觀也,然但習肉食充腸,安佚四肢不能馳驟,則見禽不顧,而忽遇路傍腐骨,卽就而嚙之,嚙畢不動矣。從獵者知其原同一母而出,則異之。

312. When evil people see others indulging in pleasure and they themselves are without it, they grow envious. When good people see this happening they, on the contrary, feel pity and say to themselves: "That they should so like, and be so greedy for, things that are impure and base! Since I have my mind on higher things, can I be so lazy and cease to strive to progress even higher merely because I cannot taste certain things or fulfil certain desires?"

313. For the calamity which has befallen mankind is that having become sick in mind, men no longer know the excellent flavor of virtue. If they knew [the excellent flavor of virtue], they would look with disdain on even the most exotic food, since they would have found happiness within the cultivation of virtue. These two kinds of flavors, [the pleasures of the mind and the pleasures of the mouth], are constantly exchanged, leaving and entering our minds, for they cannot exist together at one and the same time. If you want the happiness of the mind you must first rid yourself of the [pleasures of the mouth and stomach].

314. Formerly, someone brought as tribute to one of our countries in the West two hunting dogs, both of good pedigree. The king placed one of them in the family of a noble minister and the other in the care of a peasant family outside the city. When the two dogs had grown to maturity the king rode out to the hunt and released both dogs into the fields to test them. The dog reared in the peasant family was thin and light, and whenever it smelled the scent of an animal it pursued it, seizing innumerable prey. Although the hunting dog reared in the nobleman's family was fat and clean and extraordinarily good to look at, it was used to eating its fill of meat and to living at ease. It was incapable of running very fast, so that when it saw the prey it had to ignore it. Happening to notice a decayed bone by the side of the road it went and gnawed at it, and when it had finished gnawing it, it refused to move. Those who were following the hunt knew that the two dogs had in fact been born to the same mother, and they were therefore amazed.

315 王曰：「此不足怪。豈惟獸哉，人亦莫不如是也，皆係於養耳矣。養之以佚玩亦不暇，必思焉而殉理義耳。此齋素正志之說三也。」若曰，凡人習於饌美厚膳，見禮義之事不暇；養之以煩勞儉約，必不惺君所望矣。習於精禮微義，遇飲食之翫飫飽，必無所進于善也；人習於饌美厚膳，見禮義之事不暇；養之以煩勞儉約，必不惺君所望矣。

316 夫齋有多端，予偏延天下多國，已備聞之：或不拘餐味，但終晝不食，迨星夜雜食眾味，此謂時齋；或不論時餐，惟戒諸葷，而隨時茹素，此謂味齋；或不擇味、時，特一日間食一餐耳，此謂餐齋；或餐、時、味皆有所拘，茹素一頓，而惟禁止肉食屬陽者，其海味屬陰者不戒，此謂公齋；或禁止火食，只午時終身山穴，專以野草根度生，茲歐邏巴山中甚眾，此謂私齋也。

辯排輪廻六道、戒殺生之謬說，而揭齋素正志

315. The king said: "There is nothing to be surprised at in this.

Not only are animals like this, but men too. It all depends on how they are reared. If they are reared so that they become habituated to indulgence in pleasure and to being too well-fed, they will be incapable of making progress in goodness. If, on the other hand, they are reared in such a way that they have become used to work and frugality, they will definitely not fail to live up to your hopes for them." Thus, one can say, any man who has grown used to delicacies and generous quantities of food will have little time for propriety and righteousness and will only be concerned to apply himself to eating and drinking. A person who is used to seeking deeply after truth and righteousness, on the other hand, will not dwell on drink, food, and leisure when he meets with these things, but will consider how to pursue truth and righteousness. This is the third true reason for fasting.

316. I have passed through a great number of countries in the world and know that there are many kinds of fasting. There are those who, regardless of the different kinds of food available eat nothing during the day, and then eat whatever they like when night falls. This is called fasting for a time. Then there are those who place no restraint on their times of eating, but limit themselves to a vegetarian diet which they eat whenever it suits them. This is called fasting based on types of food. Others are not concerned about types of food or when they eat, but limit themselves to one meal a day. This is called meal fasting. Others again control the number of meals they take, their times of eating and the kinds of food they eat, eating only at midday, and refusing to eat the flesh of warm-blooded animals, although they will permit themselves seafood and the like. This is called public fasting. Some forbid the eating of cooked food and live out their lives as hermits in caves deep in the mountains, relying solely on grass and roots to stay alive. At the present time in Europe there are many such recluses in the mountains. This kind of fasting is called private fasting.

辯排輪廻六道、戒殺生之謬說，而揭齋素正志

317 然夫數等之所齋，總歸責屈本己，要在視其人、視其身何如耳：富貴膏粱，減取其常亦可謂齋；彼賤家民，時習粗糲不可以為齋也。又須量本身之力何如：有衰病者，未免時以滋味養身也；有行役者，勞其四肢不容久饑。故天主公教制老者六旬巳上、穉者二旬巳下、身病者、乳子者、勞力為僕夫者皆不在齋程之內。

318 夫戒口之齋非齋也，乃齋之末節也；究齋之意，總為私欲之過，不可不敦不盡矣。是以持齋而捨敬戒，譬如藏璞而弛其玉，無知也。

319 中士曰：善哉！法語真齋之正旨也。吾俗行齋者，非緣貧乏而持齋以餬口，必其偷取善名而陰以欺人者也，當眾而致齋，幽獨而無人，酒色忿怒、不義

280

317. But the overall purpose of these many kinds of fasting is the mortification of oneself. The kind of fasting undertaken is determined by the kind of person and the kind of body to be mortified. The wealthy and noble constantly eat fine food. If the amount they eat and drink each day is reduced, this, too, can be called fasting. Although the common people are used to consuming coarse and mean food they cannot for this reason be said to be fasting all the time. If this could be termed fasting, then beggars could be said to be on a perpetual fast. Further, one must determine the health and strength of the body. Those who are sick and whose bodies are weak must have frequent nourishment to strengthen themselves. Those who labor and toil hard expend their physical energy, and cannot sustain a long period of hunger. Therefore, the rule of the universal religion of the Lord of Heaven is that persons over the age of sixty, and young people under the age of twenty, the sick, mothers suckling their young, and laborers, all fall outside the rules governing fasting.

318. The fact is that the rules prohibiting eating and drinking count for very little and are only the unimportant details of fasting. When one searches for the meaning of fasting one finds that it is concerned with the repression of man's selfish desires; therefore, one must strive for this with complete honesty and with all one's might. To fast, and at the same time to abandon the precept which commands the practice of reverence, is like cherishing uncarved stone whilst neglecting a beautiful piece of jade—it is an act of ignorance.

319. *The Chinese scholar says:* You have explained the true meaning of fasting extremely well. When we commonly speak of a man who fasts we either mean one who fasts because of poverty and who uses this method to stay alive, or we mean one who uses fasting to win a good reputation for himself, secretly deceiving people. Such a person will fast in public, but when he is alone he indulges in wine, women, and great anger; he acquires wealth unethically, and slanders the worthy and the good. Alas! If he cannot

辯排輪廻六道、戒殺生之謬說，而揭齋素正志

貨財、讒賢毀善，無所不有。嗚呼！人目不能逃，能矇上帝乎？幸領高諭，尚願盡其問。

320

西士曰：道遂，不博問不可且廣約守。詳問即誠意之效也，何傷夫？

escape the eyes of men, how can he hope to deceive the Sovereign on High? It is fortunate that I have been able to listen to your lofty teaching. I should like to continue receiving instruction from you.

320. *The Western scholar says:* The Way is most profound.

Without extensive questioning it would be impossible to arrive at its essential meaning. Detailed questioning is the result of a sincere mind, so please do not feel you are embarassing me.

第六篇

釋解意不可滅。幷論死後必有天堂地獄之賞罰，以報世人所為善惡。

321 中士曰：承教，一則崇上帝為萬尊之至尊，一則貴人品為至尊之次。但以天堂地獄為言，恐未或天主之教也。夫因趣利避害之故為善禁惡，是乃善利惡害，非善善惡惡正志也。吾古聖賢教世弗言利，惟言仁義耳。君子為善無意，況有利害之意耶？

322 西士曰：吾先答子之末語，然後答子之本問。彼滅意之說固異端之詞，非儒人之本論也。儒者以誠意為正心、修身、齊家、治國、平天下之根基，何能無意乎？高臺無堅基不克起，儒學無誠意不能立矣。

---

1 This is a reference to the opening words of the *Book of Mencius*. See *The Chinese Classics*, II, pp. 125-127.
2 One of the main themes of this chapter is motivation. Ricci uses the character *i* (意) throughout this chapter. According to the context we render it as "motive," "intention," "will."

Chapter 6

AN EXPLANATION AS TO WHY MAN CANNOT BE FREE OF MOTIVES, AND A DISCUSSION ON WHY THE GOOD AND EVIL DONE ON EARTH BY MAN MUST BE REWARDED OR PUNISHED IN HEAVEN AND HELL.

321. *The Chinese scholar says:* The instruction I have received from you has taught me, first, that the Sovereign on High is to be adored as the most highly honored of all beings; and, second, that man ranks next [to the Sovereign on High]. But surely talk of Heaven and Hell has no place in the teachings of the Lord of Heaven. To persuade people to do good or to prohibit them from doing evil because of the gain or loss that will accrue from such conduct is to try to profit from good deeds and to avoid harm by refraining from evil; it is not to delight in goodness or to hate evil, [which should be man's] true ambition. Our ancient sages and worthies taught men not to discuss profit, but only humanity and righteousness.[1] The superior man does good without any ulterior motive,[2] and certainly without any thought of gain or loss.

322. *The Western scholar says:* I shall first comment on your final sentence, [the superior man does good without any ulterior motive], and then answer your question. The theory that a superior man has no hidden motive comes from other schools of thought and is not an original doctrine of Confucianism. Confucianism regards the motive of sincerity as the foundation for the rectification of the mind, for self-cultivation, for the regulation of the family, for the ordering of the state, and for the bringing of

設自正心至平天下，凡所行事事皆不得有意，則奚論其意誠乎？虛乎？譬有琴於市，使吾不宜奏，何以售之？何拘其古琴、今琴歟？

323 且意非有體之類，乃心之用耳，用方為意，即有邪正。若令君子畢竟無意，不知何時誠乎？大學言齊治均平必以意誠為要，不誠則無物矣。意於心，如視於目；目不可卻視，則心不可除意也。君子所謂無意者，虛意、私意、邪意也；如云滅意是不達儒者之學，不知善惡之原也。

324 善惡德慝，俱由意之正邪，無意則無善惡、無君子小人之判矣。

325 中士曰：「毋意，毋善毋惡。」世儒固有其說。

釋解意不可滅。并論死後必有天堂地獄之賞罰，以報世人所為善惡。

---

3 A summary of the teaching found in the *Great Learning*. See Chan, *A Source Book in Chinese Philosophy*, pp. 84-94, and *The Chinese Classics*, I, pp. 355-381.

4 The reference is, no doubt, to the *Analects*, IX, 4: "There were four things from which Confucius was entirely free. He had no foregone conclusions, no arbitrary predeterminations, no obstinacy, and no egoism." See *The Chinese Classics*, vol. I, p. 217. Here, it is obvious that Ricci misunderstood "have no foregone conclusions" as "have no motives," and further added "no good and no evil."

286

peace to the world.[3] How, then, can one say that there is no hidden motive? A tower cannot be built without firm foundations, and if Confucianism lacked the element of the motive of sincerity it could not have been established. If no motive may intrude into any of the activities, ranging from the rectification of the mind to the bringing of peace to the world, how can one talk of the motive of sincerity or of mendacity? How can a person sell musical instruments in the marketplace if he does not permit people to play them? It will matter not at all whether the instruments are ancient or modern.

323. Moreover, motive is not a thing which has substance, but is a functioning of the mind. Motive results from this functioning, and it is only when there is motive that a distinction can be made between evil and good. If you say that the superior man has no hidden motive, it is difficult to see how he can have sincerity. The teaching in the *Great Learning* concerning the regulation of the family, the ordering of the state, and the bringing of peace to the world has sincerity of motive as its most necessary ingredient, for if there is no sincerity nothing can be accomplished. The hidden motives in the minds of men are like the sense of sight in the eyes. Just as the eyes cannot rid themselves of "sight," so men's minds cannot eliminate "motive." What the superior man means when he says he has no motive is that he has no vain, selfish, or evil motive. If you say that he has no motive, then you do not understand Confucianism, and you do not know the source of good and evil.

324. Good and evil, virtue and vice all stem from right or corrupt motives. If there are no motives there can be no good or evil or any distinction between superior and inferior men.

325. *The Chinese scholar says:* But certain Confucian scholars distinctly assert: "Have no motives, no good and no evil."[4]

326 西士曰：此學欲人為土石者耳。謂上帝宗義，有是哉？若上帝無意無善，亦將等之乎土石也。謂之「理學」？悲哉！悲哉！

327 昔老莊亦有「勿為、勿意、勿辯」之語，然已所著經書，其從者所為註解，意固欲易天下而僉從此一端。夫著書，獨非為乎？意易天下，獨非意乎？既不可辯是非，又何辯「辯是非」者乎？辯天下名理，獨非辯乎？則既已自相戾矣，而欲師萬世也，難哉！

328 吾觀世人為事，如射焉，中「的」則謂善，不中則為惡。天主者，自然中于「的」者也，有至純之善，無纖芥之惡，其德至也；吾儕則有中、有不中矣，其所修之德有限，故德有不到，即行事有所不中，而善惡參焉。為善禁惡，縱有意猶恐不及，況無意乎？

釋解意不可滅。并論死後必有天堂地獄之賞罰，以報世人所為善惡。

---

5 The Chinese term *li-hsüeh* (理學) may also be translated "rational philosophy." See Chan, *A Source Book in Chinese Philosophy*, p. 751.
6 Lao Tzu (老子), the reputed author of the *Tao-te Ching* and Chuang Tzu (莊子, bet. 399-295 B.C.) are traditionally regarded as the first exponents of Taoist philosophy.

Motivation, Reward, and Punishment

326. *The Western scholar says:* Such a thesis puts man on a par with soil and stones. Can the teaching of the Sovereign on High really harbor such a view? If the Sovereign on High is devoid of motives and goodness he too must be regarded as being on the same level as soil and stones. To call this "moral science"[5] is lamentable!

327. Formerly, Lao Tzu and Chuang Tzu[6] also taught that people should "not act, have no motives, and not dispute." Nevertheless, they themselves produced canonical writings and books, and their followers added notes and commentaries. Clearly, their motive was a desire to transform the world, and to persuade all people to follow their teachings. Was not the writing of books an activity? And was not their intention to transform the world a motive? If they were not permitted to argue over the nature of right and wrong, why did they engage in disputes with those who made a point of arguing over such matters? Were the disputes over logical principles not then disputes? It is no easy matter for a person to become a teacher of men in all ages when he so contradicts himself.

328. In my view, when people do things they are like archers. Those who hit the target are said to be good, whereas those who miss it are bad. And what of the Lord of Heaven? He naturally achieves what he sets out to do and is therefore perfectly good and without the slightest trace of evil. His virtue has already reached its fullest extent. We men, however, sometimes achieve what we set out to do, but we also sometimes fail. Because the extent to which we cultivate our virtue is limited, we are never perfectly virtuous, which is to say that we are not always successful in what we do; this is why there is good and evil. When we seek to do good and to curb evil our one concern is that our motivation may not be sufficient for the task. But how much more should we be concerned when there is no motivation?

329 其餘無意之物,如金石草木類,然後無德無愆,無善無惡。如以無意無善惡為道,是金石草木之,而後成其道耳。

330 中士曰:老莊之徒,只欲全其天年,故屏意棄善惡以絕心之累也。二帝、三王、周公、孔子皆苦心極力脩德於己,以施及於民,縱充其百歲之壽,亦不能及一龜一朽樹之壽也,而徒以加二三旬之暫,於此穢身竟何濟哉?然氏無足訊。所言「德愆善惡俱由意」,其詳何如?聞夫順理者即為善,而稱之德行,犯理者即為惡,而稱之不才,則顧行事如何,於意似無相屬。

331 西士曰:理易解也。凡世物既有其意,又有能縱止其意者,然後有德、有愆、有善、有惡焉。意者心之發也,金石草木無心,則無意。故鎮鋣

釋解意不可滅。并論死後必有天堂地獄之賞罰,以報世人所為善惡。

7 The mythical emperors Yao and Shun and the founders of the Hsia, Shang, and Chou dynasties.

329. Things which lack motives are such things as metal, stone, grass, and trees. Only such things as these can be devoid of virtue, corruption, goodness, and evil. If lack of motive and lack of good and evil are to be the hallmark of the Way, then this is tantamount to saying that only after men have changed into metal, stone, or vegetation will they be able to attain to the Way.

330. *The Chinese scholar says:* Lao Tzu, Chuang Tzu and their followers were only interested in preserving their natural span of life and therefore abandoned motivation and cast aside good and evil in order to eradicate all burdens from the mind. The Two Emperors and the Three Kings,[7] as well as the Duke of Chou and Confucius, all strove painstakingly to cultivate their virtues in order to bestow blessings upon the people; they dared not rest until they had attained supreme goodness. Who among them worked only for the preservation of his own body and cast aside his motives, roaming free and unrestrained so that he could live to the ripe old age of one hundred? Further, though a man may live to be one hundred, his age will still not match that of the tortoise or an old tree. Of what use is it to add a mere twenty or thirty years to this contaminated body? But the two gentlemen, Lao and Chuang, are not worth discrediting; the virtue and vice, good and evil of which you spoke are all products of the will. What are your views in greater detail? I have heard it said that to act in accordance with reason is good and that this is called virtuous conduct, and that to offend against reason is evil, and that this is called being devoid of talent. Provided one determines the nature of a man on the basis of his actions, his motives would seem to be of no consequence.

331. *The Western scholar says:* Reason is easy to explain. Everything in the world which has a will can allow the will to achieve its end or can restrain it, and a distinction is thereby made between virtue and vice, good and evil. The will issues from the mind. Metal, stone and vegetation are devoid of mind and therefore of will. Thus, if a man is injured by a sword, his avenger will not break the sword in two. If a tile falls and injures a man's head, the man who is harm-

傷人，復讐者不折鎮鋣；瓦蔽風雨，民無酬謝。所為無心無意，是以無德無應、無善無惡，而無可以賞罰之。

332 若禽獸者，可謂有禽獸之心與意矣，但無靈心以辯可否，不能以理為之節制，其所為是禮非禮不但不得已，且亦不自如，有何善惡之可論乎？是以天下諸邦所制法律，無有刑禽獸之應、賞禽獸之德者。

333 惟人不然。行事在外，理心在內，是非當否嘗能知覺，兼能縱上；雖有獸心之欲，若能理心為主，獸心豈能違我主心之命？故吾發意從理，即為德行君子，天主佑之；吾溺意獸心，即為犯罪小人，天主且棄之矣。

334 嬰兒擊母，無以咎之，其未有以檢己意也；及其壯，而能識可否，則何待于擊，稍逆其親即加不孝之罪矣。

釋解意不可滅。并論死後必有天堂地獄之賞罰，以報世人所為善惡。

Motivation, Reward, and Punishment

ed will not bear a grudge against the tile. One does not impute merit to a sword because it can sever things. Tiles keep wind and rain out of a house, but men do not offer them thanks. Because they have no mind and no will they are devoid of virtue and vice, goodness and evil, and one cannot reward or punish them.

332. As to animals, we can say that they have the minds and wills of animals, but that they have no intelligent mind with which to distinguish between right and wrong. They follow their senses, and are unable to regulate their reactions with reason. Everything they do, whether it be fitting or not, is done without their being able to be masters of their actions and without any self-awareness; how, then, can one begin to speak of good and evil? Thus, of the laws enacted in the countries of the world, there is not one which punishes an animal for wrong-doing, or which rewards an animal for its virtue.

333. But man's conduct is quite otherwise. His actions are external, but his reasoning mind lies within him. Not only is he aware that his actions are right or wrong, correct or otherwise, but he is also capable of allowing them to run riot or of bringing them to a halt. Although he possesses desires proper to the minds of animals, if he can use his rational faculty to exercise control over them, his animal mind will not be able to disobey the commands of the master of his mind. Consequently, if I determine to follow what is right and rational, I am a superior man in my moral conduct and will obtain the protection and support of the Lord of Heaven. If, instead, I am dissolute, and determine to obey my animal mind, I am an inferior man who transgresses the law and will be renounced by the Lord of Heaven.

334. If a child strikes its mother it is not accounted a transgressor, because it still lacks that by which it can restrain its will. When the child reaches maturity, however, and is capable of knowing whether he may or may not do a thing, then, even before he strikes her, if he shows the slightest tendency to disobey his parents, he will be accused of being unfilial.

335 昔有二弓士。一之山野,見叢有伏者如虎,慮將傷人因射之,偶誤中人;一登樹林,恍惚傍視,行動如人亦射刺之,而實乃鹿也。彼前一人果殺人者,然而意在射虎,斷當寬;後一人雖殺野鹿,而意在刺人,斷當貶。則意為善惡之原,明著矣。美由焉?由意之美醜異也。

336 中士曰:子為養親行盜,其意善矣,而不免于法,何如?試言其故:

337 西士曰:吾西國有公論曰:「善者成乎全,惡者成于一。」所謂「西子蒙不潔,則人皆掩鼻而過之。」譬如水甕週圍厚堅,惟底有一鏬,水從此漏,此甕決為無用碎瓦。人既為盜,雖其餘行悉義,但呼為惡,不可稱善。

338 惡之為情甚毒也,捨己之財普濟貧乏,以竊善聲而得非所得之位,所為雖當,其意實枉,則其事盡為不直,蓋醜意污其善行也。子為親竊人財物,其事既惡,何有善意?

釋解意不可滅。幷論死後必有天堂地獄之賞罰,以報世人所爲善惡。

8 *Chinese Classics*, II, p. 330. Lady Hsi (西子, around 500 B.C.) was renowned for her beauty.

294

Motivation, Reward, and Punishment

335. Once upon a time there were two famous archers. One went out into the wilds where he saw something in the woods, crouching like a tiger. Seriously concerned lest the tiger harm someone, he shot at it, but accidentally hit a man. The second archer climbed up a tree, and thought he noticed a movement which seemed to be that of a human being. He also shot an arrow at the moving object, but it turned out, in fact, to be a deer. The first hunter most assuredly shot and killed a man, but his intention was to shoot a tiger, and he was judged worthy of praise. Although what the second hunter shot was merely a wild deer, because his intention had been to kill a human being, he was judged worthy of blame. And why? Because a distinction was made between good and bad intentions. Thus, it is very clear that the source of good and evil is the will.

336. *The Chinese scholar says:* If a son steals and robs to support his parents his intentions are good, but if he is unable to avoid the sanctions imposed by the law, what then?

337. *The Western scholar says:* In our Western countries there is a generally accepted view according to which goodness results from wholeness, and evil from fragmentation. I shall now try to explain the causes underlying this view. Although the rest of his conduct may be righteous, if a person steals and robs he is accounted an evil-doer and cannot be called good. "If the Lady Hsi had been covered with a filthy headdress, all people would have stopped their noses in passing her."[8] We can also use a water jar as an example; its walls may be firm and thick on all sides, but if there is a small hole in the bottom of it, the water will leak out and it will be absolutely useless—a broken piece of pottery.

338. Evil is a very poisonous thing. If one bestows one's wealth widely to succor the poor, but with the intention of stealing a fine reputation for oneself and of gaining a position to which one is not entitled, then, although what one has done is right and proper, one's motive is in reality wrong, and everything one has done is twisted and dishonest. This is because the ugliness of one's motive

339 吾言正意為為善之本，惟謂行吾正，勿行吾邪；偷盜之事固邪也，雖襲之以義意，不為正矣。為纖微之不善可以救天下萬民，猶且不可為，矧以育二三口乎？

340 為善正意，惟行當行之事，故意益高則善益精，若意益陋則善益粗，是故意宜養、宜誠也，何滅之有哉？

341 中士曰：聖人之教，縱不滅意，而其意不在功效，只在脩德之美，不指賞；阻惡而言惡之罪，不言罰。

342 西士曰：聖人之教在經傳，其勸善必以賞，其阻惡必以懲矣。舜典曰：「象以典刑，流宥五刑。」又曰：「三載考績；三考，黜陟幽明。庶績咸熙，分北三苗。」

釋解意不可滅。幷論死後必有天堂地獄之賞罰，以報世人所爲善惡。

9 Ibid., III, p. 38.
10 Ibid., III, p. 50.

296

Motivation, Reward, and Punishment

has infected one's good deeds. If a son steals other people's property for his parents, the act is evil. How then can one say that his motive is good?

339. When I say that right motives are the root of good conduct, I am only saying that my actions ought to be upright and not wicked. Stealing and robbery are assuredly wicked, and even though one may impute a righteous motive to them, they still cannot be said to be right. Even if only the smallest of evil deeds is required to save everyone in the world, it still may not be done; how much more must this be so, then, when it is for the purpose of feeding only two or three people?

340. The right motive for doing good is to do what one ought to do. The higher a man's motives, the more perfect will be his good deeds. The more base a man's motives, the more mean will be the good he does. Thus, the will must be trained and must be sincere. How can one eliminate motive?

341. *The Chinese scholar says:* Motive is not eliminated in the teachings of the sages and worthies, but it is directed only towards moral cultivation and not towards its effectiveness; therefore, when they persuade people to do good, they only point to the beauty of moral conduct, and say nothing of rewards; when they teach people to reject evil, they only speak of the wrongness of evil, and say nothing of punishment.

342. *The Western scholar says:* The teachings of the sages are recorded in the canonical writings and their authoritative commentaries. The sages invariably employed rewards in order to induce people to do good, and punishments to make them avoid evil. In the "Canon of Shun" we read: "He gave delineations of the statutory punishments, enacting banishment as a mitigation of the five great inflictions."[9] We also read: "Every three years there was an examination of merits, and after three examinations the undeserving were degraded, and the deserving promoted. By this arrangement the duties of all the departments were fully discharged. The people of San-miao were discriminated and separated."[10]

343 皋陶謨曰：「天命有德，五服五章哉；天討有罪，五刑五用哉。」益稷謨曰：「帝曰：迪朕德，時乃功惟敍。皋陶方祇厥敍，方施象刑，惟明。」

344 盤庚曰：「無有遠邇，用罪伐厥死，用德彰厥善。邦之臧，惟汝衆；邦之不臧，惟予一人佚罰。」又曰：「乃有不吉不迪，顛越不恭，暫遇奸宄，我乃剗殄滅之，無遺育，無俾易種于茲新邑。」

345 泰誓武王曰：「爾衆士，其尚迪果毅，以登乃辟。功多有厚賞，不迪有顯戮。」又曰：「爾所弗最，其于爾躬有戮。」康誥曰：「乃其速由文王作罰，刑茲無赦。」

346 多士曰：「爾克敬，天惟畀矜爾；爾不克敬，爾不啻不有爾土，予亦致天之罰于爾躬。」多方又曰：「爾乃惟逸爲頗，大遠王命

釋解意不可滅。幷論死後必有天堂地獄之賞罰，以報世人所爲善惡。

11 Ibid., III, p. 74.
12 Ibid., III, p. 86.
13 Ibid., III, p. 231.
14 Ibid., III, p. 241.
15 Ibid., III, p. 296.
16 Ibid., III, p. 304.
17 Ibid., III, p. 393.

Motivation, Reward, and Punishment

343. In the "Counsels of Kao-yao" we read: "Heaven graciously distinguishes the virtuous; are there not the five habiliments, five decorations of them. Heaven punishes the guilty; are there not the five punishments to be severally used for that purpose?[11] In the "Counsels of I and Chieh" we have the following: "The emperor said, 'That my virtue is followed, this is the result of your meritorious services, so orderly displayed. And now Kao-yao is respectfully carrying out your arrangements, and employing the represented punishments with entire intelligence.' "[12]

344. P'an Keng said: "There is with me no distinction of distant and near. The criminal shall die the death; and the good-doer shall have his virtue displayed. The prosperity of the country must come from you all. If it fail in prosperity, that must arise from me, the one man, erring in the application of punishment."[13] P'an Keng also said: "If there be bad and unprincipled men, precipitously or carelessly disrespectful to my orders, and taking advantage of this brief season to play the part of villains or traitors, I will cut off their noses, or utterly exterminate them. I will leave none of their children. I will not let them perpetuate their seed in this new city."[14]

345. King Wu says in the third part of "The Great Declaration":
"Do you, all my officers, march forwards with determined boldness, to sustain your prince. Where there is much merit, there shall be large reward. Where you advance not so, there shall be conspicuous disgrace."[15] In "The Speech at Mu" he says: "If you are not thus energetic, you will bring destruction on yourselves."[16] In "The Announcement to the Prince of K'ang" we read: "You must deal speedily with such parties according to the penal laws of King Wen, punishing them severely and not pardoning."[17]

346. In the book entitled "The Numerous Officers" it is stated:
"If you can reverently obey, Heaven will favor and be compassionate toward you. If you cannot reverently obey, you will not only not have your lands, but I will also carry to the utmost Heaven's

347 此二帝三代之語，皆言賞罰，固皆併利害言之。

348 中士曰：春秋者，孔聖之親筆，言是非，不言利害也。

349 西士曰：俗之利害有三等：一曰身之利害，此以肢體寧壽為利，以危夭為害；二曰財貨之利害，此以廣田畜、充金貝為利，以減耗失之為害；三曰名聲之利害，此以顯名休譽為利，以譴斥毀污為害也。

350 春秋存其一，而不及其二者也。然世俗大概重名聲之利害，而輕身財之損益，故謂：「春秋成，而亂臣賊子懼。」亂臣賊子奚懼焉？非懼惡名之為害不已乎？孟軻首以仁義為題，厥後每會時君，勸釋解意不可滅。并論死後必有天堂地獄之賞罰，以報世人所為善惡。

18 Ibid., III, p. 462.
19 Ibid., III, pp. 506-507.
20 The work is attributed to Confucius by Mencius. It records events from the standpoint of the state of Lu (魯) during the Spring and Autumn period (722-481 B.C.).
21 Chinese Classics, II, p. 283.

Motivation, Reward, and Punishment

inflictions on your persons."[18] In "The Numerous Regions" it is also stated: "Thus will you be proved slothful and perverse, greatly disobedient to the charges of your sovereign. Throughout your many regions, you will bring on yourselves the terrors of Heaven, and I also will inflict its punishment, removing you far from your country."[19]

347. These are all sayings from the times of the two emperors [Yao and Shun] and the three dynasties [Hsia, Shang, and Chou]. They all speak of rewards and punishments, and all, in fact, carry with them consequences of gain and loss.

348. *The Chinese scholar says:* The *Spring and Autumn Annals*[20] was written personally by the sage, Confucius, and this work speaks only of right and wrong without any reference being made to gain or loss.

349. *The Western scholar says:* Three kinds of gain and loss exist in the world. The first kind is gain and loss in terms of the body where health and long life are regarded as gain and calamity and brevity of life as loss. The second kind is gain and loss from the standpoint of wealth and goods. From this point of view gain is represented by large holdings of land, animals, and money, and loss by the reduction and loss of wealth. The third kind of gain and loss falls within the sphere of reputation. Gain in this case is the acquiring of a great name and fame, whereas loss is to suffer reprimand and the destruction of one's reputation.

350. The *Spring and Autumn Annals* speaks only of one of these kinds of gain and loss and says nothing of the other two. Because people probably emphasize the gains and losses of reputation more than anything else, and take less heed of the gains and losses which affect their bodies and wealth, it was said: "Confucius completed the 'Spring and Autumn,' and rebellious ministers and villainous sons were struck with terror."[21] And why were the rebellious ministers and villainous sons struck with terror? Were they not fearful of the harm that would be done to them as a result

行仁政，猶以「不王者，未之有也」為結語。

351 王天下顧非利哉？人孰不悅利于朋友？利于親戚？如利不可經心，則何以欲歸之友親乎？仁之方曰：「不欲諸己，勿加諸人。」既不宜望利以為己，猶必當廣利以為人。以是知利無所傷于德也。

352 利所以不可言者，乃其偽，乃其悖義者耳。易曰：「利者，義之和也。」又曰：「利用安身，以崇德也。」論利之大，雖至王天下，猶為利之微。況戰國之主，雖行仁政，未必能王；雖使能王，天下一君耳，不取之此，不得予乎彼，夫世之利也如是耳矣。

353 吾所指來世之利也，至大也，至實也，而無相礙，縱盡人得之，莫相奪也。以此為利，王欲利其國，大夫欲利其家，士庶欲利其

釋解意不可滅。幷論死後必有天堂地獄之賞罰，以報世人所為善惡。

22 *Analects*, XV, 23.
23 *I Ching*, p. 408.
24 Ibid., p. 390. Ricci would probably have preferred a translation in which the word *li* (利) was translated "profit," "advantage," or "gain." He may have preferred a rendering which would have read: "When gain is used to provide security, our virtue is thereby exalted."
25 403-221 B.C.

302

of their reputations being damaged? Mencius took humanity and righteousness as his theme. Later, each time he paid an official call on the ruler of a state he would plead with him to practice humane government and even argued that everyone who had done this had succeeded in ruling the world.

351. Do you mean to say that the exercise of kingship over the world does not represent gain? What person is not happy when his friends or relatives benefit in some way? If gain is something we should not be concerned with, why do we wish our friends and relatives to enjoy it? The method of cultivating humanity is as follows: "Never do to others what you would not like them to do to you."[22] Though one ought not to look for personal gain, one ought, nevertheless, to extend benefits to others. One should realize from this that the gain [discussed above] is not harmful to virtue.

352. The gain one may not speak of is false gain, and gain which flouts righteousness. In the *Book of Changes* we read: "What is called 'the advantageous' is the harmony of all that is right."[23] And, "When that application becomes the quickest and readiest all personal restfulness is secured, our virtue is thereby exalted."[24] When we come to speak of gain in its greatest sense, we find that rulership of the world ranks very low. Moreover, even if the lords of the Warring States[25] had exercised humane government, there is no certainty that they would all have been able to rule the empire. There can only be one ruler of the world; and if a state is to be enlarged, it can only be at the expense of another. Gain in this world amounts to no more than this.

353. The benefits I am referring to, however, are the benefits of the world to come which are both supremely great and supremely real and which hurt no one. Since everyone can obtain them there is no need to fight each other for them. If these benefits are regarded as gain, then kings will want their states to enjoy them,

身，上下爭先，天下安方治矣。重來世之益者，必輕現世之利，輕現世之利而好犯上爭奪、弒父弒君，未之聞也。使民皆望後世之利，為政何有？

354 中士曰：嘗聞之：「何必勞神慮未來？惟管今日眼前事。」此是實語，何論後世？

355 西士曰：陋哉！使犬彘能言也，無異此矣。西域上古有一人立教，專以快樂無憂為務，彼時亦有從之者，自題其墓碑曰：「汝今當飲食歡戲，死後無樂兮。」諸儒稱其門為「豬豢門」也。詎貴邦有暗契之者。夫無遠慮，必有近患。獸之不遠，詩人所刺。吾視人愈智，其思愈遐；人愈愚，其思愈邇。

釋解意不可滅。幷論死後必有天堂地獄之賞罰，以報世人所為善惡。

304

the great officers will want to provide them for their families, and both the educated and common people will want to acquire them for themselves. All classes of men will rush to be first [to obtain this kind of benefit], and only then will the world be at peace and be properly governed! People who emphasize the benefits of the world to come are bound to look with disdain on the benefits provided in this world. I have never heard of people who look with disdain on the benefits to be gained in this world, and who, at the same time, enjoy defying authority, struggling for power and gain, and murdering and assassinating fathers and rulers. If one can make all the people look forward to the benefits of the next life, one will have no difficulty in ruling the state.

354. *The Chinese scholar says:* I have heard it said: "Why trouble oneself about the future? The best thing to do is to limit one's concern to the matters before one today." These are realistic words; why talk about the world to come?

355. *The Western scholar says:* What a superficial way to look at things! If pigs and dogs could speak, this is the kind of thing they would say. In ancient times in the West there was a founder of a school of thought who concentrated on happiness and gave no consideration to anything mournful or distressing. At the time a number of people accepted his teaching. He wrote an inscription for his own tombstone which read: "You ought to eat, drink, and be merry for there is no happiness after death." Many scholars referred to his followers as disciples of the pigpen. Could it be that in your noble country there are those who secretly agree with this philosophy? Any man who lacks foresight is bound to experience immediate troubles. A man with limited vision must suffer the ridicule of the satirist. In my view the wiser a person is, the more far-ranging will be his thought, while the more dull-witted a person is, the more shallow and immediate will be his thinking.

356 凡民之類,豈可不預防未來,先謀未逮者乎?農夫耕稼於春,圖秋之穡。松樹百年始結子,而有藝之,所謂:「圃翁植樹,爾玄孫攀其子者。」行旅者,周沿江湖,冀老之安居鄉土;百工勤習其業,期獲所賴;士髫卝勤苦博學,欲後輔國匡君;夫均不以眼前今日之事為急者也。不肖子敗其先業,虞公喪國,夏桀殷紂失天下,此非不慮悠遠、徒管今日眼前事者乎。

357 中士曰:然。但吾在今世則所慮雖遠,止在本世耳;死後之事,似迂也。

358 西士曰:仲尼作春秋,其孫著中庸,厥慮俱在萬世之後,夫慮為他人,而諸君子不以為迂;吾慮為己惟及二世,而子以為迂乎?童子圖既老之事,未知厥能至壯否,而莫之謂遠也。吾圖死後之事,或卽詰

釋解意不可滅。并論死後必有天堂地獄之賞罰,以報世人所為善惡。

26 Another name for the Shang dynasty.
27 Confucius' grandson is Tzu Ssu (子思). At the time of Ricci the majority of Confucian scholars believed Tzu Ssu was the author of the *Doctrine of the Mean*. Today the majority of the scholars believe the work was composed one hundred or two hundred years later.

Motivation, Reward, and Punishment

356. There is not a man who does not provide against the future and who does not consider things before they arise. The farmer ploughs and sows in spring, hoping for a harvest in the autumn. The pine tree grows for a hundred years before it produces any seeds, and yet men plant them. As the saying goes: "The gardener plants the tree, but the later generations will pluck its fruit." A traveller will travel the length and breadth of rivers and lakes, always hoping that when old age creeps up on him he will be able to live contentedly in his home town. Artisans diligently practice their trades in the hope that people will depend on them [for the skills they have perfected]. In his youth a scholar will labor diligently over his books so that his learning will be broad and penetrating and he will eventually be able to support his king and be of benefit to his nation. None of these people will regard matters immediately before him, or of the day, as requiring his most urgent attention. The destruction of the life-work of his ancestor by an unfilial son; the Duke of Yü's loss of his State, and the loss of the world by King Chieh of the Hsia dynasty and King Chou of the Yin[26] dynasty were all due, were they not, to the failure on the part of these men to exercise foresight and to their sole concern for the things immediately before their eyes.

357. *The Chinese scholar says:* That is so. But, although I may be far-sighted in this present world, I am still limited to this present world. To consider what happens after death seems to be so impractical.

358. *The Western scholar says:* Confucius compiled the *Spring and Autumn Annals* and his grandson wrote the *Doctrine of the Mean*.[27] They both gave thought to all the generations which were to follow them. Superior men did not regard thoughtfulness for other people as too impractical. If I give some thought to myself it is simply for my after-life; do you consider this impractical? Children plan for their old age without knowing whether they will grow to maturity; yet no one will say they are being too far-sighted.

朝之事,而子以為遠乎?子之婚也,奚冀得子孫?

359 中士曰:以有治喪葬、墳墓、祭祀之事也。

360 西士曰:然。是亦死後之事矣。吾既死,所留者二:不能朽者為切,子尚以速腐者為慮,可謂我迂乎?

361 中士曰:行善以致現世之利、遠現世之害,君子且非之;來世之利害之影耳,利害之影又何足論歟?

362 西士曰:來世之利害甚真大,非今世之可比也。吾今所見者,利害之影耳,故今世之事,或凶或吉俱不足言也。

363 吾聞師之喩曰:「人生世間,如俳優在戲場;所為俗業,如搬演雜劇。諸帝王、宰官、士人、奴隷、后妃、婢媵,皆一時粧飾之耳。則其所衣衣,非其衣;所逢利害,不及其躬。搬演旣畢,解去粧飾,漫然不復相關。故俳優不以分

釋解意不可滅。并論死後必有天堂地獄之賞罰,以報世人所爲善惡。

308

Motivation, Reward, and Punishment

When I plan for what happens following my death I may be planning for something that will happen tomorrow. Would you consider that too distant an event? Why do you hope for sons and grandsons when you get married?

359. *The Chinese scholar says:* So that after I die there will be someone to oversee my burial and to offer sacrifices at my tomb.

360. *The Western scholar says:* But these too are events which follow your death. When I die I shall leave two things behind me: (1) an incorruptible spirit, and (2) a corpse which will rapidly become corrupt. I regard my incorruptible soul as that which requires my urgent attention, but you are chiefly concerned over a body which speedily decays. Can you accuse me of being impractical?

361. *The Chinese scholar says:* A superior man is not concerned to do good in order to win benefits in this life and to steer clear of worldly loss. How, then, can the question of gain or loss in the next life be worth discussing?

362. *The Western scholar says:* The question of gain or loss in the next life is a very real and very great question, and cannot be compared with gain and loss in this life. What I see now are no more than the shadows of gain and loss. Therefore, the matters of this world, whether bad or good, are not worth talking about.

363. I once heard my teacher tell the following allegory: When a man is born into this world he is like an actor on a stage. His practice of a profession in this common world is like the playing of a role in a comedy. People such as kings, prime ministers, officials, educated men and slaves, queens, imperial concubines, female slaves, wives and concubines are all no more than actors temporarily made up and playing a part. The garments they wear are not their own clothes and the beneficial or hurtful circumstances they encounter cannot affect them. When the acting ends, and they

位高卑長短爲憂喜，惟扮所承腳色，雖巧子亦真切爲之，以中主人之意耳已。蓋分位在他，充位在我。」

364 吾曹在于茲世，雖百歲之久，較之後世萬祀之無窮，烏足以當冬之一日乎？不論君子小人，咸赤身空出，赤身空返，臨終而去雖遺金千笈，積在庫內不帶一毫，何必以是爲留意哉？今世僞事已終，即後世之真情起矣；而後乃各取其所宜三貴賤也。若以今世利害爲真，何異乎蠢民看戲，以粧帝王者爲真貴人，以粧奴隸者爲真下人乎？

365 意之爲情，精粗不齊。員敎世之責者，孰先布其麤，而後不闡其精？必旣切琢，而後磋磨矣。需醫者，惟病者，非謂瘉者也；需吾敎者，惟小人耳已，釋解意不可滅。并論死後必有天堂地獄之賞罰，以報世人所爲善惡。

have divested themselves of their costumes and removed their make-up, these things cease to be of any concern to them. Thus, an actor is neither distressed nor elated by the rank or qualities of the person he plays. He simply dressed up for the parts, and even if he is to play a beggar he will do it as conscientiously as he can, thinking only of how he might satisfy the intentions of his master. An actor is assigned a part by his master, but the filling of his role rests with the actor himself.

364. Although we may live to be a hundred in this world, our lives will not even be the equivalent of the shortest day in winter when they are compared with the endless ages of the after-life. The riches we acquire are merely borrowed for our use, and we are not the true masters of them. Why, then, should we rejoice over the amassing of wealth, and be distressed when it is reduced? Whether people be superior or inferior, they all enter this world naked and depart from it naked. Although we may have a thousand cases of gold stored away in a treasury when we are at the point of death, we can take nothing of it with us. Why, then, should we concern ourselves with it? The ending of the vain affairs of this life represents the beginning of the real things in the next life when each person will occupy the position, whether honorable or mean, for which he is most suited. If you treat the gains and losses of this life as real, will you not be like those foolish people who go to the theater and believe that the actor dressed up in the role of an emperor is really a man of nobility, or that the one dressed up as a slave really is a man of low degree?

365. A man's motives can be either refined or vulgar. Is there anyone among those who have taken upon themselves the responsibility for offering guidance to mankind who does not begin with crude statements before proceeding to more subtle discourse? After one has studied and learnt by mutual discussion one must go on to refine one's knowledge through the hard grind of further study. Only the sick need a physician; not those who say they have

君子固自知之，故教宜曲就小人之意也。孔子至衛，見民眾，欲先富而後教之。詎不知教為滋重乎？但小民由利而後可廸乎義耳。

366　凡行善者，有正意三狀：下曰，因登天堂免地獄之意也；中曰，因報答所重蒙天主恩德之意；上曰，因翕順天主聖旨之意也。教之所望乎學者，在其成就耳，不獲已，而先指其端焉。民溺于利久矣，不以利廸之、害駭之，莫之引領也。

367　然上意至，則下意無所容而去矣，如縫錦繡之衣必用絲線，但無鐵鍼，線不能入，然而其鍼一進卽過，所庸留於衣裳者絲線耳已。吾欲引人歸德，若但舉其德之美，夫人已昧於私欲，何以覺之乎？言不入其心，卽不願聽而去，惟先怵惕之以地獄之苦，誘導之以天堂之樂，將必傾耳欲聽，而漸就乎善善惡惡之成旨，成者至，則缺者化去，而獨其成就恒存焉。故曰：「惡者惡惡，因懼刑也；善者惡惡，因愛德也。」

釋解意不可滅。并論死後必有天堂地獄之賞罰，以報世人所為善惡。

28 Cf. *Chinese Classics*, I, pp. 262-267.

Motivation, Reward, and Punishment

been cured. It is only the inferior who require our guidance—the superior man will assuredly already know the truth. Instruction, therefore, must be accommodated to the ways of thinking common to the inferior man. When Confucius went to the State of Wei and saw the people there, he wanted first to enrich them and only then to instruct them.[28] Was he not aware that education is of far greater importance than wealth? But humble people must begin from the standpoint of gain; only then can they be led to accept a higher standard of morality.

366. There are three correct motives for doing good works. The lowest involves doing good in order to get to Heaven and to avoid going to Hell; the second, doing good in order to repay the Lord of Heaven for His profound favors; and the highest, doing good in order to harmonize with, and to obey, the Lord of Heaven's sacred will. A teacher inevitably hopes that his students will be successful; he has no alternative, however, but to begin by teaching them first principles. The masses have long been fond of gain, and if one does not guide them with the promise of gain, or frighten them by warning them of the losses they can incur, one will not be able to lead them.

367. But when higher motives are reached, the lower cannot co-exist with them and are eliminated. For example, silk thread is employed in the embroidering of clothes, but if steel needles are not used, the thread will not be able to penetrate the cloth. On the other hand, once the needle penetrates the material through which it passes, all that is left in the garment is the silk thread. If we wish to lead people so that they will take refuge in virtue and only point out to them the beauty of moral conduct, they will never discover it for themselves, because their minds are clouded by selfish desires. The things we say will not penetrate their minds and, because they do not wish to listen, they will depart. Only by first using the sufferings of Hell to frighten them, and the joys of Heaven to entice them, will they eventually be inclined to listen and gradually to ap-

368　往時敝邑出一名聖神，今人稱為拂郎祭斯穀，首立一會，其規戒精密，以廉為尚，今從者有數萬友，皆成德之士也。初有親炙一友，名曰如泥伯陸，會中無與比者，其學豁然，日增無息。有一邪鬼憎妒，欲阻之，偽化天神，旁射輝光，夜見於聖神私居曰：「天神諭爾，如泥伯陸德誠隆也，雖然，終不得擠天堂，必墮地獄。天主嚴命已定，不可易也。」

369　言訖弗見。拂郎祭斯穀驚，秘不敢洩，而心深痛惜。每見如泥伯陸不覺涕淚，如尼伯陸屢見而疑之，已齋宿，赴師座問曰：「某也日孜孜守戒，奉敬天主，幸在憫敎，通日以來，覺先生目有異也，何以數涕淚于弟子？」

釋解意不可滅。幷論死後必有天堂地獄之賞罰，以報世人所爲善惡。

29 *Sheng-shen* (聖神). See chapter 2, n. 7.
30 *Fu-lang-chi-ssu-ku* (拂郎祭斯穀). The expression used today is *Fang-chi-ko* (方濟各).
31 *Ju-ni-po-lu*. The characters used by Ricci were 如泥伯陸 ; today other characters which have a better meaning are used to indicate the same sound: 猶尼伯祿．

Motivation, Reward, and Punishment

proach that realm of perfection in which they delight in goodness and despise evil. When they attain to the realm of perfection deficiencies will be removed, and only their achievements will forever remain. This is why it is said that the bad avoid evil out of a fear of punishment and the good avoid evil out of a love of virtue.

368. Formerly, in my humble country, there appeared a saint.[29] People today call him Francis.[30] He established an order whose rules are most exact and which exalts purity of life. Members of that order now run into the tens of thousands, and all of them have reached a degree of success in the cultivation of virtue. At the beginning there was a member of this order called Juniper[31] whom Francis had trained himself, and there was no one in the order who could compare with him; his learning was brilliant, and he made continuous progress every day. There was a certain evil spirit which hated and envied him and which wanted to destroy him. It pretended to be an angel, and, shining, appeared one night in the saint's cell. It said: "This angel tells you clearly that although Juniper performs great moral feats he will not finally go to Heaven but will, eventually, descend to Hell; the awesome will of the Lord of Heaven has already determined it, and His will cannot be changed."

369. When he had finished speaking he disappeared. Francis was quite startled by what he had heard, but dared not reveal it to anyone, his heart being deeply grieved. Every time he saw Juniper he could not keep himself from weeping. When Juniper had seen this happen on a number of occasions he began to wonder what was the matter. He went to his master and asked: "Each day I diligently and unweariedly keep the rules and reverently serve the Lord of Heaven; I have been fortunate in winning your sympathy and in being taught by you. But over the past few days I have felt that there has been an unusual look in your eyes; why have you wept for me on a number of occasions?"

370 拂郎祭斯毅初不肯露,再三懇請,盡述向所見聞。如尼伯陸怡然曰:「是何足憂乎?天主宰人物,惟其旨所置之,上天下地,吾儕無不奉焉。吾所為敬愛之者,非為天堂地獄,為其至尊至善,自當敬、自當愛耳。今雖棄我,何敢毫髮懈惰,惟益加敬慎事之,恐在地獄時,即欲奉事而不可及矣。」

371 拂郎祭斯毅覩其容也,聽其語也,恍然悟而嘆曰:「愧哉前者所聞,有學道如斯,而應受地獄殃者乎?天主必擠爾天堂矣。」

372 夫此天堂地獄,其在成德之士,少借此意以取樂而免苦也,已矣。何者?天堂非他,乃古今仁義之人所聚光明之宇;地獄亦非他,乃古今罪惡之人所流穢污之域。升天堂者,已安其心乎善,不能易也;其落地獄者,已定其心乎惡,不克改也。吾願定心於德,勿移于不善;吾願長近仁義之君子,

釋解意不可滅。幷論死後必有天堂地獄之賞罰,以報世人所為善惡。

Motivation, Reward, and Punishment

370. At first Francis was unwilling to reveal what was on his mind, but after Juniper had pleaded with him repeatedly he told him everything that he had seen and heard. Juniper said, contentedly: "What cause for grief is there in this? The Lord of Heaven controls mankind and all things, and everything is ordered according to His sacred will. Heaven above and the earth beneath, and all of us serve Him. It is not on account of Heaven and Hell that I reverently love Him. Because [the Lord of Heaven is] the most noble and the most good, He ought naturally to be worshipped and adored. Although He may reject me, how dare I be at all delinquent in my duties. I must reverence and serve Him with even greater care lest, in Hell, I be unable to do so even if I should want to."

371. When Francis looked into Juniper's face and heard what he said, the truth suddenly dawned on him and with a sigh he said: "What I listened to before really was error. How can anyone who has practiced self-cultivation and studied the truth like this ever experience the perils of Hell? The Lord of Heaven is certain to promote you to Heaven."

372. People who have attained to perfection in their moral conduct seldom depend on the joy of Heaven or the suffering of Hell to motivate them. What is important for the majority is the cultivation of humanity and righteousness. And why should this be so? It is because Heaven is nothing other than that glorious place where those of the past and present who have cultivated humanity and righteousness foregather. And Hell is nothing other than that filthy place where the wrong-doers of past and present drift, homeless. Those who go to Heaven have already set their minds on goodness, and cannot be changed. Those who go to Hell have fixed their minds on evil and can no longer change them. I want to fix my mind on virtue and never to change course and turn to evil. I want constantly to associate with those superior men who practice humanity and righteousness and to withdraw from wrong-doing, inferior men for ever. Who says it is wrong to distinguish

永離罪惡之小人；誰云以利害分志，而在正道之外乎？儒者攻天堂地獄之說，是未察此理耳已。

373 中士曰：茲與浮屠勸世、輪廻變禽獸之說，何殊？

374 西士曰：遠矣。彼用「虛」「無」者偽詞，吾用「實」「有」者至理；彼言輪廻往生，止于言利；吾言天堂地獄利害，明揭利以引人于義。豈無辯乎？且夫賢者修德，雖無天堂地獄，不敢自已，況實有之。

375 中士曰：善惡有報，但云必在本世，或不於本身，必於子孫耳，不必言天堂地獄。

376 西士曰：本世之報微矣，不足以充人心之欲，又不滿誠德之功。公相之位，極重之酬矣，若以償德之價，萬不償一矣，天下固無可以償德之價者也。修德者雖不望報，上帝之尊豈有不報之盡滿者乎？王者

釋解意不可滅。并論死後必有天堂地獄之賞罰，以報世人所為善惡。

between men's ambitions on the basis of gain and loss? The reason why Confucianism attacks the doctrine of Heaven and Hell is that it has not investigated this truth.

373. *The Chinese scholar says:* What is the difference between this doctrine and the teaching of the Buddhists which uses reincarnation and rebirth in animal forms to induce people to do good?

374. *The Western scholar says:* There is a great difference between them. Whereas they use the false terms "empty" and "nonexistent," we use the supreme truth [contained in the words] "real" and "existent." They speak only of gain when they talk of reincarnation and past existences. When we talk of gain and loss in terms of Heaven and Hell we make the relationships between these things abundantly clear so that we can lead men to righteousness. How can there be no difference? Further, good men do not dare to refrain from cultivating their virtue even when [they believe] there is no Heaven and Hell. How much more will this be so when [it is realized that Heaven and Hell] really do exist?

375. *The Chinese scholar says:* Goodness is rewarded with goodness and evil with evil, but one need only assert that these rewards are bound to be met with in this world, if not by oneself, then by one's sons and grandsons. There is no need to introduce the doctrine of Heaven and Hell.

376. *The Western scholar says:* Rewards in this life are very small indeed and cannot satisfy the longings of men's minds; they are inadequate to the merit of virtue sincerely cultivated and are insufficient to express the power of the Sovereign on High to reward goodness. Aristocratic and ministerial ranks represent very great rewards, but if they are used as remuneration of the value of virtue they will not equal one ten thousandth of that value. There is nothing in the world which can match the value of virtue. Although men who cultivate virtue may not seek for any reward, would anyone as honorable as the Sovereign on High refrain from rewarding such virtue in full? Kings reward ministers for their ser-

酬臣之功,賞以三公足矣,上帝之酬而於是乎止乎?人之短于量也如是。

377 子孫自為子孫,夫我所親行善惡,盡以還之子孫,其可為公乎?且問天主既能報人善惡,何有能報其子孫,而不能報及其躬,何以捨此而遠俟其子孫之子孫?且其子孫又有子孫之善惡,何以為報?亦將俟其子孫之子孫,以酬之歟?

378 夫世之仁者不仁者,皆屢有無嗣者,其善惡何如報也?我自為我,爾為善,子孫為惡,則將舉爾所當享之賞,而盡加諸其為惡之身乎?可謂義乎?爾為惡,子孫為善,則將舉爾所當受之刑,而盡置諸其為善之躬乎?可為仁乎?非但王者、卽霸者之法,亦不如是。更善惡之報於他人之身,宰宇內之恒理,而俾其本身,而惟胃是報耶?天主捨民疑上帝之仁義,無所益於為政,不如各任其報耳。

釋解意不可滅。幷論死後必有天堂地獄之賞罰,以報世人所爲善惡。

Motivation, Reward, and Punishment

vices by simply conferring one of the three ranks of nobility upon them. But would the Sovereign on High consider such a reward sufficient? Man's way of looking at things is ultimately as limited as this.

377. Both the humane and the inhumane in this world are frequently without progeny; how are they to be rewarded for the good and evil they do? I am myself and children and grandchildren are themselves. Is it justice if the rewards and punishments for the good and evil that I personally do were to fall solely on the persons of sons and grandsons? May I ask why it is that, since the Lord of Heaven is able to reward and punish people for the good and evil they do, He is only able to reward and punish their sons and grandsons and not the people themselves? And if He is able to reward them, why does He neglect them and wait instead until their sons and grandsons come along? Moreover, sons and grandsons perform their own good and evil deeds; how are they to be rewarded? Has [the Lord of Heaven] to wait until their sons and grandsons are living before dispensing retribution?

378. If you do good and your sons and grandsons are evil, will it be right for the reward you ought to receive to be given to your evil sons and grandsons? If you do evil and your sons and grandsons do good, is it humane if the punishments due to you fall on your good sons and grandsons? Not only the laws of a good king, but even those of a tyrant will not make later generations culpable for the crimes of their forbears; will the Lord of Heaven then allow a man's offences to pass and visit them upon his descendents? Further, to allow rewards and punishments for good and evil to fall on someone else is to introduce confusion into the constant principles of the Universe and to cause people to doubt the humanity and righteousness of the Sovereign on High. It would be of no advantage to His rule, and it would be better, therefore, for each man to bear his own rewards and punishments.

379 中士曰：先生曾見有天堂地獄，而決曰有？

380 西士曰：吾子已見無天堂地獄，而決曰無？何不記前所云乎？智者不必以肉眼所見之事，方信其有，理之所見者，真于肉眼。夫耳目之覺，或常有差；理之所是，必無謬也。

381 中士曰：願聞此理。

382 西士曰：一曰：凡物類各有本性所向，必至是而定止焉；得此，則無復他望矣。人類亦必有止，然觀人之常情，未有以本世之事爲足者，則其心之所止不在本世明也。不在本世，非在後世天堂歟？蓋人心之所向，惟在全福，眾福備處乃謂天堂，是以人情未迄于是，未免有冀馬。全福之內含壽無疆，人世之壽——雖欲信天、地、人三皇及楚之冥釋解意不可滅。幷論死後必有天堂地獄之賞罰，以報世人所爲善惡。

Motivation, Reward, and Punishment

379. *The Chinese scholar says:* Sir, have you seen Heaven and Hell that you should assert their reality so firmly?

380. *The Western scholar says:* Have you, Sir, seen that there is no Heaven and Hell that you should so firmly assert their non-existence? Why do you not remember what I said earlier on; that the wise man will have no need to delay belief in something until he has seen it with his physical eyes. What reason brings to light is even more real than what is seen with the physical eyes. What ears and eyes hear and see is frequently in error, but what reason has determined cannot be in error.

381. *The Chinese scholar says:* I would like to hear your grounds for such an assertion.

382. *The Western scholar says:* First, things have goals to which their natures direct themselves, and they must attain to these goals if they are to enjoy serenity and stability. When they have attained them they will have no further desire. Men too must have a goal [which, when reached, will give them serenity and stability]. Nevertheless, when one observes man's normal circumstances, one finds that nothing in this present life fully satisfies him, and it becomes clear that the serenity and stability which will satisfy his mind is not to be found in this life. If it is not to be found in this life, must it not be found in Heaven in the next life? For that for which a man's mind craves is only to be found in perfect blessedness, and the place where all blessings are perfectly complete is called Heaven. Thus, so long as man has not reached Heaven, his state of mind will constantly be one of unsatisfied hopes. Perfect blessedness includes an unlimited life. Although one may wish to believe that some lives in this world are like the three powers of heaven, earth, and man, and that a man may live as long as the ming-ling tree of the State of Ch'u and the Great Ch'un of ancient times,[32] in the final analysis his life will still have a definite limit set to it. What this implies is that this life is full of shortcomings, and that no perfect blessedness exists in this so-called world of men.

靈、上古大椿——其壽終有界限，則現世悉有缺也。所謂世間無全福，彼善於此則有之﹔至于天堂，則止弗可尚，人性于是止耳。

383 二曰：人之所願，乃知無窮之真，乃好無量之好。夫性是天主所賦，豈徒然賦之？必將充之，亦必於來世盡充之。

384 三曰：德于此無價也，雖舉天下萬國而市之，則有德者不得其報稱矣。得罪上帝，其罪不勝重，雖以天下之極刑誅之，不滿其咎，苟不以地獄永殃之，則有罪者不得其報稱矣。天主掌握天下人所行，而德罪無報稱，未之有也。

385 四曰：上帝報應無私，善者必賞，惡者必罰。如今世之人，亦有為惡而富貴安樂，為善而貧賤苦難者，上帝固待其人之既死，然後取其善者之魂而天堂福之，審其惡者之魂而地獄刑之。不然，何以明至公、至審乎？

釋解意不可滅。并論死後必有天堂地獄之賞罰，以報世人所為善惡。

One can say that one thing is better than another, but when it comes to Heaven we have a state of perfection to which nothing can be added, and in which man's nature is fully satisfied.

383. Secondly, man's wish is to know inexhaustible truth and to enjoy unlimited goodness. But truth in this world is exhaustible, and goodness is limited; neither, then, can satisfy the desires of man's nature. Man's nature was bestowed on him by the Lord of Heaven, and He would hardly have bestowed it on him to no purpose. He is bound to cause it to be satisfied, and He is bound to satisfy it completely in the next life.

384. Thirdly, virtue is a priceless treasure and the possession of all the nations of this world would not be sufficient to compensate for its loss. If it is not rewarded with the eternal blessedness of Heaven then a virtuous person will not be rewarded with a fitting reward. To offend against the Sovereign on High is the most serious of crimes; and although one may punish the wrong-doer by means of the severest punishments to be found in this world, it will not suffice to make up for his transgression. Unless he is punished with the eternal sorrows of Hell he will not receive a fitting punishment. The Lord of Heaven holds the deeds of all men in the world in His hand, and there has never been an occasion when virtue or wrong-doing has failed to receive its just rewards.

385. Fourthly, the Sovereign on High is without prejudice in His rewards and punishments; where there is goodness it must be rewarded, and where there is evil it must be punished. In this world evil-doers sometimes enjoy wealth, honor, contentment, and joy; and men who do good sometimes experience poverty, loneliness, suffering, and hardship. This is most assuredly because the Lord on High wishes to wait until these people have died before raising the souls of the good to Heaven to enjoy a life of blessedness, and before judging the souls of the evil so that they might suffer the punishments of Hell. If this were not so, how could He manifest His perfect fairness and total lack of prejudice?

386 中士曰：善惡之報，亦有現世何如？

387 西士曰：設令善惡之報咸待于來世，則愚人不知來世之應者，何以驗天上之有主者？將益放恣無忌。故犯纂者，時遇饑荒之災，以懲其前而戒其後；順理者，時蒙吉福之降，以酬于往而勸其來也。然天主至公，無不盡賞之善，無不盡罰之惡。故終身為善不易其心，則應登天堂，享大福樂而賞之；終身為惡至死不悛，則宜墮地獄，受重禍災而罰之。

388 其有為善而貧賤者，或因為善之中有小過惡焉，故上帝以是現報之，至於歿後，旣無所欠，則入全福之域，永享常樂矣。亦有為惡而富貴者，乃行惡之際並有微善存焉，故上帝以是償之，及其死後，旣無可舉，則陷深陰之獄，永受釋解意不可滅。幷論死後必有天堂地獄之賞罰，以報世人所爲善惡。

386. *The Chinese scholar says:* But some good and evil is rewarded in this life. How do you account for this?

387. *The Western scholar says:* If rewards for good and evil were all postponed to the next life, how would it be possible to prove to those foolish people who have no knowledge of the rewards and punishments in the next life that there is a Lord in Heaven? The result would be that they would give even greater rein to evil, and would fear nothing. Thus, those who offend against the moral code frequently experience the disasters of hunger and famine as a warning before they act, or as a punishment following their offence. Those who act in accordance with their rational faculty frequently enjoy good fortune, either as a reward for what they have done in the past, or as an encouragement to do good in the future. But the Lord of Heaven is most fair; there is no goodness which is not fully rewarded, and no evil which is not fully punished. So it is that a man who consistently does good throughout his life is rewarded by being allowed to ascend to Heaven and to enjoy great blessings and happiness. A man who does evil, and who does not repent before he dies, is punished by being sent to Hell where he suffers great disasters.

388. There are those who do good but who are nevertheless poverty-stricken and lowly. This could be because small transgressions are to be found among their good deeds, and the Sovereign on High is therefore rewarding them with these things so that after death they will have no further debts to pay, and will be able to enjoy eternal happiness in that place of perfect blessedness. Then, there are those who do evil but who nevertheless enjoy wealth and honor. This is because there are some good deeds amidst all the evil they do, and the Sovereign on High is rewarding these deeds so that after death, when nothing more can be done to encourage them, the evil-doers will sink into the depths of Hell to experience for all eternity the suffering they must undergo for their wrongdoing. Do disaster and good fortune, both within and beyond the

罪苦矣。夫宇宙內外，災祥由天主歟？由命歟？天主令外，固無他命也。

389 中士曰：儒者以聖人為宗，聖人以經傳示敎，遍察吾經傳，通無天堂地獄之說，豈聖人有未達此理乎？何以隱而未著？

390 西士曰：聖人傳敎，視世之能載，故有數傳不盡者；又或有面語，而未悉錄于冊者；或已錄而後失者；或後頑史不信，因削去之者。況事物之文，時有換易，不可以無其文卽云無其事。

391 今儒之謬攻古書，不可勝言焉。急乎文，緩乎意，故今之文雖隆，今之行實衰。詩曰：「文王在上，於昭于天；文王陟降，在帝左右。」又曰：「世有哲王，三后在天。」召誥曰：「天旣遐終大邦殷之命。茲殷多先哲王在天。」夫在上、在天、在帝左右，非天堂之謂，其何歟？

釋解意不可滅。并論死後必有天堂地獄之賞罰，以報世人所爲善惡。

33 *Chinese Classics*, IV, pp. 427-428.
34 Ibid., IV, p. 458.
35 Ibid., III, p. 426.

328

universe, come from the Lord of Heaven or are they due to fate? Apart from the commands of the Lord of Heaven there can definitely be no other kind of fate.

389. *The Chinese scholar says:* Confucians regard the sages as authoritative examples [for the rest of mankind], and the sages used the canonical writings and their authoritative commentaries as media of instruction; but in all our canonical writings and their authoritative commentaries there is not a single mention of Heaven and Hell. Are you trying to say that the sages were ignorant of this teaching? Why is it concealed and not mentioned?

390. *The Western scholar says:* The teaching handed down from the sages was geared to what people were capable of accepting; thus, there are many teachings which, though handed down for generations, are incomplete. Then there are teachings which were given direct to students and which were not recorded in books or, if recorded, were subsequently lost. There is also the possibility that later, perverse historians removed parts of these records because they did not believe in their historical veracity. Moreover, written records are frequently subject to alteration, and one cannot say that because there is no written record certain things did not happen.

391. Confucians today constantly misinterpret the writings of antiquity; and because they put greater emphasis on style than on content, therefore, although the essay flourishes, [the quality of] its content has declined. In the *Book of Odes* we read: "King Wen is on high; Oh! bright is he in heaven ... King Wen ascends and descends, on the left and right of [the emperor]."[33] We also read: "For generations there had been wise kings; The three sovereigns were in heaven."[34] In the "Announcement of the Duke of Shao" in the *Book of History* we read: "When Heaven rejected and made an end of the decree in favor of the great State of Yin, there were many of the former intelligent kings of Yin in heaven."[35] When these various texts use the expressions "on high," "in heaven" and "to the left and right of [the emperor]," to what are they referring if not to Heaven?

329

392 中士曰：察此經語，古今聖人已信死後固有樂地為善者所居矣。然地獄之說，絕無可徵于經者。

393 西士曰：有天堂自有地獄，二者不能相無，其理一耳。如真文王、殷王、周公在天堂上，則桀、紂、盜跖必在地獄下矣。行異則受不同，理之常，因不容疑也。緣此，人之臨終，滋賢者則滋舒泰而略無駭色焉，滋不肖則滋逼迫而以死為痛苦不幸之極焉。

394 若以經書之未載為非真，且悞甚矣。西庫論之訣曰：「正書可證其有，不可證其無。」吾西國古經載昔天主開闢天地，即生一男，名曰亞黨，一女，名曰阨襪，是為世人之祖，而不書伏羲、神農二帝。吾以此觀之，可證當時果有亞黨、阨襪二人，伏羲，神農二帝也。然而不可證其後之無伏羲、神農二帝也。

釋解意不可滅。并論死後必有天堂地獄之賞罰，以報世人所為善惡。

36 Chih (跖) was the greatest robber in ancient times. Cf. *Chinese Classics*, II, p. 285.
37 Ricci used the characters 亞黨 "Ya-tang"; today 亞當 "Ya-tang" are used.
38 Ricci used 阨襪 "O-wa"; today 厄娃 "E-wa" are used.
39 Fu-hsi (伏羲), a legendary ruler to whom has been ascribed the Eight Trigrams employed for divination purposes. Shen-nung (神農), also a legendary ruler and cultural hero who was said to be the inventor of agriculture.

Motivation, Reward, and Punishment

392. *The Chinese scholar says:* When one investigates these classical texts one finds that the sages of ancient times already believed that after death there assuredly was a place of joy reserved for the good. But you definitely cannot discover any reference to Hell in the canonical writings.

393. *The Western scholar says:* If there is a Heaven there must be a Hell; the one cannot exist without the other because the reason for the one is the reason for the other. If King Wen, the kings of Yin and the Duke of Chou really are in Heaven, then the two great brigands, King Chieh [of the Hsia dynasty] and King Chou [of the Shang dynasty], and the Robber Chih[36] must be in Hell. Where each behaves in a different way, each is rewarded and punished differently. This is a constant principle which does not permit doubt. Thus, when people are about to die, the more virtuous they have been the more composed will they appear, and show no sign of fear; however, the more a person has broken the rules of conduct and behaved immorally the more anxious and fearful he will appear, and he will regard death as suffering and as a great misfortune.

394. If one says that Hell is not real because it is not referred to in the canonical writings one will be making a great mistake. According to the method of disputation in Western learned academies, an orthodox book can prove the existence of a fact, but it cannot prove the non-existence of a fact. In the ancient canonical writings of our Western nations, it is recorded that formerly, when the Lord of Heaven created heaven and earth, he created a man, who was called Adam,[37] and a woman, called Eve,[38] the first ancestors of all people in this world. These canoncial writings make no mention, however, of the two emperors Fu Hsi and Shen Nung.[39] We can prove from this that there really were two people called Adam and Eve, but we cannot prove that later there was no Fu Hsi and Shen Nung.

331

395 若自中國之書觀之，可證古有伏羲、神農于中國，而不可證無亞黨、陡禨二祖也。不然，禹蹟不寫大西諸國，可謂天下無大西諸國哉？故儒書雖未明辯天堂地獄之理，然不宜因而不信也。

396 中士曰：善者登天堂，惡者墮地獄，設有不善不惡之輩死後當往何處？

397 西士曰：善惡無間，非善即惡，非惡即善，惟善惡之中有巨微之別耳。善惡譬若生死，人不生則死，未死則生，固無弗生弗死者也。

398 中士曰：使有人先為善，後變而為惡；有先為惡，後改而為善；兹二人身後何如？

399 西士曰：天主乃萬靈之父，限本世之界以勸告儕于德，必以瀕死之候為定。故平生為善，須臾變心向惡而死，便為犯人，則受地獄常永之殃，其前善惟末減耳；平生為惡，今日改心歸善而死，則天主必扶而宥之，免前罪而授天堂，萬年永常受福也。

釋解意不可滅。并論死後必有天堂地獄之賞罰，以報世人所為善惡。

Motivation, Reward, and Punishment

395. If we look at things from the standpoint of the Chinese canonical writings, however, we can prove that in ancient China there were two men called Fu Hsi and Shen Nung, but we cannot prove that our first parents, Adam and Eve, did not exist. If this were not so, would it not be possible to say that the many countries in the West do not exist simply because there is no mention of them in the records which give an account of Yü [of the Hsia dynasty]? Thus, although the books of Confucianism do not argue clearly for the doctrine of Heaven and Hell, one should not for this reason refuse to believe it.

396. *The Chinese scholar says:* So good people go to Heaven and evil people to Hell. But what if there is someone who is neither good nor evil; where ought he to go when he dies?

397. *The Western scholar says:* There is nothing intermediate between good and evil. If something is not good, then it is evil; and if it is not evil, then it is good. In good and evil there are only distinctions of degree. Good and evil are like life and death. If a person is not alive he is dead, and if he is not dead he is alive. There has never been anyone who was neither alive nor dead.

398. *The Chinese scholar says:* What happens after death to one person who is at first good, and then later turns into a bad person; and to another person who is at first bad, and then later changes into a good person?

399. *The Western scholar says:* The Lord of Heaven is the father of all intellects and sets the limits to this life. Since he exhorts us to be virtuous, he is bound to wait until we are about to die before determining what will happen to us. Thus, if a person does good throughout his life, but then dies after suddenly turning in the direction of evil, he is a wrong-doer and will therefore suffer the eternal misfortunes of Hell; but, because of his former goodness, his punishment may be lightened. A person who spends his whole life doing evil but who dies after changing his mind and reforming is bound

400 中士曰：如此，則平生之惡無報焉？

401 西士曰：天主經云：「人改惡之後，或自悔之深，或以苦勞本身自懲，于以求天主之宥，天主必且赦之，而死後即可昇天也。倘悔之不深，自苦不及前罪，則地獄之內另有一處以置此等人，或受數日數年之殃，以補在世不滿之罪報也，補之盡則亦躋天。」其理如此。

402 中士曰：心悟此理之是，第先賢之書云：「何必信天堂地獄？如有天堂，君子必登之；如有地獄，小人必入之。吾當為君子則已。」此語庶幾得之？

403 西士曰：此語固失之。何以知其然乎？有天堂，君子登之必也，但弗信天堂地獄之理，決非君子。

404 中士曰：何也？

405 西士曰：且問乎子，不信有上帝，其君子人歟？否歟？

釋解意不可滅。并論死後必有天堂地獄之賞罰，以報世人所為善惡。

40. Ricci is referring to the doctrine of purgatory, in Chinese *lien-yü* (煉獄).

to be supported and pardoned by the Lord of Heaven. His former trangressions will be forgiven, and he will be rewarded by being allowed to ascend to Heaven where he will enjoy eternal felicity.

400. *The Chinese scholar says:* In that event, the evil he has done throughout his life will not reap its appropriate reward.

401. *The Western scholar says:* In the canonical writings of the Lord of Heaven it is stated that if a man turns from evil to do good, or profoundly repents his former evil, or strives to atone for the past and disciplines himself, and by these means seeks for the forgiveness of the Lord of Heaven, he is bound to be pardoned by the Lord of Heaven and to be able to go to Heaven following his death. If his repentance is insufficiently profound, and if the atonement he makes for his former sins is inadequate, then, within Hell, there is another place where such a person can be appropriately dealt with and given punishment lasting several days or several years to make up for the inadequate retribution he experienced for his wrong-doing whilst on earth.[40] When full atonement has been made he may then go to Heaven. Such is the doctrine.

402. *The Chinese scholar says:* I understand this doctrine now; but in the writings of former worthies it is stated: "Why must one believe in Heaven and Hell? If there is a Heaven the superior man is bound to go there, and if there is a Hell the inferior man is bound to go there. We ought simply to be superior men." Surely such an assertion cannot be wrong!

403. *The Western scholar says:* There is something lacking in this statement; and why? If there is a Heaven, then the superior man will certainly go to Heaven. But anyone who does not believe in the truth of Heaven and Hell is definitely not a superior man.

404. *The Chinese scholar says:* Why?

405. *The Western scholar says:* Let me ask you, Sir: can a person who does not believe in the existence of the Lord on High be accounted a superior man?

406 中士曰：否。詩曰：「維此文王，小人翼翼，昭事上帝。」孰謂君子而弗信上帝者？

407 西士曰：不信上帝至仁至公，其君子人歟？否歟？

408 中士曰：否。上帝為仁之原也，萬物公主也，孰謂君子而弗信其至仁至公者耶？

409 西士曰：仁者為能愛人、能惡人。苟上帝不予善人升天堂，何足云能愛人？不逆惡人于地獄，何足云能惡人乎？夫世之賞罰大略，未能盡公，若不待身後以天堂地獄，還各行之當然，則不免乎私焉。弗信此，烏信上帝為仁、為公哉

? 釋解意不可滅。并論死後必有天堂地獄之賞罰，以報世人所爲善惡。

410 且夫天堂地獄之報，中華佛老二氏信之，儒之智者亦從之，太東太西諸大邦無疑之，天主聖經載之，吾前者揭明理而顯之，則拗逆者必非君子也。

41 See *The Chinese Classics*, IV, p. 433.

336

406. *The Chinese scholar says:* No. In the *Book of Odes* it is stated: "This King Wen, watchfully and reverently, with entire intelligence served the Sovereign on High."[41] How can anyone who refuses to believe in the existence of the Sovereign on High be called a superior man?

407. *The Western scholar says:* Can a person be a superior man when he does not believe that the Sovereign on High is supremely humane and supremely just?

408. *The Chinese scholar says:* No. Because the Sovereign on High is the source of humanity and the just lord of all things. How can anyone be called a superior man when he refuses to believe that [the Sovereign on High] is supremely humane and supremely just?

409. *The Western scholar says:* One who is humane can both love people and hate them. If the Sovereign on High does not grant good men the right to go to Heaven, how can He be said to love people; and if He does not spurn evil men and punish them by sending them to Hell, how can He be said to hate them? Rewards and punishments in this world can probably never be entirely just; if Heaven and Hell are not given to men following their deaths as rewards and punishments rightly due to them for what each has done, then it will not be possible to avoid partiality. How can anyone believe that the Sovereign on High is humane and just and yet refuse to believe this?

410. Moreover, both Buddhists and Taoists in China believe in the rewards of Heaven and Hell, and the wise among the Confucians also accept this teaching. The people of many great nations in both the East and the West voice no doubt concerning this doctrine. It is also recorded in the sacred canonical writings of the Lord of Heaven. The day before yesterday I clarified this doctrine and proved its truth. Those who obstinately oppose it definitely cannot be superior men.

411 中士曰：如此，則固信之矣，然尚願聞其說。

412 西士曰：難言也。天主經中特舉其概，不詳傳之。然夫地獄之刑於今世之殃略近，吾可借而比焉；彼天堂之快樂，何能言乎？夫本世之患有息有終，地獄之苦無間無窮。

413 聖賢論地獄分其苦勞二般；或責其內中，或責其表外。若凍熱之不勝，臭穢之難當，饑渴之至極，是外患也；若戰慄視厲鬼魔威，恨妬膽天神福樂，愧悔無及憶己前行，乃內禍也。雖然，罪人所傷痛莫深乎所失之巨福也，故常哀哭自悔曰：「悲哉！吾生前為淫樂之微，失無窮之福而溺于此萬苦之聚谷乎，今欲改過免此而已遲。欲死而畢命以脫此而不得，蓋此非改過之時。」

414 天主公法所使：以刑具苦痛其人，不令毀滅其體，而以悠久受殃也。夫不欲死後落地獄，全在生時思省，思其苦，思其勞，思其戒，戒則不為陷溺之事釋解意不可滅。幷論死後必有天堂地獄之賞罰，以報世人所為善惡。

Motivation, Reward, and Punishment

411. *The Chinese scholar says:* In that case I assuredly believe this doctrine. But I should still like to be given additional reasons for accepting it.

412. *The Western scholar says:* It is a very difficult subject to explain. The canonical writings of the Lord of Heaven only provide a general outline of it and do not teach it in detail; nevertheless, natural disasters in this life approximate somewhat to the punishments of Hell, and can be used to illustrate them. How can the happiness of Heaven be described in words? The travails of this life cease and have an end. The sufferings of Hell are continuous and inexhaustible.

413. When sages and worthies discuss Hell they divide its travails into two categories: (1) internal suffering, and (2) external suffering. External sufferings are unbearable cold and heat, intolerable odors and extreme hunger and thirst. Internal sufferings include shuddering from fear at the sight of the severity and awesomeness of the Devil; envy on seeing the blessed joys of the angels, and the impossibility of repenting sufficiently for former wrong-doings now remembered. Even so, what hurts the guilty most is their loss of great blessings. They therefore constantly mourn and cry with regret: "Alas! When I was alive I gave up inexhaustible blessings and joy for the sake of a little lewd pleasure, and have now fallen into this deep ravine where all sufferings are accumulated. Even though I now want to reform and to escape these sufferings it is too late. Even if I wish to seek death by committing suicide in order to escape from this place I cannot do so, since the time for reform and renewal has already passed."

414. The just laws of the Lord of Heaven are such that he uses punishment to cause men to suffer, but he does not permit men to destroy their bodies which must experience prolonged suffering. If a person does not wish to go to Hell after he dies, all will depend on whether he has engaged in self-reflection during his

，而地獄可免焉。

415 天主所備以待仁人者，目所未見，耳所未聞，人心所未及忖度者也。」從是可徵其處為眾吉所歸，諸凶之所遠焉。

416 夫欲度天堂光景，且當縱目觀茲天地萬物，現在奇麗之景多令人歎息無已者，而即復推思，此乃上帝設之以為人民鳥獸共用之具，若其獨為善人造作全福之處，更當何哉？必也：常為暄春，無寒暑之迭累；常見光明，無暮夜之屢更；其人常快樂，大壽無憂怨哀哭之苦；常舒泰，無危險；韶華之容，常駐不變；歲年來往，無減；常生不滅，周旋左右于上帝。世俗之人烏能達之？烏能言釋之哉？

設地獄之嚴刑不足以動爾心，天堂之福當必望之。經曰：「天堂之樂，

釋解意不可滅。并論死後必有天堂地獄之賞罰，以報世人所為善惡。

42 See I Cor 2:9.

340

Motivation, Reward, and Punishment

lifetime: whether he has considered the sufferings and tribulations of Hell. If he has thought of these things he will caution himself and, having cautioned himself, will not sink into bad habits, and will avoid descending into Hell.

415. If the severe punishments of Hell are incapable of moving your mind, you ought to hope for the blessings of Heaven. The canonical writings state: "The Lord of Heaven has prepared the joys of Heaven for humane men. They are joys which no eye has ever seen, no ears have ever heard of, and no mind of man has ever conceived."[42] From this one can prove that in Heaven everything good and beneficial is gathered together, and that it is distantly separated from all that is evil.

416. If a person wishes to conjecture the circumstances of Heaven, he ought to observe heaven, earth and all things. Many of the strange and beautiful things that exist elicit from people unceasing admiration. Later, on giving these things further thought, they realize that the Sovereign on High has provided these things for the use and enjoyment of men and animals. Although this world is a dwelling place for both good and evil men alike, still it has been created as well as it has. How much better, then, must a place of perfect blessedness be which has been prepared for the good alone? It must provide constant, mild spring weather with none of the troubles of winter and summer; it must constantly be light, and there must be no night. The inhabitants [of such a place] must constantly be happy and suffer no grief, anger, or tears. They must enjoy constant comfort and never experience danger. The countenance of spring must be constant and unchanging; the years may come and go, yet men's lives must not be shortened because they must live for ever and not die, ever dwelling to the left and right of the Lord on High. How can the vulgar of this world understand; and how can human language explain such a place?

417 夫眾福吉之浴泉,聖神所常嗜、所常食,嗜而未始乏,食而未始饜也。此者?各滿其量也。譬長身者長衣,短身者短衣,長短各得其所,欲何憎之有?眾善為侶,和順親愛,俯視地獄之苦,豈不更增快樂也乎?白者比黑而彌白,光者比暗而彌光也。

418 天主正教以此頒訓于世,而吾輩拘於目所恆覩,不明未見之理。比如囚婦懷胎產子暗獄,其子至長而未知日月之光,山水人物之嘉,只以大燭為日,小燭為月,以獄內人物為齊整,無以尚也,則不覺獄中之苦,始以為樂不思出矣。若其母語之以日月之光輝、貴顯之粧飾、天地境界之文章、廣大數萬里

釋解意不可滅。幷論死後必有天堂地獄之賞罰,以報世人所爲善惡。

43 *Li* (里) and *chang* (丈) are units of measure. See chapter 2, n. 35.

342

Motivation, Reward, and Punishment

417. The abundant springs of blessings, joy, and goodness tasted by the saints never run dry, and [the inhabitants] are satiated as a result of drinking from these springs. Because of merit gained whilst alive people enjoy varied blessings. The blessings they receive are proportionate to the merit they have won, yet no one harbors a grudge against another. And why is this so? Because each is satisfied according to his own capacity. It is like the human body which, if large, wears ample garments, but which, if small, wears small garments. If the large and the small, the tall and the short, all get what they require, there is no reason for one to harbor a grudge against another. All good people [in Heaven] are companions; they are accommodating and loving, and when they look down at the sufferings of Hell their happiness and rejoicing is increased. White is even whiter when compared with black, and light is even lighter when compared with darkness.

418. The orthodox religion of the Lord of Heaven employs this doctrine to instruct and guide the people of the world; but we who are surrounded by things constantly seen with our eyes cannot understand this truth which cannot be seen with the physical eye. It is like a woman with child who is incarcerated in prison. She gives birth to the child in the dark prison, and the child knows nothing of the light of sun and moon or of the goodness of mountains, rivers, and people until it has grown to maturity. Only the light of a large candle serves as his sun and the light of a small candle as his moon. He regards the people in prison as being exceedingly orderly, and perhaps even feels that the sufferings he experiences in prison are happiness, and consequently does not think of leaving prison. If his mother should explain to him the nature of the light of sun and moon; show him the dress and adornments of noble men, and acquaint him with the unexpected size of each of the realms of heaven and earth—their breadth which extends to tens of thousands of *li*,[43] and their height which measures millions of

、高億萬丈,而後知容光之細、桎梏之苦、囹圄之窄穢,則不肯復安爲家矣。世人不信天堂地獄,或乃始晝夜圖脫其手足之桎梏,而出尋朋友親戚之樂矣。世人不信天堂地獄,或疑,或誚,豈不悲哉?

中士曰:悲哉!世人不爲二氏所誕,則蕩蕩如無牧之群,以苦世爲樂地天堂耳。茲語也,慈母之訓也。吾已知有本家,尚願習回家之路。

西士曰:正路茅塞,邪路反闢,固有不知其路而妄爲引者。真似僞也,僞近真也,不可錯認也,向萬福而卒至萬苦皋,彼行路,慎之哉?

釋解意不可滅。并論死後必有天堂地獄之賞罰,以報世人所爲善惡。

44 Ricci no doubt had in mind certain superficial similarities between Buddhism and Christianity.

chang, he will then come to realize how small are the lights in the prison; how painful the shackles on hands and feet, and how narrow and filthy is the prison. When he has realized all this, he will no longer be willing to accept the prison as his home, and he will begin, day and night, to work out how to rid his hands and feet of their shackles, and how to leave the prison in order to look for the happiness of friends and relatives. Of those in the world who do not believe in Heaven and Hell, some are sceptical and others ridicule. Are they not to be pitied?

419. *The Chinese scholar says:* They are indeed to be pitied! People who do not accept the musings of the Buddhists and Taoists drift through this world like sheep without a shepherd, regarding this cruel world as a paradise or as Heaven. These words of yours are the teachings of a compassionate mother. I now know that human beings have a real home, and I should like to learn of the path which leads to that home.

420. *The Western scholar says:* The correct path is full of stumbling-blocks, whereas the heterodox path is open and broad. Then, there are those who do not know the way and who serve as false guides. The true path resembles the false path, and the false path looks much like the true path, so one must not be mistaken concerning the path one chooses.[44] If one intends to travel in the direction of perfect happiness and finds, in the end, that one has arrived at the place where all is suffering, the blame must be laid on the path that was chosen. Can one fail to exercise caution?

第七篇

論人性本善，而述天主門士正學

421

中士曰：先辱示以天主為兆民尊父，則知宜慕愛。次示人類靈魂身後不滅，則知本世暫寄，不可為重。復聞且有天堂為善者昇焉，居彼已定心修德以事上帝，與神人為侶，況有地獄；居彼已定心不改惡，以受刑殃致萬世不可脫也。茲欲詢事天主正道。夫吾儒之學，以率性為修道，設使性善，則率之無錯；若或非盡善，性固不足恃也，奈何？

Chapter 7

A DISCUSSION ON THE [CONFUCIAN] TEACHING THAT HUMAN NATURE IS FUNDAMENTALLY GOOD, AND AN EXPOSITION OF THE ORTHODOX [WAY OF] LEARNING OF THOSE WHO ADHERE TO THE RELIGION OF THE LORD OF HEAVEN.

421. *The Chinese scholar says:* I have already been favored with your instruction in which you have indicated that the Lord of Heaven is the most honored father of all people, and I have been made to realize that I ought to love and respect Him. You have also pointed out that the soul of man is not destroyed following the death of his body, and I am therefore aware that this present world is only a temporary abode and that I may not ascribe undue importance to it. I have also heard you say that a person who does good ascends to Heaven, and that those who have already fixed their minds on the cultivation of virtue in order to serve the Sovereign on High will there be the companions of angels and sages. Furthermore, [you have taught that] there is a Hell, and that those who have already determined not to turn from their evil ways will be punished there forever, and will never be able to escape from it. I would now like to ask you about the right way to serve the Sovereign of Heaven. According to our Confucian teachings, the cultivation of the Way lies in following human nature. If human nature is good, then one cannot go wrong if one is able to follow it. If human nature is not entirely good, however, it will be unreliable. What is to be done then?

論人性本善，而述天主門士正學

422 西士曰：吾觀儒書嘗論性情，而未見定論之訣，故一門之中恆出異說。知事而不知己本，知之亦非知也。

423 欲知人性其本善耶，先論何謂性、何謂善惡。夫「性」也者非他，乃各物類之本體耳。曰各物類也，則同類同性，異類異性。曰「本」也者，則凡不在其物之體界內，亦非性也。但物有自立者，而性亦為自立；有依賴者，而性兼為依賴。

424 可愛可欲謂善，可惡可疾謂惡也。通此義者，可以論人性之善否矣。

425 西儒說「人」云，是乃生覺者、能推論理也：曰生，以別于金石；曰能推論理，以殊乎鳥獸；曰推論不直曰明達，又以分之乎鬼神。鬼神者，徹盡物理如照如視，不待推論；人也者，以其前

---

1 Mencius and Hsün Tzu (荀子), both of whom were Confucians, appeared to be diametrically opposed on this issue. Mencius taught that human nature was good and Hsün Tzu said it was bad. Later Confucians sought to reconcile these two views.

The Cultivation of Virtue

422. *The Western scholar says:* From my reading of Confucian literature I have found that human nature is continually discussed, but I have never found any unanimity of opinion. Thus, in any one school one can discover a variety of teachings.[1] [Scholars] are aware of [the natures of] all things, but not of [the true nature of] themselves; what they originally knew cannot be reckoned knowledge.

423. If one wants to know whether human nature is fundamentally good or not one ought first to discuss what is meant by nature and what is meant by good and evil. "Nature" is nothing other than the fundamental essence of each category of things. When one speaks of "each category" of things one concludes that things of the same category have similar natures and that things of different categories have different natures. When one uses the word "fundamental" one means that anything included in the principles of other categories is not the fundamental nature of this category. When one speaks of "essence" one means that anything beyond the boundaries of the essence of this thing is not the nature of this thing. But, when things are substance, their natures are also autonomous; and when things are accident, their natures are also dependent.

424. Whatever is lovable and desirable is termed good, and whatever is loathsome and hateful is termed evil. When one understands these definitions one can then go on to discuss whether human nature is good or not.

425. Western scholars define "man" in the following manner: He is [a creature] who has life and awareness, and who is also capable of reason. When he is said to have life he is distinguished from metal and stone; when he is said to have awareness he is distinguished from vegetation, and when he is said to be capable of reason he is distinguished from birds and animals. When man is said to be capable of reason but not of immediate comprehension, he is distinguished from spiritual beings, because spirits have

論人性本善，而述天主門士正學

推明其後，以其顯驗其隱，以其既曉及其所未曉也。故曰能推論理者立人於本類，而別其體於他物，乃所謂人性也。仁義禮智，在推理之後也。

426 解者曰：「人得性之正，禽獸得性之偏也。」「理」則無二無偏，是古之賢者固不同「性」於「理」矣。

427 「理」也，乃依賴之品，不得為人性也。古有岐人性之善否，誰有疑「理」為有弗善者乎？孟子曰：「人性與牛犬性不同。」

428 釋此，庶可答子所問人性善否歟？若論厥性之體及情，均為天主所化生。而以理為主，則俱可愛可欲，而本善無惡矣。至論其用機，又由乎我，我或有可愛、或有可惡，所行異則用之善惡無定焉，所為情也。

2 According to Neo-Confucianism, *jen* (仁, "humanity"), *i* (義, "righteousness"), *li* (禮, "decorum") and *chih* (智, "wisdom") are essential characteristics of human nature which men receive from Heaven.

3 According to Neo-Confucianism, *li* (理) is the Absolute which in man is called *hsing* (性, "nature"), and in God (Heaven) is called *ming* (命, "order," "destiny," "mandate of Heaven"), so it seems that *li* means more than "reason." Ricci did not understand this and so he interprets *li* merely as "reason."

4 See *Chinese Classics*, II, p. 397.

The Cultivation of Virtue

a thorough and complete understanding of the principles of things. For them, knowledge is like a reflection in a mirror: When they see things they understand them, and have no need to reason them out. Men can infer what will happen in the future from what has happened in the past; they employ what is manifest to prove what is hidden. They use what they already know to deduce that of which they are still ignorant. [Western scholars] therefore say that the capacity to reason establishes man in his own category; that it distinguishes man from all other things, and that it is that which is called human nature. Humanity, righteousness, decorum, and wisdom[2] are subsequent to the capacity to reason.

426. "Reason"[3] itself is accident and cannot be said to be human nature. In ancient times people were divided over the question of whether human nature is good or not; but who would doubt the goodness of reason? Mencius asserted that man's nature is different from the natures of oxen and dogs.[4] Some have explained this by saying that man received nature in all its uprightness, whereas animals received it in its obliqueness. But there is no such thing as two reasons or an oblique reason; therefore, worthy men of ancient times did not equate nature with reason.

427. Now that I have explained the several points above I can answer your question: Is human nature good? If we say that the essence of human nature together with [human] feelings are all produced by the Lord of Heaven, and if we let reason be the master of them, then [we can also say that] they are lovable and desirable and are essentially good and not evil.

428. When we come to the uses to which these things are put, however, we find that it all depends on the individual. I can be lovable, but I can also be loathsome; my actions vary, and therefore it is uncertain as to whether the use to which I put [my endowments] will be good or bad. This is where my feelings or passions come into play.

429 夫性之所發，若無病疾必自聽命于理，無有違節，即無不善。然情也者性之足也，時著偏疾者也，故不當壹隨其欲，不察于理之所指也。身無病時，口之所啖，甜者甜之，苦者苦之；乍遇疾變，以甜為苦，以苦為甜者有焉。性情之已病，而接物之際惧感而拂于理，其所愛惡，其所是非者，鮮得其真、鮮合于理者。然本性自善，此亦無碍于稱之為善，蓋其能推論理，則良能常存，可以認本病，而復治療之。

430 中士曰：貴邦定善之理曰：可愛；定惡之理曰：可惡。是一說固盡善惡之情。敝國之士有曰：「出善乃善，出惡乃惡。」亦是一端之理。若吾性既善，此惡自何來乎？

431 西士曰：吾以性能行善惡，固不可謂性自本有惡矣。惡非實物，乃無善之謂，如死非他，乃無生之謂耳。如士師能死罪人，詎其有「死」在己乎？苟世人者生而不能不為善。從何處可稱成善乎？天下無無意于為善而可以為善也。

429. If a man's nature is free of any ailment it is bound to follow the dictates of reason in whatever it sets out to do. If it does not step beyond its proper bounds, it will do nothing but good. But the feelings and passions are the "feet" of human nature, and they are frequently afflicted with selfishness. One should not therefore constantly follow one's desires without investigating whether or not one is in accord with the dictates of reason. When the body is free of disease the sweet things one eats taste sweet, and the bitter, bitter. It sometimes happens, however, that when a man suddenly falls ill, sweet things taste bitter, and bitter things sweet. Because our natures have been infected with disease, when we come into contact with things we gain a mistaken impression of them which is not in accordance with reason; our loves and hates and our judgments concerning the rightness and wrongness of things are seldom correct and seldom true. Nevertheless, our fundamental nature was originally good. So that there is no reason why one should not say it is good. Because it has the capacity to reason, its "innate ability" is always in existence, and this can be used to recognize one's own sickness, and to effect a recovery.

430. *The Chinese scholar says:* In your esteemed country you have defined goodness as that which is lovable and evil as that which is hateful. This statement assuredly gives a full account of the nature of good and evil. But in my humble country there are those who say that goodness emerges from goodness and evil from evil. This, too, is a statement of truth. If my nature is good, where does evil come from?

431. *The Western scholar says:* I can do both good and evil with my human nature, but one cannot say that human nature was originally evil. Evil is not a thing with substance, but rather a way of referring to a lack of goodness. It is like death, which is nothing but a way of speaking of a lack of life. The chief criminal judge can apply the death penalty to criminals, but one can hardly say that he carries death on his person. If men were unable to do anything but good from the moment of birth, how could one speak

論人性本善，而述天主門士正學

432 吾能無強我為善而自往為之，方可謂善之君子。天主賦人此性能行二者，所以厚人類也，其能取捨此善，非但增為善之功，尤俾其功為我功焉。故曰：「天主所以生我，非用我；所以善我，乃用我。」此之謂也。即如設正鵠，射者失之；亦猶惡情於世，非以使人為之。彼金石鳥獸之性不能為善惡，不如人性能之以建其功也。其功非功名之功，德行之真功也。人之性情雖本善，不可因而謂世人之悉善人也，惟有德之人乃為善人。德加于善，其用也在本善性體之上焉。

433 中士曰：性本必有德，無德何為善？所謂君子，亦復其初也。

434 西士曰：設謂善者惟復其初，則人皆生而聖人也，而何謂「有生而知之，有學而知之」之別乎？如謂德非自我新知，而但返其所已有；已失之大犯罪，今復之不足以為大功。

5 See Chan, *A Source Book in Chinese Philosophy*, pp. 278, 84-85.

The Cultivation of Virtue

of anyone becoming good? There is no such thing in the world as unintentional goodness.

432. I can refrain from doing good, and it is only when I decide to go and do good that I can be said to be a superior man who does good works. When the Lord of Heaven bestowed this nature on man, man was capable of doing both good and evil, and man was enriched thereby. Because man can take or reject goodness, not only is the merit of goodness increased, but that merit becomes man's own. It is therefore said that when the Lord of Heaven produced man He made no use of him, but that when He wanted him to be good He had to make use of him. A target is not set up so that the bowman will miss it; and evil is not in the world to encourage people to do it. The natures of metal, stone and animals are incapable of doing good and evil. Human nature is different; it is capable of doing either the one or the other and thereby establishing merit. The merit I am speaking of here has nothing to do with the merit of honor or rank but only with the true merit of virtue. Although human nature is fundamentally good, one cannot for this reason say that all men are good. Only those who possess virtue can be called good. Virtuous conduct added to goodness is the expression [of that goodness]. This is how man perfects that which is fundamentally good.

433. *The Chinese scholar says:* Nature must always harbor virtue; if it does not, how can it be good? That is why it is said that the superior man is simply the one who restores the nature he originally possessed!

434. *The Western scholar says:* If goodness merely means the restoration of original nature, then every person would be a sage at birth. Why should a distinction be made between "knowing it at birth and knowing it through education"?[5] If you say that virtue does not represent new knowledge, and that it is merely a restoration of what I already have, then its loss was a great offence. To restore what one has lost cannot be said to be a work of great merit.

論人性本善，而述天主門士正學

435 則固須認二善之品矣：性之善，為良善；德之善，為習善。夫良善者，天主原化性命之德，而我無功焉；我所謂功，止在自習積德之善也。

436 孩提之童愛親，鳥獸亦愛之；常人不論仁與不仁，乍見孺子將入於井，即皆怵惕；此皆良善耳。彼或有所未能、或有所未暇視義，無以成德也。鳥獸與不仁者何德之有乎？見義而即行之，乃為德耳。

437 故謂人心者，始生如素簡無所書也，又如艷貌女人，其美則可愛，然皆其父母之遺德也，不足以見其本德之巧；若視其衣錦尚絅，而後其德可知也，茲乃女子本德矣。吾性質雖妍，如無德以飾之，何足譽乎？

438 吾西國學者謂德乃神性之寶服，以久習義、念義行生也。謂「服」，則可著、可脫，而得之于忻然為善之念，所謂聖賢者也。不善者反是。但德與罪皆無形之服也，而惟無形之心—即吾所謂神者—衣之耳。

6 This example is quoted from Mencius. See *Chinese Classics*, II, p. 202.

The Cultivation of Virtue

435. You must admit, then, that there are two kinds of goodness!

The goodness of human nature is "innate goodness," whereas the goodness of virtue is " acquired goodness." "Innate goodness" is the virtue originally bestowed on man by the Lord of Heaven, and man can claim no merit for that. The merit I am speaking of here is limited to the goodness of that virtue which man himself accumulates through his own efforts.

436. Children love their parents, but so do animals. When ordinary people suddenly see a child about to fall into a well they will feel fearful and apprehensive for it whether they are humane or not.⁶ Such concern results from "innate goodness." But what virtue is there in this when even animals and the inhumane [all possess this kind of "innate goodness"?] Virtue can only be regarded as such when a person does what he sees to be right. If people are unable to do what is right when they see it, or are neglectful of it, they will not be able to be virtuous.

437. It has therefore been said that when a child is born its mind is like a sheet of white paper on which nothing has been written. It is also like the beauty of a woman's face which, though lovable, is a virtue inherited from her parents and which is an insufficient indication of the qualities of her own virtue. If one sees her wearing an outer garment over a silk dress, one will know the nature of her virtue—a virtue which is her own. I may have beautiful qualities, but if I do not adorn them with virtue, of what can I boast?

438. The learned men of our Western countries say that virtue is the precious adornment of the spirit, and that if one habitually thinks of righteousness this will result in righteous behavior. Now, adornments can be either worn or discarded. To attain to [righteousness] by happily thinking of doing good is to be what is called a sage or a worthy man, who is opposed by the wicked. But virtue and wrong-doing are both incorporeal adornments, and only the incorporeal mind—what I have called the spirit—can wear such adornments.

357

439 中士曰：論性與德，古今眾矣，如闡其衷根，則茲始聞焉。夫為非義，猶以汙穢染本性；為義，猶以文錦彰之。故德修而性彌美焉，此誠君子修己之功。然又有勉于外事，而不復反本者。

440 西士曰：惜哉！世俗之盡日周望，殫心力以疊偽珍悅肉眼，而不肯略啟心目以視千萬世之文彩、內神之真寶也；宜其逐日操心困苦，而臨終之候，哀痛俱慄如畜獸被牽於屠矣。

441 天主生我世間，使我獨勤事于德業，常自得無窮之福，不煩外借焉；而我自棄之，反以行萬物之役，趨百危險，誰咎乎？誰咎乎？

442 夫人非願為尊富，惟願恒得其所欲耳。得所欲之路無他，不在我者焉。我固有真我也，我自害之心之害乃真害也。人以形神兩端相結

439. *The Chinese scholar says:* In both ancient and modern times there have been many opinions expressed concerning human nature and virtue, but this is the first time I have heard the fundamentals of these topics described with such clarity. Your exposition of wrong-doing makes it appear as though something filthy has infected man's fundamental nature, and that the doing of what is right is like the adorning of oneself with multi-colored embroidered garments, so that after a person has cultivated his virtue, his nature becomes even more beautiful. This is truly the task of the superior man. But there are also those who put all their efforts into external things and fail to concern themselves with any personal, inner cultivation.

440. *The Western scholar says:* Alas, the vulgar man spends the whole of each day hoping for, and applying his whole mind to, the accumulation of false treasure which will please his physical eyes, and he is unwilling to open the eyes of his mind in the slightest degree to the beauties which are new in every age, and to the genuine treasures of his inner spirit. Because of this every day of his life is filled with anxiety and suffering, and when he reaches the point of death, he is filled with grief and fear, and is like an animal about to be led to its death in the slaughterhouse.

441. When the Lord of Heaven ushered me into this world he wanted me only to strive dutifully to cultivate virtue so that I might always obtain inexhaustible felicities by myself, without any need to trouble, or to rely unduly on, things external to me. If I instead give myself up to self-abandonment and make myself the slave of all things, casting myself into every kind of danger, whose fault is this?

442. People are not particularly concerned with honor and wealth so long as they can obtain what they want; and there is no other way to gain what one wants than to limit one's demands to those things which are within one's grasp. There is no doubt that

成人，然神之精超于形，故智者以神為真己，以形為藏己之器。古有賢臣亞那，為篡國者所傷，泰然曰：「爾傷亞那之器，非能傷亞那者也。」此所謂達人者也。

443 中士曰：人亦誰不知違義之自殃，從德者之有大吉盛福，而不須外具也。然而務德者世世更稀，其德之路難曉乎？抑難進乎？

444 西士曰：俱難也，進尤甚焉。知此道而不行，則倍其怒且減其知。比于食者，而不能化其所食，則充而無養，反傷其身。力行焉踐其所知，即增闢其才光，益厚其心力，以行其餘。試之則覺其然焉。

445 中士曰：吾中州士，古者學聖教而為聖，今久非見聖人，則竊疑今之學非聖人之學，茲願詳示學術。

The Cultivation of Virtue

I genuinely exist, and if I harm my own mind that harm is real. Man is a unity of body and spirit, but his spirit transcends his body; and a wise person will therefore regard his spirit as his true self, and his body as a vessel in which his self is hidden. In ancient times there was a certain good minister called Yana who, when stabbed by a usurper, said, quite unperturbed: "You have stabbed Yana's vessel, but Yana himself cannot be stabbed." This was a truly enlightened man.

443. *The Chinese scholar says:* Is there anyone who is not aware that a person who turns his back on righteousness will encounter misfortune, and that a person who follows after virtue will automatically enjoy good fortune and many blessings and will have no need to rely unduly on things external to himself? But each generation sees fewer and fewer men devote themselves solely to the cultivation of virtue. Is this because the path of virtue is difficult to understand or because it is difficult to proceed along it?

444. *The Western scholar says:* Both the understanding and the practice of virtue are difficult, although its practice is the more difficult of the two. He who knows what is right but who fails to act on it is doubly culpable and will also find his understanding reduced. It is like a person who eats something. If he is unable to digest what he eats not only will what he eats fail to nurture him, but it will even harm him. To strive to act on what one knows is to increase one's knowledge and ability, and to augment still further one's will to continue unceasingly in one's endeavours. If you were to try it you would realize that this is so.

445. *The Chinese scholar says:* Formerly, Chinese scholars studied the teachings of our sages and themselves became sagely men; but for a long time now no sage has arisen, and I am therefore led to doubt whether present-day learning is the learning of sages. May I ask you, Sir, to give me detailed instruction on how to study the Way.

論人性本善，而述天主門士正學

446 西士曰：嘗竊視群書，論學各具己私，若已測悟公學，吾何不聽命，而復有稱述西庠學乎？顧取捨之在子耳。夫學之謂，非但專效先覺行動語錄謂之學，亦有自己領悟之學，有視察天地萬物而推習人事之學，故曰智者不患乏書冊、無傳師，天地萬物盡我師、盡我券也。

447 學之為字，其義廣矣，正邪、大小、利鈍均該焉。吾所論學惟內也。彼邪學固非子之所問，其勢利及無益之習，君子不以營心焉。吾所論學惟內也，為己也，約之以一言，謂成己也。世之弊非無學也，是乃徒習夫寧無習之方，乃竟無補乎行。

448 吾儕本體之神，非徒為精貴，又為形之本主，故神修即形修，神成即形無不成矣。是以君子之本業特在于神，貴邦所謂無形之心也。

362

The Cultivation of Virtue

446. *The Western scholar says:* I have read a great many books, and have found that those who discourse on learning have each their own personal views; but if you are thoroughly to comprehend general principles, how can I refuse your request and refrain from discoursing on Western learning? You can accept or reject what I shall say as you see fit. The word "learning" has not only a specialized connotation according to which one emulates the deeds and words of past men of vision as these have been recorded for us, but it also refers to personal understanding and to the significance for man of deductions arrived at as a result of investigating heaven and earth and all phenomena. It is therefore said that he who is wise does not fear lest he have no books or teachers since heaven, earth, and all things are his teachers and his books!

447. The meaning of the word "learning" is so broad that it embraces orthodoxy and heterodoxy, what is great and what is small, what is sharp and what is blunt. Now I am quite sure you are not inquiring about heterodoxy; and those forms of learning which speak only of personal advantage, and which are of no benefit, will not concern the man of superior worth. The learning I shall now discuss is a learning entirely to do with the inner life and which is for oneself—in a word, it is that learning whereby a man is made whole. The ills of the world are not due to a lack of learning, but rather to the learning of things which are better not learnt, and which, in the end, contribute nothing to the betterment of man's behavior.

448. Not only are our spirits of great worth, but they are also the lords of our bodies, so that spiritual cultivation is also the cultivation of the body. When our spirits are cultivated to perfection, our physical bodies will be perfectly cultivated. Therefore, the superior man devotes himself solely to the spirit or what the men of your esteemed country refer to as the formless or incorporeal mind.

449 有形之身得耳、口、目、鼻、四肢、五司,以交覺于物;無形之神有三司,以接通之:曰司記含、司明悟、司愛欲焉。凡吾視聞啖覺,即其像由身之五門竅,以進達于神,而神以司記者受之,如藏之倉庫,不令忘矣,後吾欲明通一物,即以司明者取其物之在司記者像,而委曲折衷其體,協其性情之真于理當否:其善也,吾以司愛者愛之、欲之;其惡也,吾以司愛者惡之、恨之。蓋司明者,達是又達非,司愛者,司善善又司惡惡者也。

450 三司已成,吾無事不成矣。又其司愛、司明者已成,其司記者自成矣,故講學只論其二爾已。司明者尚真,司愛者尚好。是以吾所達愈真,其真愈廣潤,則司明者愈成充;吾所愛愈好,其好愈深厚,則司愛愈成就也。若司明不得真者,司愛不得好者,則二司者俱失其養,而神乃病餒。

451 司明之大功在義,司愛之大本在仁,故君子以仁義為重焉,二者相須,一不

The Cultivation of Virtue

449. The physical body uses ears, eyes, the mouth, the nose, the four limbs and five senses to make contact with and to perceive the physical objects [in the world outside itself]. The formless spirit [within man] employs memory, the intellect and the affections to communicate with the outside world. The images of what I see, hear, taste, or feel enter the five portals of my body to reach the spirit [within my body], and the spirit employs the faculty of memory to receive these things and to store them, as it were, in a storehouse so that they are not forgotten. Later, should I wish to understand something thoroughly, I employ my intellect to weigh up the true nature of the things stored away in my memory in order to determine whether they are true or not. If they are good, my affections will delight in them; but if they are bad, my affections will loathe and hate them, for my intellect can thoroughly understand what is right and what is wrong, and my affections cause me either to delight in what is good, or to hate what is evil.

450. When the work of these three controlling factors has been done there is nothing which remains unaccomplished. Further, when the controller of my affections and the controller of my understanding have completed their tasks, my memory will also be complete. When discussing learning, therefore, only the intellect and the affections are taken into account. The object of the intellect is truth; the object of the affections is goodness. Therefore, the more true my understanding and the more extensive that truth, the more complete and substantial will be my intellect; and the better and more profound the things I have an affection for, the more perfect will be my affections. If the intellect were unable to arrive at truth and the affections were unable to attain to goodness, then both these controlling factors would be incapable of preserving their health, and the spirit would fall sick.

451. The supreme task of the intellect is the clarification of what is right, and the greatest foundation of the affections is humanity; therefore, the constant concern of the superior man is

可廢。然惟司明者明仁之善，而後司愛者愛而存之；司愛者愛義之德，而後司明者察而求之。但仁也者，又為義之至精，仁盛，則司明者滋明，故君子之學又以仁為主焉。

452 仁，尊德也。德之為學，不以強奪，不以久藏毀而殺，施之與人而更長茂，在高益珍，所謂德在百姓為銀，在牧者為金，在君為貝也。

453 嘗聞智者為事，必先立一主意，而後圖其善具以獲之，如旅人先定所往之域，而後尋詢去路也。終之意固在其始也。

454 夫學道亦要識其向往者，吾果為何者學乎？不然則貿貿而往，自不知其所求。或學特以知識，此乃徒學；或以售知，此乃賤利；或以使人知，此乃罔勤；或以誨人，乃所為慈；或以淑己，乃所為智。

論人性本善，而述天主門士正學

for humanity and righteousness. These two things are related to each other, and neither the one nor the other can be neglected. But is is only after the intellect has made it clear that humanity is good that the affections are able to develop an affection for it and to preserve it; and it is only after the affections have formed an affection for righteousness that the intellect will examine it and seek after it. But humanity is the essence of righteousness, so that a man who is rich in humanity is bound to have an intellect capable of even greater understanding. Thus, the education of a superior man is principally concerned with humanity.

452. Humanity is the noblest of virtues, and the study and nurture of it cannot be hurt or destroyed by force or through its long concealment. Bestowed on others, it grows ever more luxuriant; in men of high estate it is particularly precious. Virtue in the common man is like silver; in the man who exercises control over others it is like gold, but in the ruler it is treasure.

453. I have heard it said that when a wise man does anything he is sure to begin with an aim and then to employ the best methods to achieve it. For example, a man who is about to travel a great distance must first decide where he wishes to go, and must then inquire which road will lead him there. His ultimate destination must be decided on at the very beginning.

454. When we come to moral training we must also know the nature of our goal—why do I wish to undergo moral training?—otherwise it will be haphazard in character, and we shall not know why we are doing what we do. Perhaps it will simply be to acquire a little knowledge, in which case our learning will all be to no purpose; or perhaps to be able to sell knowledge—a base way to gain any profit; or perhaps so that others will come to know about us, which is vanity; or perhaps to make use of such knowledge in order to be able to instruct others, which signifies concern for others; or perhaps to use it for self-cultivation, which is wisdom.

455 故吾曰學之上志惟此成己，以合天主之聖旨耳，所謂由此而歸此者也。

456 中士曰：如是，則其成己為天主也，非為己也，則毋奈外學也。

457 西士曰：烏有成己而非為己者乎？其為天主也，正其所以成也。余曰仁也者，乃愛天主與夫愛人者，崇其宗原而不遺其枝派，何以謂外乎？人之中雖親若父母，比于天主者，猶為外焉，況天主常在物內，自不當外。意益高者學益尊，如學者之意止於一己，何高之有？至于為天主，其尊乃不可加矣，孰以為賤乎？

458 聖學在吾性內，天主銘之人心原不能壞，貴邦儒經所謂明德、明命是也。但是明為私欲蔽掩以致昏瞑，不以聖賢躬親喻世人，豈能覺？恐以私欲悞認明德，愈悖正學耳。

7 Ibid., I, p. 260.
8 Ibid., I, p. 356.

The Cultivation of Virtue

455. Thus, I would say that the highest aim of learning is the perfection of oneself, so that one can accord with the holy will of the Lord of Heaven. This is to return to one's origin.

456. *The Chinese scholar says:* In that case, the perfection of oneself is for the Lord of Heaven and not for oneself. Does this not mean that one is concentrating on externals?

457. *The Western scholar says:* How can a man perfect himself without doing it for himself? To act for the Lord of Heaven is to perfect himself! When Confucius talked of humanity he simply spoke of loving others,[7] yet Confucians do not regard this as a form of learning which concentrates only on externals. When I speak of a humane person I am speaking of one who loves both the Lord of Heaven and man; who emphasizes the root, but is not neglectful of the branches. How can one call this "concentrating on externals"? Although a person may be as close to one as one's parents, that person must still be counted an outsider when compared with the Lord of Heaven. Moreover, the Lord of Heaven is constantly within things, and should therefore not be regarded as something external. The higher our aims, the nobler will be our learning. If the learner's aims are merely limited to himself, what nobility is there in that? If, on the other hand, they are directed towards the Lord of Heaven, their nobility will be such as to be incapable of augmentation. How can this be called base?

458. The sagely learning within our natures has been engraved on our minds by the Lord of Heaven and is, in consequence incapable of destruction. This is what is meant when the Confucians of your esteemed country speak in the Classics of "illustrious virtue"[8] and "glorious decrees." But the illustriousness has been clouded by man's selfish desires to the point where it has been engulfed in darkness, and had it not been for the sages and worthies who devoted themselves to the instruction of mankind, man would have had no way to become aware [of his true nature], and would, I fear, have mistakenly equated selfish desire with illustrious virtue, and thus departed even further from true learning.

459 然此學之貴，全在力行，而近人妄當之以講論，豈知善學之驗在行德，不在言德乎。然其講亦不可遺也，講學也者，溫故而習新，達蘊而釋疑，奮己而勸人，博學而篤信者也。善之道無窮，故學為善者與身同終焉，身在不可一日不學。凡曰已至，其必未起也；凡曰吾已不欲進於善，即是退復於惡也。

460 中士曰：此皆真語，敢問下手工夫？

461 西士曰：吾素譬此工如圃然，先繕地，拔其野草，除其瓦石，注其泥水於溝壑，而後藝嘉種也。

462 學者先去惡而後能致善，所謂有所不不為方能有為焉。未學之始，習心橫肆，其惡根固深透乎心，抽使去之，可不畾畾乎？勇者克己之謂也。童年者蚤卽于學，其工如一，得工如十，無前習之累故也。

The Cultivation of Virtue

459. But the value of this learning depends entirely on its vigorous implementation, whereas people in recent times have falsely imagined that all that is required is the exposition and discussion of it. How are they to know that the efficacy of such learning lies in the practice of virtue and not in talk about it? Nevertheless, one cannot neglect such discussion. The exposition and discussion of knowledge can help us review what has been learnt and cause us to learn something new; it can help us gain a thorough understanding of mysteries and resolve doubts. He who strives hard and exhorts others to do the same is a person of extensive learning and one who is trustworthy. The way of goodness is inexhaustible, and therefore any man who learns to do good must be prepared to study throughout his life. Every day that he lives must be devoted to its study. Any man who says he has reached his goal has simply not begun, and anyone who says he no longer wishes to make progress in goodness has again reverted to evil.

460. *The Chinese scholar says:* All that you have said is true. May I ask how one sets about it?

461. *The Western scholar says·* I always compare this kind of task with the planting of vegetables: First one prepares the soil, pulls up the weeds, rids the ground of broken earthenware and stones, and guides accumulated water so that it flows into ditches. Only when all this has been done does one plant the seeds.

462. The student of morality must first rid himself of evil habits before he can enter the realm of goodness. There must be things one must refrain from doing before one can begin to act. Before beginning one's study every effort must be made to uproot outrageous and dissolute habits and evil practices which are firmly rooted and which have penetrated deep into the mind. The meaning of courage is self-conquest. If a person applies himself to study whilst still a child, the efficacy of a moment's effort will be magnified ten times. The reason for this is that a child does not carry the burden of earlier habits.

論人性本善，而述天主門士正學

463 古有一善教者，子弟從之必問曾從他師否，以從他師者，為其已蹈襲時之懊，必倍其將誠之儀，一因改易其前懊，一因教之以知新也。

464 既已知學矣，尚迷乎色慾，則何以建於勇毅？尚驕傲自滿欺人，則何以進乎謙德？尚惑非義之財物，不返其主，則何以秉廉？尚溺乎榮顯功名，則何以超乎道德？尚將怨天尤人，則何以立於仁義？秬囹盈以醯鹽，不能斟之鬱鬯矣。知己之惡者，見善之倪，而易入于德路者也。

465 欲剪諸惡之根，而興己於善，不若守徼會規例，逐日再次省察。凡己半日間，所思所言所行善惡：有善者，自勸繼之；有惡者，自懲絕之。久用此功，雖無師保之責，亦不患有大過。

9 See St. Ignatius of Loyola, *Spiritual Exercises*, [24-43] and *Constitutions of the Society of Jesus*, [261, 342, 344].

The Cultivation of Virtue

463. In ancient times there was a man who was skilled in the instruction of others, and when disciples came to follow him as their master he invariably inquired of them whether they had had other teachers. From those who had had other teachers he would demand twice his normal fee on the grounds that they had already entered into error and that they would first have to have their errors corrected before he could instruct them in new knowledge.

464. How is a spirit of courage to be established in a student whom we know has fallen into concupiscence because of what he has learnt thus far? How can the virtue of modesty be fostered in one who is still arrogant, and who thinks only of cheating others? How can a person preserve his honesty when he is still bewitched by ill-gotten wealth and refuses to return it to its rightful owner? How can a person possess a superior morality when he is still drowned in greed for glory and fame? How can one who is forever blaming Heaven and man stand firm on humanity and righteousness? If vinegar and the like is poured into ritual vessels meant for the offering of wine in sacrifice they can no longer be used by a priest for their original purpose. A man who knows his faults will find it easy to move on to the path of virtue when he sees the first shoots of goodness.

465. If you wish to eradicate the many roots of evil and establish yourself in goodness, you can do no better than to keep the rules of my humble Society, and to examine yourself twice a day, reviewing each half-day's thoughts, words, and actions to determine whether they have been good or evil. Where they are found to be good, one strives to continue with them, and where they are bad, one disciplines oneself and cuts them off.[9] If this practice is continued over a long period of time one is not likely to fall into any great error, even if one has no teacher or protector to exercise close supervision.

論人性本善，而述天主門士正學

466 然勤修之至，恒習見天主於心目，儼如對越。至尊不離于心，枉念自不萌起，不須他功，其外四肢莫之禁，而自不適於非義矣。故改惡之要，惟在深悔，悔其昔所已犯，自誓弗敢再蹈，心之既沐，德之寶服可衣焉。

467 夫德之品衆矣，不能具論，吾今為子惟揭其綱，則餘者隨之，故易云：「元者，善之長；君子體仁，足以長人。」得其綱，則仁其要焉。

468 夫仁之說，可約而以二言窮之，曰：「愛天主，為天主無以尚；而為天主者，愛人如己也。」行斯二者，百行全備矣。然二亦一而已，篤愛一人，則幷愛其所愛者矣；天主愛人，吾真愛天主者，有不愛人者乎？此仁之德所以為尊，其尊非他，乃因上帝。借令天主所以成我者，由他外物，又或

10 *I Ching,* p. 408.
11 See Matthew 22:34-40; Mark 12:28-34; Luke 10:25-28.
12 See Romans 8:10
13 See I John 4:7-21.

The Cultivation of Virtue

466. When one has worked diligently to improve one's moral conduct and has attained to the highest level of perfection, one will habitually see the Lord of Heaven in the eye of one's mind as if one is really face to face with Him. When the supremely honored [Lord of Heaven] does not leave a man's mind, evil thoughts will naturally cease to put forth shoots, and there will be no need to employ any other technique. A man's four limbs will naturally cease to engage in unrighteous activities, and will need have no restraint put on them. The most essential thing in turning away from evil is a profound remorse; one will determine that the wrongs done prior to being deeply remorseful will not be committed again. Since the mind is cleansed, it then becomes possible to put on the precious garment of virtue.

467. There are, of course, many grades of virtue, and I cannot enumerate them all here. I shall therefore provide you with a number of examples of which humanity is the most imporant. When you have been provided with these major examples, you will find that the remainder simply follow on. Thus, the *Book of Changes* states: "What is called 'the great and originating' is (in man) the first and chief quality of goodness ... The superior man, embodying benevolence, is fit to preside over men."[10]

468. The definition of humanity can be summed up in the following two sentences: Love the Lord of Heaven, for He is supreme; and love others as you love yourself for the sake of the Lord of Heaven.[11] If you carry out these two commands, everything you do will be perfect.[12] But these two commands are, after all, only one command. If one loves a person passionately one will love what that person loves. The Lord of Heaven loves people; if I genuinely love the Lord of Heaven can I fail to love the people He loves?[13] The reason why the virtue of humanity is so noble is precisely that it signifies love for the Sovereign on High. If the Lord of Heaven were to rely on some other external thing to bring me to perfection

求得之而不能得，則尚有歉。然皆由我內關，特在一愛云耳，孰曰吾不能愛乎？天主諸善之聚，化育我，施生我，使我為人不為禽蟲，且賜之以作德之性，吾愛天主，即天主亦寵答之，何適不詳乎？

469 人心之司愛向于善，則其善彌大，司愛者亦彌充。天主之善無限界，則吾德可長無定界矣，則夫能充滿我情性惟天主者也。然于善有未通，則必不能愛。故知寸貝之價當百，則愛之如百；知拱璧之價當千，則愛之如千。是故愛之機在明達，而欲致力以廣仁，先須竭心以通天主之事理，乃識從其教也。

470 中士曰：天主事理目不得見，所信者人所言錄耳，信人之知，惟恍惚之知，何能決所向往？

471 西士曰：人有形者也，交于人道者，非信人不可，況交乎無形者耶？今余不欲揭他遠事也。子孝嚴親無所不至，然子何以知孝？惟信人之言，知其乃生

The Cultivation of Virtue

I might seek for it without being able to obtain it and thereby remain in a state of imperfection. But everything rests with my inner mind—on love. Who can say I cannot love? The Lord of Heaven is the sum of all goodness, and in creating me He has caused me to be a man and not a bird, animal, or insect; moreover, He has given me a human nature which is constituted for virtue. I love the Lord of Heaven and the Lord of Heaven also loves me, in this way there is nothing that can be inauspicious.

469. If the affections of men's minds are directed towards goodness, the greater the goodness, the more satisfied will be the affections. The Lord of Heaven is unlimited goodness, and therefore our virtue is capable of unbounded growth; therefore, only the Lord of Heaven can satisfy our nature. But if we do not completely understand goodness we will not be able to love it. If we know that an inch-long cowry is worth a hundred, we shall love it to that extent. If we know that a circlet of jade is worth a thousand, we will love it accordingly. Thus, the motivation to love lies in understanding, and if one is to strive to broaden one's humanity, one must first use all one's mind to understand the truth concerning the Lord of Heaven. Only so will one be able to recognize and follow His teachings.

470. *The Chinese scholar says:* To serve the Lord of Heaven is to serve something one cannot see with one's eyes; and what one [is asked] to believe are all teachings and writings of other men. If one puts one's faith in the knowledge of others, and that knowledge itself is none too clear, how can it determine the direction one's [mind] should take?

471. *The Western scholar says:* Man has a physical body, and any association with others on the human level demands that we place our trust in people. How much more must this be so in our association with the metaphysical? I do not wish at this point to concern myself with such remote matters, [but simply to explain what I mean in terms of] the concern of children to be extraordinarily

己之父也,非人言,自何以知之乎?

472 子又忠於君,雖捐命無悔,其為君,亦只信經書所傳耳,臣孰自知其為己君乎?

473 則吾所信有實據,不可謂不真切明曉,足以為仁之基也。況夫天主事,非一夫之言,天主親貽正經,諸國之聖賢傳之,天下之英俊僉從之,信之固不為妄,何恍惚之有?

474 中士曰:如此則信之無容疑矣。但仁道之大,比諸天地無不覆載,今日一愛已爾,似乎太隘。

475 西士曰:血氣之愛尚為群情之主,矧神理之愛乎?試如逐財之人,以富為好,以貧為醜,則其愛財也。如未得,則欲之;如可得,則望之;如不可得,則棄志;既得之,則喜樂也。若更有奪其所取者,則惡之;慮為人之所奪,則避

論人性本善,而述天主門士正學

thorough in the filial service of their parents. How do children know that they should be filial? Only by trusting what others have told them and thereby knowing that a certain man is the father who has begotten them. If they do not trust what others have told them, how can they know the truth?

472. A minister serves his sovereign loyally and will have no regrets even though he may have to give up his life for him. That he is his sovereign is something he accepts on trust from official records. Since when has a minister been able to know of his own accord that his sovereign is really his sovereign?

473. Now, what I believe is provided with real proof, and you cannot say it is not real and not clear. It is sufficient to serve as the foundation for [growth into] humanity. Furthermore, when we speak of matters concerning the Lord of Heaven we are not dealing with the teaching of an ordinary man. The Lord of Heaven personally gave man orthodox canonical writings which sages and worthies of many nations have transmitted to us and which heroes and men all over the world believe and follow. This kind of belief is no mere shallow acceptance; how then can my teaching be regarded as lacking in clarity?

474. *The Chinese scholar says:* In that case, I need have no reason for doubt. But humanity is an enormous subject and, like heaven and earth, embraces all things; to limit it now to a discussion only about love would seem to restrict the concept unduly.

475. *The Western scholar says:* Physical love is the leader of the other emotions; how much more of a leader, then, is spiritual and rational love? Let us test this truth by looking at a person who seeks after riches; such a person regards wealth as good and poverty as loathsome. If he covets riches yet has so far failed to obtain them, he will desire to obtain them. If he is on the way to obtaining them he will hope to obtain them; but if he has no way of obtaining them he will cease to be concerned over them. If he has already obtained

之。如可勝，則發勇爭之；如不可勝，則懼之；一旦失其所愛，則哀之；如奪我愛者強而難敵，則又或思禦之，或欲復之而忿怒也。此十一情者，特自一愛財所發。

476 總之，有所愛，則心搖，其身體豈能靜漠無所為乎？故愛財者，必逝四極，交易以殖貨；愛色者，必朝暮動費以備嬖妾；愛功名者，終身經歷百險，以逞其計謀；愛爵祿者，攻苦文武之業，以通其幹才。天下萬事皆由愛作，而天主之愛獨可已乎？愛天主者，固奉敬之，必顯其功德，揚其聲教，傳其聖道，鬭彼異端者。

477 然愛天主之效，莫誠乎愛人也。所謂仁者愛人，不愛人，何以驗其誠敬上帝歟？愛人非虛愛，必將渠饑則食之，渴則飲之，無衣則衣之，無屋則舍之，憂患則恤之、慰之，愚蒙則誨之，罪過則諫之，侮我則恕之，既死則葬之

14 As mentioned above: desire, hope, peace, joy, hatred, avoidance, struggle, fear, grief, resistance, and anger.

them he will be joyful; if someone else robs him of what he has he will hate that man. Worried lest someone will rob him of his goods he will hide them. If he can be victorious he will dare offer resistance; but if he cannot gain the victory he will be fearful. Should a man one day lose the thing he loves he will experience profound grief. If the person who robs me of what I love proves to be strong and difficult to resist I shall think of some way to obstruct him or angrily take my revenge on him. These eleven kinds of "love"[14] are all produced from a mind devoted to riches.

476. To sum up, whenever there is a special fondness for something a man's mind will move, his body will be incapable of calm, and he will engage in activity. Thus, a man who loves riches must travel in every direction to engage in trade and plan for profit; a man who is fond of women will go to great expense morning and evening to provide for his favorite concubines. A man who is fond of fame will undergo many dangers throughout his life in order to achieve his ends; and a person who loves rank and official emoluments will apply himself through all trials and tribulations to the study of civil and military arts in order that he might become thoroughly skilled in them. Everything in the world is done for love; must love of the Lord of Heaven be the one exception? Those who love the Lord of Heaven are naturally able to serve Him, are bound to make His meritorious works widely known, proclaim His teachings, spread His holy doctrine, and put a stop to heterodoxy.

477. Sincere love for men is the greatest result of a love for the Lord of Heaven. This is what is meant by the expression "Humanity is the love of man." If a man does not love his fellow-men, how can one tell that he sincerely respects the Lord on High? The love of man is no feigned love since it must result in the feeding of the hungry, in the giving of drink to the thirsty, in the clothing of those without clothes, and in the provision of places to live for the homeless. Love has compassion for and comforts those who

論人性本善，而述天主門士正學

，而為代祈上帝，且死生不敢忘之。故昔大西有問于聖人者曰：「行何事則可以至善與？」曰：「愛天主，而任汝行也。」聖人之意乃從此哲引者固不差路矣。

478 中士曰：司愛者用于善人可耳；人不皆善，其惡者必不可愛，況厚愛乎？若論他人，其無大損；若論在五倫之間，雖不善者，我中國亦愛之，故父為瞽瞍，弟為象，舜猶愛友焉。

479 西士曰：俗言仁之為愛，但謂愛者可相答之物耳，故愛鳥獸金石非仁也。然或有愛之而反以仇，則我可不愛之乎？

480 夫仁之理，惟在愛其人之得善之美，非愛得其善與美而為己有也。譬如愛醴酒，非愛其酒之有美，愛其酒之好味，可為我嘗也，則非可謂仁于酒矣。愛己之子，則愛其有善，即有富貴、安逸、才學、德行

15 See Matthew 25:31-46.
16 See St. Augustine, *Sermons on I John*, VII, 8.
17 *Wu-lun*（五倫）. See Ricci's Introduction, n. 2.
18 Tu Sou（瞽瞍）was a man unable to distinguish between right and wrong.
19 Hsiang（象）was always thinking of ways to harm Shun.

The Cultivation of Virtue

experience disaster; it instructs the ignorant, corrects the wrong-doers, forgives those who humiliate me, buries the dead, and dares not forget to pray the Sovereign on High for all men, living or dead.[15] Therefore, in former times in the West, there was a certain man who went to inquire of a sage what he must do to be good. The answer was: "Love the Lord of Heaven and do as you wish."[16] What the sage meant was that if a man chose to follow this wise advice he would, as a matter of course, be unable to take the wrong path.

478. *The Chinese scholar says:* One may love a good man, but not all men are good, and an evil man may not be loved, let alone deeply loved. No great harm can come of this if we are thinking of those with whom we have no connection, but if we are considering those who fall within the range of the Five Cardinal Relationships,[17] then we Chinese love them even when they are bad; thus, [Emperor] Shun's father was Tu Sou[18] and his younger brother was Hsiang[19] yet Shun still loved them.

479. *The Western scholar says:* In common parlance humanity is equated with love, but this love is limited only to things which can repay debts of gratitude, and, therefore, the love of animals, metals, and stone is not called humanity; but if I love someone and that person responds to my love with hostility, am I to stop loving that person?

480. The principle of humane-love consists solely in gladness that another person should obtain the beauty of goodness, and not in the desire to obtain that goodness and beauty for oneself. For example, when one loves sweet wine, one does not love the beauty of the wine but the fact that it has a good flavor and that one can taste it. One cannot say that one experiences a feeling of humanity towards that wine. But when one loves one's son one loves his goodness; one loves the fact that he possesses wealth and honor,

，此乃謂仁愛其子；若爾愛爾子，惟為愛其奉己，此非愛子也，惟愛自己也，何謂之仁乎？

481 惡者固不可愛，但惡之中亦有可取之善，則無絕不可愛之人。仁者愛天主，故因為天主而愛己愛人，知為天主則知人人可愛，何特愛善者乎？愛人之善，緣在天主之善，非在人之善。

482 故雖惡者亦可用吾之仁，非愛其惡，惟愛其善者之或可以改惡而化善也。況雙親兄弟君長與我有恩、有倫之相繫，吾宜報之；有天主誡令慕愛之，吾宜守之；又非他人等乎，則雖其不善，豈容斷愛耶？人有愛父母不為天主者，茲乃善情非成仁之德也，雖虎之子為豹，均愛親矣。故有志於天主之旨，則博愛于人以及天下萬物，不須徒膠之為一體耳。

論人性本善，而述天主門士正學

384

The Cultivation of Virtue

ease and talents, learning and virtue: this is what is meant by loving one's son. If you only love your son because he can care for you, this is not love of your son, but only love of yourself. How can this be called humane-love?

481. Evil is certainly unlovable, but even in an evil man one can find some goodness; thus, there is no one who is totally unlovable. The humane man loves the Lord of Heaven and, in consequence, loves himself and others. When he realizes that it is on account of the Lord of Heaven [that he is to love his fellow men], he becomes aware that every man is lovable. How, then, can one limit one's love to the good? One loves what is good in man because it is a goodness which comes from the Lord of Heaven, and not because it is man's goodness.

482. Therefore, though a man may be evil, I can use my humane-love, not to love his evil, but to love the possibility that the evil man might turn from evil to goodness. In addition, my parents, brothers, elders and I are bound to one another with ties of affection, and by the bonds of morality governing human relationships, and these I am obliged to respond to positively. Then there are the commandments of the Lord of Heaven which demand that I cherish [my relations], and which I must also keep. Obviously, then, other people cannot be placed on an equal footing [with my relatives]. How can I be permitted to sever my love for them even when they are bad? There are those who love their parents, but not for the sake of the Lord of Heaven: this is a good emotion but not the virtue of perfect humanity. Even if a tiger's cub turns out to be a leopard, the tiger will love what it has begotten. Thus, he whose mind accords with the will of the Lord of Heaven will love all men, and all things under heaven, without any need to become organically one with them.

論人性本善，而述天主門士正學

483 中士曰：世之誦讀經書者，徒視其文而聞其旨。某曩者嘗誦詩云：「維此文王，小心翼翼，昭事上帝，聿懷多福，厥德不回。」今聞仁之玄論轉于天主，而始知詩人之旨也：志事上帝即德無缺矣。然仁旣惟愛天主，則天主必眷愛仁人，何須焚香禮拜、誦經作功乎？吾檢慎于日用，各合其義，斯已焉。

484 西士曰：天主賜我形神兩備，我宜兼用二者以事之。天主繁育鳥獸，昭布萬像，而其竟莫有知所酬報者，獨人類能建殿堂、設禮祭，祈拜誦經以申感謝，何者？天主之愛人甚矣。大父之慈，恐人以外物幻其內仁，則命聖人作此外儀，以啓吾內德而常存省之，俾吾日日仰目禱祈其恩，旣得之，則讚揚其

20 *Chinese Classics*, IV, p. 433.

386

483. *The Chinese scholar says:* Those who recite the canonical writings merely read the words without being able to understand their purport. I once read the following words in the *Book of Odes:* "This King Wen, watchfully and reverently, with entire intelligence served the Sovereign on High, and so secured the great blessings. His virtue was without deflection."[20] Now, having heard you discourse on the profundities of humanity and how you have related it to the Lord of Heaven I understand for the first time what the writer of that ode had in mind: anyone who serves the Sovereign on High will not be lacking in virtue. But since humanity means nothing else but love of the Lord of Heaven, the Lord of Heaven is bound to love the humane man; what need is there, then, to burn incense, to offer worship, to recite scriptures and to establish one's merit? Surely, all I need to do is to be cautious in my daily activities and to review them thoroughly so that they are in harmony with the moral principles governing human relationships.

484. *The Western scholar says:* The Lord of Heaven has bestowed on man both a physical body and a spirit, and both are complete in every respect. I ought to use both of them to serve Him. The Lord of Heaven created every kind of bird and beast and arranged all things, but none has any idea as to how to repay Him. Man alone is capable of building palaces and sacred halls; of worshipping, of offering sacrifices and of reciting scriptures as an expression of thanks. Any why is this? It is because the Lord of Heaven has a great love for us men and, fearing lest physical things in the world outside man will transform the humanity in men's minds into something chimerical, He has, out of His fatherly love, commanded sagely men to set up these external rites and ceremonies in order to educate our inner virtue so that we can constantly preserve and examine it, and so that we will daily look up to and pray for the grace [of the Lord of Heaven]. And when I have received what I have asked of Him, I praise Him for his bounty, and never

盛而感之不忘,且以是明我本來了無毫髮之非上賜,而因以增廣吾仁,且今後世彌厚享賞也。

485 天主之經無他,只是欽崇上帝恩德而讚美之,或祈恕宥昔者所犯罪惡,或乞恩祐以勝危難、以避咎衍、以進于至德,故數數誦之者,必益敦信此道,愈闢心明以達學術之隱也。又恐污邪妄想,侵滑人心,因而渙散,于是天主又敎之以禮,不拘男女咸日誦經拜叩以閑其邪。

486 夫吾天主所授工夫,匪佛老空無寂寞之敎,乃悉以誠實引心于仁道之妙,故初使掃去心惡,次乃光其闇惑,卒至合之于天主之旨,俾之化為一心,而與天神無異,用之必有其驗,但今不暇詳解耳。

fail to express my gratitude. As a result of this, moreover, I am made to understand that even every hair on my head has been bestowed on me from above, and my sense of humanity is extended. Further, my rewards in the next life will be rich indeed.

485. The words contained in the canonical writings of the Lord of Heaven are concerned with nothing else than the adoration of the grace of the Sovereign on High and the praise of Him. Whether one is seeking for forgiveness for past wrong-doing, or for the support of grace so that one may overcome difficulties and danger, avoid wrong-doing, and make progress in the direction of sublime virtue, when reciting [these scriptures] one must strengthen one's faith in all these doctrines and increase the light in one's mind so that one may comprehend the hidden places of this learning. Fearing lest evil thoughts should invade men's minds and cause them to become dissipated, the Lord of Heaven also employed rites and ceremonies as a means of instructing them; and so, whether they be men or women, they should recite the scriptures and offer worship daily in order to put a stop to evil thoughts.

486. The Way of cultivation which the Lord of Heaven has taught to men has nothing to do with the doctrines of voidness and nirvana taught by the Buddha and Lao Tzu, but is concerned only with leading men's minds, through sincerity, into the wonderful mystery of humanity. Thus, the first step must be to sweep all evil thoughts from the mind, so that light can illuminate man's darkness and doubts, and man can finally be in harmony with the will of the Lord of Heaven. His mind will then be at one with that of the Lord of Heaven, and he will be no different from the angels. If you use this method of self-cultivation you are bound to find it effective; but I have no time now to expound it in further detail.

論人性本善，而述天主門士正學

487 吾竊視貴邦儒者病正在此，第言明德之修，而不知人意易疲，不能自勉而修，又不知瞻仰天帝以祈慈父之佑，成德者所以鮮見。

488 中士曰：拜佛像，念其經，全無益乎？

489 西士曰：奚啻無益乎，大害正道。惟此異端，愈祭拜尊崇，罪愈重矣。

490 一家止有一長，二之則罪；一國惟得一君，二之則罪；乾坤亦特由一主，二之豈非宇宙間重大罪犯乎？儒者欲罷二氏教于中國，而今乃建二宗之寺觀，拜其像，比如欲枯槁惡樹而厚培其根本，必反榮焉。

491 中士曰：天主為宇內至尊無疑也，然天下萬國九州之廣，或天主委此等佛

21 *Ch'ien-k'un*. See Ricci's Introduction, n. 5.

390

487. When I observe the learned men of your esteemed country I find that their common failing is to be found precisely at this point. They speak of the need to cultivate one's illustrious virtue, but are unaware of the fact that man's will tires easily, and that the will cannot strive to cultivate virtue by the will's own strength. They are not aware that they must look up to the Sovereign on High to plead for the protection and support of their compassionate Father. It is for this reason that one so rarely sees a man whose virtue has been cultivated to perfection.

488. *The Chinese scholar says:* Is there nothing to be gained from venerating the image of the Buddha and reciting Buddhist scriptures?

489. *The Western scholar says:* Why stop at "There being nothing to be gained"? The fact is that activities such as these are of great harm to the orthodox Way. The more one indulges in this type of heterodox worship and veneration the more serious will be one's crime.

490. A family can have only one head; it is wrong to have two. A nation can have only one sovereign; it is wrong to have two. The Universe[21] too is controlled by one lord. Is it not the most heinous crime in the universe to say there are two? Confucians wished to rid China of the two religions of Buddhism and Taoism, yet now we see them building Buddhist and Taoist temples and worshipping idols. This is like wanting noxious trees to wither and die whilst at the same time doing everything possible to nourish their roots. The result is bound to be that they will flourish again.

491. *The Chinese scholar says:* I have no doubt that the Lord of Heaven is the one most deserving of respect in the universe; but the world, with its numerous nations and nine regions, is so extensive that perhaps the Lord of Heaven has deputed such beings as the Buddha, the Immortals, and the Bodhisattvas to protect each place. Would it not be like the Son of Heaven, [the

論人性本善，而述天主門士正學

祖、神仙、菩薩保固各方，如天子宅中，而差官布政于九州百郡，或者責方別有神祖耳。

492 西士曰：此語本失而似得，不細察則誤信之矣。天主者非若地主但居一方，不遣人分任即不能兼治他方者也。

493 上帝知能無限，無外為而成，無所不在，所御九天萬國，體用造化，比吾示掌猶易，奚待彼流人代司之哉？

494 且理無二是，設上帝之教是，則他教非矣；設他教是，則上帝之教非矣。朝廷設官分職，咸奉一君，無異禮樂，無異法令。彼二氏教自不同，況可謂天主同乎？彼教不尊上帝，惟尊一己耳已，昧于大原大本焉，所宣晦諭大非天主之制具，可謂自任，豈天主任之乎？

495 天主經曰：「妨之妨之：有着羊皮而內為豺狼極猛者；善樹生善果，惡樹生

Emperor], who resides at the center and deputes his officials to exercise government on his behalf in the nine regions and hundred districts? Perhaps your esteemed country has other deities.

492. *The Western scholar says:* What you say may seem to be right, but it is, in fact, wrong. If one does not examine it with great care one might mistakenly believe it to be true. The Lord of Heaven is not like a landlord who lives only in one place, and who cannot control other places without delegating his responsibilities.

493. The knowledge and capabilities of the Sovereign on High are unlimited, and He can complete any task without any external action. The [Sovereign on High] is omnipresent and exercises control over the "nine heavens and all nations." He controls creation more easily than I can lift my hand, so He would hardly have to wait for all those people to deputize for Him.

494. Further, there cannot be two truths which are both correct. If the religion of the Sovereign on High is true, then all other religions are wrong. If any one of the other religions is true, then the religion of the Sovereign on High is wrong. The Court may arrange for a great number of officials to share the burdens of office, but they all serve one sovereign, and there is one system of rites and music and one system of law. Buddhism and Taoism are essentially different from one another; how much more, then, must they be different from the religion of the Lord of Heaven? Those religions refuse to respect the Sovereign on High and simply respect themselves. They have no understanding of the Great Source and Root [of all things] and what they proclaim and teach is decidedly not what the Lord of Heaven ordained. One might say that they are self-appointed; one can hardly say that the Lord of Heaven has appointed them to act on His behalf, can one?

495. In the canonical writings of the Lord of Heaven we read:
"Beware of those who wear sheepskins but who are really ravening wolves. A good tree bears good fruit, and a bad tree bad

論人性本善，而述天主門士正學

496 惡果；視其所行，即知何人。」謂此輩耳。

凡經半句不真，決非天主之經也。天主者，豈能欺人，傳其偽理乎？異端偽經，虛詞誕言難以勝數，悉非由天主出者，如曰「日輪夜藏須彌山之背」；曰「天下有四大部州，皆浮海中，半見半浸」；曰「阿函以左右手掩日月，為日月之蝕」。此乃天文地理之事，身毒國原所未達，吾西儒笑之而不屑辯焉。

497 吾今試指釋氏所論人道之事三四處，其失不可勝窮也。曰四生六道，人魂輪迴，又曰殺生者靈魂不昇天堂，或歸天堂亦復回生世界，以及地獄充滿之際，復得再生于人間，又曰禽獸聽講佛法亦成道果，此皆拂理之語，第四、五篇已明辯之。

498 又言婚姻俱非正道，則天主何為生男女以傳人類，豈不妄乎？無婚配，

22 See John 10:1-17; Matthew 12:33-37.
23 See chapter 5, n. 1.

fruit. You will know what kind of men they are by their deeds."²²
These words are directed precisely towards such people as these!

496. In the canonical writings of the Lord of Heaven not even half a sentence can be false. How could the Lord of Heaven cheat men by transmitting false doctrines? The false canonical writings of the heterodox are filled with fantasies too numerous to count, and none comes from the Lord of Heaven. For example, it is stated that at night the sun is hidden behind Mount Sumeru; that there are four continents in the world which are floating on the ocean, half rising above sea level and half submerged. It is also stated that Arhan covered the sun and moon with his left and right hands, and that this caused an eclipse of the sun and the moon. These are all matters to do with astronomy and geography of which [the people of] India have in fact no understanding. Our learned men of the West ridicule them and disdain to argue these matters with them.

497. The mistakes made by Buddhists are beyond reckoning, but let me refer to three or four in the field of human affairs. They speak of four forms of birth and say reincarnation in the human soul experiences the Six Directions.²³ They also teach that the soul of a man who kills a living creature will not ascend to Heaven, or, if it does, it will later return to be reborn on earth. They even go on to assert that if a person in Hell has undergone sufficient tribulation, he is reborn into this world. They further assert that when birds and beasts listen to the teachings of the Buddha they too can become enlightened. These are all irrational assertions which I have clearly exposed in chapters four and five.

498. He also teaches that marriage is wrong. Why, then, did the Lord of Heaven create men and women to propagate mankind? Is such teaching not preposterous? If there were no marriage

499 佛從何生乎？禁殺生復禁人娶妻，意惟滅人類而讓天下於畜類耳。

又有一經，名曰大乘妙法蓮花經，囑其後曰：「能誦此經者，得到天堂受福。」今且以理論之，使有罪大惡極之徒，力能置經誦讀，則得升天受福；若夫修德行道之人，貧窮困苦買經不便，亦將墜於地獄與？

500 又曰呼誦「南無阿彌陀佛」不知幾聲，則免前罪，而死後平吉了無凶禍，如此其易即可自地獄而登天堂乎？豈不亦無益於德，而反導世俗以為惡乎？小人聞而信之，孰不遂私欲、汙本身、侮上帝、亂五倫，以為臨終念佛者若干次，可變為仙佛也。

501 天主刑賞，必無如是之失公失正者。夫「南無阿彌陀佛」一句有何深妙，即可逃重殃而著厚賞？不讚德，不祈祐，不悔己前罪，不述宣守規誡

24 *Saddharma-pundarika*.
25 *Wu-lun* (五倫). See Ricci's Introduction, n. 2.

from what would the Buddha have been born? By forbidding the taking of life and marriage, his obvious intention was to destroy mankind and to leave the world to the animals.

499. Then, there is a scripture called the *Mahayana Lotus Sutra of the Wonderful Law*[24] which informs men of later times that if they can recite this scripture they will go to Heaven and there enjoy a life of blessedness. We may now say, then, that should a great criminal and evil-doer be able to make preparations to chant this scripture he will rightfully ascend to Heaven and enjoy its blessings. However, if a person cultivates his virtue and practices the Way, but cannot conveniently purchase this scripture, he will descend to Hell.

500. It also teaches that the person who invokes the name of Amida Buddha over and over again will be forgiven his former wrong-doings, and that following his death he will enjoy peace and good fortune and will experience nothing ill. If it is so easy to go from Hell to Heaven, will this not prove an impediment to [the cultivation of] virtue and even encourage people to do evil? If the inferior man hears such a thing and believes it, how will he refrain from following his selfish desires and passions, befouling his person, insulting the Sovereign on High, and bringing confusion into the Five Cardinal Relationships,[25] believing that when about to die the invocation of the Buddha's name a number of times, will ensure his becoming an Immortal or a Buddha?

501. The rewards and punishments of the Lord of Heaven could never be so unfair or so improper. What is so marvellous about the name Amida Buddha that its mere recitation can effect an escape from severe punishment and cause someone to obtain generous rewards? If a man refrains from praising virtue, or from praying for protection and help, or from repenting of his former wrong-

,則從何處立功修行哉？世人交友，或有一二語誑，終身不敢盡信其言；今二氏論大事，許多誕謬，人尚畢信其餘，何也？

502 中士曰：佛神諸像何從而起？

503 西士曰：上古之時，人甚愚直，不識天主，或見世人略有威權，或自戀愛己親，及其死而立之貌像，建之祠宇廟禰，以為思慕之跡，暨其久也，人或進香獻紙以祈福祐。

504 又有最惡之人以邪法制服妖怪，以此異事自稱佛仙，假布誑術，詐為福祉，以駭惑頑俗，而使之塑像祀奉，此其始耳。

505 中士曰：非正神，何以天主容之，不滅之；且有焚禱像下，或致感應者。

The Cultivation of Virtue

doings, and takes no cognizance of the rules of conduct [he is obliged to keep], then where is he to begin to establish his merit and to cultivate moral conduct? When a man makes a friend, should he happen to utter one or two deceitful remarks, the other man will never again dare trust his word completely. Now these two men, [Buddha and Lao Tzu], have made a great number of false statements in their comments on the most important of matters, yet people still put implicit faith in the remainder of their teachings. Why is this so?

502. *The Chinese scholar says:* How did the numerous images of the Buddha and deities first come to be used?

503. *The Western scholar says:* In ancient times people were very artless, and because they did not know the Lord of Heaven, they set up images of those who more or less represented authority, or of departed relatives for whom they felt great affection, and they built ancestral temples as memorials to them. After the passage of much time, people would burn incense and offer paper money in order to seek their blessing and protection.

504. Then, there were very evil men who employed witchcraft to subdue goblins and phantoms. Because of these unusual activities they called themselves Buddhas and Immortals and, relying on the dissemination of their precepts and arts, they deceitfully promised to bestow blessings and happiness in order to frighten and mislead the stupid and vulgar, causing them to make images of these men and to sacrifice to them. This was how it all began.

505. *The Chinese scholar says:* If they are false spirits why does the Lord of Heaven allow them to exist instead of destroying them? Moreover, there are occasions when people experience a response after burning incense and bowing their heads to the ground in prayer before an idol.

論人性本善，而述天主門士正學

506 西士曰：有應也，亦有不應也，則其應非由彼神邪像也。人心既自靈，或有非理，常自驚詫己而規其隱者，不須外感也。又緣人既為非，則天主棄之不佑，故邪神魔鬼潛附彼像之中，得以侵迷誑誘，以增其愚。夫人既奉邪神，至其已死，靈魂墜於地獄，卒為魔鬼所役使，此乃魔鬼之願也。

507 幸得天主不甚許此等邪神發見於人間，見亦少以美像，常睹醜惡，或一身百臂，或三頭六臂，或牛頭，或龍尾等怪類，正欲人覺悟，知其非天上容貌，乃諸魔境惡相耳。而人猶迷惑，塑其像而置之金座，拜之，祀之，悲哉。

508 夫前世貴邦三教各撰其一，近世不知從何出一妖怪，一身三首，名曰三函教。庶氓所宜駭避，高士所宜疾擊之，而乃倒拜師之，豈不愈傷壞人心乎？

26 The spirit of eclecticism appears to have been particularly strong during the Ming dynasty (1368-1644). A useful summary of the forces which helped to stimulate this spirit is found in chapter five of Arthur F. Wright's *Buddhism in Chinese History,* (London, 1959), pp. 86-107. Note especially The recently published work by Judith A. Berling, *The Syncretic Religion of Lin Chao-en,* (New York, 1980).

400

The Cultivation of Virtue

506. *The Western scholar says:* Some prayers are answered and some are not, but the answers do not come from the impious image of that spirit. The mind of man is possessed of its own intelligence, and if something arises which is improper, it will usually react spontaneously in shocked surprise and reprove its own secret desires; it has no need of any external influence. But, since men do improper things, the Lord of Heaven abandons them and ceases to offer them His protection; in consequence, evil spirits and the Devil which lie hidden in the images are able to violate them, mislead them, deceive them, and seduce them, adding to their foolishness. Since men serve evil spirits, their souls fall into Hell after their deaths, and they end up as the servants of the Devil, the Devil having thereby achieved his aim.

507. Fortunately the Lord of Heaven seldom permits such evil spirits to appear in the world, and those we do see seldom possess a beautiful image. Most of them have an ugly appearance: either a single body and a hundred arms, three heads and six arms, or the head of an ox or the tail of a dragon and other such abnormalities, which cause people to come to their senses and to realize that these are not heavenly countenances, but rather the many evil faces of the Devil. Yet, people are still misled. They carve and shape these images; place them on golden thrones, and worship and sacrifice to them. Is this not sad?

508. Formerly, in your esteemed country, each of its three religions had its own image. In recent times a monster has appeared from I know not where: it has one body and three heads and is called the Religion of the Three in One.[26] The common people ought to have been frightened of it, and the lofty scholars should have attacked it with all speed; in fact, however, they have prostrated themselves in worship before it and made it their master. Will this not corrupt men's minds even further?

論人性本善，而述天主門士正學

509 中士曰：曾聞此語，然儒者不與也，願相與直指其失。

510 西士曰：吾且具四五端實理，以證其誣。一曰：三教者，或各真全，或各偽缺；或一真全，而其二偽缺也。苟各真全，則專從其一而足，何以其二為乎？苟各偽缺，則當竟為卻屏，奚以三海蓄之哉？使一人習一偽教，其誤已甚也，況兼三教之偽乎？苟惟一真全，其二偽缺，則惟宜從其一真，其偽者何用乎？

511 一曰：輿論云：「善者以全成之，惡者以一耳。」一艷貌婦人，但乏鼻，人皆醜之。吾前明釋二氏之教，俱各有病，若奉三函之教，豈不俾心分于三路，信心彌薄乎？

512 一曰：正教門，令入者篤信，心一無二，若欲包含為一，不免惡謬矣。

513 一曰：三門由三氏立也。孔子無取于老氏之道，則立儒門。釋氏不足于道、

402

The Cultivation of Virtue

509. *The Chinese scholar says:* I have heard of such a thing, but Confucians would never go along with it. I would like you, Sir, to be forthright in pointing out its faults.

510. *The Western scholar says:* I shall employ four or five solid reasons to provide proof of the fallacies contained within it. First, the Three Religions are either all true and complete or they are all false and incomplete; or one of them is true and complete and the other two are false and incomplete. If each of the [Three Religions] is true and complete then it is enough to believe one of them; why should one have to practice the other two? If they are all false and incomplete then they ought all to be rejected. Of what use is it to embrace all three of them? To cause a man to practice one false religion is a sufficiently grave error; how much greater, then, will the error be if he is made to practice three false religions? If only one is a true and complete religion and the two others are false and incomplete, then one ought to follow the one true religion. Of what use are the false ones?

511. Secondly, it is commonly accepted that goodness is the result of wholeness and evil the result of incompleteness. For example, a beautiful woman who lacks only a nose is considered by everyone to be ugly. I have already clearly explained above how the teachings of the Buddha and Lao Tzu are all faulty. If these are now to be merged, this will inevitably result in a compounding of error.

512. Thirdly, right religion will cause the minds of its converts to believe firmly in the one and only truth. If they enter the Religion of the Three in One, this will surely result in the division of their minds so that they follow three different paths. Will this not weaken their faith?

513. Fourthly, the three religions involved were established by three different men. Confucius refused to accept the teachings

儒之門，故又立佛門於中國。三宗自己意不相同，而二千年之後測度彼三心意，強為之同，不亦誣歟？

514 一曰：三教者，一尚「無」，一尚「空」，一尚「誠」「有」焉。天下相離之事，莫遠乎虛實有無也。借彼能合有與無、虛與實，則吾能合水與火、方與圓、東與西、天與地，而天下無事不可也。

515 胡不思每教本戒不同，若一戒殺生，一令用牲祭祀，則函三者欲守此固違彼，守而違，違而守，詎不亂教之極哉？

516 於以從三教，等無一教可從。無教可從，必別尋正路，其從三者，自意教為有餘，而實無一得焉。

517 不學上帝正德，而殉人夢中說道乎？

of Lao Tzu and therefore set up a Confucian school of thought; the Buddha was dissatisfied with the Taoist and Confucian schools, and therefore established Buddhism in China. The views of each of these religions are different from those of the others; is it not deceitful, then, for someone, two thousands years later, to try to guess their founders' intentions and to force them into being identical?

514. Further, in the teachings of the Three Religions, Taoism emphasizes "nothing," Buddhism "voidness," and Confucianism "sincerity" and "being." In the world of opposites there are no greater distinctions than those between emptiness and fulness and between existence and non-existence. If existence and non-existence, emptiness and fullness can be harmonized, then fire and water, squareness and roundness, east and west, and heaven and earth can all be harmonized, and there will be nothing in the world which will not be possible.

515. Why is no attention given to the dissimilarities of the basic precepts of each religion? If one religion prohibits the taking of life and another commands the use of a slaughtered animal for sacrificial purposes, then, the adherent of the Three in One Religion will find that when he wishes to keep the precepts of one religion he will have to disobey the precepts of the other. If by obeying one precept, he disobeys another, and by disobeying this one, he keeps that one, will this not result in total confusion?

516. Those who believe all three religions will find themselves without a single religion to follow, and, deprived of any religion, they are bound to search elsewhere for a correct path. Those who put their faith in the Religion of the Three in One will think that their faith extends beyond the boundaries of one religion whereas, in fact, they are not even putting their faith in one.

517. Do you wish to follow a religion which has been dreamed up by some human being before you have learnt to recognize

518 夫真維一耳，道契於其真，故能榮生。不得其一，則根透不深；根不深，則道不定；道不定，則信不篤。不一、不深、不篤，其學烏能成乎？

519 中士曰：噫嘻！寇者殘人，深夜而起；吾儕自救，猶弗醒也。聞先生之語，若霹靂馬動吾眠，而使之覺。雖然，猶望卒以正道之宗援我。

520 西士曰：心既醒矣，眼既啓矣，仰天而祈上佑，其時也夫。

The Cultivation of Virtue

the true Way of the Sovereign on High?

518. There is only one truth, and the Way lies in harmonizing oneself with that truth. Only so may one live a life of abundance. If you fail to find [the true Way] your roots will not go deep, and if your roots do not go deep, your way will prove uncertain; and if your way proves uncertain, your faith will lack sincerity. To have more than one [system of roots]; to lack depth, and to be devoid of sincerity can only mean that even should you wish to study the Way, you are not likely to succeed.

519. *The Chinese scholar says:* Alas! Robbers have taken advantage of the depth of night to injure people, and we have still not roused ourselves to guard against them. Your words as I have listened to them have been like a clap of thunder, causing me to wake from my slumbers. Notwithstanding, I still hope that in the end you will help me by means of the right Way.

520. *The Western scholar says:* Since your mind has been wakened and your eyes opened wide, the time has come for you to look up to Heaven and pray for blessings from above.

第八篇

總舉大西俗尚，而論其傳道之士所以不娶之意，幷釋天主降生西土來由。

521 中士曰：貴邦旣習天主之敎，其民必醇樸，其風必正雅，願聞所尚。

522 西士曰：民之用功乎聖敎，每每不等，故雖云一道，亦不能同其所尚。然論厥公者，吾大西諸國且可謂以學道爲本業者也，故雖各國之君，皆務存道正傳。

523 又立有最尊位，曰敎化皇，專以繼天主頒敎諭世爲己職，異端邪說不得作于列國之間，主敎者之位，享三國之地，然不婚配

1 *Chiao-hua huang* (敎化皇), the one who brings enlightenment to the people.
2 According to the common teaching of Western Catholic theology, the pope has an authority of "orders," as the head of the Church's hierarchy, of "jurisdiction," as the universal pastor of the faithful, and "in temporal matters," formerly as head of the papal states, and presently as the ruler of Vatican City State.

Chapter 8

A SUMMARY OF WESTERN CUSTOMS, A DISCUSSION OF THE MEANING AND HISTORY OF CELIBACY AMONG THE CLERGY, AND AN EXPLANATION OF THE REASON WHY THE LORD OF HEAVEN WAS BORN IN THE WEST.

521. *The Chinese scholar says:* Since your esteemed country practices the teaching of the Lord of Heaven, its people must be simple and honest and its customs correct and refined. I would like to hear about your customs.

522. *The Western scholar says:* People who believe in our sacred religion express their faith in different ways: thus, although one can say that they all believe the same doctrine, one cannot say that they all have the same customs. Nevertheless, our countries of the West can be said, on the whole, to regard the study of the Way as their fundamental task. Thus, even the sovereigns of each of these nations pay close attention to the need to preserve the orthodox transmission of the Way.

523. But another office which commands the highest respect has also been established, the holder of which is called the pope.[1] His sole task is to promulgate teachings on behalf of the Lord of Heaven and to instruct the world. Heterodoxy and false teachings cannot gain a footing in those [Western] countries. The pope enjoys a threefold authority,[2] but because he does not marry he has no heirs to his patrimony; instead, a good man is elected to succeed him. The sovereigns and ministers of the remaining states all swear allegiance to him. Because he is free of all family ties he

409

，故無有襲嗣，惟擇賢而立，餘國之君臣皆臣子服之。蓋旣無私家，則惟公是務；旣無子，則惟以兆民爲子，是故廸人於道，躬所不能及，則委才全德盛之人，代誨牧于列國焉。

524 列國之人，每七日一罷市，禁止百工，不拘男女尊卑，皆聚于聖殿，謁禮拜祭，以聽談道解經者終日。

525 又有豪士數會，其朋友出遊于四方，講學勸善。間有徹會，以耶穌名爲號，其作不久，然已三四友者，廣聞信於諸會，皆願求之以誘其子弟於眞道也。

526 中士曰：擇賢以君國，布士以訓民，尚德之國也，美哉風矣！又聞尊敎之在會者無私財，而以各友之財共焉；事無自專，每聽長者之命焉。其少也，成己德、博己學耳；壯者，學成而後及于人。以文會，以誠約，吾中夏講道者或難之。

總擧大西俗尚，而論其傳道之士所以不娶之意，并釋天主降生西土來由。

is able to devote himself solely to the public good, and since he has no children, he regards the numberless people as his sons and daughters, and exerts all his mind and energies in the guidance of the masses. What he is unable to accomplish himself he delegates to talented and virtuous men who teach and govern on his behalf in a great number of countries.

524. The people of each country cease all trading for a whole day every seventh day. Every kind of work is prohibited, and men and women, both the noble and the plebeian all gather together in sacred temples to pay their respects, to offer sacrifices, and to listen to the preaching of doctrine and the exposition of the canonical writings.

525. Then there are several societies to which men of honor and courage belong. The members of these associations travel far and wide lecturing on academic subjects and encouraging people to do good. Among these associations is my own humble Society which has taken as its name the name Jesus. It has only recently been established, but has already produced three or four members whose fame has spread to many countries. Every country is anxious to have its members so that they might guide and instruct children in the true Way.

526. *The Chinese scholar says:* A nation which elects the good to rule over its people and which sends scholars in all directions to instruct the common people is a nation which emphasizes virtue. This is an excellent custom. I am also given to understand that those who enter a society of your revered religion have no private possessions; that the wealth of each member is held in common; that nobody works solely for himself; that whenever something has to be done the members all obey the orders of their superior; that when they are young they concentrate on the perfection of virtue and the acquisition of learning, and that only when they are mature and have completed their learning do they extend their knowledge to others, forging friendships through scholarship, and discussing

527 然有終身絕色、終不婚配之戒，未審何意？夫生類自有之情，宜難盡絕，上帝之性，生生為本，祖考百千，其世傳之及我，可卽斷絕乎？

528 西士曰：絕色一事，果人情所難，故天主不布之于誡律，強人盡守，但令人自擇，願者遵之耳。然其事難能，大抵可以驗德，難乎精嚴正行。

529 凡人旣引于德，則路定而不易矣。君子修德不憚劬苦，吾方寸之志已立，則世上無難事焉，使以難為，為非義，則甚難為義者也。

530 生生者上帝，死死者誰乎？二者本一，非由二心。未開天地乎萬世以前，上帝無一生者，生生之性何在乎？人心卑瞑，莫測尊極之心，剏云

總舉大西俗尚，而論其傳道之士所以不娶之意，并釋天主降生西土來由。

412

Western Customs and God's Saving Work

matters of faith with sincerity. There have been some Chinese exponents of moral questions who have been embarrassed by this.

527. But what is the idea behind life-long chastity and the life-long rule forbidding marriage? It must be difficult to refrain completely from what is natural to living creatures. Love of life is the very foundation of the nature of the Sovereign on High. Can I cut off what has been handed down to me by my ancestors over hundreds and thousands of generations?

528. *The Western scholar says:* It is of course difficult for a man to be chaste, and therefore the Lord of Heaven has not promulgated in His commandments that all men should keep such a rule. He has simply instructed men to choose for themselves what they should do. Those who wish to remain chaste can do so. Although such a thing is difficult, it can be used to test a man's virtue. Its difficulty lies in the extremely strict nature of right conduct.

529. Any man who has already been led into the path of virtue will have decided firmly on his route and will not deviate from it. The superior man will fear no hardship as he cultivates his virtue. If my life's ambition has already been firmly established, then nothing in the world will prove difficult for me. If people equate everything that is difficult with unrighteousness, it will prove difficult to be a righteous man.

530. It is the Sovereign on High who causes man to live; and who then causes him to die? Both [life and death] stem from the one [and only Sovereign on High] and not from anyone else. Thousands of ten thousand generations ago, before heaven and earth came into existence and before the Sovereign on High had created a single living creature, where was that nature of His which is fond of life? The mind of man is lowly and in darkness and cannot fathom the most noble of all minds; how, then, can one attribute

咎之哉?且人以上帝之心為心,非但以傳生為義,亦有陳生之理。

531 夫天下人民,總合言之,如一全身焉,其身之心意惟一耳,各肢之所司甚重。令一身悉為首腹,胡以行動?令全身皆為手足,胡以見聞、胡以養生乎?比此而論,不宜責一國之人各同一轍。

532 若云以此生人、又兼司教以主祭祀始為全備;竊謂:婚姻之情固難竟絕,上帝之祀又須專潔,二職渾責一身,其于敬神之禮必有荒蕪。夫人奉事國君,尚有忍趄本身者;奉事上帝,詎不宜克己慾心哉?

533 古之民寡而德盛,而一人可以兼二職;今世之患,非在人少,乃人眾而德衰耳。圖多子而不知教之,斯乃祇增禽獸之群,豈所云廣人類者歟?

總舉大西俗尚,而論其傳道之士所以不娶之意,并釋天主降生西土來由。

error to it? Moreover, if man considers the mind of the Sovereign on High as [true] mind, then not only must the transmission of life be its intention, but it must also be capable of refusing to produce life.

531. Mankind, viewed as a whole, is like a body complete in all respects. But, although there can only be one purpose in the mind of that body, the function of the individual members of the body are numerous. If the whole body were a head or a stomach how would it be able to move? If the body were all hands or feet, how would it see or hear? How would it nourish its own life? In the light of this the people of a nation ought not to be condemned to uniformity. If you say that a person must marry and have children as well as manage the education of the Church and be responsible for the maintenance of the sacrificial system before he can be complete, I would say that marriage is certainly not something that can easily be eliminated, and that the offering of sacrifice to the Sovereign on High demands men who are devoted to nothing else and who are pure in body.

532. If a man bears both responsibilities it is bound to result in the neglect [of certain of his duties] connected with the rites and ceremonies of worship. When a man serves his sovereign he must practice a certain ruthless self-denial; should not a man then deliberately curtail his passions when he enters the service of the Sovereign on High?

533. In ancient times the population was small, and it was a period when virtue flourished; thus, one man was capable of combining both responsibilities. The troubles of today are not due to the smallness of the population, but to the fact that the population has grown large without a corresponding growth in virtue. To plan to have many children and to be ignorant of how to instruct them is merely to increase the animal population. Can you really call that adding to the population of mankind?

534 有志乎救世者，深悲當世之事，制為敝會規則，絕色不娶，緩於生子，急於生道，以挺援斯世墮溺者為意，其意不更公乎？

535 又傳生之責，男與女均。今有貞女各聘未嫁而夫卒者，守義無二，儒者嘉之，天子每旌表之。

536 彼其棄色而忘傳生者，第因守小信於匹夫，在家不嫁，尚且見褒。吾三四友人，因奉事上帝，欲以便于遊天下、化萬民，而未暇一婚，乃受貶焉，不亦過乎？

537 中士曰：婚娶者，於勸善宣道何傷乎？

538 西士曰：無相傷也。但單身不娶，愈靖以成己，愈便以及人也。吾為子揭其便處，請詳察之，以明敝會所為有所據否？

總舉大西俗尚，而論其傳道之士所以不娶之意，并釋天主降生西土來由。

534. Those concerned for the salvation of the world feel deep pity for the situation in the world today, and have therefore made chastity and celibacy rules of my humble Society. Curtailing the birth of children we urgently beget the Way, and have as our sole aim the salvation and help of fallen men in this present age. Is not such an aim even more public-spirited?

535. Further, men and women are equally responsible for handing on human life. There are at this time certain chaste women whose menfolk, to whom they have been betrothed, have died before they were married. To maintain their honor such women have refrained from a second betrothal. Confucians praise such action and emperors give public recognition to it.

536. Chastity of the kind which results in a refusal to transmit life to later generations is merely due to a desire to keep faith with a spouse; and yet to remain at home and to refrain from further espousals results in public tribute being paid to that person. Is it not unfair that we few friends should be censured when, due to our work for the Sovereign on High, and so that we might conveniently travel throughout the world in order to transform all men, we have not time to concern ourselves with marriage?

537. *The Chinese scholar says:* How can marriage be harmful to anyone wishing to publicize the Way and to urge people to lead a good life?

538. *The Western scholar says:* It is not harmful. It is simply that to remain single and unmarried allows one greater tranquility to perfect oneself, and makes it easier for one to extend [the perfection] to others. Let me explain the convenience of celibacy to you under a number of headings so that you will be able to see whether or not this practice of the members of my humble Society is well founded.

539 一曰：娶者，以生子為室家耳；既獲幾子，必須養育，而以財為置養之資，為人之父不免有貨殖之心。今之父子眾，求財者眾也；求之者眾，難以各得其願矣。吾以身纏拘於俗情，不能超脫無溺，必將以苟且為幸也，欲立志責人於義，豈能興起乎？夫修德以輕貨財為首務，我方重愛之，何勸爾輕置之哉？

540 二曰：道德之情至幽至奧，人心未免昏昧，色慾之事又恆鈍人聰明焉。若為色之所役，如以小燈藏之厚皮籠內，不益矇乎？豈能達于道妙矣。絕色者如去心目之塵垢，益增光明，可以窮道德之精微也。

541 三曰：天下大惑，維由財色二欲耳，以仁發憤救世者，必以解此二惑為急。醫家以相悖者相治，故熱病用寒藥，寒病用煖藥，乃能療之。茲吾惡富總舉大西俗尚，而論其傳道之士所以不娶之意，并釋天主降生西土來由。

539. First, marriage is for the begetting of children and the setting up of families. If one begets several children one must provide them with love and care and accumulate wealth to provide for their nurture. A father cannot avoid thinking about trade and commerce. Since in these days there are many fathers and sons the number engaged in acquiring wealth is also considerable. As the numbers of those who seek to acquire wealth grow, it becomes increasingly difficult for each man to obtain what he wants. If I were to allow myself to be involved in secular affairs I would be unable to detach myself from the mundane, and would be bound to count myself fortunate if I were merely able to remain alive. How could **I carry out my ambition to encourage people to live a righteous life?** The most important thing in the cultivation of virtue is to despise wealth and goods. How can I persuade others not to concern themselves with wealth and goods if I pay serious attention to, and have an inordinate affection for, such things?

540. Secondly, the nature of morality is most profound and most mysterious, but the minds of men are unavoidably steeped in darkness. Further, man's quickness of understanding is constantly blunted by passion. If a man becomes a slave to passion it is as if a small light has been hidden inside a lamp-shade of thick skin, and he is plunged into even greater darkness. How, then, will he be able to attain to the most sublime levels of morality? A person who has undertaken to be chaste is like one who has cleansed the eye of his mind of all dust and who has therefore increased the volume of light, and can thoroughly comprehend the subtlest truths of morality.

541. Thirdly, the people of this world have been greatly misled by covetousness and by lust. The man who firmly resolves to save the world by means of humanity must regard the rescue of men from these two great temptations as his most urgent task. A medical practitioner employs antidotes to heal people of their sicknesses; thus, cold medicine is applied to those suffering from

之害，而自擇為貧者；畏色之傷，而自擇為獨夫者，處己若此，而後無義之財、邪色之欲始有省焉。故儆會友捐己義得之財物，以勸人勿于非義之富；為修道以卻正色之樂，以勸人勿迷于非禮之色也。

542

四曰：縱有俊傑才能，使其心散而不專乎一，則所為事必不精。克己之功難于克天下，自古及今，史傳英雄攻天下而得之者多矣，能克己者幾人哉？志欲行道于四海之內，非但欲克一己，兼欲防遏萬民私欲，則其功用之大，曷可計乎？專之猶恐未精，況宜分之他務？爾將要我事少艾而育小兒乎？

543

五曰：善養馬者，遇騏驥騂騮，可一日而馳千里，則謹收以期戰陣之用，懼有劣嫻於色者，別之於群，不使與牝接焉。天主聖教亦將尋豪傑之人，能周編四方之疆界者，以明道禦侮，息異論，逆邪說，而永存聖教之正也，豈欲輟其

---

3 *Li* (里), a unit of measure. See chapter 4, n. 27.

總舉大西俗尚，而論其傳道之士所以不娶之意，并釋天主降生西土來由。

feverishness, and hot medicine to those with cold ailments; only so can these sickness be cured. Because we loathe the harm caused by wealth we have chosen poverty; and because we fear the hurt caused by lust we have chosen to remain single. Only by so disciplining ourselves can we become fully aware of the injustices of wealth and of the nature of evil desires. Thus, the members of my humble Society sacrifice their own legitimate wealth in order to persuade people not to scheme for unjust wealth; they leave home for the monastic life so that they may cultivate the Way, and renounce the joys of legitimate sexuality in order to persuade people not to be tempted by improper passions.

542. Fourthly, a person may possess the talent and ability of the most extraordinary of men, but if his mind is undisciplined and lacks singleness of purpose, then everything he does will be devoid of refinement. The task of self-conquest is more difficult than the conquest of the world. From ancient times to the present, history has recorded the names of numerous heroes who have captured the world, but not many have been victorious over themselves. Anyone with an ambition to promote the Way in every place must not only gain control over himself, but must also seek to take defensive measures to halt the selfish desires of all men. The greatness of such an activity is beyond measure. Even with complete singleness of mind it is doubtful whether one will be able to carry it out to perfection, but how much more will this be so if one's mind is also occupied with other things? Do you want me to serve an attractive young woman and to beget children?

543. Fifthly, an expert in the rearing of horses who comes across good horses like piebalds and chestnuts which can travel a thousand *li*[3] in a day will rear them with all care so that they may be prepared for the front line of battle. Fearful lest they be immersed in sexual activity he removes them from the herd and denies them any contact with the opposite sex. The holy religion of the Lord of Heaven also seeks out men of valor who will be able to travel

心以色樂,而不欲培養其果穀以克私慾之習乎?故西士之專心續道,甚于專事嗣後者也,譬天欽收五穀萬石,未有盡播之田中以為穀種者,必將擇其一以貢君,一以藝稼為明年之穡。曷獨人間萬子皆罄費之以產子,而無所全留以待他用者耶?

544

六曰:凡事有人與鳥獸同者,不可甚重焉。勞身以求食,求食以充饑,充饑以蓄氣,蓄氣以敵害,敵害以全己性命也,咸下情也,人於鳥獸此無殊也。若謹慎以殉義,殉義以檢心,檢心以修身,修身以廣仁,廣仁以答天主恩也,此乃生人切事,可以稱上帝之大旨。

總舉大西俗尚,而論其傳道之士所以不娶之意,并釋天主降生西土來由。

Western Customs and God's Saving Work

to the remotest corner of the earth in order to explain the principles of the Way, defend them against slander, pacify conflicting opinions, eradicate heterodox teachings, and always to preserve the holy Church's orthodox tradition. Do you want to weaken their resolve by means of the pleasures of sexuality; and do you wish to refrain from supporting them in their heroic attempts to subdue evil habits stemming from the passions? Thus, Western scholars are more concerned to inherit the Way than they are to provide themselves with progeny. The farmer who harvests ten thousand measures of grain provides a good illustration of what I mean. He would never use all this grain for seed and plant it in his fields. He would be bound to select one portion of it to present to his sovereign as tribute; another portion he would use for seed so that he might reap a harvest the following year. Why should all the millions of men and women in this world be spent in transmitting life to later generations, and none be reserved for other purposes?

544. Sixthly, whatever is common to both men and animals should not be valued too highly. Men labor to provide food; they seek food to satisfy their hunger; they satisfy their hunger in order to nourish their vital energy; they nourish their vital energy in order to resist harm, and they resist harm in order to preserve their lives. All these things have to do with man's lower nature, and there is little difference between man and the animals in this respect. When it comes to the careful following after righteousness we find that one follows righteousness in order to scrutinize one's motives; one scrutinizes one's motives in order to cultivate oneself; one cultivates oneself in order to extend one's humanity; one extends one's humanity in order to repay the Lord of Heaven for His favors. These are important matters in human existence and they allow men to bring themselves into harmony with the will of the Sovereign on High.

545 從此觀之，則匹配之情之務道之意，孰重乎？天下寧無食，不寧無道；天下寧無人，不寧無教。故因道之急，可緩婚；因婚之急，不可緩道也。以遵頒天主聖旨，雖棄致己身以當之可也，況棄婚乎？

546 七曰：敝會之趣無他，乃欲傳正道於四方焉耳。苟此道於西不能行，則遷其繫身于一處，必周流以濟各處之病，方為博施。吾徒畫身於一境乎？醫之仁者，不友于東，於東猶不行，又將徙於南北。

547 婚配之身纏繞一處，其本責不越于齊家，或迨于一國而已耳，故中國之傳道者，未聞其有出遊異國者，夫婦不能相離也。吾會三四友，聞有可以行道之域，雖在幾萬里之外，亦即往焉，無有託家寄妻子之慮，則以天主為父母，以世人為兄弟，以天下為己家焉，其所涵胸中之志如海天然，豈一匹夫之諒乎？

總舉大西俗尚，而論其傳道之士所以不娶之意，并釋天主降生西土來由。

545. When we look at things from this point of view, which is the more important: marriage or the determination to devote oneself to the cultivation of the Way? I would rather there be nothing to eat in the world than that there should be no Way; I would rather there be no people in the world than that there be no education. Because of the urgent need for the Way we may neglect marriage, but we cannot neglect the Way because of the urgent need to marry. If it is right for me to give up my own body in order to serve the Lord of Heaven by promulgating His sacred will, how much more is it right for me merely to give up marriage?

546. Seventhly, my humble Society has no other aim than the promulgation of the orthodox Way to all quarters of the earth. If this Way cannot make headway in the West, then the members of my order are transferred to the East; and if it cannot make headway in the East they are transferred to the South or to the North. Why should I confine myself in vain to one place? A benevolent physician does not confine himself to one place, but goes from place to place in order to save the sick. Only so can he be said to bestow his skills widely.

547. A man who is married is tied to one place and his natural duties do not extend beyond the ordering of his family or, at most, the governing of a state. Thus, I have never heard of a Chinese preacher who has travelled beyond the confines of China [to preach religion]. This is because husbands and wives cannot leave each other! If the members of my Society hear of a place where they can promote their teachings, they can go there immediately even if the place be more than tens of thousands of *li* away. With no need to worry about entrusting wives and children to the care of others we regard the Lord of Heaven as our father and mother and all men as our brothers. We look on the whole world as our family; and the ambition we harbor in our breasts is as great as the wide ocean and the vault of heaven. The spirit of the ordinary man hardly measures up to this.

548 八曰：凡此與彼彌似，則其性彌近。天神了無知色者，絕色者其情通乎天神矣；夫身在地下，而比居上天者；以有形者而效無形者，此不可謂鄙人庸學也。似此清淨之士有所祈禱于天主，或天之旱，或妖鬼之怪也，或遇水火災異之求解也，天主大都鑒而聽之，不然上尊何寵之哉？

549 然吾此數條理，特具以解儆會不婚之意，非以非婚姻者也：蓋順理娶也，非犯天主誡也；又非謂不娶者皆通神人也：設令絕婚屏色，而不捲捲于秉彝之德，豈不徒然乎？

550 乃中國有辭正色而就狎斜者，去女色而取頑童者，此輩之穢污，西鄉君子弗言，恐浼其口；雖禽獸之彙亦惟知陰陽交感，無有反悖天性如此者。人弗報馬，則其犯罪若何？吾儆同會者收全己種，不之藝播于田畝，而子猶疑其可否，況棄之溝壑者哉！

總舉大西俗尚，而論其傳道之士所以不娶之意，并釋天主降生西土來由。

548. Eighthly, whenever two things grow more alike their natures increasingly approximate each other. The angels are devoid of sexual desire, and the nature of a chaste person approximates to that of the angels because, although his body is here on earth he is similar to those who live in Heaven. Men with physical bodies who nevertheless imitate the metaphysical angels cannot be said to be vulgar men and mediocre scholars. Whatever such pure students of the Way ask of the Lord of Heaven in prayer—whether the requests be concerned with drought, the abnormal behavior of evil spirits or with relief from the effects of fire and flood—the Lord of Heaven will probably condescend to listen to them; if this were not so, how could the Honor on High be said to love such people?

549. But, although I have employed these several arguments specifically to explain why members of my Society do not marry, I have not adduced them in order to oppose marriage for, to take a wife is a right and proper thing to do and can certainly not be regarded as breaking any commandment of the Lord of Heaven; nor is it to say that all who remain single are of angel-like appearance. If a person refrains from sexual activity and does not marry, but at the same time does not pay careful attention to the virtue bestowed on him, is not his abstinence in vain?

550. In China there are those who reject correct sexual behavior and visit houses of ill fame; who put aside sexual intercourse with women and amuse themselves with young boys. Superior men in the West do not speak about such foul individuals for fear of contaminating their own mouths. Even animals know only of sexual intercourse between males and females and would be incapable of so running counter to their natures. If a man lacks a sense of shame, to what lengths of wrong-doing will he go! The members of my humble Society are like the farmer who retains his seed and does not scatter it in his fields. If you still believe this to be indefensible, how much more indefensible must it be to cast it carelessly into a ditch!

551 中士曰：依理之語以服人心，強于利刃也。但中國有傳云：「不孝有三，無後為大者。」如何？

552 西士曰：有解之者云：「彼一時，此一時；古者民未衆，當充擴之，今人已衆，宜姑停焉。」予曰此非聖人之傳語，乃孟氏也：或承悞傳，或以釋舜不告而娶之義，而他有托焉。禮記一書多非古論議，後人集禮，便雜記之于經典。

553 貴邦以孔子為大聖，學庸論語孔子論孝之語極詳，何獨其大不孝之戒，群弟子及其孫不傳，而至孟氏始著乎？孔子以伯夷叔齊為古之賢人，以比干為殷三仁之一，既稱三子曰仁

總舉大西俗尚，而論其傳道之士所以不娶之意，并釋天主降生西土來由。

4 *Chinese Classics*, II, p. 313.
5 Ibid..
6 Though one of the Five Classics of Confucianism, the *Li Chi* (禮記) or *Book of Rites* did not reach its present form until well into the Han dynasty (206 B.C.—220 A.D.)
7 Po I (伯夷) and Shu Ch'i (叔齊) were brothers and men of high principle who lived towards the end of the Shang dynasty. They were highly regarded by both Confucius and Mencius. See *Chinese Classics*, I, pp. 181, 199 and II, p. 193.
8 For Confucius' evaluation of Pi Kan (比干), see *Chinese Classics*, I, p. 331.

428

551. *The Chinese scholar says:* The truth can subdue men's minds more readily than a sharpened sword. But in our canonical writings there is the statement: "There are three things which mark a man as being unfilial, and the greatest of these is to have no progeny."[4] What have you to say about that?

552. *The Western scholar says:* Some would explain it by saying that times have changed. In ancient times the population was small, and it was right for mankind to proliferate; now that men have become so numerous, however, they ought temporarily to slow down the birth-rate. My view, however, is that the words you have quoted were not handed down from the Sage, but were uttered by Mencius. It may be that he received a faulty statement in the [oral] transmission [of the Sage's teachings], or perhaps he was using these words to explain the significance of the emperor Shun taking a wife[5] without reporting the fact, and that others employed deliberately misleading terminology. In the *Book of Rites* there are many passages which do not give an account of ancient times and where men of later times have gathered together the rites of their own day, recording them haphazardly in this Classic.[6]

553. In your esteemed country you regard Confucius as a great Sage. In the *Great Learning,* the *Mean,* and the *Analects of Confucius* Confucius discusses filial piety in great detail. Why is it, then, that he, his disciples and his grandson all fail to make any mention of regulations concerning this most unfilial piece of human conduct? Why was it not until the time of Mencius that such a doctrine was first recorded? Confucius regarded Po I and Shu Ch'i[7] as good men of ancient times and Pi Kan[8] as the most humane of the three humane men of the Yin dynasty. Since Confucius used the words "humane" and "good" to praise these three men, we can be sure he believed their virtue to be perfect and lacking in nothing; nevertheless, none of these three men had an heir. If Mencius thought them unfilial and Confucius considered them

、曰賢,必信其德皆全而無缺矣。然三人咸無後也,則孟氏以為不孝,孔子以為仁,且不相戾乎?是故吾謂以無後為不孝,斷非中國先進之旨。

554 使無後果為不孝,則為人子者,宜旦夕專務生子以續其後,不可一日有間,豈不誘人被色累乎?如此則舜猶未為至孝耳,蓋男子二十以上可以生子,舜也三十而娶,則二十逮三十匪孝乎?古人三旬已前不婚,則其一旬之際皆匪孝乎?

555 譬若有匹夫焉,自審無後非孝,有後乃孝,則娶數妾,老于其鄉生子至多,初無他善可稱,可為孝乎?學道之士,平生遠遊異鄉,輔君匡國,敎化兆民,為忠信而不顧產子,此隨前論乃大不孝也;然於國家兆民有大功焉,則輿論稱為大賢。

556 孝否在內不在外,由我豈由他乎?得子不得子也,天主有定命矣,有求子者而不得,烏有求孝而不得孝者乎?孟氏嘗曰:「求則得之,舍則失之,是求有益於得

總舉大西俗尚,而論其傳道之士所以不娶之意,幷釋天主降生西土來由。

humane is there not a contradiction here? I therefore assert that the view which holds that to lack heirs is to be unfilial is abolutely not an early Chinese idea.

554. If it really were the case that a lack of progeny represents an unfilial attitude, then every son ought to devote himself from morning to night to the task of begetting children in order to ensure the existence of later generations. He should not interrupt his task even for a day. But does this not mean leading a man into bondage to sex? Put in this way, even Emperor Shun cannot be regarded as a very filial man. Since a man can certainly beget children from the age of twenty, and Emperor Shun waited until he was thirty before he took a wife, the period from twenty to thirty years of age must be regarded as a time when he was unfilial. If the ancients did not marry before they were thirty, then for ten years they were all unfilial.

555. Take, for example, a fellow who thinks to himself that he is being unfilial if he has no progeny, and that he will only be filial if he has heirs. He takes several wives in succession and begets a great number of sons, but keeps them all in his home town and never does another good thing. Can such a man be called filial? Then take a student of the Way who spends his whole life travelling to other towns, supporting his sovereign and giving aid to the nation, teaching and guiding people to be loyal and trustworthy yet disregarding his duty to beget children. According to the theory stated earlier, such a person would be adjudged greatly unfilial; nevertheless, he would have accomplished highly meritorious deeds for the nation and the people, and public opinion would acclaim him as a great and good man.

556. The fact is that filial piety or the lack of it resides in the mind and is not something external; it stems from me and not from someone else. Whether we have sons or not is determined by the Lord of Heaven. There are those who seek to have sons but never have them; but how can there be anyone who seeks to be filial and yet fails to be so? Mencius once said: "When we get by our seek-

也，求在我也；求之有道，得之有命，是求無益於得也，求在外也。」以是得嗣無益於得，況為峻德之效乎？

557 大西聖人言不孝之極有三也：陷親於罪惡，其上；弒親之身，其次；脫親財物，又其次也。天下萬國通以三者為不孝之極。至中國而後，聞無嗣不孝之罪，於三者猶加重焉。

558 吾今為子定孝之說，欲定孝之說，先定父子之說。凡人在宇內有三父：一謂天主，二謂國君，三謂家君也；逆三父之旨者，為不孝子矣。天下有道，三父之旨無相悖，蓋下父者，命己子奉事上父者也，而為子者順乎，一即兼孝三焉；天下無道，三父之令相反，則下父不順其上父，而私子以奉己，弗顧其上，其

總舉大西俗尚，而論其傳道之士所以不娶之意，并釋天主降生西土來由。

9 Ibid., II, p. 450.

432

ing and lose by our neglecting, in that case seeking is of use to getting, and the things sought for are those which are in ourselves. When the seeking is according to the proper course, and the getting is only as appointed, in that case the seeking is of no use to getting, and the things sought are without ourselves."[9] If you employ this method to acquire sons there is no certainty that you will get them; how much less, then, are you likely to acquire the results of virtue?

557. Western sages say that the following are the three most unfilial acts: causing one's parents to do wrong, murdering one's parents, robbing one's parents of their wealth. Many nations in the world regard these three things as the most unfilial deeds possible. It was only after I arrived in China that I heard it said that a failure to produce progeny represented a lack of filial piety and an act, moreover, more grave than the three mentioned above.

558. I have now determined the limits within which filial piety may be discussed. To determine the meaning of filial piety we must first determine the relationship between father and son. In this world a man has three kinds of father, the first is the Lord of Heaven, the second the sovereign of his state, and the third the father of his family; to disobey these three fathers is to be unfilial. When all men follow the Way the wills of these three kinds of fathers will not be in conflict since the father of lowest rank will command his own son to serve the senior fathers, and he who is a son will observe all three kinds of filial piety by obeying his one father. When the Way does not hold sway in the world, however, the commands of the three kinds of father will conflict with each other; the father of the lowest rank will fail to obey the senior fathers, will seek to benefit his own selfish ends, and will instruct his sons to serve himself and to ignore his other fathers. A son ought to obey the commands of his most senior father even if they run counter to those of his father of lowest rank. In so doing he does no violence to his filial

為子之者，聽其上命，雖犯其下者，不害其為孝也，若從下者逆其上者，固大為不孝者也。

559 國主於我相為君臣，家君於我相為父子，若使比乎天主之公父乎，世人雖君臣父子，平為兄弟耳焉，此倫不可不明矣。

560 夫萬國通大西之境界，皆稱為出聖人之地，蓋無世不有聖人焉。吾察百世以下，做土聖人之尊者，咸必終身不娶，聖人為世之表，豈天主立之為表，而處己於不義之為哉？彼有不娶而為積財貨，或為糊口，或為偷安懶惰，其卑賤之流，何足論者？

561 若吾三四友，一心慕道以事天王，救世歸元，且絕諸色之類，使其專任鄙見，無理可揭，誠為不可。然而群聖以其身先之，萬國賢士美之，有實理合之

總學大西俗尚，而論其傳道之士所以不娶之意，并釋天主降生西土來由。

conduct. If, on the other hand, he obeys his father of lowest rank and thereby disobeys his senior fathers he will naturally be reckoned the most unfilial of sons.

559. The supreme head of a nation and I stand in relationship to each other as sovereign to subject, and the head of my household and I stand in the mutual relationship of father to son. Although human beings make distinctions between sovereign and subject, father and son, when they are seen in their relationship to the common fatherhood of the Lord of Heaven they all become brothers with an equal standing; it is essential to understand this principle.

560. The nations of the Far West are places known for the sages they produce since every generation produces its own sage. When I examine the many generations that have gone before I find that among the most highly honored of the sages of my own humble land there has not been one who has not remained single throughout his life. Sages are models for the rest of mankind. The Lord of Heaven would hardly raise them up as models if their conduct was in any way unrighteous. Those who refrain from marrying because they wish to amass a fortune, or for reasons of their livelihood, or because they are lazy and have no other ambition but to get by in this life, are men of inferior quality and are not worth mentioning.

561. When it comes to the members of my Society, however, we find that they are wholeheartedly devoted to the Way, that they serve the Lord of Heaven, that they save mankind by causing men to return to their source, and that they forsake sexual passion. But if we only had their word for it there would be no truth to present, and it would be quite wrong to refrain from marriage. However, many sages who have been examples in themselves have preceded them [as models], and since these have been praised by worthy scholars of all nations, and since their [decision to remain unmarried] is supported by solid reasons and by the [authority of]

,有天主經典奇之,亦可姑隨其志否耶?

562 以繼後為急者,惟不知事上帝,不安于本命,不信有後世者,以為生世之後已盡滅散,無有存者,真可謂之無後。吾今世事奉上帝,而望萬世以後猶悠久常奉事之,何患無後乎?吾死而神明全在,當益鮮潤;所遺虛軀殼,子葬之亦腐,朋友葬之亦腐,則何擇乎?

563 中士曰:為學道而不婚配,誠合義也。我大禹當亂世治洪水,巡行九州八年於外,三過其門而不入。今也當平世,士有室家何傷焉?

564 西士曰:嗚呼!子以是為平世乎?誤矣。智者以為今時之災比堯時之災愈洪也,群世人而盲聾,不之能視焉,則其殘不亦深乎?古之所謂不祥,從外而來,人猶易見而速防,其所傷不踰財貨,或傷膚皮;今之禍自內突

總舉大西俗尚,而論其傳道之士所以不娶之意,幷釋天主降生西土來由。

10 Ibid., II, pp. 250-251.

436

Western Customs and God's Saving Work

the canonical writings of the Lord of Heaven, we can surely follow their lead for the time being!

562. The reasons why the continuity of successive generations is considered so urgent a duty are that people have no knowledge as to how they should serve the Sovereign on High, that they are not content with the commands of Heaven, and that they do not believe in life after death. To believe that once a person has died he is completely dissolved and that nothing of him remains is truly to assert that a man has no posterity. If I serve the Lord on High in this present life and hope that for all generations to come I shall continue to serve Him, how can I have any anxiety over a lack of progeny? After I die my spirit will be preserved in its entirety and will be even more fresh and healthy. Whether the empty body I leave behind is buried by sons or by friends, it will rot away. What other choice is there?

563. *The Chinese scholar says:* It is truly fitting that a man should not marry for the sake of studying the Way. When Emperor Yao [of our Hsia dynasty] set himself the task of controlling the flood in an age of disorder he went on a tour of inspection through all nine regions and was away from home eight years! He passed the door of his house three times without entering it.[10] But these are peaceful times, so what harm is there in people having their own homes?

564. *The Western scholar says:* Alas! You are wrong to say that we are living in peaceful times. Wise men believe that the **disasters of the present day are greater than the natural disasters of** the times of Emperor Yao! Mankind is both blind and deaf. Is not the loss of sight a most serious injury? The misfortunes of ancient times came from outside; people found it easy to see them and were able to take precautions quickly so that all that was harmed was their property and their skins. Today's calamities, however, sud**denly** emerge from within men. When wise men become aware of them, they find it difficult to avoid them; how much more must

發,哲者覺之而難避也,況于恒人?故其害莫甚焉。如風雷妖怪之擊人,不損乎外,而侵其內者也。

565
夫化生天地萬物乃大公之父也,又時主宰安養之,乃無上共君也。世人弗仰弗奉,則無父無君,至無忠、至無孝也;忠孝蔑有,尚存何德乎?

566
夫以金木土泥鑄塑不知何人偽像,而倡愚氓往來拜禱之,曰此乃佛祖、此乃三清也。且興淫辭奸說以壅塞之,使之氾濫中心,而不得歸其宗。且以人類與天主為同一體,非將以上帝之尊,而侔之於卑役者乎?恣其誕妄,以天主無限之感靈,而等之於土石枯木,以其無窮之仁,覆為有玷缺,而寒暑災異,憫且尤之,侮狎君父一至于此,蓋昭事上帝之學,久已陵夷。

總舉大西俗尚,而論其傳道之士所以不娶之意,并釋天主降生西土來由。

11 *San Ch'ing* (三清). The Three Pure Ones are the three heavens of the three supreme gods of Taoism. The term also applies to the gods themselves.

this be so for ordinary men? Thus, there can be nothing more serious than the harm caused by these calamities. More fearsome than storms and monsters, they do not affect people externally, but invade their inner beings.

565. The creator of heaven, earth, and all things is the father of all, and as the controller and sustainer of all things He is also the supreme sovereign of all. If mankind does not reverence Him and serve Him it will lack both father and sovereign, and this is to be totally disloyal and altogether lacking in filial piety. Can one be virtuous at all if one is disloyal and is lacking in filial piety?

566. To cast and sculpt false images of every kind of people out of metal, wood, and earth in order to lead the uneducated masses into worshipping them and praying to them and to say that this is the Buddha or those are the Three Ch'ing;[11] to employ immoral terms and villainous talk to obstruct [the true Way] and to cause them to flood the hearts of men so that they are unable to return to the truth; and to make "voidness" and "nothing" into the source of all things, is to make the Lord of Heaven void and non-existent. To regard mankind and the Lord of Heaven as being organically one is to place the honor of the Sovereign on High on an equal footing with the lowliest of slaves. To allow such false ideas is to put the unlimited prestige of the Lord of Heaven on the same footing as earth, stone, and withered trees. The overthrowing of the inexhaustible humanity of [the Lord of Heaven] so that it becomes flawed and imperfect creates unhappiness and resentfulness in people when there are natural disasters in winter and summer. That people go as far as they now do in slandering their sovereign and fathers is entirely due to the fact that the teaching which commands the service of the Sovereign on High has long been neglected.

567 不思小吏聊能阿好其民，已為建祠立像，布滿郡縣皆是生祠，佛殿神宮彌山徧市，豈其天主尊神無一微壇，以禮拜敬事之乎？

568 四友，有子之情，有兄弟之情，視此為何如時哉？今世，非但八年在外，必其絕不有家，終身周巡于萬國，而不忍還矣。爾欲吾三世人也，皆習詐偽，偽為眾師，以揚虛名，供養其口，昌民父母，要譽取資，至于世人大父、宇宙公君，泯其跡而僭其位，殆哉！殆哉！吾意大禹適在

569 中士曰：以是為亂，則亂固不勝言矣。時賢講學，急其表而不究其裏，故表裏終于俱壞，蓋未聞積惡於內，而不發于外者也。

570 間有儒門之人，任其私智，附會二氏以論來世，如丐子就乞餘飯，彌紊正學；不如貴邦儒者乃有歸元，此論既明，人人可悟，但肯用心一思眾物之態，必

總舉大西俗尚，而論其傳道之士所以不娶之意，并釋天主降生西土來由。

440

Western Customs and God's Saving Work

567. To curry favor with the populace, minor officials build shrines and set up images for them. In every part of every prefecture and county there are to be found memorial temples to living persons. On every mountain and in every city one comes across Buddhist monasteries and Taoist temples. How is it that there is not even a small altar for the reverencing and worshipping of the most honored deity of all, the Lord of Heaven?

568. Mankind is given over to the practice of deceit. Men who pretend to be guides come and proclaim false names, serving their own mouths and stomachs. Then there are those who pretend to be parents but who only seek fame and money. These men seek to obliterate all traces of the great father of mankind and of the sovereign of the universe, usurping His authority. The times are dangerous indeed! I think if Emperor Yü of the Hsia dynasty were alive today he would not only travel abroad for eight years, but would absolutely refuse to have a family so that he could devote his whole life to travelling around and inspecting every part of the world. He would not be able to bear the thought of returning home. What kind of times do you think we live in that you should want the few members of our Society to concern ourselves with children and brothers?

569. *The Chinese scholar says:* If these are to be called turbulent times then there can be no end to the defining of turbulence. Worthy men of today who lecture on academic subjects are only concerned with externals and are careless of what goes on within men; the result has been a deterioration in both the external and inner world. Because they have so far heard nothing to the contrary evil has accumulated within and gradually this has manifested itself externally.

570. There are even Confucians who, following their own private wisdom have adopted the opinions of Buddhism and Taoism on the life to come. Like beggars seeking to eat other people's leftovers, they have brought confusion into orthodox learning. They

知物有始元,非物可比。

571 聖也、佛也、仙也,均由人生,不可謂無始元者也,則不為真主何能輒立世誡?夫知有歸元,則人道已定,舍事天又何學焉?譬如一身,四肢各欲自存也,然忽有刀鎗將擊其首,手足自往救護,雖見傷殘,終不能已。

572 尊教洞曉天主為眾物元,則凡觀惡行、聞惡語,凡有逆于理、違于教者,若矛刃將刺天主然,亟迫往護,此亦惟知有天主之在上,而寧知天下有他物可尚乎?故不但不念妻子財資,吾身生命猶將忘之。

573 吾輩俗心錮結,佛彷慕企,輒淺信從,奚云捨生命、棄妻子?有因上帝道德之故,通移半步,遙費一芥,且各惜之矣。嗟呼!

總舉大西俗尚,而論其傳道之士所以不娶之意,并釋天主降生西土來由。

are unlike the learned men of your esteemed country who all refer to one original source to which nothing else can be compared. Since such teaching is clear, everyone can understand it; all that is required is that thought be given to the condition of things. If this is done one will come to realize that all things have a first cause to which nothing else can be compared.

571. Sages, Buddhas, and Immortals are all born of man and none can be said to be without a first cause. What is not the first cause is not the true Lord of Heaven. How then can such a person proclaim commandments for the whole world? Where a first cause is known the principles governing man's place in the world are already definite and sure. What more important learning can there be than that which is concerned with the service of Heaven? It is like the four limbs of the body. Each wishes to maintain its own existence; but, when a sudden attack is made on the head with sword and spear, hands and feet naturally attempt to save and protect it, and they are unable to desist even when it is obvious that they will suffer mutilation.

572. Because your honored religion has a penetrating understanding of the fact that the Lord of Heaven is the first cause of all things, whenever it observes any evil practice or hears any evil word which runs counter to the truth or disobeys [the teachings of] the Church and which, like lance or sword, is about to be used to attack the Lord of Heaven, it hurriedly rushes to protect Him. This is because it knows that the Lord of Heaven is above all things, and that there is no thing under heaven which merits greater emphasis. Thus [the Church's representatives] not only give up all thought of wives, children, and wealth, but are even careless of their own lives.

573. The minds of all of us are already shackled by the customs and manners of the world. We would appear to admire and look up to the Lord of Heaven, but our faith is shallow, and we

574 然吾頻領大教，稱天主無所不通，無所不能，其既為世人慈父，烏忍我儕久居闇晦，不認本原大父，貿貿此道途？曷不自降世界親引群迷，俾萬國之子者明覩真父，了無二尚，豈不快哉？

575 西士曰：望子此問久矣。苟中華學道者常詢此理，必已得之矣。今吾著世界治亂之由者，請子服膺焉。

576 天主始制創天地、化生人物，汝想當初乃即如是亂苦者歟？殊不然也。天主之才最靈，其心至仁，亭育人群以造天地萬物，豈忍置之於不祥者乎哉？

577 開闢初生，人無病夭，常是陽和，常甚快樂，令鳥獸萬彙順聽其命，毋敢侵害，惟令人循奉上帝，如是而已。夫亂、夫災，皆由人以肯理犯天主命，人

總舉大西俗尚，而論其傳道之士所以不娶之意，并釋天主降生西土來由。

can hardly begin to talk of such things as giving up our lives, our wives, and our children. Sometimes we are mean when all we have to do is to take half a step or donate the smallest possible sum of money for the Sovereign on High or for reasons of morality. How tragic!

574. But I have now received instruction from you on numerous occasions and therefore regard the Lord of Heaven as omnipresent and omniscient. Since He is the compassionate father of mankind, how can He bear to allow us to live in darkness for so long, not knowing the great father who is our source, and wandering to and fro along this road of human existence. Why does He not come down to earth Himself and personally lead the masses who have lost their way so that the people of every nation will be able to recognize their true father and thereby know that there is no other [god]. Would this not be the most straightforward thing to do?

575. *The Western scholar says:* I have long hoped that you would ask just such a question. If students of the Way in China had constantly asked this question, they would already have received an answer. Let me now explain how the turbulence in the world is to be corrected. Please listen carefully.

576. Do you think there was as much turbulence and suffering in the world as there is today when the Lord of Heaven first created heaven and earth and produced man and all other things? Far from it! The talent and capabilities of the Lord of Heaven are most efficacious and His heart is most humane. How could He bear to place man in this unsettled and **unfortunate place when** He begat him and created heaven, earth and all things?

577. In the beginning when the world was created, man was free of sickness and death. The weather was constantly spring-like and mild, and he was constantly happy. [The Lord of Heaven] commanded birds, beasts, and all things to obey man's commands, and

既反背天主，萬物亦反背于人，以此自為自致，萬禍生焉。

578 世人之祖已敗人類性根，則為其子孫者沿其遺累，不得承性之全，生而帶疵人所已習可謂第二性，故其所為難分由性由習，雖然，性體自善不能因惡而滅，所以凡有發奮、遷善、轉念可成，天主亦必祐之。，又多相率而習醜行，則有疑其性本不善，非關天主所出，亦不足為異也。

579 但民善性既滅，又習乎醜，所以易溺于惡，難建于善耳。天主以父慈愍之，自古以來代使聖神繼起，為之立極，逮夫淳樸漸漓，聖賢化去，從欲者日眾，循理者日稀。

總舉大西俗尚，而論其傳道之士所以不娶之意，并釋天主降生西土來由。

446

Western Customs and God's Saving Work

none dared harm him; but he also commanded man to obey and to serve the Sovereign on High. Rebellion and natural disasters are all due to the fact that man turned his back on truth and offended against the Lord of Heaven's commands. Because man disobeyed the Lord of Heaven, all things in turn disobeyed man. Because of the effects of his own deeds numerous disasters followed.

578. Man's first ancestor had already corrupted the roots of man's nature so that later generations of sons and grandsons all suffered residual harm and were unable to receive perfect natures. There were imperfections from the moment of birth, and everyone mostly copied the ugly deeds of everyone else. Some men began to doubt that human nature really had been good at the outset; however, although this was hardly to be wondered at, the fault did not lie with the Lord of Heaven. Man's habits can be said to be his second nature, and it is therefore difficult to decide what stems from man's original nature, and what from his habits. Nevertheless the essence of man's nature is good and cannot be destroyed because of evil deeds; therefore, anyone who is determined to turn from evil to goodness has only to change his mind in order to succeed, and the Lord of Heaven is sure to offer him His protection and support.

579. But because man's goodness has already been impaired and he has become used to evil, he finds it easy to fall into evil and difficult to do good. Out of fatherly pity for mankind the Lord of Heaven has from ancient times to the present caused saints (sages) to appear in succeeding generations to serve as examples to the rest of mankind. But in the end the purity of customs steadily degenerated and sages and worthies died off. The situation was reached where the number of people who followed their selfish desires increased daily, and the number of those who followed after truth daily decreased.

580 於是大發慈悲，親來救世，普覺群品，於一千六百有三年前，歲次庚申，當漢朝哀帝元壽二年冬至後三日，擇貞女為母，無所交感，託胎降生，名號為耶穌——耶穌即謂救世也——躬自立訓，弘化于西土三十三年復昇天。此天主實蹟云。

581 中士曰：雖然，抑何理以徵之？當時之人何以驗耶穌實為天主，非特人類也？若自言耳，恐未足憑。

582 西士曰：大西法稱人以聖，較中國尤嚴焉，況稱天主耶？夫以百里之地君之，能朝諸侯得天下，雖不行一不義、不殺一不辜以得天下，吾西國未謂之聖；亦有超世之君，却千乘以修道，屏榮約處，僅稱謂廉耳矣；其所謂聖者，乃其勤崇天主，卑謙自牧，然而其所言所為過人，皆人力所必不能及者也。

總舉大西俗尚，而論其傳道之士所以不娶之意，并釋天主降生西土來由。

12 *Keng-shen* (庚申). See Ricci's Introduction, note 20. *Keng* is one of the Celestial Stems; *Shen* is one of the Terrestrial Branches.
13 *Ai Ti Yüan-shou erh-nian,* (哀帝元壽二年).
14 Here Ricci compares the Western and Chinese notions of "saint."

448

Western Customs and God's Saving Work

580. [The Lord of Heaven] thereupon acted with great compassion, descended to this world Himself to save it, and experienced everything [experienced by man]. One thousand six hundred and three years ago, in the year *Keng-shen*,[12] in the second year after Emperor Ai of the Han dynasty adopted the reign title Yüan-shou,[13] on the third day following the winter solstice, He selected a chaste woman who had never experienced sexual intercourse to be His mother, became incarnate within her and was born. His name was Jesus, the meaning of which is "the one who saves the world." He established His own teachings and taught for thirty-three years in the West. He then reascended to Heaven. These were concrete actions of the Lord of Heaven.

581. *The Chinese scholar says:* You may say this, but what proof is there of these events? How did the people of that time test the claim that Jesus was not only a man, but was really the Lord of Heaven? If the claim was made by Him alone His word would hardly be sufficient proof to command belief!

582. *The Western scholar says:* In the West the rules governing the bestowal of the title "saint" (sage)[14] are even more strictly applied than they are in China; how much more must this be so, then, when it comes to the title "Lord of Heaven"? A prince who governs territory a hundred *li* square in size; who is able to command tribute from feudal lords and who gains the whole world would not be called a saint in the West, even though he may never do anything unjust, and never put the innocent to death. Then there are outstanding kings who have given up their nations of a thousand chariots to enter the monastic life. They have cast aside all glory and lived the simplest of lives, and yet we have only called them "honest." A saint is one who strives to adore the Lord of Heaven and who is modest and self-disciplined, and yet whose words and deeds surpass those of all other men and are beyond the power of men to accomplish.

583 中士曰：何謂過人？

584 西士曰：誨人以人事，或以往者，或今有者，皆自強而為焉。若以上帝及未來之事訓民傳道，非但聖而後能之，有志要名者以人力得之，不宜以之驗聖也。惟天主也。以藥治病，服之即療，學醫者能之；以賞罰之公，治世而世治，儒者可致；茲俱以人力得之，不宜以之驗聖也。

585 若有神功絕德，造化同用，不用藥法，醫不可醫之病，復生既死之民，如此之類人力不及，必自天主而來，敝國所稱聖人者，率皆若此。

586 倘有自伐其聖，或朋輩代為誇伐，或不畏天主，用邪法鬼功為異怪，以惑愚俗，好自逞而悖天主之功德，此為至惡，大西國防之如水火，何但弗以稱聖之力，天主則何有所假哉？

587 天主在世之時，現跡愈多，其所為過于聖人又遠，聖人所為奇事，皆假天主乎？

總舉大西俗尚，而論其傳道之士所以不娶之意，并釋天主降生西土來由。

Western Customs and God's Saving Work

583. *The Chinese schoar says:* What do you mean by the words: "surpass those of all other men?"

584. *The Western scholar says:* One can instruct people about past or present human events without being a saint. Anyone who wishes to make a name for himself can do so simply by firmly resolving to do so and by working hard. But is human strength sufficient for the task if one determines instead to instruct people in matters pertaining to the Sovereign on High and in things which are yet to happen, and to proclaim the Way? Only the Lord of Heaven can do such things. A physician is able to cure people by using medicine, and Confucians are adept at preserving order in the world through the employment of rewards and punishments. These are things which can be done by human effort, and ought not to be used as proof of sainthood.

585. But if a man's astounding actions and virtue are equal to [the actions and virtue required in] creation; if he cures incurable diseases without medicine, brings the dead back to life, and performs other similar deeds, which cannot be done by human power but only by power which comes for the Lord of Heaven, then my humble country calls such a person, and others like him a saint.

586. If a person boasts of his own saintly virtues, or friends do so on his behalf; and if he shows no reverence for and fear of the Lord of Heaven and does supernatural things with the aid of witchcraft and black magic in order to lead the foolish and vulgar astray, being fond of self-assertion and offending against the meritorious works of the Lord of Heaven, then this is a very great evil, and the nations of the West not only refuse to call such a man a saint, but react toward him as they would to fire and flood.

587. When the Lord of Heaven came down and lived in this world He showed many signs, and His actions greatly surpassed those of all other saints. The unusual things done by saints were all accomplished through their reliance on the power of the Lord

588 西土上古多有聖人，于幾千載前，預先詳誌于經典，載厥天主降生之義，而指其定候，迨及其時，世人爭共望之而果遇焉。

589 驗其所為，與古聖所記如合符節：其巡遊詔諭于民，聾者命聽即聽，瞽者命視即視，瘖者命言即言，躄者命行即行，死者命生即生，天地鬼神悉畏敬之，莫不聽命也。既符古聖所誌，既又增益前經，以傳大教于世，傳道之功已畢，自言期候，白日歸天。

590 時有四聖錄其在世行實及其教語，而貽之於列國，則四方萬民群從之，而世守之。自此大西諸邦教化大行焉。

591 考之中國之史，當時漢明帝嘗聞其事，遣使西往求經，使者半塗誤值身毒之國，取其佛經傳流中華。迨今貴邦為所誑誘，不得聞其正道，大為學術之禍，豈不慘哉？

總舉大西俗尚，而論其傳道之士所以不娶之意，并釋天主降生西土來由。

of Heaven. The Lord of Heaven, on the other hand, depends on no one's power.

588. In primordial times in the West there were many saints, and several thousand years ago they forecast in detailed records in the canonical writings that the Lord of Heaven would be born on earth, and went so far as to indicate the predetermined time of this birth. When the time came people vied with each other in looking out for Him and, indeed, they found Him.

589. When one investigates His actions one finds that they tally completely with the records of the saints of old. He travelled extensively, instructing the people; when He commanded the deaf to hear, they heard; when He commanded the blind to see, they saw; when He commanded the mute to speak, they spoke; and when He commanded the lame to walk, they walked; He also commanded the dead to return to life, and they did so. Ghosts and spirits in heaven and earth all feared and reverenced Him and all obeyed His commands. Since His actions accorded with the records of the sages in ancient times, the canonical writings of former times were supplemented so that these great teachings could be transmitted to the world. When His work of preaching was complete He ascended to Heaven in broad daylight at a time clearly forecast by Himself.

590. Four saints recorded the deeds He had performed whilst on earth, as well as His teachings. These were transmitted to many countries, and large numbers of people from all quarters believed in Him, keeping His commandments from one generation to another. From this time onwards many nations in the West took great strides along the road to civilization.

591. When we examine Chinese history we find that Emperor Ming of the Han dynasty heard of these events and sent ambassadors on a mission to the West to search for canonical writings. Midway these ambassadors mistakenly took India to be their goal, and returned to China with Buddhist scriptures which were then cir-

592 中士曰：稽其時則合，稽其人則通，稽其事則又無疑也。某願退舍沐浴而來領天主真經，拜為師，入聖教之門之外，今世不得正道，後世不得天福也。不知尊師許否？

593 西士曰：祇因欲廣此經，吾從二三英友棄家屏鄉，艱勤周幾萬里，而僑寓異土無悔也。誠心悅受乃吾大幸矣。然沐浴止去身垢，天主所惡乃心咎耳；故聖教有造門之聖水，凡欲從此道，先深悔前時之罪過，誠心欲遷于善，而領是聖水，即天主慕愛之，而盡免舊惡，如孩之初生者焉。

594 吾輩之意，非為人師，惟恤世之錯，回元之路，而為一引于天主聖教，則充之皆為同父之弟兄，豈敢苟圖稱名辱師之禮乎哉？天主經文字異中國，雖譯未盡，而其要已易正字。但吾前所談論總舉大西俗尚，而論其傳道之士所以不娶之意，并釋天主降生西土來由。

15 According to one tradition Emperor Ming (58-75 A.D.) of the Han dynasty had a dream in which he saw a large golden figure. Having been assured by a minister that the figure was that of the Buddha he sent ambassadors in search of him. These ambassadors are credited with introducing Buddhism into China between 64 and 75 A.D.

16 Buddhists had earlier described water for which healing properties were claimed as *sheng shui* (聖水, "holy water").

culated throughout the nation.[15] From then until now the people of your esteemed country have been deceived and misled. That they have not heard the correct Way is truly a great tragedy for the field of learning. Was it not a disaster?

592. *The Chinese scholar says:* When we investigate the time of His appearance we find it agrees with earlier predictions. When we investigate the man Himself we find Him to be a master of all things, and when we investigate His deeds we find nothing suspicious about them. After going home and taking a bath I shall return to receive the true canonical writings of the Lord of Heaven; to take you, Sir, as my teacher, and to enter the gate of your sacred Church; for I clearly know that unless I pass through this gate I shall find no other correct way in this world, nor heavenly blessing in the world to come. Will you, revered teacher, allow me to do this?

593. *The Western scholar says:* For the sake of making these canonical writings widely known I and two or three valiant colleagues have given up our families and left our home towns to travel tens of thousands of *li*, undergoing untold hardships in order to dwell in a strange land. But we have no regrets whatsoever. It is a great joy to me that you should now sincerely wish to listen to and to accept my teaching. But a bath can only remove the dirt on one's body, and what the Lord of Heaven loathes are the transgressions of mind and heart. The holy Church therefore has sacred[16] water which it uses on those who enter its gates. Everyone who wants to follow this Way, who deeply repents his past wrongdoings, and who sincerely wants to turn away from his transgressions to do good and to receive this sacred water, will receive the love of the Lord of Heaven, and will have all his former evil forgiven. He will be like a new-born child.

594. Our purpose is not to be teachers of men. It is simply that because we feel pity for men's mistakes we wish to lead them back to their original path and into the holy Church of the Lord of Heaven. We are all brothers who share the same father; how

致端,僉此道之肯綮,願學之者,退而玩味于前數篇事理,了已無疑,則承經領聖水入教,何難之有?

595 中士曰:吾身出自天主,而久昧天主之道,幸先生不辭八萬里風波,遠傳聖教,彪炳異同,使愚聆之豁然深悟昔日之非,獲惠良多,且使吾大明之世,得承大父聖旨而遵守之也。

596 吾靜思之不勝大快,且不勝深悲焉。吾當退于私居溫繹所授,紀而錄之以志不忘,期以盡聞歸元直道。所願天主佐佑先生仁指,顯揚天主之教,使我中國家傳人誦,皆為修善無惡之民,功德廣大,又安有量歟。

總舉大西俗尚,而論其傳道之士所以不娶之意,并釋天主降生西土來由。

dare we accept the title of "teacher" and offend against the rites which govern teachers of men? The script used in the canonical writings of the Lord of Heaven is different from the Chinese script. Although I have not finished translating them, I have complete translations of the essential parts. But what I have discussed earlier are all key elements of this teaching. I hope that those who study the Way will go home and savour the teachings which I have propounded in the several foregoing chapters. If you have no further doubts about what I have said, what is there to hinder you accepting the canonical writings, receiving the sacred water and entering the Church?

595. *The Chinese scholar says:* This body of mine comes from the Lord of Heaven, yet I have long been ignorant of the doctrine concerning the Lord of Heaven. Now by good fortune you have fearlessly travelled eighty thousand *li* and braved wind and water to come to this distant land to transmit those sacred teachings and to point out both the similarities and dissimilarities [between our two parts of the world] so that I might learn of them, understand in what ways I have been wrong in the past and gain numerous benefits. Further, you have caused us in this age of the Great Ming dynasty to receive the sacred will of our great father and to keep it.

596. As I silently think things over I find myself experiencing both great joy and a deep feeling of sorrow. I must return home, review the teachings I have heard, and write them down so that I do not forget them. I hope I can hear everything about this true doctrine concerning man's return to his source! I trust that the Lord of Heaven will protect you so that you may promulgate His teachings, so that each family in China will hand them down from generation to generation, so that every person will chant them, and so that everyone will cultivate goodness and cease to do evil. The contribution this would make to the general welfare of mankind would be so great as to be beyond calculation!

時萬曆三十一年歲次癸卯七月既望利
瑪竇書

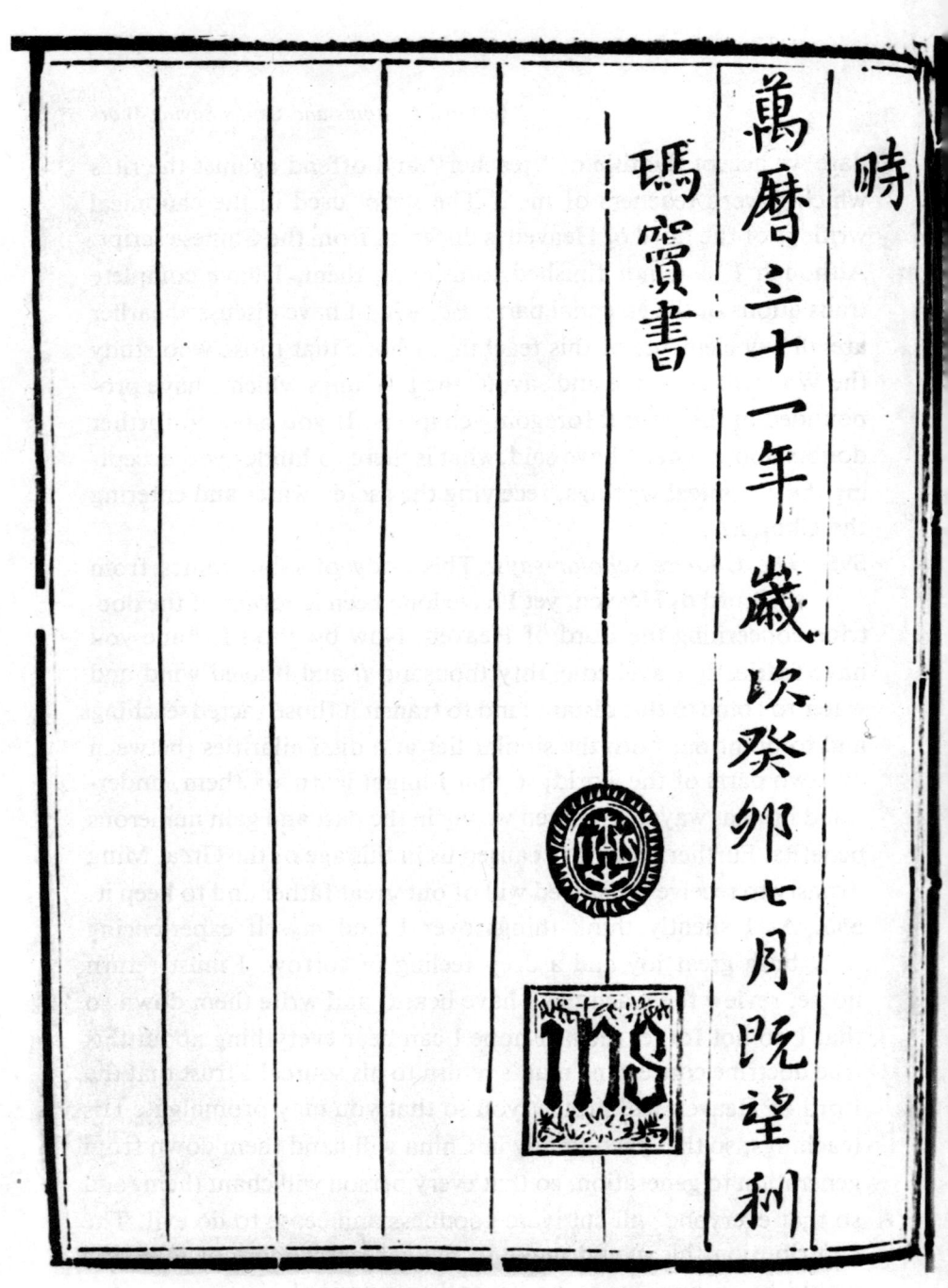

Figure 4. The date and Ricci's Chinese name with the seal of the Society of Jesus, at the end of his introduction to the first edition of The True Meaning of the Lord of Heaven, *first Peking edition, 1603. With permission of Biblioteca Casanatense, Rome.*

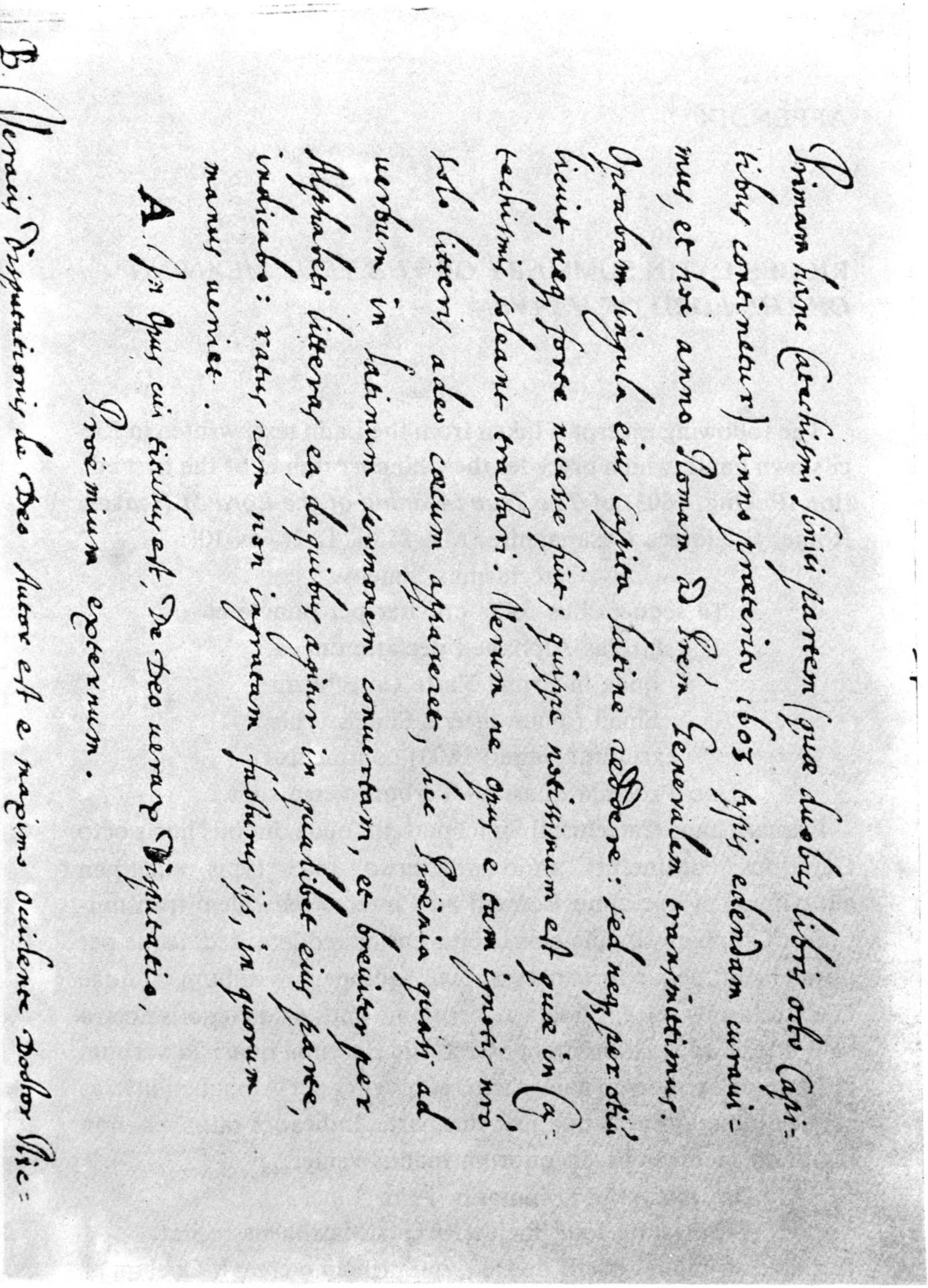

Primam huius Catechismi solius partem (quae duobus libris octo Capi=
tibus continetur) anno praeterito 1603 typis edendam curavi=
mus, et hoc anno Romam ad Rev. Pr. Generalem transmittimus.
Operam singula eius Capita latine reddere: sed nequaquam otii
licuit, neque forte necesse fuit; quippe notissimum est quae in Ca=
techismis soleant tradi. Verum ne opus e cuius ignotis nitro
isto litteris, ades caecum appareret, hic Synopsis quasi ad
verbum in latinum sermonem conversam, et breviter per
Alphabeti litteras ea, de quibus agitur in qualibet eius parte,
indicabo: ratus non ingratum fachurus iis, in quorum
manus veniet.

A. Sit Opus cui titulus est, De Deo verag Disputatio,
Proemium sexternum.

B. Veracis Disputationis de Deo Autor est e maximis Occidentis Doctor Ilic=

Figure 5. The Latin autograph of Ricci's preface to his translation of the Chinese prefaces to his work, and to his own Latin summary of the book, first Peking edition, 1603. With permission of Biblioteca Casanatense, Rome.

APPENDIX

RICCI'S LATIN SUMMARY OF *THE TRUE MEANING OF THE LORD OF HEAVEN*

The following excerpt is taken from the Latin text, written in Ricci's own hand, which precedes the Chinese original of the first edition (Peking, 1603) of *The True Meaning of the Lord of Heaven*. Rome, Biblioteca Casanatense, Ms. 2136, 1, 2r, 4v-10r.

    Catechismus Sinicus
In sequentibus foliis breviter per puncta et
litteras Alphabeti declarantur ea,
quae in Prima Parte Catechismi
Sinici (quam litteris Sinicis typis
excudimus anno 1603) continentur.
Duo Proemia quasi ad Verbum versa sunt...

Primam hanc Catechismi Sinici partem (quae duobus libris octo Capitibus continetur) anno praeterito 1603 typis edendam curavimus, et hoc anno Romam ad Patrem Generalem transmittimus. Optabam singula eius capita Latine reddere: sed neque per otium licuit, neque forte necesse fuit; quippe notissimum est quae in Catechismis soleant tractari. Verum ne opus e tam ignotis nostro solo litteris adeo caecum appareret, hic Proemia quasi ad verbum in Latinum sermonem convertam, et breviter per Alphabeti litteras ea, de quibus agitur in qualibet eius parte, indicabo: ratus rem non ingratam facturus iis, in quorum manus veniet...

    G. De Deo verax Disputatio. Prior Liber.
    H. E Societate Iesu Socius Riccius Matthaeus recitat.
    I. Caput primum disserit de Deo, qui principio creavit Coelum et

Appendix: Ricci's Latin Summary

terram cum rebus omnibus, eaque gubernat atque conservat.
- **K.** Inducuntur duo litterati, unus Sina alter Europaeus: et Sina quidem rogat de rebus fidei Christianae, Europaeus autem respondet ad ea quae rogatur. In hoc loco Sina dicit se multum diuque de vera doctrina ambiguum fuisse; et diligentissime perscrutatum, et multa de rebus huius vitae percepisse, de rebus vero vitae futurae nihil, ductumque fama Patrum Occidentalium accessisse ut ab eis doceatur.
- **L.** Europaeus litteratus pollicetur se ad singula responsurum, atque ita exorditur disputationem de Deo.
- **M.** Europaeus primo aliquid praefatur de humanae intelligentiae praestantia. Et in hoc libro edicit se praecipue acturum rationibus, parum authoritatibus.
- **N.** Hic tribus rationibus incipit probare aliquam esse causam primam invisibilem, qui hunc mundum gubernet et regat.
- **O.** Sina rationibus assentitur. Et quia dubitat an idem fuerit auctor universi, probatur tribus rationibus eundem Deum qui gubernat universum, creasse illud principio.
- **P.** Probatur Deum esse unum, et non posse esse plures. Et ut melius hoc cognoscatur, et explicatur quo genere causarum sit Deus prima causa causarum, declarantur paucis quatuor genera causarum, simulque agitur de causis mediatis et immediatis, primis etc. Quae doctrina Sinis ut nova et vera, ita accidit gratissima et maxime probatur.
- **Q.** Sina rationibus advictus credit Deum esse, et rogat quid sit Deus.

Europaeus primo exemplo Philosophi qui rogatus quid esset Deus, indies plures sibi petebat dari dies a Rege qui rogabat ad respondendum, et D. Augustini cui puer apparuit in littore maris in parvo serobiculo aquam maris infundente, declarat non posse hominem penitus Deum intelligere. Et de eius natura multa melius intelligi per negationem quam per affirmationem. Et hac occasione multa docet de perfectionibus et attributis divinis, usque ad finem capitis. Et sic primo capiti finis imponitur.
- **R.** Caput secundum. Declarantur errores multorum, qui perperam

Appendix: Ricci's Latin Summary

sensere de prima causa.

S. Sina repetit disputationem et adnectens colloquium hesternum, brevibus profert tres sectas quae vigent in hoc regno et eorum principia, rogans Europaeum ut statuat quaenam vero sit proxima. Europaeus maxime damnat sectam Xekiai et Laotii, quorum alter asserit Vacuum, alter sentit Nihilum esse rerum omnium principium. Et ait litteratorum sectam, quae principium facit ens solidum, laudandam.

T. Sina affert fundamentum eorum qui dicunt Nihilum et Vacuum esse rerum primum principium efficiens. Quod ab Europaeo impugnatur et evertitur.

V. Declaratur id quod affertur, prius res non esse et deinde esse, nullo modo posse intelligi de Deo primo ente et causa universalissimo omnis entitatis.

X. Litteratus Sina rationibus convictus damnat, et merito ait damnatas a litteratis illas duas sectas; et quaerit quid sentiat de Taikieo, quod litterati asserunt esse principium rerum.

Z. Haec doctrina de Taikieo nova est, et quingentos ante annos nata et in quibusdam si attente consideretur pugnat cum Sinarum antiquis sapientibus, qui rectius de Deo sensere. Ex iis quae de Taikieo loquuntur, nihil mea quidem sententia aliud est, quam id quod nostri Philosophi dicunt primam materiam. Quia id et minimae entitatis esse, immo aiunt non esse rem, et esse in omnibus rebus tamquam illarum partem, non esse spiritum neque intelligere. Et licet dicant aliqui esse rerum rationem, non intelligunt per rationem aliquid substantiale, neque intelligens: et magis accedit ad rationem ratiocinatam quam ad ratiocinantem. Demum non solum inter illos varia est eius interpretatio, sed multa dicunt absurda quare satius esse duximus in hoc libro impugnare, quam ea quae dicuntur congruenter ad Deum detorquere; ne videremur nos magis sequi Legem Sinicam quam facere et interpretari Sinicos autores ut sequantur nostram Legem. Et quia litterati qui Sinam gubernant, maxime nobis infensi sunt ob huius principii impugnationem, nisi sumus magis

Appendix: Ricci's Latin Summary

impugnare explicationem huius principii quam principium. Et in fine si Taikieum intelligerent esse primum principium substantiale, intelligens, et infinitum: illud asserimus quidem esse Deum et nihil aliud.

a. Hic declaratur doctrina et divisio rerum in substantiam et accidens, quae quidem Sinis litteratis maxime probatur, et numquam audita antea fuit apud illos: ut ostendatur Deum primam causam debere esse omnino substantiam et non accidens, ut interpretes Taikiei asserunt.

b. Declaratur rationem accidentalem nunc non posse producere res, atque adeo neque principio.

c. Declaratur causam efficientem non posse esse inferiorem re, cuius est causa, neque non intelligentem producere intelligentem.

d. Ostenditur Deum eminenter continere omnes rerum perfectiones; atque adeo licet non sit aliqua ex rebus creatis, posse tamen res omnes creatas producere.

e. Europaeus interpretatur hic quendam locum Confutii, qui maxime est apud eos autoritatis et sanctitatis, qui quingentos ante Christum natum annos floruit, et multa optime scripsit, et usurpatum est hoc nomen Taikiei in quibusdam commentariis, et ait intelligendum esse de materia prima de qua pollicetur se alibi acturum.

> Marginal note: Quidam vir primarius et maximae autoritatis videns hunc locum, enixe contendit cum nobis ut haec doctrina de materia prima enuclearemus, **asserens maximum fore beneficium Regno Sinico sed hactenus per otium non licuit.**

f. Hic declarantur multa loca in sex libris antiquis veterum Philosophorum Sinarum, qui veluti Sacri apud eos habentur. Quid intelligendum sit pro Rege superno, pro Caelo, pro Domino Rege: atque adeo non esse pro Caelo intelligendum hoc caelum materiale, ut quidam autores et vulgus autumant, sed inmateriale, vel esse phrasem Sinicam; quidem nunc in communi sermone Regem appellantes vocant eum Aulam Regiam, et alibi modus loquendi Sinarum continens pro contento accipit, ut multis exemplis clarissime

Appendix: Ricci's Latin Summary

probatur. Deducitur et maximum incoveniens et contradictio, si per Caelum et Terram accipiantur haec materialia, quia nullo modo possunt esse unum principium ut ipsimet dicunt, cum caeli sint novem et terra a Caelo distincta sit. Et usque ad finem capitis prosequitur Europaeus hanc materiam.

g. Caput 3m. disputat de anima hominis, et asserit eam esse immortalem et valde diversam ab anima reliquorum animalium.

h. Antequam agatur de animae immortalitate, introducitur Sina graviter conquerens de natura, quod reliqua animalia in magna quiete creaverit, libera a multis curis, solum hominem qui debuit potiores partes in hoc mundo habere, in multis miseriis nasci et vivere voluerit. Et hic multa a nostris libris mutuata dicuntur de miseria humana, quibus Sinae omnes maxime permoventur.

i. Europaeus respondens contra conqueritur de hominum stultitia, qui in hisce miseriis finem suum ponat, hic velint diu vivere, et felices esse, atque adeo duos nostros Philosophos Heraclitum et Democritum affert, quorum alterum semper risisse perhibent, alterum semper plorasse hanc hominum miseriam. Demum exponit Deum non creasse hominem ut semper hic viveret tanquam in loco proprio, sed tanquam in exsilio et probatione. Verum locum et patriam hominum esse Caelum.

k. His animo erectus Sina rogat quibus rationibus nitatur haec doctrina de animarum immortalitate.

l. Europaeus exponit hanc doctrinam de immortalitate animarum, et vitam beatam quae in Paradiso bonis praeparata est, ex sua origine a Lege Christianorum habuisse principium: atque alias sectas ut sua falsa dogmata divulgarent, haec etiam in suis libris inseruisse. Quare nos in hoc non sequimur Idolotaeos, sed quod proprium est unum tractamus. Et ut melius hoc probari possit, principio declarat tria esse genera animarum, et quomodo inter se distinguantur, quae doctrina etiam nova est apud Sinas. Insuper exponitur animae sensitivae et vegetativae actiones a corpore pendere, secus est de operationibus animae intellectivae. Et causas interitus animalium esse compositione ex quatuor elementis inter se contrariis:

Appendix: Ricci's Latin Summary

animam vero esse spiritualem et non componi ex contrariis.

m. Probatur sex rationibus animas hominum esse spiritus.

n. Hic aliis quinque rationibus probatur animas hominum esse immortales.

o. Hic usque ad finem improbatur quoddam commentum quod nunc maxime invaluit in secta litteratorum, et creditur pro vero, nempe animas bonorum bonitate coagulari, atque adeo post mortem non mori: animas vero malorum malitia dissipari, atque adeo post mortem dispergi et ad nihilum redigi.

p. Caput 4m. exagitat et refellit pravas opiniones de spiritibus et animis hominum, et probat omnia quae sunt in mundo non posse dici unam esse substantiam.

q. Cum hodie multi ex litteratis non credant vere esse in caelo et in mundo spiritus, in quibus et Deus et animae hominum continentur: Europaeus probat ex antiquis libris sectae ipsorum, spiritus vere cognitos et creditos esse Antiquis, et iis ipsis qui apud Sinas Sancti habentur.

r. Refellit hoc loco ineptum et imperitum dictum eorum, qui dicunt non debere credi ut certa nisi ea quae videntur oculis, et probat certiorem esse fidem quam faciunt rationes, quam quam faciunt oculi: cum oculi errent saepissime, ratio vero nunquam.

s. Rogat Sina de quodam, qui olim post mortem visus esse in libris litteratorum scribitur, et multa docuisse: quo modo fieri possit ut spiritus videatur, et mortuus plura sciat quam dum viveret. Quae omnia ab Europaeo declarantur, et causa affertur cur nos omnes post mortem videantur, et cur aliquibus a Deo permittatur redire in mundum.

t. Confutatur opinio eorum, qui dicunt animam hominis esse aerem.

u. Probatur animam esse partem hominum, spiritus vero qui in terris versantur esse substantias per se subsistentes, diversas a rebus. Alioqui cum spiritus ubique sint, ut ipsi concedunt, omnes res essent intelligentes quod multi Sinarum sentiunt.

x. Ex divisione rerum in insensibiles et sensibiles, animatas vero

Appendix: Ricci's Latin Summary

in intelligentes et non intelligentes, non posse esse res omnes anima rationali praeditas. Et hac occasione apposuimus figuram praedicamenti substantiae quae res est nova et Sinis iucundissima, ex qua magnum aliquid concipiunt de nostris scientiis.

z. Tabula praedicamenti substantiae, et aliorum praedicamentorum in summarium redacta. Divisimus ens in substantiam et accidens, et substantiam tantum fuse prosequti sumus.

AA. Confutatur opinio eorum qui dicunt animas hominum ab animis animantium differe tantum secundum magis et minus, rectum et pravum intelligens. Et animantia ea quae intelligere videntur, tantum esse ex instinctu naturali, non ex propria intelligentia.

BB. Confutatur opinio eorum qui dicunt res distingui inter se, et etiam in genera et species distribui tantum per figuram.

CC. Proponitur opinio eorum qui dicunt homines esse eiusdem substantiae et unam rem cum Deo, rerum procreatore, et confutatur.

DD. Europaeus asserit hunc errorem esse omnium praeteritorum maxime execrandum, et in sectam litteratorum inductum solum ex commercio cum secta Idolotaeorum qui hoc sentiunt: imo ortum habuisse a Lucifero qui similis Deo esse voluit, cuius historia hac occasione narratur; et de origine Daemonum et Inferni, qui primorum Daemonum causa constitutus est.

EE. Respondetur ad obiectiones Idolotaeorum, quibus probant homines esse eandem rem cum Deo.

FF. Adhuc proponuntur tres modi dicendi, Deum esse unum cum hominibus, et singuli multis rationibus confutantur.

GG. Cum homo non sit compositus ex Deo tanquam sui parte, colligitur hominis nihil post mortem in Deum redire et converti.

HH. Quot modis aliquid dicatur esse in aliquo, et quo modo Deus dici possit esse in homine et in creaturis.

II. Adhuc proponitur opinio eorum qui dicunt res creatas omnes unum esse inter se, et confutatur.

Appendix: Ricci's Latin Summary

Marginal note: Haec opinio et superior maxime nunc viget et pro vera habetur inter litteratos, ideo necesse fuit bene confutari.

KK. Quot modis aliqua dicantur unum inter se.

LL. Quo modo res possint dici unum, et quomodo non possint usque ad finem capitis.

MM. De Deo verax disputatio. Liber posterior.

NN. Quintum Caput disserit de falso dogmate transmigrationis animarum de corpore in corpus per sex itinera, et de abstinentia ab occisione animalium, et affert rectam ieiunii causam.

OO. Afferuntur a Sina tres opiniones de anima; et rogat cur opinio de transmigratione animarum in alia corpora, et mutationes in animalia non admittatur a fide Christiana.

PP. Declarat Europaeus hunc errorem a Pythagora nostro Philosopho antiquo habuisse originem, et inde eum Idolotaeos mutuasse, et inseruisse suis libris.

QQ. Hac occasione Europaeus indicat Sinis regnum Industanorum, unde secta Idolotaeorum profecta est ad Sinas, non esse regnum alicuius nominis, imo parvum et sine litterarum scientiis, longeque inferius huic magno Sinarum regno, laris nobilitate et fertilitate soli, quod longe aliter Sinae opinantur ducti libris Idolotaeorum, qui suum regnum exaltant, atque adeo multi cupiunt apud Sinas mori et nasci iterum ibi. Inducitur autem Sina ex descriptione orbis terrarum, quam nuper edidimus, haec quae Europaeus dicit verissime credere.

RR. Hic probat quinque sexve validissimis rationibus, vanum esse commentum transmigrationis animarum in alia corpora, sive hominum sive animalium. Respondetque dubitationibus quae a Sina afferuntur.

SS. Hic deducit Europaeus nullum esse mandatum a Deo, quo abstineamus ab esu carnium vel piscium, vel ab interfectione vivorum. Et respondet propositae dubitationi, cur animae genitorum hominum si vivunt, non repleant orbem terrarum multitudine.

TT. Dixerat Europaeus supra omnia quae in mundo sunt creata

Appendix: Ricci's Latin Summary

propter hominem. Hic respondet roganti Sinae, ea quae videntur nullo esse usui, imo hominibus esse nocumento, quo modo a Deo creata sint propter hominem, et aliquid tangit de inobedientia primorum parentum.

VV. Dat Sina Idolotaeorum distinctionem, cur edant olera quae itidem viventia sunt, et non animalia, nempe quia illa neque sentiunt neque habent sanguinem. Cui respondet Europaeus et plantas habere sanguinem licet aliquem non rubeum, et usum veluti equorum et bovuum in vectione et aratione multo esse laboriosiorem ac magis dedecori illis, quam mortem: et tamen illi eos iis adhibent usibus.

XX. Hic asseruntur tres causae ieiunii et paenitentiae, et fit digressio ad voluptates adeo hominibus pernitiosas.

ZZ. Hic adducuntur varia genera abstinentiarum, et quod sit ieiunium nostrae Legis usque ad finem capitis.

aa. Sextum caput primo oppugnat errorem quorundam qui dicunt nullam operibus nostris debere adhiberi intentionem. Postea probat post mortem esse praemium bonorum in Caelo, et poenam malorum in Inferno, utrumque sine fine.

bb. Sina nititur probare facere bona propter metum poenae, et propter spem praemii esse malum, et nullam intentionem habere in nostris operibus esse maximae perfectionis.

cc. Europaeus respondet posteriori parti dubitationis, et probat omnino necessariam esse intentionem, quia bona et mala opera pensantur maxime ex intentione ob nostri arbitrii libertatem, idque probat autoritate suorum librorum.

dd. Respondet priori dubitationi, et primo probat autoritatibus suorum librorum, deinde multis rationibus licere abstinere a malo et benefacere metu poenarum et spe praemii: licet perfectius sit haec facere amore Dei et virtutis. Postremo declarat poenas et praemia alterius vitae esse veras poenas et vera praemia, huius vitae praemia et poenas esse breves et parvas.

ee. Refellitur dictum impudens quorumdam Sinarum litteratorum,

Appendix: Ricci's Latin Summary

nihil curandum esse nisi ea quae ante oculos sunt, et nihil laborandum de futuro.

ff. Adhuc instat Sina laborandum esse de futuro, sed non de his quae post mortem sunt. Ad haec Europaeus multa incipit disserere de vita futura.

gg. Proponitur sententia modernorum litteratorum, qui praemia et poenas bonorum et malorum rependi a Deo in hoc mundo, vel iis qui ea agunt, vel suis posteris: et refellitur ab Europaeo tanquam falsa et impossibilia, cum multi posteros non habeant.

hh. Probatur quatuor rationibus necessarie dari Paradisum et Infernum, pro praemio bonorum et poena malorum, quae fuit in hoc mundo.

ii. Respondetur dubitationi, cur bona multa a Deo persolvantur in hoc mundo bonis, et multa mala puniantur. Et cur multi boni poenis in hoc mundo afficiantur, multi vero mali habeant multa bona temporalia.

kk. Rogat Sina, cur prisci sancti Sinarum non locuti sunt de Paradiso et de Inferno. Quare afferuntur ab Europaeo multa loca pulcherrima priscorum librorum, in quibus viri illi qui sancti apud litteratorum sectam habentur, non obscure de gloria locuti sunt, et declarantur causae cur prisci reliquerint hanc rem non fuse tractatam, et forte libros amissos in quibus de hac re agebatur.

ll. Confutatur hic commentum Idolotaeorum qui dicunt aliquos homines mori, qui nec boni nec mali sunt, et propterea ponunt transmigrationem animarum et declarantur aliqua de Purgatorio, in quo destinentur qui decesserunt in gratia Dei, sed non integre persolverunt poenas pro peccatis praeteritis.

mm. Confutatur alius error cuiusdam Philosophi magni nominis inter litteratos, qui scriptum reliquit non necesse esse credere Paradisum et Infernum, sed tantum nitendum esse bonos viros et non malos. Quippe si Paradisus sit boni intrabunt in eum, si Infernus sit mali detrudentur in eum.

nn. Sina inducitur iam nihil dubitare de Paradiso et Inferno, et petere sibi declarari quae in eo sunt. Et hac occasione Europaeus

Appendix: Ricci's Latin Summary

multa de Inferni poenis, et de Paradisi gloria dicit usque ad finem capitis.

oo. Caput 7m. declarat hominis naturam esse bonam, et in quibus virtutibus maxime exercitantur Christianae Religionis homines.

pp. Sina proponit dubitationem suam, an cor hominis ex se sit bonum.

qq. Europaeus primo exponit quid sit homo, et quid sit natura humana, quid sit bonum, et quid sit malum. Postea constituit quomodo natura dicenda sit bona, et quo modo dicenda sit mala.

rr. Declaratur illa propositio quomodo natura ex se bona possit tamen facere malum ex libertate liberi arbitrii, quod non possunt facere animalia illo destituta.

ss. Incipitur disputatio de exercitio boni hominis.

tt. Declarantur tres animae potentiae, et perfectionem consistere in perfectione harum trium potentiarum, quae iustitia et charitate maxime perficiuntur.

uu. Varii dicendi fines, et quis omnium optimus.

xx. Respondetur ad obiectionem Sinae, qui improbat finem hominum esse Deum, rem externam ipsi homini, et vult finem ponere seipsum.

zz. Quid principio ei qui studet bene vivere, faciendum sit; ubi varia exercitia proponuntur.

α. Proponit Europaeus fidem christianam esse positam in duobus praeceptis. 1. Amare Deum supra omnia creata, et Proximum sicut se ipsum.

β. Disserit de fide, et probat fidem divinam, qua humana Religio continetur, esse certiorem qualibet scientia, et maxime convenientem ad homines docendos.

γ. Declarantur undecim passiones et earum deductio, ut ostendatur amorem esse earum caput et efficacissimam.

δ. De operibus charitatis et misericordiae.

e. Inducitur ipsemet Sina afferre aliqua ex suis libris in hanc sententiam.

Appendix: Ricci's Latin Summary

ζ. De Religione et cultu etiam externo qui Deo debetur, et de fine et emolumento nostrarum precum.

η. Impugnatur secta Idolotaeorum, et deducuntur multa nocumenta ex recitatione dotrinae eius sectae et veneratione Idolorum; quae licet eis non credamus, neque externo cultu licet cuique colere, quod vitium commune est litteratis.

θ. Impugnatur error quam plurimorum Sinarum, qui dicunt omnes sectas et Religiones esse veras et in unum recidere. Et probat Relgionem Christianam esse veram, et a lege Idolotaeorum maxime differe, quippe unum recognoscat verum principium.

ι. Afferuntur varia erronea et falsa ex lege Idolotaeorum, et rationibus impugnantur.

κ. Declaratur origo Idolorum.

λ. Redditur ratio cur aliqua Idola vera respondeant.

μ. Quinque rationibus usque ad finem capitis impugnatur nova quaedam opinio quae nunc in Sina multum viget, quae asserit debere et posse servari ab omnibus trium sectarum Sinicarum praecepta.

ν. Caput 8m. summatim aliqua dicit de moribus et legibus Europaeis, et redditur causa quam ob rem Evangelii annunciatores uxorem non ducant, et de Dei Incarnatione apud occidentales populos.

ξ. Quaerit Sina ut aliquid dicat de moribus Europaeis. Europaeus dicit ibi communem esse Religionem Christianam, quam reges ipsi colunt et observant. Et adhuc esse ibi dignitatem maximam summi Pontificis, qui est caput et magister Christianae Religionis, quem Reges ut patrem et magistrum observant, qui constituit episcopos et paelatos in qualibet orbis parte, cum variis familiis religiosis.

ο. Redduntur variae causae et rationes cur Christiane religionis propagatores ut in plurimum caelibem vitam agunt, et caelibem vitam non adversari naturae praeceptis.

π. Probatur octo rationibus sacerdotes, qui sacrificant Deo et rem Christianam curant, debere esse caelibes.

Appendix: Ricci's Latin Summary

ϱ. Declarat Europaeus se haec non disseruisse adversus matrimonium, quia id prohibitum non est lege Christiana, immo commendatum ad prolem propagandam, et damnantur multi Sinarum qui uxores non ducunt et variae libidini indulgent. Quare maxime aversandi et damnandi sunt, nec in hoc caelibum numero continentur.

σ. Respondet autoritati cuiusdam dicti in una ex suis sex doctrinis inserti, quae ait inobedientiae tria esse genera, sed maximum omnium esse non habere filios. Haec autoritas magnum nobis facessit negotium apud litteratos. Quare primum negamus hoc dictum esse alicuius sancti antiqui, sed temere ibi insertum, ut multa sunt inserta passim in illa doctrina, ut ipsi fatentur. Deinde variis probamus esse falsum et nulla ratione niti.

τ. Deplorat hic Europaeus confusionem maximam, quae Legum facta est in Sina, et longe maiorem quam in saeculis praeteritis, quando una tantum erat Religio in Sina.

υ. Ostendit mundum in sua prima creatione non fuisse creatum a Deo in tantis miseriis, sed hasce miserias a peccato primorum parentum habuisse originem.

φ. Breviter Europaeus affert causas, quare Christus incarnari voluerit, et nasci, et Legem divinam promulgare in mundo, et quo tempore id fuit.

χ. Exponitur quibus rationibus, miraculis, et prophetiis ducti primi illi fideles crediderint Jesum Christum verum Deum fuisse. Et de praedicatione Evangelii.

ψ. Sina auditis his petit Doctrinam Christianam, quia Christianus fieri vult. Sed respondet Europaeus eum Christianum fieri posse, si alia discat esse quae non sunt in hoc libro: praesertim si suscipiat aquam sancti baptismi, et percipiat ea quae in Doctrina Christiana, quam vertimus in litteras Sinicas, ediscat.

ω. Sina pollicetur se haec, quae his octo capitibus continentur, maturius consideraturum, et rediturum ut caetera addiscat.

BIBLIOGRAPHY

Compiled by
Edward J. Malatesta, S.J.

In addition to sources consulted in the preparation of this book, we include here, without attempting to be exhaustive, other studies which may be of interest to our readers.

PRIMARY SOURCES

Ricci, Matteo, S.J. *China in the Sixteenth Century: The Journals of Matthew Ricci 1583-1610.* Translated from the Latin of Nicholas Trigault, S.J. by Louis J. Gallagher, S.J. New York, 1953.
_____. *Opere storiche.* 2 vols. Edited by Pietro Tacchi Venturi, S.J. Macerata, 1911-1913.
_____. *T'ien-chu shih-i (The True Meaning of the Lord of Heaven).*
  Chinese editions
    Peking, 1603, first edition. Biblioteca Casanatense, Rome, Manuscript no. 2136.
    Canton, 1605, second edition.
    Hangchow, 1607, third edition.
    Hangchow, n.d.
    Fukien, n.d.
    Shanghai, 1904, 1930, 1935.
    Hsien-hsien, 1933.
    Yenzhow, 1938.
    Hong Kong, 1939.
    Tientsin, 1941, original text together with a rendering into contemporary Chinese by Chu Hsing-yuan and T'ien Ching-hsien.
    Taichung, Taiwan, 1966, original text together with a rendering into contemporary Chinese by Liu Shun-te. Reprinted Taipei, 1967.
  Japanese edition
    Tokyo, Mei toku shuppan sha, 1971, selections of the Chinese text with translation and commentary by Goto Motomi.

Bibliography

French translation
"Entretiens d'un Lettré Chinois et d'un docteur Européen, sur la vraie idée de Dieu." Translated by Charles-Jean-Baptiste Jacques, S. J. (1688-1728) in *Lettres édifiantes et curieuses, écrites des missions étrangères.* Nouvelle édition. Mémoires des Indes et de la Chine. Toulouse, 1811. Vol. 25, pp. 143-385. Also published in *Choix de lettres édifiantes.* 2e édition. Bruxelles, 1838. Vol. 2, pp. 1-179.

Ricci, Matthieu, S.J. and Nicolas Trigault, S.J. *Histoire de l'expédition chrétienne au royaume de la Chine 1582-1610.* Introduction par Joseph Shih, S.J., pp. 11-59. Etablissement du texte et annotations par Georges Bessière. Tables et index par Joseph Dehergne, S.J. Paris and Montreal, Desclée De Brouwer and Editions Bellarmin, 1978. Collection "Christus", no. 45.

SECONDARY SOURCES

Baker, Donald L. "Neo-Confucians Confront Theism: Korean Reactions to Matteo Ricci's Arguments for the Existence of God." *The Journal of the Institute for East Asian Studies,* 2 (1983), 157-179.

Beauchamp, Paul, S.J. et al. "La partie historique de l'oeuvre de Ricci. Table ronde," in *Une Rencontre de l'Occident et de la Chine: Matteo Ricci.* Paris, Centre Sèvres, 1983, pp. 119-128.

Berling, Judith A. *The Syncretic Religion of Lin Chao-en.* New York, 1980.

Bernard, H., S.J. *L'apport scientifique du Père Matthieu Ricci à la Chine.* Tientsin, 1934. English translation by Edward C. Werner, *Matteo Ricci's Scientific Contribution to China.* Peiping, Henri Vetch, 1935.

_____. "L'art chrétien en Chine au temps du P. Matthieu Ricci." *Revue d'histoire des missions,* 12 (1935), 199-229.

_____. *Le Père Matthieu Ricci et la société chinoise de son temps (1552-1610).* 2 vols. Tientsin, 1937.

_____. "Musica e canti italiani a Pechino, marzo-aprile 1601." *Rivista degli Studi Orientali,* 30 (1955), 131-141.

Bettray, J., S.V.D. *Die Akkommodationsmethode des P. Matteo Ricci S.J. in China.* Excerpt from a doctoral dissertation. Rome, Gregorian University, 1955.

Bertuccioli, Giuliano. "Matteo Ricci and Taoism." *ISCWCI,* pp. 41-49.

Bortone, Fernando, S.J. *P. Matteo Ricci S.I., Il "Saggio d'Occidente.* Rome, 1965.

Brou, Alexandre, S.J. "Les tatonnements du Père Matthieu Ricci," *Revue d'Histoire des Missions,* 15 (1938), 228-244.

Caraci, G. "Nuovi studi sull'opera cartografica del P. Matteo Ricci." *Rivista Geografica Italiana,* 47 (1940), 25-66; 124-273.

Cartier, Michel. "Aux Origines de la politique des Lumières. La Chine vue par Matteo Ricci." *Actes du IIe Colloque International de Sinologie, Chantilly, 16-18 september 1977.* Paris, 1980, pp. 39-48.

Chan, Albert, S.J. "Early Missionary Attempts in Korea." *The Journal of East Asian Studies*, 2 (1983), 131-155.
Chan, Wing-tsit. *A Sourcebook in Chinese Philosophy*. Princeton, 1963.
_____, trans. *Instructions for Practical Living and Other Neo-Confucian Writings by Wang Yang-ming*. New York, 1963.
_____, trans. *Reflections on Things at Hand: The Neo-Confucian Anthology compiled by Chu Hsi and Lü Tsu-ch'ien*. New York, 1967.
Chang, Aloysius, S.J. "A Living Dialogue with Matteo Ricci." *Collectanea Theologica Universitatis Fujen*, no. 57 (1983), 353-359. (In Chinese.)
_____. "Father Matteo Ricci and the Enculturation of the Catholic Church in China." *ISCWCI*, pp. 79-83. (In Chinese.)
_____. "Father Matteo Ricci and Indigenization." *Collectanea Theologica Universitatis Fujen*, no. 56 (1983), 339-351. (In Chinese.)
_____. "Matteo Ricci's Contribution to the Chinese Church: Ecclesial Dimensions of the Intellectual Apostolate." *Collectanea Theologica Universitatis Fujen*, no. 55 (1983), 37-41. (In Chinese.)
_____. "Methods of Evangelization from Francis Xavier to Matteo Ricci." *Collectanea Theologica Universitatis Fujen*, no. 55 (1983), 43-48. (In Chinese.)
Chang, Mark, S.J. "A Concise Biography of Father Matteo Ricci." *Collectanea Theologica Universitatis Fujen*, no. 56 (1983), 167-179. (In Chinese.)
_____. "Father Matteo Ricci, S.J. and his Fellow Chinese Jesuits." *Collectanea Theologica Universitatis Fujen*, no. 58 (1983), 507-519. (In Chinese.)
_____. "Pioneer Missionaries to China Prior to Father Matteo Ricci." *Collectanea Theologica Universitatis Fujen*, no. 56 (1983), 157-166. (In Chinese.)
_____. "The Latin Phoneticization of Chinese Characters of Matteo Ricci and Nicolas Trigault." *ISCWCI*, pp. 88-96. (In Chinese.)
Chao, Albert, C.S.J.B. "Chinese-Western Cultural Interchange from the Perspective of the Make-up of Culture." *ISCWCI*, pp. 101-106. (In Chinese.)
Charbonnier, Jean, M.E.P. "China-Christian Relations in the Spirit of Matteo Ricci." *Tripod*, no. 12 (Hong Kong, 1982), 102-111.
Ch'en Kenneth S. "A Possible Source for Ricci's Notices on Regions Near China." *T'oung Pao*, 34 (1938), 179-190.
_____. *Buddhism in China. A Historical Survey*. Princeton, 1964.
_____. *The Chinese Transformation of Buddhism*. Princeton, 1973.
_____. "Matteo Ricci's contribution to, and influence on, geographic knowledge in China." *Journal of the American Oriental Society*, 59 (1929), 325-359; 509 corrections.
Cheng, Bishop Paul. "Father Matteo Ricci and Confucianism." *Collectanea Theologica Universitatis Fujen*, no. 56 (1983), 219-225. (In Chinese.)
Chiang, Fu-tsung. "The History of Matteo Ricci's Mission to China and the Meaning of His Book The True Idea of God." *ISCWCI*, pp.

139-144. (In Chinese.)
Ching, Julia. *Confucianism and Christianity*. Tokyo, 1977.
_____. tr. *The Philosophical Letters of Wang Yang-ming*. Canberra, 1972.
_____. *To Acquire Wisdom: The Way of Wang Yang-ming*. New York, 1976.
Choe, Andrew. "Korean Confucianist Opinions on Matteo Ricci's *The True Doctrine of the Lord of Heaven*." *Journal of the Institute for East Asian Studies*, 2 (1983), 1-25. (In Korean.)
Chu, Mark, S.J. "Searching the Psychology of Matteo Ricci." *Collectanea Theologica Universitatis Fujen*, no. 57 (1983), 361-368. (In Chinese.)
Corradini, Piero. "Actuality and Modernity of Matteo Ricci, a Man of the Renaissance in the Framework of Cultural Relations between East and West." *ISCWCI*, pp. 174-180.
_____. "Ricci, homme de la Renaissance?" in *Une Rencontre de l'Occident et de la Chine: Matteo Ricci*. Paris, Centre Sèvres, 1983, pp. 25-30.
Cronin, Vincent. *The Wise Man from the West*. London and New York, 1955. Revised edition, 1984.
Dai, David W.Y. "Matteo Ricci and Hsü Kuang-chi." ISCWCI, pp. 183-194. (In Chinese.)
de Bary, William Theodore, Wing-tsit Chan, and Burton Watson, eds. *Sources of Chinese Tradition*. New York, 1960.
Dehergne, Joseph, S.J. "L'appel de Matteo Ricci aux Jésuites français," in *Une Rencontre de l'Occident et de la Chine: Matteo Ricci*. Paris, Centre Sèvres, 1983, pp. 111-116.
_____. "The Request from Ricci Sent to the Confessor of the King of France." *ISCWCI*, pp. 198-210.
D'Elia, Pasquale M., S.J. "Due amici del P. Matteo Ricci ridotti all' unità *Archivum Historicum Societatis Iesu*, 6 (1937), 303-310.
_____. "Ermeneutica Ricciana." *Gregorianum*, 34 (1953), 669-679.
_____. ed. *Fonti Ricciane*. 3 vols. Rome, 1942-1949.
_____. "Further Notes on Matteo Ricci's *De Amicitia*." *Monumenta Serica*, 15 (1956), 356-377.
_____. "Il domma Cattolico integralmente presentato da Matteo Ricci ai letterati della Cina." *Civiltà Cattolica*, 86 (1935,II), 35-53.
_____. *Il mappamondo cinese del P. Matteo Ricci, S.J., conservato presso la Bibliotheca Vaticana, commentato, tradotto e annotato*. Rome, 1938.
_____. "Il metodo di adattamento del P. Matteo Ricci S.I. in Cina." *Civiltà Cattolica* 107 (1956,III), 174-182.
_____. "Il P. Matteo Ricci introduce definitivamente il Cristianesimo in Cina." *Gregorianum*, 34 (1953), 482-526.
_____. "*Il Trattato sull'Amicizia*. Primo Libro scritto in cinese da Matteo Ricci." *Studia Missionalia*, 7 (1952), 425-515.
_____. "I primordi delle missioni cattoliche in Cina secondo una lettera inedita del P. Matteo Ricci." *Civiltà Cattolica*, 86, (1935,IV), 25-37.

———. *Le origine dell'arte cristiana cinese (1583-1640)*. Rome, 1939.
———. "Matteo Ricci S.I. nell'opinione dell'alta società cinese. Secondo nuovi documenti (1600-1604)." *Civiltà Cattolica*, 110 (1959, II) 26-40.
———. "Poeti cinesi in lode dei missionari gesuiti italiani del Seicento." *Civilità Cattolica*, 98 (1947,IV), 560-569.
———. "Presentazione della prima traduzione cinese di Euclide." *Monumenta Serica*, 15 (1956), 161-202.
———. "Prima Introduzione della Filosofia Scolastica in Cina (1584, 1603)." *The Bulletin of the Institute of History and Philology, Academia Sinica*, 28. Studies presented to Dr. Hu Shih on his sixty-fifth birthday, Taipei, Taiwan, December, 1956, pp. 141-196.
———. "Quadro storico-sinologico del primo libro di dottrina cristiana in cinese." *Archivum Historicum Societatis Iesu*, 3 (1934), 193-222.
———. "Roma presentata ai letterati cinesi da Matteo Ricci S.I." *T'oung Pao*, 41 (1952), 149-190.
———. "Recent discoveries and new studies (1938-1960) on the world map in Chinese of Father Mattaeo Ricci S.J." *Monumenta Serica*, 20 (1961), 82-164.
———. "Sonate e canzoni italiane alla corte di Pechino nel 1601." *Civiltà Cattolica*, 96 (1945, III), 158-165.
———. "Sunto poetico-ritmico di *I dieci paradossi* di Matteo Ricci S.I." *Rivista di Studi Orientali*, 27 (1952), 111-138.
Desbuquois, L. "Matthieu Ricci." *Revue d'Histoire des Missions*, 1 (1924), 52-70.
Destombes, Marcel. "Wang P'an, Liang Chou et Matteo Ricci. Essai sur la cartographie chinoise de 1593 à 1603." *Actes du IIIe Colloque International de Sinologie, Chantilly, 11-14 septembre 1980*. Paris, 1983, pp. 47-65.
Dudink, A. *Een westerse godsdienst oostwaarts: Matteo Ricci en zijn introduktie van het christendom in het China van de Late Ming.* Unpublished doctoral dissertation, University of Amsterdam, 1979.
Duvingneau, A.B. "Cartographie chinoise. A propos de Matthieu Ricci." *Bulletin Catholique de Pékin,* 22 (1935), 258-263; 304-310; 373-380; 430-434; 482-488.
D'Orleans, Pierre Joseph, S.J. *La vie du Père Matthieu Ricci de la Compagnie de Jésus.* Paris, 1693.
Dunne, George H., S.J., *Generation of Giants*. Notre Dame and London, 1962.
Fan, James C.P. "The Reverend Matteo Ricci's Contributions to the Modernization of China." *ISCWCI*, pp. 232-254. (In Chinese.)
Fang, Hao. "Notes on Matteo Ricci's *De Amicitia*." *Monumenta Serica*, 14 (1948-1955), 574-583.
Foss, Theodore, N. "How They Learned: Jesuits and Chinese, Friends and Scholars." *ISCWCI*, pp. 255-263.
———. "Nicholas Trigault, S.J.—Amanuensis or Propagandist?" *ISCWCI*,

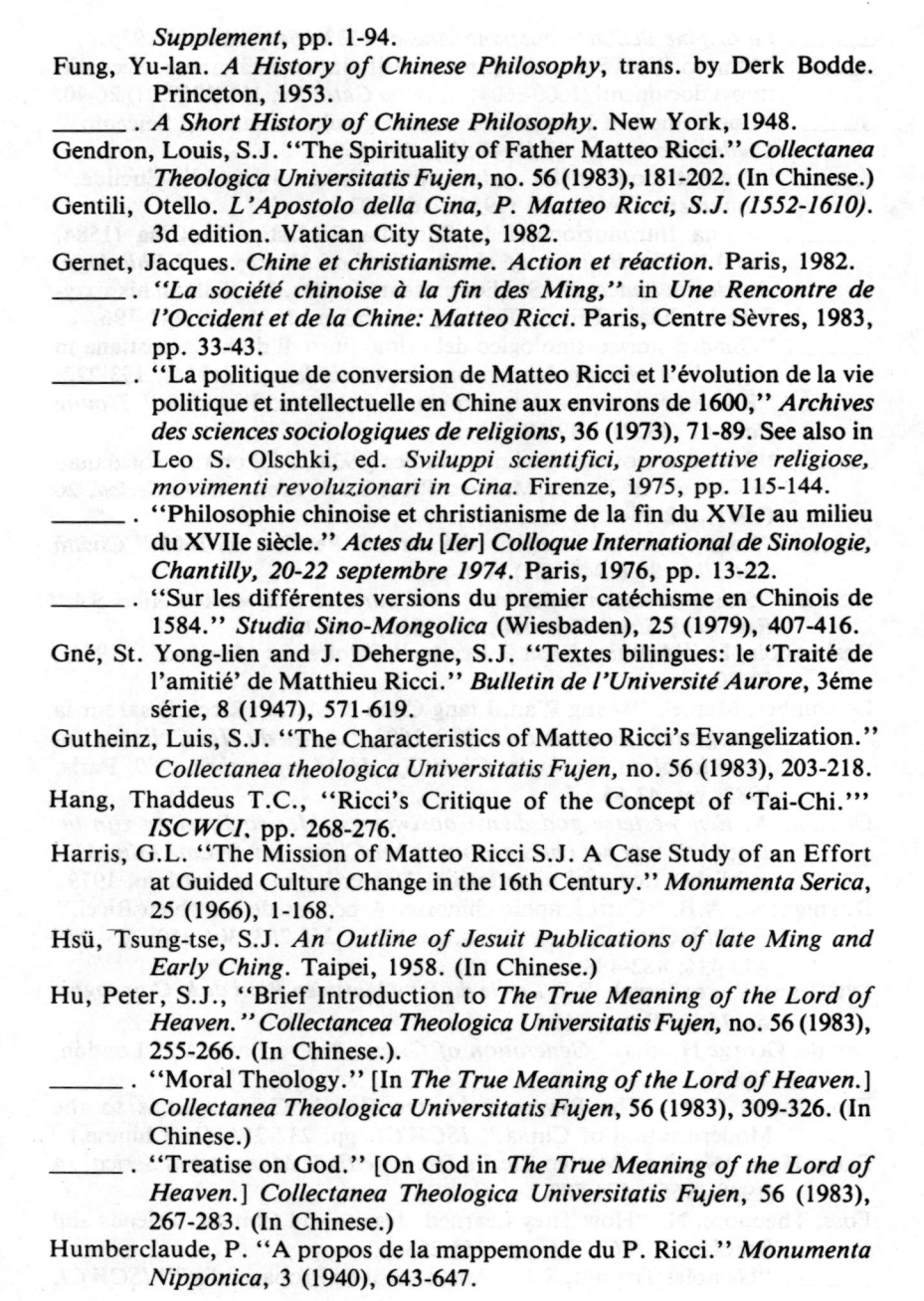

Supplement, pp. 1-94.
Fung, Yu-lan. *A History of Chinese Philosophy,* trans. by Derk Bodde. Princeton, 1953.
_____ . *A Short History of Chinese Philosophy.* New York, 1948.
Gendron, Louis, S.J. "The Spirituality of Father Matteo Ricci." *Collectanea Theologica Universitatis Fujen,* no. 56 (1983), 181-202. (In Chinese.)
Gentili, Otello. *L'Apostolo della Cina, P. Matteo Ricci, S.J. (1552-1610).* 3d edition. Vatican City State, 1982.
Gernet, Jacques. *Chine et christianisme. Action et réaction.* Paris, 1982.
_____ . "La société chinoise à la fin des Ming," in *Une Rencontre de l'Occident et de la Chine: Matteo Ricci.* Paris, Centre Sèvres, 1983, pp. 33-43.
_____ . "La politique de conversion de Matteo Ricci et l'évolution de la vie politique et intellectuelle en Chine aux environs de 1600," *Archives des sciences sociologiques de religions,* 36 (1973), 71-89. See also in Leo S. Olschki, ed. *Sviluppi scientifici, prospettive religiose, movimenti revoluzionari in Cina.* Firenze, 1975, pp. 115-144.
_____ . "Philosophie chinoise et christianisme de la fin du XVIe au milieu du XVIIe siècle." *Actes du [Ier] Colloque International de Sinologie, Chantilly, 20-22 septembre 1974.* Paris, 1976, pp. 13-22.
_____ . "Sur les différentes versions du premier catéchisme en Chinois de 1584." *Studia Sino-Mongolica* (Wiesbaden), 25 (1979), 407-416.
Gné, St. Yong-lien and J. Dehergne, S.J. "Textes bilingues: le 'Traité de l'amitié' de Matthieu Ricci." *Bulletin de l'Université Aurore,* 3éme série, 8 (1947), 571-619.
Gutheinz, Luis, S.J. "The Characteristics of Matteo Ricci's Evangelization." *Collectanea theologica Universitatis Fujen,* no. 56 (1983), 203-218.
Hang, Thaddeus T.C., "Ricci's Critique of the Concept of 'Tai-Chi.'" *ISCWCI.* pp. 268-276.
Harris, G.L. "The Mission of Matteo Ricci S.J. A Case Study of an Effort at Guided Culture Change in the 16th Century." *Monumenta Serica,* 25 (1966), 1-168.
Hsü, Tsung-tse, S.J. *An Outline of Jesuit Publications of late Ming and Early Ching.* Taipei, 1958. (In Chinese.)
Hu, Peter, S.J., "Brief Introduction to *The True Meaning of the Lord of Heaven.*" *Collectancea Theologica Universitatis Fujen,* no. 56 (1983), 255-266. (In Chinese.).
_____ . "Moral Theology." [In *The True Meaning of the Lord of Heaven.*] *Collectanea Theologica Universitatis Fujen,* 56 (1983), 309-326. (In Chinese.)
_____ . "Treatise on God." [On God in *The True Meaning of the Lord of Heaven.*] *Collectanea Theologica Universitatis Fujen,* 56 (1983), 267-283. (In Chinese.)
Humberclaude, P. "A propos de la mappemonde du P. Ricci." *Monumenta Nipponica,* 3 (1940), 643-647.

Jeanne, Pierre, M.E.P. "Ricci: Precursor of Inter-Cultural Exchange." *Tripod*, no. 12 (1982), 122-136.
Ku, Ignatius, S.J. "The Chinese Writings of Father Matteo Ricci." *Collectanea Theologica Universitatis Fujen*, no. 56 (1983), 239-253. (In Chinese.)
_____. "The Introduction of Western Science in China Since the Time of Matteo Ricci." *Collectanea Theologica Universitatis Fujen*, no. 55 (1983), 1-35. (In Chinese.)
Ku, Joseph, K.H. "Hsü Kuang-ch'i: Chinese Scientist and Confucian (1562-1633)." Unpublished doctoral dissertation, St. John's University, Jamaica, New York, 1973.
Lancashire, Douglas. "Anti-Christian Polemics in Seventeenth Century China." *Church History*, 38 (1969), 218-241.
_____. "Buddhist Reaction to Christianity in Late Ming China." *Journal of the Oriental Society of Australia*, 6 (1968-1969), 82-103.
Larre, Claude, S.J. "Christianisme et Confucianisme dans la perspective de Ricci," in *Une Rencontre de l'Occident et de la Chine: Matteo Ricci*. Paris, Centre Sèvres, 1983, pp. 73-80.
_____. "Le Pere Matteo Ricci." *Bulletin du Club français de la médaille*, 51-52 (1976), 52-61.
Latourette, Kenneth S. *A History of Christian Missions in China*. New York and London, 1929.
Lau, Maria Goretti. "Some Eschatological Thoughts in Matteo Ricci's *The True Idea of God*." *Tripod*, no. 12 (1982), 93-101.
Lawlor, R.V. *The Basic Strategy of Matthew Ricci S.J. in the Introduction of Christianity in China*. Excerpt from a doctoral dissertation. Rome, Gregorian University, 1951.
Lazzarotto, Angelo S. "An Appeal for Dialogue from Ricci's Tomb." *Tripod*, no. 12 (1982), 74-76.
Lee, Ding-Hok. "The influence of Matteo Ricci's missionary efforts on successive generations. A summary." *Tripod*, no. 12 (1982), 137-139.
Legge, James, trans. *The Chinese Classics*. 5 vols. Oxford, 1893-1895. Reprinted with the addition of corrections, concordance tables, and a biographical note. Hong Kong, 1960.
_____, trans. *I Ching: Book of Changes*. Oxford, 1882. Reprinted with an introduction by Ch'u Chai and Winberg Chai. New York, 1969.
_____, trans. *Li Chi: Book of Rites*. 2 vols. Oxford, 1885. Reprinted with an introduction by Ch'u Chai and Winberg Chai. New York, 1967.
Lin, Tong-yang. "Several Problems Concerning Matteo Ricci's *The True Meaning of the Lord of Heaven* and *Ten Chapters by a Nonconformist*." *Ta-lu tsa-chih*, 56 (1978), 26-44. (In Chinese.)
_____. "The World Map of Matteo Ricci and Its Influence in the Chinese Intellectual Circle at the End of the Ming Dynasty." *ISCWCI*, pp. 311-378. (In Chinese.)

Bibliography

Lokuang, Archbishop Stanislaus. "Father Matteo Ricci and Buddhism." *Collectanea Theologica Universitatis Fujen*, no. 56 (1983), 227-237. (In Chinese.)
_____. "Matteo Ricci's Contribution to Chinese Academic Thought." *ISCWCI*, pp. 400-405. (In Chinese.)
Lu, Shih-chiang. "A Survey of the Chinese Intellectuals' Anti-Christian Opinions as Related to the Cultural Exchange between China and the West (1583-1723)." *ISCWCI*, pp. 411-430. (In Chinese.)
Luk, Bernard Hung-key. "The Background in European History of Matteo Ricci's Mission." *Tripod*, no. 12 (1982), 77-84.
Luo, Thomas Yu. "The Grandeur of Matteo Ricci Viewed from His Letters." *ISCWCI*, pp. 433-435. (In Chinese.)
Malatesta, Edward, S.J., "Matteo Ricci, Friend of China." *Tripod*, no. 12 (1982), 85-92
Martzloff, Jean-Claude. "Sciences et techniques dans l'oeuvre de Ricci," in *Une Rencontre de l'Occident et de la Chine: Matteo Ricci*. Paris, Centre Sèvres, 1983, pp. 83-95.
_____. "The Influence of Matteo Ricci's Mathematical Works." *ISCWCI*, pp. 438-453.
Mungello, David E. "The First Complete Translation of the Confucian Four Books in the West." *ISCWCI*, pp. 516-539.
_____. *Leibniz and Confucianism. The Search for Accord*. Honolulu, 1977.
Nalet, Yves, S.J. "Ricci et son oeuvre vus par la République populaire de Chine," in *Une Rencontre de l'Occident et de la Chine: Matteo Ricci*. Paris, Centre Sèvres, 1983, pp. 101-110.
Needham, Joseph. *Chinese Astronomy and the Jesuit Mission: An Encounter of Cultures*. China Society Occasional Papers, no. 10. London, 1958.
Park, Seong-Rae. "Matteo Ricci and the Introduction of Western Science into Korea." *The Journal of the Institute for East Asian Studies*, 2 (1983), 27-49. (In Korean.)
Raguin, Yves, S.J. "Father Ricci's Presentation of Some Fundamental Theories of Buddhism." *Chinese Culture*, 10 (1969), 37-43.
_____. "Matteo Ricci aujourd'hui," in *Une Rencontre de l'Occident et de la Chine: Matteo Ricci*. Paris, Centre Sèvres, 1983, pp. 5-21.
_____. "Matteo Ricci Today." *ISCWCI*, pp. 544-554.
Rowbotham, Arnold H. *Missionary and Mandarin, the Jesuits at the Court of China*. Berkeley, 1942.
Rule, Paul A. "The Confucian Interpretation of the Jesuits." *Papers on Far Eastern Studies*. (Department of Far Eastern Studies, Australian National University), 6 (1972), 1-61.
_____. "Jesuit or Confucian: Chinese Religion in the *Journals* of Matteo Ricci, 1583-1610." *Journal of Religious History*, 5 (1969), 105-124.
_____. *K'ung tzu or Confucius? The Jesuit Interpretation of Confucianism*. Unpublished doctoral dissertation, Australian National University, Canberra, 1972.

Sainsaulieu, Jean. "Le Confucianisme des Jésuites." *Actes du [Ier] Colloque International de Sinologie, Chantilly, 20-22 septembre 1974.* Paris, 1976, pp. 41-57.

Schütte, Franz Josef, S.J. *Valignano's Mission Principles for Japan.* Translated by John J. Coyne, S.J. Part I: *The Problem (1573-1580);* Part II: *The Solution (1580-1582).* St. Louis, 1980, 1985.

Sebes, Joseph, S.J. "A 'Bridge' between East and West: Father Matteo Ricci, S.J. His Times, His Life, and His Method of Cultural Accommodation." *ISCWCI*, pp. 556-615 (discussion draft); *ISCWCI*, Supplement, 70 pages (final draft).

―――. "Father Matteo Ricci S.J.: An Intellectual Biography." *The Journal of the Institute for East Asian Studies*, 2 (1983), 83-102.

Shen, Vincent. "Some Philosophical Reflections on Matteo Ricci's Cultural and Scientific Approaches in China." *ISCWCI*, pp. 621-632 (in English); pp. 633-640 (in Chinese).

Shih, Joseph, S.J. *Le Père Ruggieri et le problème de l'évangelisation en Chine.* Excerpt from a doctoral dissertation. Rome, Gregorian University, 1964.

―――. "Les étapes de l'itinéraire de Ricci en Chine," in *Une Rencontre de l'Occident et de la Chine: Matteo Ricci.* Paris, Centre Sèvres, 1983, pp. 51-61.

―――. "Matteo Ricci as Missionary." *ISCWCI*, pp. 645-654.

Spalatin, Christopher A., S.J. "Matteo Ricci and a Confucian Christianity." Unpublished doctoral dissertation, Gregorian University, Rome, 1974.

―――. "Matteo Ricci's Approach to 16th Century Confucian China." *ISCWCI*, pp. 660-676.

―――. "Matteo Ricci's Understanding of the Natural Law in Confucianism." *The Journal of the Institute for East Asian Studies*, 2 (1983), 51-72.

―――. *Matteo Ricci's Use of Epictetus.* Taegu (Korea), Waegwan Press, 1975.

―――. "Matteo Ricci's Use of Epictetus' *Encheiridion*." *Gregorianum*, 56 (1975), 551-557.

Spence, Jonathan D. *The Memory Palace of Matteo Ricci.* New York, 1984.

Spengler, Tilman. "European and Chinese Evaluations of the History of Chinese Science—A Story of Collective Neglect and Unsuccessful Theorizing." *ISCWCI*, pp. 680-694.

Sprenger, Arnold, S.V.D. "Science and Religion for Matteo Ricci; Science and Religion for Today." *ISCWCI*, pp. 703-727.

Sung, Thomas, C.S.J.B. "Spirituality." [In *The True Meaning of the Lord of Heaven.*] *Collectanea Theologica Universitatis Fujen*, no. 56 (1983), 327-338. (In Chinese.)

Bibliography

Toshihiko, Yazawa. "Fr. Matteo Ricci's World Map and Its Influence on East Asia." *The Journal of the Institute for East Asian Studies,* 2 (1983), 185-202.
Tong, John. "Ricci's Contribution to China. A Reflection on the Insights of Two Modern Chinese Scholars [Qian Mu and Hou Wailu]." *Tripod*, no. 12 (1982), 112-121.
Tsien, Andrew. "New Perspectives of Chinese Culture under the Inspiration of Fr. Matteo Ricci." *ISCWCI*, pp. 778-781.
Vanderstappen, Harrie, S.V.D. "Some Reflections on Chinese Reactions to European Art Introduced by Catholic Missionaries in the Seventeenth and Eighteenth Centuries." *ISCWCI*, pp. 786-800.
Van Kley, Edwin J. "Buddhism in Early Jesuit Reports: the Parallel Cases of China and Tibet." *ISCWCI*, 804-815.
_____. "Some Seventeenth Century European Protestant Responses to Matteo Ricci and His Mission in China." To be published in a forthcoming *Festschrift* honoring Donald F. Lach, Bernadotte Schmitt professor of Modern History, the University of Chicago.
Voss, Gustav, "Missionary Accommodation and Ancestral Rites in the Far East." *Theological Studies*, 4 (1943), 525-560.
Waley, Arthur, trans. *The Confucian Analects*. London, 1938.
_____. trans. *The Way and its Power*. London, 1934.
Wang, Ping. "The Influence of Matteo Ricci's Introduction of Western Science into China." *ISCWCI*, pp. 821-826. (In Chinese.)
Watson, B., trans. *The Complete Works of Chuang-tzu*. New York, 1968.
Weingartner, Fredric F., S.J. "Sources for a Treatise on the Ten Commandments Based on the Writings of Early Jesuits in China." *ISCWCI*, pp. 830-838.
Werner, E.T.C. *Myths and Legends of China*. London, 1922.
Wright, Arthur F. *Buddhism in Chinese History*. Palo Alto, 1959.
Wu, J.C.H., trans. *Lao-tzu, Tao-te Ching*. New York, 1961.
Yang, C.K., *Religion in Chinese Society*. Berkeley, 1961.
Young, John D., *Confucianism and Christianity. The First Encounter*. Hong Kong, 1983.
_____. *East-West Synthesis: Matteo Ricci and Confucianism*. Hong Kong, 1980.
_____. "'Original Confucianism' versus Neo-Confucianism: Matteo Ricci's Chinese Writing." *Actes du XXIXe Congrès International des Orientalistes: Chine Ancienne*. Paris, 1977, pp. 371-377.
Yü Chün-fang, *The Renewal of Buddhism in China: Chu-hung and the Late Ming Synthesis*. New York, 1981.
Yueh, Paul. "Treatise on the Soul." [On the soul in *The True Meaning of the Lord of Heaven.*] *Collectanea Theologica Universitatis Fujen*, no. 56 (1983), 285-307. (In Chinese.)
Zürcher, E. "The First Anti-Christian Movement in China (Nanking, 1616-1621)" in *Acta Orientalia Neerlandica*, Leiden, 1971.

INDEX OF CHINESE CLASSICAL TEXTS

The English titles for the Chinese classical texts are taken from Legge with some exceptions. References are to paragraph numbers of the present translation of *The True Meaning of the Lord of Heaven*.

I. 書經 : Shu Ching: The Book of History
    唐書 The Book of T'ang
        堯典 Canon of Yao   242
        舜典 Canon of Shun   242
        皋陶謨 Counsels of Kao-Yao   343
        益稷 Counsels of I and Chieh   243
    商書 The Books of Shang
        湯誓 Speech of T'ang   108
        湯誥 Announcement of T'ang   108
        盤庚 P'an-kêng   172, 344
        西伯戡黎 Chief of the West's
            Conquest of Li   172
    周書 The Books of Chou
        泰誓 Great Declaration   345
        牧誓 Speech at Mu   345
        金縢 Metal-bound Coffer   108, 174
        康誥 Announcement to [the
            Prince of] K'ang   345
        召誥 Announcement to [the
            Duke of] Shao   174, 391
        多士 Numerous Officers   346
        多方 Numerous Regions   346

II. 詩經 : Shih Ching: The Book of Odes
    大雅 Major Odes
        文王 Wên Wang   105, 406, 483
        大明 Ta Ming   174, 391
        下武 Hsia Wu   155, 278
        烝民 Chêng Ming   391
    周頌 Hymns to Chou
        執競 Chih Ching   105

Index of Chinese Classical Texts

	臣工 Ch'ên Kung	105
商頌 Hymns to Shang		
	長發 Ch'ang Fa	105

III. 易經 : I Ching: The Book of Changes
    乾文言 Wên Yen of Ch'ien   252, 467
    繫辭傳上十一 Hsi-ts'u Chuan, I, 11   66
    繫辭傳下四 Hsi-ts'u Chuan, II, 4   80
    繫辭傳下五 Hsi-ts'u Chuan, II, 5   252
    說卦傳 Shuo Kua Chuan   106

IV. 禮記 : Li Chi: The Book of Rites
    月令 Yüeh Ling   107
    表記 Piao Chi   107

V. 春秋左傳 : Ch'un-ch'iu Tso Chuan: Tso's Commentary of Ch'un-Ch'iu Annals
    召公七年 The Seventh Year of the Duke of Shao   184-185

VI. 四書 : The Four Books
    大學 The Great Learning   84, 322, 457
    中庸 The Doctrine of the Mean
        一章 chapter 1   421
        十六章 chapter 16   171, 191
        十九章 chapter 19   104, 154
        二十章 chapter 20   234
        二十二章 chapter 21   117
    論語 Analects
        八佾 Pa I   206
        公冶長 Kung Yeh Chang   295, 553
        雍也 Yung Yeh   206
        述而 Shu Êrh   553
        顏淵 Yen Yüan   351, 457
        子路 Tzu Lu   365
        憲問 Hsien Wên   72
        衛靈公 Wei Ling Kung   98, 351
        季氏 Chih Shih   434
        微子 Wei Tzu   553
    孟子 The Book of Mencius
        梁惠王 Liang Hui Wang   193, 296, 321, 350

Index of Chinese Classical Texts

	公孫丑 Kung Sun Ch'ou	350, 436, 553
	滕文公 T'êng Wên Kung	254, 350, 395, 563
	離婁 Li Lou	168, 304, 339, 551, 552
	告子 Kao Tzu	60, 155, 203, 350, 436, 553
	盡心 Chin Hsin	553
VII.	老子 : Lao Tzu	
	四十章 chapter 40	66
VIII.	莊子 : Chuang Tzu	
	逍遙遊 Hsiao Yao Yu	382